THE MORAL NEXUS

CARL G. HEMPEL LECTURE SERIES

The Moral Nexus

R. JAY WALLACE

PRINCETON UNIVERSITY PRESS

PRINCETON & OXFORD

Copyright © 2019 by Princeton University Press

Published by Princeton University Press
41 William Street, Princeton, New Jersey 08540
6 Oxford Street, Woodstock, Oxfordshire OX20 1TR

press.princeton.edu

Jacket art: Cy Twombly, *Untitled*, 1966. Oil-based house paint, wax crayon
on canvas. 74 3/4 × 78 3/4 in. © Cy Twombly Foundation. © Museum für
Gegenwartskunst Siegen. The Lambrecht-Schadeberg Collection / Winners of
the Rubens Prize of the City of Siegen, Germany

LCCN 2018958378
ISBN 978-0-691-17217-0

British Library Cataloging-in-Publication Data is available

Editorial: Rob Tempio and Matt Rohal
Production Editorial: Kathleen Cioffi
Jacket Design: Layla MacRory
Production: Jacquie Poirier
Publicity: Jodi Price
Copyeditor: Hank Southgate

This book has been composed in Arno

Printed on acid-free paper. ∞

Printed in the United States of America

10 9 8 7 6 5 4 3 2 1

For Katharina, again

CONTENTS

Acknowledgments ix

1 Introduction   1

   1.1. Elements of Relational Normativity   5

   1.2. Overview of the Argument   12

2 The Problem of Moral Obligation   24

   2.1. Practical Requirements: The Basic Challenge   26

   2.2. Moral Obligation: The Specific Challenge   34

   2.3. A Relational Approach to Moral Obligation   47

   2.4. Refining the Picture   54

3 Morality as a Social Phenomenon   66

   3.1. The Interpersonal Significance of Moral Right and Wrong 67

   3.2. Individualistic and Relational Conceptions of the Moral Right 76

   3.3. The Relational Structure of Interpersonal Accountability 86

   3.4. The Relational Content of Blame   95

4 Relational Requirements without Relational Foundations   105

   4.1. Obligations and Relationships   107

   4.2. Self-Standing Relational Requirements   115

   4.3. Anti-Individualism about the Normative   125

   4.4. Agent-Relativity and Morality as an Ideal   135

5 From Interests to Claims   146

   5.1. Defining the Manifold: Who Are the Claimholders?   148

5.2. Interests, Claims, and Moral Wrongs 156

5.3. Moral Justification and Moral Reasoning: From Interests
to Claims 165

5.4. A Theory of Relational Morality? 176

6 Some Practical Consequences 190

6.1. Foreseeability, Claims, and Wrongs 192

6.2. Claims without Rights: Imperfect Moral Duties 201

6.3. Numbers and Non-Identity 210

6.4. Extramoral Concern for Moral Persons 221

Notes 235

Bibliography 275

Index 285

ACKNOWLEDGMENTS

MY MOST SALIENT DEBT in connection with this volume is to the Department of Philosophy at Princeton University, which invited me to deliver the Carl G. Hempel Lectures in May of 2015.[1] As a Princeton graduate alumnus, I was deeply honored to receive this invitation, and I am grateful to the members of the Princeton philosophy community for their warm hospitality during my week among them. Discussions with those in attendance for the three lectures in Princeton were exceptionally stimulating and helpful to me as I began thinking about how to expand them into a book; I profited especially from comments by John Cooper, Johann Frick, Mark Johnston, Alexander Nehamas, Gideon Rosen, Michael Smith, and several extremely sharp and interesting graduate students.

I have been thinking about the relational interpretation of morality for many years now, and shorter and longer discussions of it have cropped up in numerous papers of mine in that period. But I first succeeded in working some of my ideas up into a sustained treatment of the topic in response to an invitation to deliver the Frankfurt Lectures at the Goethe-Universität Frankfurt in July of 2013. Those lectures, presented under the title "Bilateralität in der Moral," and sponsored by the impressive Excellence Cluster on the Formation of Normative Orders, covered much of the same terrain that I treated in the Hempel Lectures, albeit in a different language and a somewhat more concise format. Discussions with philosophers and other scholars and students in Frankfurt, both at the two public lectures and in the seminar that followed them, were extremely rewarding, and they encouraged me to think that the project might be worth pursuing further. I am especially grateful to Rainer Forst for serving as the gracious host of my visit, and for the interest he has continued to show in this project in the years since I delivered my lectures in Frankfurt. I received further encouragement and helpful feedback when I presented a version of the same material as a "Voltaire Lecture" at the Universität Potsdam later in the summer of 2013; Logi Gunnarsson was my host on this occasion, and I have benefited greatly from his trenchant comments, both at the Voltaire Lecture and in several subsequent discussions.

The first drafts of the three Hempel Lectures were prepared in connection with a graduate seminar that I taught at the University of California, Berkeley, in the spring of 2015. It was immensely helpful for me to be able to discuss my ideas about the moral nexus with the participants in this seminar, who offered detailed comments on my drafts, including many constructive suggestions about how my developing argument might be clarified and improved. Among these participants were Facundo Alonso, Gabriel Beringer, Lindsay Crawford, Sophia Dandelet, Omar Fakhri, Nicholas French, Tyler Haddow, Nicolas Jaber, Ethan Jerzak, Julian Jonker, Daniel Khokhar, and James Steijger.

Material from the Princeton lectures was presented at several different venues in the years to follow, including the Murphy Institute at Tulane University, Duke University, the University of Toronto, a conference on "The Direction of Moral Duties" in Vancouver, the Humboldt-Universität zu Berlin, and the Max Planck Institute for Evolutionary Anthropology in Leipzig. The interest that audiences showed on these occasions, and the cogent questions and feedback that they provided, helped to keep the project alive during a period when I was preoccupied by heavy administrative commitments at Berkeley. I am happy to be able to single out Facundo Alonso and Ariel Zylberman, who both provided written comments on all three of my Hempel Lecture texts, as well as Arthur Ripstein, who pressed me very hard on some central issues in a series of emails after a presentation of mine in Toronto, and Michael Morgan, who has followed my project closely over the years.

A sabbatical leave from the University of California, Berkeley, in the academic year of 2016–17, provided the conditions I needed to expand the Hempel Lectures into the first draft of this book. The leave was also supported by a Humanities Research Fellowship from Berkeley, for which I am very grateful. An earlier fellowship from the same source, in the academic year of 2010–11, helped me to lay the foundations for the book project; my sabbatical leave during that year was also made possible by fellowships from the John Simon Guggenheim Memorial Foundation and the Alexander von Humboldt Foundation (in the form of a "Wiedereinladung" as "Forschungspreisträger"). Judy Chandler Webb generously endowed the professorship I hold at Berkeley, which makes available research funds that have contributed to my research on this project throughout its different stages. The support I received from these disparate sources has been invaluable, even if it took longer than originally anticipated for my ideas about the moral nexus to come together in book form.

My sabbatical in 2016–17, spent in Berlin, coincided fortuitously with the first year of my tenure as an Einstein Visiting Fellow. This fellowship, supported by the Einstein Foundation in Berlin, provides an affiliation with the Topoi Excellence Cluster and the Humboldt-Universität, as well as generous funding for the activities of a research group (the "Einstein Ethics Group," as we call ourselves). My work on the moral nexus has provided the theoretical framework for the work of the Einstein Ethics Group during the first phase of its existence, and it has been exceptionally fruitful to be able to discuss aspects of the project with the other group members. They are Jan Gertken and Felix Koch (who hold postdoctoral fellowships from the Einstein Foundation) and Daniele Bruno, Francesca Bunkenborg, and Simon Gaus (who hold or held dissertation stipends in the Einstein Group). Together, we planned and organized a series of workshops and conferences in Berlin, starting in the fall of 2016, on topics that relate in one way or another to my own work on relational normativity and morality. Themes of these workshops were "The Moral Foundations of Tort Law" (focused on Arthur Ripstein's *Private Wrongs*); "Moral Address: Responsibility as an Interpersonal Practice"; "The Nature of Moral Obligation"; and "Contractualism, Risk, and Population Ethics" (focused on some recent work by Johann Frick). We also hosted a one-week visit to Berlin by Samuel Scheffler, who discussed with us his work in two separate sessions on "Membership and Political Obligation" and "Why Care about Future Generations?"

Though my work was not officially under discussion at these sessions, they were extremely helpful to me as I was developing my own thoughts on closely related topics over the past two years. I am grateful to all who took part in our workshops, but would like to single out in particular the distinguished philosophers who accepted our invitations to come to Berlin to present work or to participate in our discussions. (They may not have realized that they would be contributing to my project by agreeing to be involved in our workshops, but the book would not have taken the final shape it did without the benefit of the stimulus I received from discussions with them.) These philosophers are Ulrike Heuer, Daniel Markovits, Erasmus Mayr, David Owens, Herlinde Pauer-Studer, and Arthur Ripstein (at "Moral Foundations of Tort Law"); Christopher Bennett, Robin Celikates, Miranda Fricker, Coleen Macnamara, Leonhard Menges, Paul Russell, and Angela Smith (at "Moral Address"); Jonathan Dancy, Stephen Darwall, Tamar Schapiro, Thomas Schmidt, Holmer Steinfath, Sarah Stroud, Ralph Wedgwood, and Susan Wolf (at "The Nature of Moral Obligation"); Christoph Fehige, Johann Frick, Tim Henning, Ulrike

Heuer, Erasmus Mayr, Kirsten Meyer, Lukas Meyer, Véronique Munoz-Dardé, Juri Viehoff, and Tatjana Višak (at "Contractualism, Risk, and Population Ethics"); and Samuel Scheffler (during his week in Berlin as our philosopher-in-residence). I would also like to thank Berit Braun, Micha Gläser, Nora Kreft, and Thomas Schmidt, who have been stalwart and valued participants in most of these events, as well as Gerd Grasshoff, the Director of the Topoi Excellence Cluster, and Kerstin Rumpeltes, who provided outstanding logistical support. Thanks above all to the Einstein Foundation for the Visiting Fellowship that made these many rewarding activities in Berlin possible.

The Einstein Ethics Group sponsored an additional workshop in May 2017, organized by Jan Gertken and Thomas Schmidt, devoted to discussion of the first complete draft of my manuscript for this book. The workshop was attended by a large group of mostly European philosophers, and I profited greatly from their acute critical and constructive suggestions during a series of intense but very productive sessions. The interest that people at the workshop seemed to take in my project was deeply gratifying, and helped to reassure me that the book might make a worthwhile contribution, on balance, despite its manifest shortcomings. The invited participants in this workshop, to whom I am especially indebted, were Monika Betzler, Christine Bratu, Tim Henning, Ulrike Heuer, Doug Lavin, Erasmus Mayr, Véronique Munoz-Dardé, and Peter Schaber. Comments by Valentin Beck, Logi Gunnarsson, Stefan Gosepath, Paul Guyer, Thomas Schmidt, and the Einstein Group members were also very helpful.

I also received valuable feedback on the first three chapters of the manuscript from participants in another workshop, in June 2017, organized in Frankfurt by the editorial board of the *European Journal of Philosophy*. Participants included Dina Emundts, Andrew Huddleston, Christoph Menke, Frederick Neuhauser, Beate Rössler, and Joseph K. Schear.

In addition, I have benefited enormously from detailed and astute written comments on the complete first draft of the manuscript from Niko Kolodny, Arthur Ripstein (who identified himself as one of the readers of the manuscript for Princeton University Press), Robert Stern, Bart Streumer, and a second reader for the Press. I have done my best to respond constructively to the feedback I have received from all of these patient and kind readers, though I am keenly aware that my revisions sometimes serve more to evade their objections than to answer them.

The Moral Nexus touches on issues in all parts of moral philosophy, very broadly conceived. As a result, its argument inevitably reflects influences that have shaped my thinking since I began the study of philosophy. I hope it will not seem presumptuous to mention here the senior figures whose work has been most inspirational to me. I still remember very vividly the feeling of exhilaration that came over me when I first worked through Thomas Nagel's *The Possibility of Altruism* during a brilliant summer week in Oxford; this book showed me that ethics could be a subject of serious philosophical study, and set me on my subsequent intellectual path. Though it took me somewhat longer to appreciate and come to terms with them, I have also been deeply influenced by the contributions to philosophical ethics of Joseph Raz, T. M. Scanlon, and Bernard Williams, which in their very different ways exemplify the capacity of philosophy to illuminate fundamental issues in this area.

As I have made my way through the stages of an academic career, I have been sustained by the loyal companionship of several extraordinary individuals who also happen to be significant contributors to contemporary moral and political philosophy, and whose influence no doubt shows up in the book that follows, if only in ways that I am no longer able to trace very precisely. I would like to mention in particular Jonathan Dancy, Samuel Freeman, Stefan Gosepath, Logi Gunnarsson, Niko Kolodny, Erasmus Mayr, Véronique Munoz-Dardé, Samuel Scheffler, Seana Valentine Shiffrin, Michael Smith, Gary Watson, and Susan Wolf. My life in philosophy has been an extremely fortunate one, but among the best things in it are philosophical friendships such as these, which have had a much more profound effect on my intellectual development than my formal education in the subject.

Rob Tempio, Matt Rohal, and Kathleen Cioffi of Princeton University Press have guided this project expertly through the process of editorial review and production. Hank Southgate's copyediting was both meticulous and unobtrusive, resulting in many improvements, and Nancy Gerth prepared the excellent index. I am grateful to all of them for their interest in my work and for the considerable efforts they have undertaken to ensure that my manuscript would become an attractive and successful book.

All these debts pale in comparison to the one I owe to Katharina Kaiser, who has not only tolerated graciously my obsessions and eccentricities and moods, but provided, in addition, an inspiring example of scholarly integrity and pedagogical commitment. Another dedication in the front of an obscure book can scarcely repay her for her many contributions to my philosophical life; but perhaps it is not nothing.

THE MORAL NEXUS

1

Introduction

PEOPLE MEAN MANY DIFFERENT THINGS when they talk about morality. In a familiar modern sense, however, morality may be thought of as a set of normative constraints on attitudes and actions that stem from the fact that we inhabit a common world together with other agents. More specifically, and more controversially, it may be thought of as a normative nexus that links us individually with each of the persons who might potentially be affected by what we do. According to what I will call the relational interpretation of it, morality involves a set of requirements on action that are constitutively connected to claims that others have against us, just insofar as they are persons. Requirements that are connected to claims in this way have a built-in directionality, specifying things that we owe it to others to do. So on the relational interpretation, morality could be said to be fundamentally a matter of what we owe *to* each other.[1]

This book offers a statement and defense of the idea that morality collects a set of fundamentally relational requirements. A leading idea of the discussion is that moral standards have some significant normative features that can be made sense of only if we interpret them in relational terms. They function to define practical requirements, which regulate the deliberations of agents in the distinctive manner of obligations; and they also have interpersonal significance, providing a normative basis for relations of moral accountability. I argue that the relational approach is better able than the alternatives to illuminate these significant aspects of the moral. In addition, I shall highlight and defend the major philosophical commitments and presuppositions of the relational interpretation, which have not been subjected to sustained critical investigation. I shall also discuss some of the first-order implications of the relational approach, for questions about what, specifically, we owe it to each other to do, and about the nature of the reasoning that goes into deciding issues of this kind.

The idea of relational requirements in the most general sense is implicit in talk of moral and legal rights. More specifically, it is familiar from discussions of claim rights, in the sense made familiar by Wesley Newcombe Hohfeld. These rights are commonly understood to be complexes of claims, privileges, and powers that are invested in agents, and that correspond to duties on the part of other agents.[2] My right to a piece of property that has legitimately come into my possession, for instance, involves a claim against other people that they should not use it without my permission, where that claim defines a duty that others are under; it involves, furthermore, a permission to do with the piece of property as I wish, as well as a power to transfer my claims in it to others as I see fit. According to this way of thinking, those who make off with my property without my authorization will violate a claim I have against them, thereby transforming their relationships to me in a way they will not change their relationships to other parties. They will have not only have acted wrongly; they will also have wronged me in particular, providing me with what we might think of as a privileged ground for objecting to what they have done.

Hohfeldian rights of this general kind are a familiar part of our normative repertoire, deeply embedded in our thinking about (for instance) the structures of private law. Contracts, for instance, seem to generate a complex of directed duties and corresponding claims, and a similar structure of claim rights is arguably implicit in the law of torts.[3] Whether there are similar claim rights at the most fundamental level of moral thought is a more controversial suggestion, one that has been questioned, in different ways, by consequentialists and proponents of certain virtue-theoretic views. Even those who are open to the idea that there are basic moral claim rights, however, naturally tend to think of them as constituting just a part of morality; the "realm of rights" that Judith Jarvis Thomson has written about, for instance, is seen by her as a subregion within a larger moral territory. Thus, there are many moral duties that people seem to be under that do not correspond to any Hohfeldian claim rights in the familiar sense, including imperfect obligations of mutual aid, duties of gratitude, environmental imperatives, and sundry requirements of moral virtue.[4]

I agree that morality cannot be understood exclusively in terms of moral rights in the narrow, Hohfeldian sense. But it nevertheless strikes me as promising to interpret morality in relational terms, as a set of requirements on agents that are like the obligations of the Hohfeldian domain in being constitutively connected to claims that other individuals have against us. Relational elements are pervasive in many significant features of modern, secular morality, and it is my belief that these elements can be brought together into a comprehensive interpretation of the moral realm. The account I defend is not a theory of moral rights, as these are conventionally understood; rather it extracts a relational core from ordinary talk about rights and directed duties, and proposes that this relational structure can be extended, in an illuminating way, into a general framework for understanding the nature and normative significance of moral requirements.

The extension of the relational model that I shall defend, however, is not meant to capture everything that might intuitively be understood to be a reason or requirement of morality. There is a broad conception of the moral according to which it collects all standards of deliberate human conduct, whatever their source. In this broad sense, it is a moral defect if someone acts with disregard for the beauty of the natural world, or attaches importance to an activity that is out of proportion to its significance and value, regardless of whether the behavior in question otherwise affects the interests or welfare of persons or other sentient individuals. Moral failings, in this very capacious usage, are to be contrasted with deficiencies that do not directly involve the will, such as chronic bodily illnesses or infirmities that interfere with an individual's biological good functioning.[5] It is no part of my brief in this book to maintain that all moral standards, in this maximally capacious sense, are defined by relational requirements that are owed to individual claimholders. The relational account I shall develop is meant to capture a moral domain that is broader than the realm of moral rights, but narrower than the set of all standards that are applicable to the rational will. This is the intermediate domain, roughly speaking, that T. M. Scanlon has referred to as "the morality of right and wrong."[6] I shall call it interpersonal morality, to emphasize the fact that the standards that are in question derive directly from the effects of an individual's actions on the interests and well-being of persons (where personhood is understood in a manner, still to be defined, that potentially diverges from membership in our biological species[7]). Interpersonal morality, in this intermediate sense, might be thought of as a set of requirements that reflect the fundamental insight that we share a world with other individuals whose interests are in some sense neither more nor less important than our own.

Not everyone who accepts this way of dividing up normative standards needs to agree about the desiderata to which an account of interpersonal morality is answerable. Some philosophers favor pluralist interpretations of interpersonal morality, tracing its requirements to fundamentally distinct values rather than imputing to them any underlying substantive unity.[8] There is room for disagreement, as well, about the precise boundaries of this intermediate domain (disagreements, that is, about some particular requirements on human agency, and whether they are to be included within the domain). The approach I favor starts from the observation that interpersonal morality intuitively exhibits more specific normative features that have been neglected in recent treatments, and that a relational conception of obligation captures the underlying unity of the interpersonal domain that exhibits these important features. A consequence of this approach is that there might be some standards of rational agency that derive from the effects of action on other persons, but that are not standards of interpersonal morality as I understand it. Standards of this kind are not obligations in the sense in which the core requirements of interpersonal morality can be understood to be, nor do they function to structure accountability relations with other persons. They define forms of what I shall call extramoral concern for moral persons—taking "morality," as I shall do in what follows, to refer to the intermediate domain of interpersonal morality, rather than to the broad set of all standards that might apply to the rational will.[9]

My discussion will at many points raise more questions than can be answered in the compass of a single volume; as will become plain in what follows, the relational interpretation touches on many large issues of both theory and practice that are worthy of extended treatment in their own right. But I write in the conviction that it is important to have a sense of the big picture before we get too bogged down in matters of fine detail and nuance.[10] Writers on moral philosophy frequently fall into a relational idiom when they talk about particular normative and philosophical issues. They assume, for instance, that individuals are typically wronged by behavior that is morally impermissible, and proceed to reflect on the implications of being treated in this way for the attitudes and behavior of the person who is wronged.[11] But the relational interpretation, even when it comes naturally to us, is also philosophically distinctive; it is fundamentally opposed by some of the most influential traditions of reflection about morality, which treat moral requirements in individualistic rather than relational terms. There is need for an overview of the relational approach to the moral that highlights its distinctive features, so that we may better appreciate both the philosophical and normative advantages of understanding morality in these terms and the obstacles that stand in the way of such an interpretation. My hope is that the discussion in the present volume will go some way toward addressing this need.

1.1. Elements of Relational Normativity

In the present section, I would like to flesh out my initial sketch of the relational conception of morality by saying a bit more about what I take to be its basic elements.[12] For purposes of exposition, it will be helpful to take as an example a case of a moral requirement that it is natural to understand as having a relational structure: that of promissory obligation. There are three important features that appear distinctive of cases of this kind, which I shall call directed obligation, claim, and normative injury; let us consider these in turn.

(a) Directed Obligation

Relational norms, on an intuitive understanding of them, serve to ground obligations, specifying things that an individual agent must do. Thus, someone who makes a promise has undertaken an obligation, one that would not obtain in the absence of the promissory exchange. If the promise was to do X, then it seems, at a minimum, that the fact of the promise gives rise to a new reason for the agent to do X. That is, there is a consideration that speaks in favor of doing X that was not in place before the promise was made. But this understates the change in the normative situation that is effected by the promise. We normally think that promisors, in offering someone else promissory assurance about what they will do, are now under a duty to fulfill the promise they have made. Promisors exercise a normative power that is available to agents to create obligations where such were not antecedently in place, binding themselves to do what they have promised. Promises are indeed among the most salient and familiar examples of the phenomenon of moral obligation, even if they differ from many alleged obligations in being created through voluntary acts.

In saying this, I do not mean to suggest that it is always morally impermissible for promisors to fail to do the very thing that they have promised. Our understanding of the morality of promissory obligation implicitly acknowledges circumstances in which promisors do not have to follow the letter of their promises. Emergencies sometimes come up, for instance, that could not have been anticipated, even by a conscientious agent, at the time when the promise was made. Under these conditions, I think it would be natural to say that it is not wrong for the promisor to fail to perform the promised action. There may be some residual obligation that the promisor is under to provide compensation for losses that the promisee might have suffered in virtue of having relied on the promisor to do the thing that was promised; strictly speaking, however, the original promissory obligation (to do X, for example, if that is what was promised) no longer obtains under such circumstances. We might put this by saying that promissory obligation is not reasonably understood to be unconditional.[13] It is, however, defeasible: so long as exceptional circumstances do not obtain, the promisor is under a moral obligation to do the thing that was promised, an obligation that was entered into through the promissory act.

It is further characteristic of these obligations that they have a built-in directionality.[14] The promissory exchange brings into existence a normative nexus between the promisor and the promisee, whereby the former owes it to the latter to do the thing that was promised. Other people, who were not themselves parties to the promissory exchange, might well take an interest in whether the promisor fulfills the obligation. But this is not something that the promisor owes it specifically to them to do. The promise creates a special relationship between the promisor and the promisee, making it the case that the new obligation that obtains is directed specifically to the promisee. Indeed, as I shall argue more extensively in chapter 2, our sense that the promise creates an obligation is connected to the fact that it links the promisor and the promisee in a new normative nexus of this kind. A requirement that is owed to another individual in particular is not the exclusive property of the agent whose actions it governs; rather it is held in common by the two people whom it links. We are "bound" when we stand in a normative relationship of this kind, in the specific sense that the requirement that we are under, as agents, binds us to another party.

(b) Claim

A directed obligation corresponds, on the side of the person to whom it is directed, to the notion of a claim. The party to whom the agent owes compliance with the obligation is someone who has a claim to such compliant behavior. Indeed, the claim in question has a built-in directionality that mirrors that of the obligation to which it corresponds; it is a claim that the party has *against* the agent to the latter's compliance with the directed requirement. In the promising case, for example, it is the promisees who have a moral claim of this kind. We might understand this as an entitlement, held against the promisors, to their seeing to it that the promises are kept.[15]

Like the directed obligation with which it is linked, the claim that is held by the other party is not necessarily unconditional. As we saw above, the promise to do X does not generate an obligation on the promisor to do X under any and all possible circumstances that might eventually come to obtain. The claim on the part of the promisee, insofar as it corresponds neatly to the promisor's obligation, is therefore likewise defeasible in character. It is a claim that the promisor should do X, barring unforeseeable conditions of the kind that would generally be understood to defeat the promisor's obligation so to act. Just as the promisor might well have various secondary obligations under such circumstances, for example to provide compensation for losses suffered, so too would the promisee have claims against the promisor to those secondary performances.

A claim, in the sense that dovetails with a directed obligation, should be distinguished carefully from the notion of an interest. To have a claim against another party or parties that they should do X is not the same as having an interest in whether they will so act. Suppose that A has promised B to do X, and that there is another person, C, whose professional projects will be furthered if A in fact does X. Under these circumstances, C has an interest in A's doing X (making C what is sometimes called a "third-party beneficiary" of A's X-ing[16]); but it does not follow from this that C has a specific claim against A that A should do X. The directed claim, insofar as there is one in this case, resides in B, the promisee. Having an interest in someone else's doing something is thus not sufficient for having a claim against that individual, in the sense that is here at issue.

It is perhaps more plausible to suppose that interests are at least necessary conditions for normative claims, but even here caution is required. When people have claims against other parties that they do X, it seems that there must be something in their situation and outlook, as individual agents, that provides a basis for their claims, and enables us to understand the claims as residing in them in particular. In some cases, this will be the fact that the claim-holders' interests would be affected negatively if the other parties were to fail to do X; consider in this connection our claims against people not to be physically assaulted by them, which presumably have something to do with the effects of assault on our basic interests in bodily integrity, self-determination, and freedom from pain and suffering.

But the general relationship between interests and normative claims is more complicated than this example might suggest. Returning to the phenomenon of promising, take the case that Philippa Foot introduced into recent discussions: a Malay servant extracts from the anthropologist Mikluko-Maklay a promise that the latter will not photograph him, believing that having his picture taken would cause harm to his spirit.[17] It seems plausible that the promise gives the servant a claim against Maklay not to be photographed by the anthropologist; and yet it seems that the servant would not really be harmed if Maklay were to break the promise surreptitiously (for example, by snapping some pictures of the servant while he is asleep).

Some have suggested that we have in this case a bare normative claim, one that is not grounded in any genuine nonnormative interests that are held by the promisee.[18] But this seems to me a questionable inference. Even if the servant would not by hypothesis be harmed if Maklay were to photograph him, he has a legitimate interest in his own autonomy—in determining for himself, and in accordance with his own convictions, how others will make use of his body and person. He also has an interest in achieving assurance from others that they will respect his wishes about such matters of personal self-determination. There are thus important interests of the servant's, in the sense of things that he takes a legitimate interest in concerning the character of his own life, that provide a basis for his claim that Maklay should keep the promise that was made in this case.

Generalizing boldly from this single example, it is tempting to conjecture that normative claims have to be anchored somehow in the interests of the claimholder, even if interests are not on their own sufficient to ground claims of the relevant kind. But is there anything in the relational interpretation of morality that would support this way of thinking about the bearing of interests on moral claims? What, more specifically, is the nature of the interests that are relevant to our specifically moral claims? And how exactly do we get from such interests to the determinate assignment of moral claims to individual claimholders, given that the bare possession of an interest does not on its own suffice to ground a normative claim? These are important questions for the relational interpretation of morality, to which I shall return in chapter 5 of this book.

In the meantime, I would caution against equating moral claims with the notion of moral rights. As I noted above, it is commonplace in the philosophical literature on rights to assume that at least some moral rights involve directed claims that are structurally like the claims that I have been discussing, insofar as they are held against other agents, correspond to directed duties on the part of those agents that are owed to the claimholder, and so on. If we are going to interpret the entire moral domain in relational terms, however, then we should not assume from the start that all moral claims involve what we would intuitively recognize as assignable individual rights. There are duties of gratitude, for instance, but it would be strange to say that these correspond to moral rights on the part of the potential beneficiaries of the duty; and we have duties to aid those who are in severe distress, without it being the case that specific rights are held by each of the potential millions of beneficiaries that each in particular should be assisted by us. We also have moral obligations to uphold and support valuable practices or conventions that we may have participated in, and yet these, too, do not seem to correspond to assignable individual rights against us.

Rights, I believe, represent a subclass of the normative claims that morality invests in individuals, but their distinguishing features are not present in all cases in which we have claims against others that they should comply with moral requirements. This will become a prominent theme in chapter 6 of this book, which addresses, inter alia, moral duties that have not seemed to be relational in character, precisely because they do not correspond to what we conventionally think of as individual moral rights.

(c) Normative Injury

The third element in the kind of relational conception that interests me is that of a normative injury. This concept is in place in situations in which agents have flouted the requirements that they stand under. Insofar as the requirement is genuine, specifying what people have to do, those who have violated it will have done something wrong. But if the requirement is a directed one, owed specifically to another party who has a claim against the agent to compliance, something further will be the case as well. The action that flouts the requirement will not merely be wrong; it will change the agent's normative relationship to another individual, wronging the person to whom compliance with the requirement was owed. This is, as it were, the ex post facto residue of the individual's claim against the agent to performance of the required action, in the case in which the claim has not been honored.

Just as normative claims are not to be equated with interests, normative injury is not the same as harm. Wrongful actions can have harmful effects on other persons without wronging them in particular, and those who are wronged by an action need not specifically be harmed by it, taking everything into account. Consider a case in which A promises B to stay away from a reception that B will be attending, but A ends up going to the reception all the same. A's wrongful presence at the reception might end up being disadvantageous to the professional interests of a third person in attendance, C, but it wouldn't necessarily follow that A had thereby wronged C. (Perhaps A ends up in a lengthy and mutually absorbing conversation with a potential client whom C had been hoping to cultivate at the reception, without it being the case that the promise was originally made by A to B out of consideration for C's professional interest in having unimpeded access to any potential clients who might be in attendance.) By the same token, A's action might wrong B, even if it leaves B better off on balance than B would otherwise have been. (Maybe B extracted the promise from A out of a concern for B's own access to potential clients at the reception, but A's presence and easy banter about fly fishing ends up facilitating B's plan to cultivate new business relationships.) If, as I suggested above, moral claims can always be traced to some interest or other on the part of the claimholder, then disregard of moral claims will involve a slight of some kind to the claimholder's interests. But it needn't be the case that claimholders are harmed, on balance, by the actions that wrong them.

These points, or analogues of them, are familiar from the literature on rights, claims, and directed obligations. But there is a further aspect of moral injury that has seldom been remarked on, namely its dependence on the attitudes of the agent. Directed obligations, and the claims that correspond to them, do not in general involve demands on the attitudes of the agents who are bound by them. In the case we have just been discussing, where A promised B to stay away from the reception, A will count as complying with the obligation, and satisfying B's literal claims, so long as A does not appear at the location of the event during the time when it is taking place; the motives out of which A satisfies this condition make no difference to the question of whether the claims and obligations have been satisfied. By the same token, A will have broken the promise if A shows up at the reception, regardless of A's reasons for so acting (assuming that no unanticipated emergencies have arisen in the meantime, of the kind that are capable of modifying the original promissory commitment).

When it comes to moral injury, by contrast, things are otherwise. It matters to the question of whether A has wronged B with what attitudes A acted. When I introduced the notion of normative injury above, I associated it with cases in which agents have flouted a directed obligation that they stand under. But to *flout* a requirement is to act with a distinctive attitude toward it, one of knowing and even open disregard. Furthermore, given the constitutive connection between the directed obligation and the claim of another party, this attitude of disregard for the obligation is eo ipso an attitude of disregard for the specific claimholder. But to be treated with this kind of disregard is crucial,

I submit, to the relevant notion of a normative injury; the wrong that has been visited on one who suffers such an injury consists, at least in part, in the attitude of indifference to or contempt for one's specific claims.

If this is right, however, then there can be cases in which agents fail to fulfill the letter of the directed obligations that they stand under, without their having thereby wronged the individuals who had claims against them to performance. Having promised not to show up at the reception, A might end up putting in an appearance inadvertently, arriving at the gallery where it is taking place out of ignorance that it was relocated there by the organizers at the last minute. The promisee, B, would not have been wronged by A's action under this scenario, precisely insofar as A's action does not reflect an attitude of disregard toward B's specific claims (though this might change if A does not leave the gallery as soon as it becomes clear that the reception is taking place there).

An attitude of disregard for another person's claims seems in this way to be a necessary element in the analysis of moral injury. Whether such an attitude is also sufficient to give rise to a moral injury is a further question, which does not need to be resolved here. To think that it is would be to suppose that people might suffer moral injuries through actions that are not morally wrong. Thus, suppose A goes to the gallery, believing that that is where the reception will be happening, and not caring about the fact that she promised B not to attend, but it turns out that the reception was all along scheduled to take place in a different venue on the other side of town. Here B would naturally feel unnerved about A's performance, if not outright resentful, despite the fact that A complied in the end with the obligation that was owed to B. But it is not clear that we would want to say that B was actually wronged by A's behavior, strictly speaking. Perhaps people suffer moral injuries, in the relevant sense, only through actions that in fact violate duties that are owed to them; or perhaps we can allow that there are cases of moral injury that do not violate any duties that are owed to the person who suffers the injury.

Whichever way we come down on this question, however, it is important to note that there will be something unsettling to claimholders about agents who comply objectively with their claims, but without acknowledging them as important constraints on their behavior. The agent's attitude of indifference to other peoples' claims is something significant that these cases have in common with the central examples of moral injury, and there will be continuities in our responses to the different cases, however we decide to classify them in the end. This is an issue to which I shall return in chapter 4 of the present volume.

1.2. Overview of the Argument

In the remainder of this book, I shall develop an interpretation of interpersonal morality as a domain of normative requirements that exhibit the three relational elements just sketched. Understanding morality in these terms, I shall argue, enables us to make sense of central features of the moral realm that are otherwise mysterious, while also shedding light on the character and content of the reasoning we engage in about particular moral issues.

The argument of the book begins, in chapter 2, with a discussion of the deliberative significance of moral considerations. The focus here is on the character of such considerations as *obligations*. Conclusions about what it is morally right or permissible to do enter the field of deliberation in a distinctive way, as presumptive constraints on the agent's activities. It is an important desideratum for moral theory to make sense of this aspect of morality, which involves (as I contend) a sui generis form of normative relation. I show that a relational interpretation of morality can illuminate the force of moral considerations as obligations of this kind, ones that derive from the basic fact that we inhabit a common world together with other individuals. Duties that are owed to another party are paradigmatically suited to the distinctive deliberative role of presumptive constraints on a person's agency. So if there are things that we owe to other persons just in virtue of their standing as persons, the ingredients will be in place for an account of interpersonal morality as a set of obligations or practical requirements on the will. In the course of developing this idea, I argue, further, that the resulting account is superior to the alternative theories of moral obligation bequeathed to us by the philosophical tradition.

In chapter 3, I turn to a different but equally important aspect of morality, which involves its social significance. Moral norms, I suggest, characteristically ground relations of accountability between individuals. Thus, we understand a group's morality, in part, by identifying the norms whose violation attracts blame and opprobrium within their community; these are norms that members of the community hold each other accountable for complying with. I argue that the features that explain the standing of moral considerations as obligations should equally shed light on their suitability to structure interpersonal accountability relations of this kind. That is, the moral qualities that function normatively in deliberation as presumptive constraints on agency should equally provide other parties with reasons to adjust their attitudes and behavior toward the agent when the constraints are flouted.

I contend that the relational interpretation is uniquely equipped to render intelligible this interpersonal dimension of the moral. If moral obligations have their basis in the things that we owe it to other individuals to do, then to act with disregard for such considerations is to display disregard for other individuals, as persons who have claims against us. To flout moral obligations, so understood, is not merely to do the wrong thing, but to wrong someone else, causing that individual what I referred to above as a moral injury. But this is the sort of thing that gives the person who is wronged reason to resent the agent, in the way that is characteristic of relations of accountability. I show, further, that our accountability practices themselves have a relational deep structure. Reactive and other forms of blame, as well as the subsequent responses they set in motion, seem to presuppose a relational interpretation of moral requirements. Thus, wrongdoers are expected to apologize to those who have been wronged by what they did, and people in this position have a power to forgive wrongdoers that does not extend to other parties. We can make sense of these features of our interpersonal practices of accountability only if the moral norms that structure them are relational in character.

Chapters 2 and 3 together make a positive case for interpreting morality as a domain of directed obligations. The argument turns on the importance of elucidating the characteristic role of morality, both within individual deliberation and as a basis for a social practice of interpersonal accountability. Both aspects of this challenge have been somewhat neglected in recent discussions.[19] To be sure, the general problem of normativity looms large in contemporary moral philosophy. But contributors to debates about this issue often ignore the distinctive role of moral considerations in practical reflection about what to do. Considerations of this kind are not merely reasons, in the now familiar sense of things that count for or against candidate actions that the agent might perform, but obligations, which structure reflection in a very different and more peremptory fashion. Similarly, the role of morality as a basis for relations of interpersonal accountability is crucial to human life, but it is often completely neglected in treatments of the nature of morality; whole treatises are written on this subject in which the topic of interpersonal accountability hardly comes up at all.[20] The lived experience of morality is as a domain of considerations that make demands on us as agents, and that also have a special kind of importance for the attitudes of other parties toward us. My contention is that the relational approach is uniquely able to shed light on these neglected aspects of interpersonal morality, and that this constitutes a powerful presumptive case for understanding the moral domain in relational terms.[21]

In the not too distant past, philosophical accounts of morality were expected to establish in some way or other the authority of moral norms to govern the activities of the individual agents to whom they apply; at least that was the expectation if they were vindicatory rather than revisionist in tenor. The background was a climate of mild skepticism about independent normative notions, and a corresponding feeling that moral requirements required some special justification if they were to succeed in prescribing what the agent is to do.[22]

More recently, the intellectual climate has evolved somewhat. Many contemporary moral philosophers are willing to take for granted some form of nonreductive realism about the normative in their philosophical investigations. Those who are not tend to focus on the metaethics of normativity in general, not the credentials of moral reasons and requirements in particular. The idea that there might be a special problem that is posed by the normativity of the moral starts to seem peculiar against the background of these assumptions. But I think there is a special problem here, one that it is important for a philosophical account of morality to address.[23] In particular, the challenge is to make sense of the fact that considerations of moral right and wrong have two very distinctive kinds of normative significance: they represent obligations or practical requirements in the first-person perspective of deliberation, and they also structure our interpersonal relations of accountability. My initial case for the relational approach is based on its success at meeting this important challenge to moral theory.

Every philosophical investigation takes some things for granted. In developing my argument for the relational approach, I shall not attempt to vindicate normative commitments in general in the face of skeptical or naturalistic worries about them. Rather, I shall assume that we can safely operate with normative notions of various kinds, and address the more specific questions sketched above, about how moral theory can make sense of the distinctive normative bearing that morality has both on individual deliberation and on our social relations. These issues, like many others in philosophy, come into sharp relief only when we focus on them at the right level of resolution. Zoom out too far—for instance, by taking up the metaethical project of placing normativity in general within the larger landscape of natural objects and processes—and the specific normative features that distinguish interpersonal morality become indistinct. These features also disappear when we zoom in very closely on the fine structure of moral requirements, as happens with many investigations in so-called normative ethics, where fantastic variants on hypothetical cases are constructed in order to elicit intuitions about the morality of right and wrong.[24] Ethical theory, as I shall be pursuing it here, cannot ignore questions in metaethics or normative ethics; but it equally cannot allow the pursuit of these questions to pull us out of the intermediate range within which the distinctive normative features of interpersonal morality become both visible and puzzling.

The background framework that I shall adopt for purposes of this intermediate investigation does not merely countenance normative commitments in general; it allows that there can be irreducibly distinct forms of normative relation.[25] Philosophers sometimes assume that normativity is exclusively a matter of reasons, where reasons are in turn considerations that count for and against attitudes and actions. But as noted earlier, this idea does not seem to fit very well with the idea that there are obligations. Considerations that practically require an agent to do something seem to figure very differently within deliberation from the kind of reasons that merely count in favor of doing the same thing. Similarly, reasons for the reactive attitudes, such as resentment or indignation, seem different in kind from the considerations that count in favor of actions we might perform; the former are considerations that render the attitudes fitting or intelligible, whereas the latter have to do with the various ways in which actions might be valuable or worthy of pursuit. My suggestion will be that the relational account is well suited to elucidate the different kinds of sui generis normative significance we attribute to morality: its standing as a source of practical requirements on the individual will, as well as its role in making it fitting or appropriate for others to respond to infractions with reactive and other forms of blame.

Directed obligations and the claims that are connected with them might be understood to constitute a normative nexus, and this is how I shall speak of the relational elements in the theory of morality that are my main target in this book. They represent a normative nexus, just in the sense that their elements have the different kinds of normative significance for agents and for claimholders that were distinguished in the preceding paragraph. But idea of a relational nexus itself—of a complex of directed obligations and claims that are linked to them—is a further element in the larger theory that I shall largely take for granted in what follows. I assume there is a range of familiar cases that we all intuitively understand to have this kind of relational structure, including the example of promissory obligations that recurs throughout the book, as well as numerous other examples from private law, institutional practice, and even games of various kinds. My aim will be to draw out some of the significant features of a normative nexus of this familiar kind, and to defend and develop the suggestion that a nexus of the same kind can be understood to constitute the deep structure of the realm of impartial morality. But I shall not endeavor to provide a reductive account of relational structures of this general type (one that might, for instance, attempt to identify nonrelational elements that together constitute necessary and sufficient conditions for the obtaining of such a structure).[26]

To summarize this catalogue of defensive stipulations, I shall develop a normative argument for the relational interpretation of the moral, but one that differs from approaches familiar in the philosophical tradition. I shall not attempt to demonstrate that all agents have reason to comply with relational moral requirements, nor do I have a transcendental argument to offer, to the effect that a commitment to relational obligations is implicit in the structure of rational agency (for instance, as a constitutive condition of its possibility). Rather, taking basic normative concepts largely as given, I shall focus on some of the things that set moral norms apart from normative notions of other kinds, including their standing in deliberation as practical requirements and their significance to our practices of interpersonal accountability. The gist of the argument is that we will best be able to understand these aspects of the moral domain if we think of it as a set of relational obligations that link us with other individuals in a pairwise normative nexus.

The normative argument of chapters 2 and 3 has a conditional structure. The general suggestion is that, if the relational model can be applied to the entire moral domain, the result will be an interpretation of it that renders fully intelligible its distinctive normative features. But it still needs to be shown that the relational model can be extended in this way. This is the task of the remaining chapters of the book. In chapter 4, I discuss some general issues that are raised by the ambition to interpret all moral obligations in relational terms. The most salient and familiar examples of directed duties arise from transactions and other forms of causal interaction between the parties that they link. A promise comes into existence through some kind of exchange between the parties to it, and duties of gratitude are created when a kindness is bestowed by one person on another; similar patterns of nonnormative interaction are found in relationships between family members and friends, which characteristically give rise to networks of claims and directed obligations.

Against this background, it is natural to wonder whether directed obligations presuppose antecedent personal relationships. If so, this would prevent the application of the model to the entire moral domain, as interpersonal morality, on the modern conception of it, is meant to define obligations that govern our conduct toward people with whom we have never before interacted. A complementary line of thought is suggested by reflection about the evolutionary history of morality, which plausibly first emerged as a set of tendencies that encourage cooperation in contexts involving close and sustained social interaction. The relational model that seems well suited to contexts of this kind might not provide a plausible framework for thinking about our duties in cases that do not involve face-to-face interaction or tribal identity.

I argue, in response to these questions, that some reflective extension of more elementary moral resources is required in any case, if we are to devise principles that are adequate to regulate our conduct in the full range of situations that must be covered by a comprehensive moral scheme. A scheme of this kind is one that acknowledges the basic modern insight that morality is a cosmopolitan phenomenon, regulating our relations to a maximally inclusive notional community of individuals whose interests are considered equally important. I suggest that there is a strong presumptive case for extending the relational model into a comprehensive framework that applies to this extensive notional community, given the ability of the model to illuminate the normative features that are distinctive of the moral realm. Doing this requires that we think of morality as a set of self-standing directed obligations, which are not grounded in any antecedent relationship that the parties to them have with each other. I consider and reject some general arguments that have been advanced for thinking that there could not be a self-standing normative nexus of this kind. I also explore some of the metaethical presuppositions of the moral nexus, construed in this way, which include an anti-individualist conception of normativity. Individualists might not be able to accept that there are self-standing relational obligations that link agents and claimholders in a common normative structure; but I show that they will equally be skeptical about ideas that are basic to any cosmopolitan conception of morality, including ideas that the relational approach is especially well equipped to illuminate.

The chapter concludes with some further reflections about the agent-relativity of moral obligations and about the values enabled by relational morality. It might initially seem that obligations are agent-relative in character in virtue of the fact that they are grounded in patterns of historical interaction between individuals, which serve to distinguish the people to whom agents specifically owe compliance with moral obligations from others who merely stand to be affected by what the agent does (perhaps in ways that also involve the agency of third parties). But this is not correct. The deeper feature that explains the agent-relativity of many standard moral requirements is simply their directed character, which connects them constitutively to the claims of other individuals. This same feature of relational morality sheds light on the values that are enabled through compliance with moral requirements, which I suggest should be understood in terms of an ideal of interpersonal recognition. We understand it to be a valuable thing to relate to others in a way that serves to realize this ideal in our own conduct, and this can help us appreciate the contribution that morality can make to the goodness of the agent's own life.

In chapter 5, I take up some questions about the structure and scope of relational morality. If the moral nexus is construed as a domain of self-standing relational obligations, the question arises as to the manifold of individuals who are potentially linked under such obligations. Prior relationships or ties are not preconditions for linkage under the relational duties and claims of morality, so what other principles might enable us to decide the issue of inclusion in the set of moral persons? I suggest that we begin by thinking of this class as including those individuals who are capable of entertaining relational moral thoughts. This group includes all normal adult members of our species, but it might conceivably include other individuals as well. I then consider various ways in which the cosmopolitan manifold of persons might be extended outward from this core, including possible extensions that result in asymmetries among the members of the manifold (where, for instance, claims are assigned to individuals who do not themselves stand under corresponding directed obligations).

It is implausible to think, however, that there are concrete duties that we owe to all of the members of the maximally extensive class of moral persons. Some individuals, for instance, lie outside our temporal or spatial reach. In thinking about the specific conditions that have to be satisfied before a concrete nexus of moral duties and claims can be in place, I suggest that we focus on the effects that our agency can potentially have on the personal interests of other individuals. Personal interests in the relevant sense are interests people have in how their own lives go. I go on to propose that interests of this kind will play a prominent role in justifications for the assignment of concrete moral claims to an individual, and that moral reasoning can be understood, in general terms, as a movement of thought that takes us from personal interests to the identification of claims. The resulting picture differs from some conventional conceptions of moral rights and duties, which conceive of these things as inputs into reflection about what it is morally permissible to do, rather than outputs of specifically moral thought.

Chapter 5 ends with a discussion of the prospects for a theoretical account of relational morality. I note that the relational approach might be advanced in an intuitionistic variant, which would hold that the movement from personal interests to claims is effected through an exercise of particularistic judgment that cannot be subsumed under any general procedures or principles. While acknowledging this possibility, however, I also think that there is a promising moral theory that can be interpreted as offering an account of morality's implicitly relational structure. That theory is moral contractualism, in the form familiar from the work of T. M. Scanlon. Contractualism offers an account of moral reasoning, describing what we might think of as a general template for extracting assignable moral claims from the personal interests of those who might be affected by an agent's actions. It can also be understood as a substantive conception of morality that specifies, in illuminating terms, what it is for a nexus of moral directed duties and claims to be in place between two individuals. Its relational character is, in my view, essential to the power and plausibility of contractualism as a substantive moral theory, something that has been lost sight of in recent debates about the role of personal interests within contractualist reasoning.[27]

The final chapter addresses some first-order practical implications of the relational interpretation. As noted above, there are some important moral duties that do not intuitively seem to be grounded in the claims of individuals. Examples include duties to future generations, where the identity of the people who will exist in the future depends on what we now decide to do; imperfect duties of mutual aid, where our actions benefit people who do not have specific claims to the goods that we provide; and situations in which the numbers count for moral reflection, which have seemed difficult to make sense of in terms of moral requirements that are owed to other individuals. I show that the relational approach can plausibly be extended to challenging cases of these kinds, though only by modifying the familiar idea of a moral claim.

The chapter begins with a discussion of some of the most familiar examples of relational obligation, which I show to be very diverse in character. Some, but by no means all of them, involve transactions through which we understand ourselves to have incurred a literal or figurative debt that stands to be repaid. But they all involve situations in which our actions have potential effects on individuals who are foreseeable at the time when we act. I go on to consider a recent suggestion to the effect that foreseeability of this kind is not a necessary condition for an action to count as one that wrongs another party. Though the suggestion seems implausible to me, I note that it could be accommodated by postulating secondary moral claims not to be harmed by the wrongful agency of another. Claims of this kind would be unlike paradigm moral rights; but on any account of relational morality, there will be numerous claims of this sort. These include the considerations involved in cases of so-called imperfect moral duty, which leave agents with considerable discretion as to how they are to be fulfilled. I discuss the cases of gratitude and mutual aid, suggesting that claims are in place even here, though they are not necessarily claims whose satisfaction would redound to the benefit of the claim-holder in particular.

The remaining sections of the chapter offer an extended discussion of some of the moral situations that have traditionally been thought especially difficult to accommodate within a basically relational framework. A particular crux is the significance of numbers and aggregation for moral thought. I recommend a form of relational morality that gives prominence to the ex ante objections that individuals might have to principles for the general regulation of behavior, and observe that it provides resources for incorporating aggregative considerations within the framework of what we owe to each other as individuals. There remain, however, some cases that cannot be understood in these terms, where philosophers have maintained that aggregate well-being has independent importance for practical thought. I note that intuitions about this matter may trade in part on a failure to distinguish between contexts of individual agency and of collective decision-making about matters of democratic public policy. I also argue that the independent importance of well-being for individual agency, to the extent it persists, should be understood to involve requirements that conflict (at best) with those of relational morality, rather than undermining or outweighing them, as some have alleged that they do.

It is not my aim in chapter 6 to resolve the thorny practical questions that are there discussed. The objective is instead to explore the resources of the relational approach for understanding the moral dimension of these important questions. As noted earlier, many contemporary discussions in normative ethics proceed through constructing elaborate hypothetical cases, which are meant to test our intuitions about what it is right or permissible to do, but in a way that is independent of theoretical debates about the nature of moral rightness or permissibility.[28] One implication of the earlier chapters of this book is that this is a questionable strategy. It is not at all clear that there is a

stable and convincing conception of moral rightness, one that is suited to the
deliberative and interpersonal roles that a conception of this kind may reasonably be expected to satisfy. Until a plausible such conception is articulated and
developed, reflection on elaborate hypothetical cases threatens to become
undisciplined, appealing to elusive ideas about morality that we do not fully
understand. It is unpromising, for instance, to argue about what we have
"moral reason" to do, or about which of various hypothetical outcomes would
be "better (from the moral point of view)," until we know what conceptions
of moral reasons and moral value might be in play.[29] So one objective of chapter 6 is to situate some of the controversies in normative ethics within the
context of an independently compelling conception of what morality is about
in the first place.

Interpersonal morality, according to the relational interpretation of it, collects a set of requirements that derive from the inherent challenges of our
social life. These requirements constitute a coherent domain of interpersonal
obligations and claims, specifying what we owe to each other insofar as we are
moral persons who stand to be affected by exertions of each other's agency.
Chapter 6 argues that this way of thinking about interpersonal morality provides a fruitful framework for understanding what is at stake in some of the
challenging practical questions that are discussed. Seen in this light, the argument of chapter 6 dovetails with the earlier chapters of the book, which identify important normative features of our moral practices that are fully intelligible only on the relational interpretation of them, and which show how the
relational framework can be extended to encompass our relations to anyone
whose interests might conceivably be affected by what we do.

The book as a whole might thus be thought of as making an interpretative
case for the relational account.[30] It sketches a distinctive approach to understanding the unity of the moral realm, highlighting normative and practical
features of morality that best make sense when morality is understood in these
terms. The burden of the argument is not to counter the kind of skepticism
about morality that questions whether we can have reason to do things that
do not directly promote our own welfare and interests; nor do I aim to establish that rational agents have to think of themselves as subject to relational
moral requirements, on pain of inconsistency or some other form of rational
instability. My discussion is targeted at those who are prepared to accept the
basic idea, already mentioned several times, that no individual is either more
or less important than any other.[31] This is a characteristically modern idea, as
it seems to me, one that may not have been fully acknowledged at all times and

places, even by agents who were otherwise thoughtful and conscientious. But for most of us today, it is an idea that seems extremely difficult to deny.[32] Even those who are willing to take on board this substantive commitment, however, might reasonably wonder how the postulate of equal standing could give rise to something recognizable as interpersonal morality: a set of obligations on agents that are also suited to structure accountability relations with other persons, and that provide an illuminating framework for negotiating first-order questions about the ways in which it is permissible for them to conduct their lives.

Thus, consequentialism in some form strikes us as an exceptionally natural way of thinking about morality, once we take seriously the idea that the circle of moral concern must expand beyond the boundaries of parochial attachment, so that we grant the interests of each individual to be equally important.[33] As T. M. Scanlon has written, consequentialism is for a wide range of people "the view towards which they find themselves pressed when they try to give a theoretical account of their moral beliefs."[34] If the interests of all persons matter equally, then it is very tempting to suppose that morality will enjoin us to maximize the impartial good, taking the good of each to be no more or less important than the good of any other. But the resulting interpretation of morality is also deeply problematic. It notoriously delivers verdicts about many questions of normative ethics that are wildly at variance with our considered convictions, failing (among other things) to acknowledge the significance for moral thought of the differences between persons and the relation between their agency and their own projects and attachments.[35] It also, as I argue in chapters 2 and 3 below, leaves us without resources to understand the character of morality as a set of obligations on agents that at the same time structure relations of accountability with others.

Some have tried to make of such apparent deficiencies a kind of theoretical virtue, arguing that secular moral philosophy is a subject in its infancy, and that it is only to be expected that the comparatively recent insights it attempts to accommodate might lead to radical revisions in received ideas about its nature and first-order consequences. It can be thrilling to think of oneself as embarked on an inquiry that is in this way untethered from conventional wisdom.[36] A different and no less plausible response is that the project of modern moral philosophy would be a failure if consequentialism (or something similar) is what becomes of it when we try to take seriously the postulate of the equal standing of everyone.[37] Both of these attitudes—the heroically optimistic as well as the pessimistic and gloomy—take for granted that central features of our interpersonal moral practices will not survive the attempt to adapt them to the cosmopolitan insight that the interests of all persons matter equally. But perhaps this common assumption is unwarranted.

I hope to show that the relational approach offers a promising paradigm for thinking about the significance of people's interests for our agency. It distills those interests into a universal normative system whose features align with our reflective understanding of interpersonal morality, construed as a unified set of obligations that equally function to structure relations of accountability. To adopt this interpretation is to see ourselves as standing in a distinctive relation to the other members of a notional domain of equal moral beings, acknowledging that we are linked to each of them through a moral nexus of directed obligations and corresponding claims. We become intelligible to ourselves, as agents who are subject to genuine moral requirements, and who rightly hold each other accountable for living up to them, when we think of the realm of interpersonal morality along these lines; we also gain insight into the first-order structure of this realm when we understand it as a collection of duties that are owed to others, just insofar as they are persons with equal standing. That, in essence, will be my argument for the relational approach.

2

The Problem of Moral Obligation

IN THIS CHAPTER, I look at the hoary issue of the normative significance of moral requirements in the first-person perspective of deliberation. Moral conclusions are customarily treated as considerations that matter within an agent's practical decision-making. That a course of action would be impermissible, for instance, or morally the right thing to do, are conclusions that appear to have direct relevance for practical deliberation, which agents who are reasoning correctly will take appropriately into account in planning their future activities. The philosophical problem in this area is accordingly often understood to be the problem of making sense of the reason-giving force of morality. That is, an account of moral rightness or permissibility should shed light on the standing of these considerations as reasons for action, which count for and against actions in the first-person perspective of agency.

In my view, however, this conventional understanding seriously underdescribes the challenge that faces a philosophical account of morality. The problem is not merely to explain why moral conclusions have some normative significance in the perspective of practical deliberation. It is to explain their apparent status as obligations, considerations that function in a very distinctive way within the practical reflection of agents who take them properly into account. This is the problem that was raised, very forcefully, in G. E. M. Anscombe's justly famous paper on "Modern Moral Philosophy."[1] Anscombe highlighted the fact that morality, on the modern conception of it, appears to involve a class of considerations that make normative demands on the agents to whom they apply. We feel that we are morally bound or obliged to act in accordance with our thinking about what it is morally right or impermissible to do. But Anscombe maintained that this conception of moral obligation is

philosophically unintelligible. We could perhaps make sense of moral obligation within the framework of a "law" conception of ethics, which holds that
moral requirements result from the demands of a beneficent and omnipotent
deity. But when we detach morality from this kind of theological framework,
as we must if we are to understand it as a secular phenomenon, the sense of
obligation proves fundamentally elusive. Anscombe concludes that we should
dispense altogether with the special notion of moral obligation, and find a way
of doing ethics without this distinctive concept.

Anscombe seems to me too quick to give up on the notion of moral obligation, which is central to our ordinary understanding of the significance that
morality has for individual deliberation. But she is right that this notion is
vulnerable if we are unable to provide a philosophical account that makes
sense of it in secular terms. My aim in this chapter is to show that the relational approach to morality is well suited to meet this important challenge.
Understanding moral obligations in relational terms, as duties that are owed
to other parties, renders them intelligible as considerations that have the distinctive normative force that Anscombe found elusive. Indeed, the relational
approach offers the most plausible way of understanding interpersonal morality as a coherent and unified set of obligations, and this is among the most
important theoretical advantages of interpreting the moral in fundamentally
relational terms.

I begin my discussion by setting out, in section 2.1, the general problem of
making sense of obligation as a deliberative phenomenon, and sketching some
of the philosophical approaches available for addressing this problem. In section 2.2, I focus specifically on moral obligation, identifying some additional
features of it that an adequate moral theory needs to accommodate; I also
canvas some familiar moral theories, highlighting the problems that those
theories inevitably face when it comes to making sense of moral obligation as
a deliberative phenomenon. In section 2.3, I present the relational account as
a superior approach to understanding the key features of moral obligation.
Duties that are owed to another party are often understood to exemplify the
original notion of an obligation, and it makes sense that we should feel ourselves bound by moral considerations if they represent directed obligations in
this very particular sense. In section 2.4, I explore some implications of the
relational account of obligation, contrasting it with the voluntarist approach
that Anscombe and many other philosophers take to be the most natural
alternative.

2.1. Practical Requirements: The Basic Challenge

Moral considerations, or at least a central class of them, familiarly exhibit what I have elsewhere called deontic structure.[2] That is, we commonly take morality to consist in large part of a set of basic requirements on the will, which preclude our doing some things and demand that we do others. Morality is not merely a set of considerations that count in favor of or against doing certain things, but a source of obligations, which are practical requirements that function as fixed constraints on what we may or may not do.

Practical requirements of this kind are highly distinctive; they differ intuitively from the reasons proper to many other normative domains, such as those of professional or personal advantage.[3] The fact that it would be entertaining for me to attend the concert next week at the Philharmonie is a reason for trying to get tickets, perhaps even a weighty or a compelling reason. But it isn't one that I take into account in reflection as a demand or an obligation. By contrast, if I've promised you that I would get us tickets to the concert, then the case acquires a moral complexion that shifts it into a different normative gear. In particular, it now seems not merely that there is something that speaks in favor of my endeavoring to get us tickets, but that I am subject to a presumptive requirement to do so.

It is something of a commonplace these days to understand normativity in terms of reasons, and to interpret reasons in turn as considerations that count in favor of the attitudes and actions that they support.[4] A reason for going to the supermarket on the way home from work is a consideration that might be set on the positive side of a notional ledger, and weighed against considerations entered on the other side, as counting against the action. But not all normative considerations are correctly understood in these terms. In particular, practical requirements seem to function very differently within deliberation than the kind of pro or contra considerations that might be weighed against each other in these ways. As Samuel Scheffler has written, such requirements intuitively function as "presumptively decisive" reasons for action and response.[5] They are not considerations that are ordinarily weighed against other, potentially competing reasons for action, but operate rather as exclusionary reasons (in Joseph Raz's influential phrase), which defeasibly block the normative force of considerations that in other contexts would serve as perfectly respectable reasons for action and response.[6]

Semantically, this dimension of practical requirements is reflected in the fact that they characteristically find expression in claims about what an agent must do, rather than about what the agent ought to do. "Must" and related deontic expressions (such as "have to") signal the peremptory or decisive aspect that distinguishes practical requirements from other kinds of normative consideration. A further dimension of the contrast between ordinary "counting in favor of" reasons and practical requirements has to do with the idea of deliberative discretion. There is a feeling that it is often up to us, in a way, whether to act on the balance of reasons when they are considerations that count for and against prospective actions in the perspective of deliberation. Failing to accord with such reasons may reflect a personal vice or a deficiency of some kind (in the dimension, say, of weakness of will), providing a potential opening for criticism and regret. But so long as our decision is supported by some sufficient reason or other, we are generally entitled to choose a course of action other than the one that is recommended by the overall balance of reasons. "Satisficing"—that is, doing something that is good enough, even if it isn't the best option available to us in the circumstances—is sometimes a legitimate way of resolving a practical problem. When this is the case, we can parry any criticism that might be directed at us by citing the discretion we have to act in ways that are less than fully rational.

But things are otherwise with practical requirements, which are considerations that we are not similarly entitled to fail to accord with. If we are under a genuine practical requirement to do something, then there is nothing analogous to satisficing with respect to it that represents an eligible way of responding to its force. The deontic structure of practical requirements in this way contrasts with the aspirational character of the familiar reasons that count for or against many alternatives for choice.[7] The rational force of such requirements is not something we have discretion to discount or ignore in deliberating about what to do.

We might summarize these distinctive features by saying that practical requirements enter the deliberative field in the guise of presumptive constraints on the agent's behavior. They function in this way, insofar as their deliberative role is to determine certain options for action to be either on or off the table from the start, fixing assumptions within and around which the rest of our planning agency will operate, as it proceeds. The natural way to register such constraints in practical reasoning would be through the formation of future-directed intentions to act in accordance with them. It is a now familiar point from the literature on such intentions that they structure deliberation in a distinctive way.[8] The fact that one intends to do X in the future is not merely one consideration among others that are to be taken into account in ongoing reflection about action, but resolves for the agent the practical question about whether or not to do X. Further deliberation will then take place against the background of the assumption that X will be done, as the agent deliberates with an eye to resolving the other questions that are left open by that assumption.[9]

Now, sometimes we form future-directed intentions of this kind after reflection in which ordinary reasons for and against the options open to us are weighed against each other. Thus, one might decide to vacation in Venice this spring, after considering the attractions and disadvantages of doing so in comparison with the alternative of spending the same period in Reggio Calabria or Alto Adige. The point, however, is that if I am aware of a normative consideration as a practical requirement, that will itself make it reasonable for me to respond to it by forming a future-directed intention to comply, without my needing to weigh the consideration in the balance against reasons on the other side. If I have promised you I would accompany you to Venice in the spring, then I already have a basis for intending so to act, independently of how its touristic attractions compare with those of other possible destinations on the Italian peninsula at the same time of year. This is how the deliberative role of practical requirements, as constraints on agency, gets operationalized in practice.

In playing this distinctive deliberative role, however, practical requirements, it is important to note, do not impose absolute constraints on the set of options about which the agent reflects. I said above that they enter the deliberative field in the guise of *presumptive* constraints, in recognition of two different kinds of unusual circumstance that can arise. First, requirements are themselves often defeasible rather than absolute. As was noted in chapter 1, the commitment that is undertaken when I promise to do X is not a commitment to do X come what may; emergencies or other special circumstances might arise that could not have been anticipated at the time when the promise was originally made, for instance, and they can have the effect that the agent is no longer required to do X (though residual obligations, such as a duty to compensate for losses, may still obtain). Second, the original requirement, though it remains in force, might conceivably conflict with a second obligation, leaving agents in a tragic situation in which there is no way forward that respects both of the operative constraints. In this situation, options for action that were initially off the table become alternatives that agents now need to bring within the compass of practical reflection. It is not that the two requirements are to be weighed against each other in this special situation, but rather that agents now need to face up to the fact that, no matter what they do, they will end up acting in a way that is strictly forbidden. For these reasons, we should understand the deliberative role of practical requirements to be that of placing presumptive rather than unconditional constraints on agency.

But this is a role that future-directed intentions are well suited to operationalize, for it is a point familiar from the literature on such intentions that they do not impose absolute and inflexible limits on practical deliberation.[10] We form intentions from a perspective of limited information about how exactly the circumstances of our agency might change over time, but also with an implicit awareness of the ways in which those circumstantial changes might turn out to be normatively significant. This is true both when intentions are based on the recognition of a practical requirement and when they result from weighing pro and con reasons against each other. (Having decided to go to Venice in the summer rather than Alto Adige on account of my interest in its touristic attractions, I should of course reconsider if the city is visited by a natural or public health calamity in the interim.) Intentions accordingly structure the deliberations of rational agents in the manner of defeasible constraints, resolving practical questions in a way that can be revisited as new information comes in that is normatively significant. In the case of practical requirements, this might be information that shows a given requirement no longer strictly to obtain, or that brings to light a conflict with a second requirement.

The preceding considerations suggest to me that the deontic character of practical requirements represents a sui generis normative relation. The presumptively constraining significance that they exhibit within deliberation is distinct from, and not reducible to, the aspirational form of normativity that is at issue with ordinary recommending reasons, of the kind that count for and against candidates for action.[11] A normative consideration, such as a promissory commitment, can require or demand that I do something like travel to Venice, and this relation differs from the one that obtains when there are considerations, such as touristic attraction, that merely count in favor of the same action.

But this idea raises a neglected philosophical question. When we encounter a putative set of obligations or practical requirements, we should be able to make sense of them not merely as considerations that possess normative force of some kind or other, but as considerations that have the deliberative features characteristic of obligations. That is, they should not merely strike us as considerations that it would be reasonable to enter into a notional ledger of factors that speak for or against a course of action that it might be open to us to pursue.

Rather, they should be intelligible as considerations that we register from the start as presumptive constraints on our agency, constraints with which we ordinarily must comply. The philosophical challenge is to develop an account of obligations that explains their suitability to structure deliberation in the way of presumptive constraints and to support practical conclusions that are expressed using the deontic "must." There are several familiar strategies for meeting this challenge in the philosophical tradition; let us consider, very briefly, some of the most prominent of them.

One approach, which we might call the dominance model, emphasizes the systematic importance and weight of the normative considerations that ground practical requirements. On this approach, there are ultimately just reasons for action of various strengths. What sets practical requirements apart within the larger normative domain is the fact that they can be traced to reasons that are weighty across a wide range of deliberative contexts, so that they nearly always dominate the considerations on the other side with which they might compete. It is the systematic importance and weight of their normative grounds that make it appropriate to express practical requirements with the deontic "must," and that explain and justify our tendency to treat them as presumptive constraints.[12] If a normative reason is such that it robustly dominates potential competitors across a wide range of contexts, then we don't really need to enter it into the deliberative ledger in order to figure out what to do, but can assume at least defeasibly that it will be dispositive. It will thus make sense to treat it as a consideration that must be complied with, one that enters deliberation in the guise of a presumptive requirement.

A different strategy appeals to the notion of identity. Some normative considerations can be traced to our self-conceptions, our sense of who we are and what is fundamentally important to us in life. In particular, there are reasons for action that are distinctively connected to threats to our identities, things that we must do if we are to hang on to our identities and to preserve them, going forward, in the face of ongoing challenges. The idea, then, is that the special nature and force of practical requirements can be traced to the special connection of the considerations that ground them to features of our practical identities.[13] We *must* do something just in case our doing it is required if we are to fend off an existential threat to who we are and to prevent the dissolution or destruction of our selves. And this same feature explains and justifies the structural role of practical requirements within deliberation, as considerations that enter the deliberative field in the guise of presumptive constraints. It makes sense to register normative considerations as constraints of this kind if they are grounded in the most basic features of our self-conceptions.

A third approach is voluntarism, which appeals to social relations of authority, tracing practical requirements to the commands of a suitably constituted legislator. Anscombe's "law" conception of ethics, referred to above, is an example of this strategy; it interprets practical requirements as imposed on human subjects by a benevolent and omnipotent divinity. The social relation that grounds obligation, on this account of it, is the relation that individual human subjects stand in to God. But other versions of the general approach are also possible, tracing practical requirements to the commands of human authorities, such as duly constituted legislative assemblies or to individuals to whom one is subordinate within a legitimate professional or family structure. This approach, too, identifies a feature of practical requirements that promises to render intelligible their distinctive deontic character and role. If we have been commanded to do something by a legitimately constituted authority, then it makes sense to treat it as a presumptive constraint on our agency that we will act in accordance with the authority's commands. Authoritative commands are considerations that are paradigmatically expressed using the practical "must," and they naturally structure our deliberations accordingly.

These three philosophical approaches, which I have of course sketched only in the broadest of strokes, strike me as among the most promising avenues for understanding the notion of a deliberative requirement. It is significant, for instance, that we can understand in terms of these models the common assumption that considerations of structural rationality represent requirements on practical thought. Thus, we generally take ourselves to be constrained to avoid contradictions and to take the necessary means to the ends we intend to achieve. But the constraints at issue here can be made sense of by assimilating them to one or another of the three models I have outlined. Those who believe that there are independent requirements of structural rationality, for instance, tend to treat such requirements as constitutive conditions of thought and action, which is to apply to them a version of the identity approach sketched above.[14] Other philosophers reject the idea that there are independent structural requirements of this kind, arguing that the cases in which such requirements appear to obtain can better be understood as ones in which the apparent balance of reasons decisively favors a given course of action over the alternatives; this assimilates the cases, in effect, to the dominance model.[15]

The three models, it should further be noted, are potentially complementary. We needn't suppose that there is only one kind of factor that can potentially make sense of practical requirements, but should be open to a kind of pluralism on this issue, which allows that practical requirements might ultimately be traced to a diversity of normative considerations. Having said that, however, I now wish to outline some challenges that each of the models faces, if only to identify issues that will need to be addressed before we can arrive at a satisfactory understanding of the nature and sources of moral requirements in particular.

The dominance model, which explains practical requirements in terms of the robust weight of certain reasons for action across a wide range of deliberative contexts, appeals to a consideration that is essentially a matter of degree. Practical requirements are, in effect, systematically weighty reasons. But weight is scalar, and so it is hard to see in this account anything that would set practical requirements apart in principle from other kinds of normative consideration. The dominance model in this way seems ill-designed to make sense of the qualitative distinction that we register in deliberation between deontic considerations and the aspirational reasons that are standardly weighed against each other.

In response, it might be noted that *dominance* is not a scalar notion, even if it is constructed out of scalar materials. But it is unclear whether we can convert scalar differences into a qualitative distinction by appeal to this notion alone. Is there, for instance, a non-arbitrary way to set the threshold of greater weight by which a reason must dominate its routine competitors before it can be considered an obligation? Furthermore, this approach seems to rule out a priori something that it is important that a theory of obligation should at least leave open, namely the possibility of conflicts of obligation. In a situation that involves this kind of conflict, a single agent stands under distinct practical requirements that pull in different directions. But if practical requirements are by definition considerations that dominate the reasons with which they might compete, there cannot be a situation of this kind; the element of normative conflict undermines the very thing that accounts for the special force of obligations in the first place.

A different problem confronts the identity-based view. On this account, practical requirements are connected to the agent's identity, and one stands under an obligation to do something just in case doing it is necessary to fend off threats to some aspect or other of who one is. A strategy that takes this form, however, will have difficulty making sense of the possibility of flouted duty, by which I mean cases in which we recognize something as an obligation, but fail to live up to it. On the identity-based approach, to acknowledge something as an obligation is to situate it in relation to a threat to one's conception of oneself, understanding that one will cease to be who one is if one does not comply with its demands. This threat, moreover, is often understood to have an existential dimension, connecting practical requirements to the core elements in one's self-conception that give one reason to go on with life in the first place. This is what is supposed to explain the appearance of peremptory necessity that sets apart those normative considerations that have the force of practical requirements. But if this is the general shape of the account, it seems to leave little space for flouted duty. If I do what I recognize will lead to the dissolution of a part of my identity, then the thing in me that is threatened cannot have the significance for my self-conception that it would have to have to ground an obligation.[16] The very fact that I am willing to countenance its loss shows that it isn't among the things that contribute importantly to my sense of what my life is basically about. The only exception to this claim will be in situations in which I flout one obligation in order to comply with a second, where the second obligation is grounded in an aspect of my identity that has even greater significance for my conception of myself. But not all cases of flouted duty take this form.[17]

The voluntarist model seems an improvement on the other two approaches in certain respects. It traces practical requirements to a consideration that sets them apart from ordinary aspirational reasons in kind and not just in degree, and that is therefore suited to make sense of their distinctive deontic character. The voluntarist approach also allows for the possibility of conflicts in obligation (insofar as there can be commands of legitimate authorities that it is not possible for a single agent to follow), and for cases in which an agent fails to live up to an obligation whose nature and force are acknowledged. Perhaps for these reasons, it is one of the most salient paradigms for understanding the phenomenon of a practical requirement in the philosophical tradition.

But voluntarism has highly particular presuppositions that limit its applicability as a general model of obligation. For one thing, there needs to be a social relationship in place of legitimate authority, whereby one party is entitled to issue directives that govern the activities of another. The notion of authority is itself complex, and there are a variety of approaches to making sense of it that have attracted philosophical attention over the years. But however they are understood, relations of authority will obtain only under severely restricted circumstances (such as those that link the members of families and other associations, or that imbue legislative assemblies with special normative insight or democratic legitimacy). Second, it must also be the case that the legitimate authority has actually issued a suitably public law or command in order for a practical requirement to have come into existence. There are certainly cases in which these conditions are satisfied, and they provide important examples of the phenomenon of a practical requirement. But many of the considerations that strike us in deliberation as familiar practical requirements do not derive from the public commands of a legitimate authority, but appear to obtain independently of the circumstances that are presupposed by the voluntarist model of obligation. Among these are the obligations of morality, to which I now turn.

2.2. Moral Obligation: The Specific Challenge

An account of the normative significance of morality faces some particular challenges, beyond those that are endemic to the general project of making sense of practical requirements. It must, first of all, explain why there are specifically moral considerations that have this distinctive kind of normative significance. Morality is not just a source of reasons for action, in the sense of things that count for and against prospective actions in the perspective of deliberation, but defines obligations, which enter the deliberative field in the guise of presumptive constraints on agency.

There are recent philosophical controversies about what exactly it is that traditional moral theories should be taken to be offering an account of. Do they purport to offer an analysis of the concept of the morally right or wrong, or of the property of being right or wrong in the moral sense? Or are such theories to be understood differently, for example as attempts to identify a general property that makes actions right or wrong in some other, not-yet-specified sense? Engaging with this issue, both Derek Parfit and T. M. Scanlon have recently proposed that there is an indefinable sense of "right" and "wrong," in which to be right or wrong just is to be something that must or must not be done.[18] Conclusions about what is right or wrong in this generic sense register the presence of what I have been calling practical requirements, construed as considerations that function deliberatively as presumptive constraints on agency.

I agree that moral theories are not plausibly understood, in the first instance, as accounts of right and wrong in this generic sense. They are neither analyses of these concepts, nor theories of the property that they consist in, for the simple reason that morality is not the only source of practical requirements on the will. As we saw in the preceding section, there can be things that one must do—that it would right for one to do, in the generic sense here at issue—for identity-based reasons, and these might not have anything to do with interpersonal morality in the conventional sense. I might rightly feel I have to do something because I am someone's parent or sibling, or because acting in this way is determined by some personal project with which I am existentially identified.

But if ethical theories are not offering accounts of this generic notion of rightness or wrongness, what is their quarry? Parfit and Scanlon propose that they be understood as attempts to specify higher-level properties that *make* actions right or wrong in the generic sense.[19] This seems to me a helpful way to think about at least one part of the project of moral philosophy, and I shall take it on board in what follows. But an important qualification is in order. To say that moral theories are attempts to describe high-level right-making properties (in the sense of properties that make actions "to-be-done" or "not-to-be-done") is not to say that they are not also putting forward interpretations of rightness or wrongness in a more specifically moral sense. Thus, utilitarians, contractualists, and Kantians clearly seem to be offering competing theories of *something*, and we can usefully think of this target of analysis as a specifically moral sense of right and wrong.

Of course, proponents of these different theories propose very different conceptions of morality, organized around completely different higher-level properties (such as maximizing the good, universalizability, etc.). This can make it difficult to see them as alternative accounts of a common concept of specifically moral rightness and wrongness (as opposed to competing proposals about high-level properties that make actions right or wrong in the generic sense of to-be-done or not-to-be-done).[20] But I am not convinced that these are the only alternatives. A different framework for thinking about the landscape of issues here might start by identifying an abstract concept of morality, marking out a domain of things that are right and wrong in a specifically moral sense. This domain collects reasons and values that have to do, in some way or other, with the social significance of our actions for the individuals who stand to be affected by them; it is the domain that I characterized in chapter 1 as interpersonal morality.

Our sense that there is a coherent domain of interpersonal reasons and values reflects our acknowledgment that there are different kinds of objections to what a person might propose to do, and that not all of these are of a moral nature. There is something morally problematic about taking advantage of other persons' vulnerability, or deliberately deceiving them about a matter that is important to them; by contrast, actions that can be criticized for reasons of style or efficiency or personal conviction need not be morally problematic in the same way.[21] The conventional concept of the moral right, in this abstract sense, might itself be historically conditioned; indeed, it seems to me plausible to suppose that the concept most of us operate with today is a distinctively modern one, incorporating elements that might have been lacking in other places and times. But for better or worse, it is our concept of the moral right, and it includes abstract features that constrain theorizing about morality in the narrower sense at issue. Moral theories can then be understood to put forward substantive conceptions of the moral right and wrong in the sense that is defined by this modern, interpersonal concept of morality.[22] Such theories are in competition with each other, insofar as they are attempts to do justice to constraints to which any account of interpersonal morality is generally understood to be answerable. But they differ from one another, insofar as they fill in the general concept in very different ways, identifying different properties with moral rightness and wrongness, and offering us different ways of understanding what it is to correctly think of something as morally right or wrong.[23]

Applying this framework to the immediate task of the present chapter, it is one of the abstract constraints on a substantive conception of interpersonal morality that it identify a high-level property that makes actions right or wrong, in the generic sense of to-be-done or not-to-be-done. This is just to say that theories of morality must make sense of the idea that there is a morally significant high-level property that correctly figures in deliberation as a practical requirement or an obligation. Meeting this desideratum, I maintain, is a distinctive and underappreciated challenge. It requires us to make sense of the properties specified by a conception of moral rightness as properties that are not merely normatively relevant to deliberations about action, but relevant in the distinctive way of practical requirements: as considerations that properly register in deliberation in the guise of presumptive constraints on agency. Of course, it is possible that this theoretical challenge is one that cannot be met. Perhaps there is no interesting high-level property that is held in common by all of the actions that we intuitively think of as morally right and wrong. Or perhaps, though there is such a property, we cannot make sense of it as one that is significant in the way of practical requirements. These possibilities point toward a skeptical or debunking account of interpersonal morality, one that denies that morality represents a unified domain of obligations. My point, however, is that a nondebunking account of moral rightness will offer a conception of it that illuminates its deontic structure, its standing as a source of practical requirements of the kind discussed in section 2.1.

A second feature of morality that I should like to emphasize is one that is characteristic of the modern concept of interpersonal morality in particular. I noted above that the concept of morality in the narrow sense collects reasons and values that connect to the social dimension of agency. But there is a specific understanding of this social aspect that is salient in modern moral thought. There are different ways to express the point, but one of them would be to say that morality defines a cosmopolitan normative structure. The moral community, according to this conception of interpersonal morality, is a maximally inclusive group of individuals whose interests are taken to matter equally. Those who are accorded equal standing by morality include, at a minimum, all human beings, though different views can be taken as to whether and in what ways the moral community extends even further, beyond the members of this class. One such further extension would be to those beings, if there are any, who share with normally developed humans the capacities for practical reason and reflective self-determination; another would be to creatures with interests that are grounded in their having a coherent point of view and a capacity for pleasure and suffering.

The general idea is that, from the moral point of view, all members of this extensive class, however precisely its limits are defined, are to be taken into account, as beings who are neither more nor less important than the other individuals in the class. This postulate of equal standing, as I referred to it in section 1.2 above, is perhaps the defining moral insight of modernity, and it has a bearing on the modern concept of morality that different theories are attempting to give an account of. Thus, the normative significance of morality for individuals is connected directly to the fact that we are members of an inclusive community of equals. On the characteristically modern way of understanding it, interpersonal morality might be thought of as the solution to the problem of how each of us is to negotiate a social world of this cosmopolitan and inclusive kind, and its verdicts matter to us, as agents, in virtue of its playing this important role.

Putting this idea together with the first, we could say that morality is the set of deontic constraints on conduct that derive from the fact that we inhabit an extensive notional community together with other beings who are "equally real" (in Thomas Nagel's striking formulation), and whose interests are no less significant than ours.[24] A philosophical account of interpersonal morality must shed light on these twin aspects of the moral, and the connection between them. Its substantive conception of moral rightness must show that the property of being morally right or wrong is not merely a presumptive constraint on the rational will, but one that reflects our common membership in an extensive community of moral equals. It should thus fall out of a substantive conception of interpersonal morality that in treating moral rightness or wrongness as practical requirements, we are acknowledging our equal standing within such a moral community.

The third feature I will mention is somewhat more controversial, and perhaps less central to the modern concept of morality. But it is very deeply embedded in our first-order moral thinking, and it is therefore a desideratum that it is reasonable for moral theories to attempt to accommodate. I have in mind here the idea that moral requirements, at least in the central cases, have an agent-relative character. That is, they do not merely define impersonal or agent-neutral values that we take it to be important that all people should promote in one way or another. Rather, they are requirements that assign to different agents different moral aims.[25] Thus, the moral significance of promissory undertakings reflects itself in the fact that we are under a presumptive obligation to keep the promises that we ourselves have entered into. It is a misunderstanding of the relevant moral desideratum to think that the fundamental value that is at stake is the impersonal value of promissory fulfillment, and that we respond correctly to it by doing everything in our power to see to it that it is maximally realized in the world. We are morally obligated to keep our own promises, even if we happen to inhabit the philosopher's distressing scenario in which our doing so will lead several other agents to break promises they would otherwise have kept.

These three features, I shall assume in what follows, are reasonable constraints that a substantive account of the moral right should aspire to meet. But it is a serious challenge to devise a theoretical account of interpersonal morality that does justice to these three constraints together. To illustrate the challenge, it may help to consider very briefly how some familiar accounts of morality would approach it.[26] I shall suggest that we can see these accounts as exploiting the different models of a practical requirement that were surveyed in the previous section; but also that those models cannot easily be married to the other specific features of moral obligation that I have just enumerated. The result is one that Anscombe anticipated, namely that moral obligation continues to seem puzzling if we think of it along the lines of the most salient modern moral theories.

Start with classical utilitarianism, which holds that those actions are morally right that maximize the net balance of pleasure over pain (producing at least as much hedonic utility as any of the alternatives that it was open to the agent to perform). As I noted in section 1.2, an approach of this kind provides an appealing account of the cosmopolitan aspect of morality. Deliberating from the Sidgwickian point of view of the universe, we are to take equally into account the interests of all of the sentient beings potentially affected by our actions, operating with austere impartiality as between those individuals. Moral requirements thus derive in a straightforward way from our acknowledgment of our equal standing with others as members of a common moral community. But if utilitarianism does well with this feature of morality, it does less well with the other two I have identified. Whatever else it might be, the principle of utility is the antithesis of an agent-relative principle; it enjoins us to promote a conception of value that is fundamentally agent-neutral in character. As long as the outcome that we bring about is impersonally optimific, it is a matter of indifference to utilitarian morality what the character is of the action that we perform. There is no room on this picture for agents to take a special concern for their own veracity or loyalty or fidelity to agreements. There is something perhaps bracing about this way of thinking of morality, but it is undeniably at odds with naïve ways of understanding what interpersonal morality asks of us.[27]

Nor does utilitarianism yield a plausible story about the deontic character of moral considerations. An action is morally right, on this approach, if it would produce at least as much total pleasure or happiness as the alternatives that it was open to the agent to choose. But why should an action's being right in this sense be a consideration that enters the deliberative field as a presumptive constraint on agency? As we saw above, there are different models for thinking about practical requirements, but utilitarian rightness doesn't seem to fit any of them. For instance, according to the dominance model, an action might be one that we are intuitively required to perform if there are decisive reasons that speak in favor of doing it, across a wide range of deliberative contexts. When this condition is satisfied, it makes sense to treat the action as one that is defeasibly fixed for purposes of future deliberation and planning, since we can be confident that the balance of reasons will continue decisively to favor the action as we progress through new situations.

But utilitarian rightness doesn't seem to function this way, for two reasons. First, to say that a course of action would produce the best consequences is not to say that it is decisively supported by the balance of reasons, even if we grant the hedonistic assumption that our reasons are exclusively tied to the production of pleasure and pain; the action that is best in these terms, after all, might merely produce a slightly better balance of pleasure over pain than one of the alternatives open to the agent. The utilitarian conception of rightness, considered on its own, thus leaves it open whether the course of action it recommends is decisively supported by the balance of reasons in any given case. Second, the action that is right in one situation, in utilitarian terms, might turn out in the very next situation one encounters to be less productive of utility than an alternative that is available in that situation. It all depends on the consequences, as the utilitarian would say. But then it wouldn't really make sense to treat the right action in this sense as something that one is committed to doing, going forward.[28]

The utilitarian might respond that this last problem stems from a fixation on the wrong level of action description. The thing that one can be confident will always be supported by the balance of reasons is not an action of some independent type that happens, in a given situation, to be the right thing to do (say, keeping one's promise or assisting a stranger in need). It is, rather, doing what would produce the best consequences, under that very description. But this does not represent a consideration that it would be intelligible to treat as a presumptive constraint on agency of the kind that we have seen practical requirements to represent. In any situation we might find ourselves in, if we are to act in accordance with the utilitarian construction of moral rightness, we will have to give some thought to the particular consequences of the options that are open to us, under the particular conditions that then obtain. Nothing is antecedently off the table, so to speak, not even in the provisional way that characterizes the deliberative role of obligations. Utilitarian rightness thus does not seem well suited to define a self-standing class of practical requirements.

We saw earlier that the dominance conception faces the difficulty of trying to extract a qualitative distinction, between ordinary reasons for action and practical requirements, from something that is essentially a matter of degree. A similar difficulty faces the utilitarian conception of the right. That conception, couched as it is in scalar terms, defines an ideal of attainment that agents could aspire to live up to, as far as it is possible for them to do so, much as the devotee of a religious doctrine might aspire to approximate to a maximally exigent standard of personal purity or devotion. Scalar ideals of this kind represent intelligible objects of personal ambition. But it is not clear that it really makes sense to treat compliance with such a scalar ideal as a presumptive constraint on one's deliberations and activities as an agent.[29] Moral rightness, as utilitarianism defines it, seems better thought of as an aspirational than as a deontic notion. It is commonly observed that the utilitarian conception of the right doesn't leave any room for the supererogatory; perhaps this is because it equally doesn't deliver a credible notion of the obligatory.[30]

Of course, refinements are possible, perhaps drawing on different intuitive models of an obligation. We saw in section 2.1, for instance, that practical requirements are often thought of in voluntarist terms, as connected to the legislative acts of authorities about the things that it is open to us to do. In this spirit, we might, following Mill, characterize moral obligations as those moral standards that it would be optimific to sanction people for flouting, interpreting the attachment of sanctions to standards as a kind of inter- or intrapersonal legislation.[31] This would arguably represent a reconstruction, in utilitarian terms, of something that is recognizable as a conception of moral obligation. It makes sense for agents to commit themselves presumptively to ensuring their compliance with standards to which internal or external sanctions are in this way attached. But the resulting account would abandon the aspiration to explain why moral considerations have the intrinsically deontic character of demands on the rational will. Thus, from the fact that an action is morally wrong, it will not follow on this approach that the agent is under an obligation not to do it. Whether that is the case or not will depend on ancillary considerations, about the consequences of a general scheme of moral sanctions that attaches penalties to people when they perform actions of the kind that is in question. The utilitarian account of what makes actions right or wrong thus does not succeed in delivering an explanation of the idea that acts that are morally wrong are ones that we have an obligation not to perform.[32]

To continue in this cartoonish vein for a moment, consider next a more robustly voluntarist position, according to which what makes actions right or wrong in the first place is the fact that they are required or prohibited by the commands of an authoritative lawgiver of some kind. On this venerable approach, there are a variety of desirable ways for people to act and to interact with each other, but it becomes right or obligatory to act in those ways only through the laying down of a corresponding requirement by an appropriately constituted authority. As noted earlier, Anscombe's critique of modern moral philosophy seems to presuppose this conception of obligation; her charge is roughly that the modern philosophical approach to morality posits universal obligations that lack the foundation in the commands of a divine authority that their intelligibility as obligations requires.[33] But there are also secular variants of the strategy, which trace requirements to the commands of a human legislator or authority.

An approach that explicates the morally right in terms of such authoritative legislative acts has some undeniably attractive features. As I observed in section 2.1, the voluntarist model, at least when its presuppositions are in place, provides an intelligible paradigm of a practical requirement, so a voluntarist theory of rightness promises to make sense of the deontic structure of the moral. The approach also seems capable of accommodating the agent-relative character of familiar moral requirements. If God, or the secular authorities, command individuals to keep the promises they have entered into, then one would be flouting the resulting requirement rather than complying with it if one were to bring about a net increase in the incidence of promise-keeping by breaking a promise one had made oneself. That is just not the thing that the relevant authority commanded one to do.

But the cosmopolitan aspect of modern morality is difficult to make sense of in voluntarist terms. The challenge here was to explain how moral rightness has its source in our common membership in an extensive community of equals. But if voluntarism takes the most common form of a divine command theory of the moral right, this desideratum seems to go by the board. The requirements that God lays down on us may enjoin us to treat other individuals with consideration and respect, as moral equals in some sense or other (perhaps as persons who are equally subject to the divine will). But this is a matter of the content of what is commanded, not of its normative status as an obligation. What makes it the case that we are practically required to comply with an injunction that has this content is solely the fact that a benevolent deity has commanded us so to act. God might equally have commanded us to comply with laws whose content has nothing to do with the equality of individual human subjects (such as dietary restrictions that prohibit the consumption of certain flora and fauna), or that even deny such equality. Or God might have imposed on the members of one tribal group requirements that are not similarly imposed on the members of other tribal groups, singling out the first community as a kind of chosen people. The divine command approach, construed as a way of understanding moral requirements, puts into the foreground the relationship between God and the individuals who are subject to God's laws, rather than the relationships that members of the broader community of moral agents stand in to each other.

It is perhaps not surprising that divine command theories have trouble accommodating what I have called the cosmopolitan aspect of morality, for it represents a distinctively modern desideratum, one that helps to define the Enlightenment project of understanding interpersonal morality as a secular phenomenon. But the problem remains intractable when we turn to voluntarist views that invoke a human rather than a religious authority. One such view holds that moral rightness is to be understood by reference to the expectations that are actually imposed on us by the members of the communities in which we happen to live. It is morally right, and hence obligatory, for me to do something, according to this approach, just in case other people in fact demand that I so act, where demands in the relevant sense are associated with informal social sanctions (including angry disapprobation and the like).[34] This social command theory, as we might think of it, borrows some of the advantages of the divine command theory for making sense of the deontic structure of the morally right. But the way that the voluntarist apparatus gets transposed into a secular key by this approach seems too crude to yield a plausible account of moral obligation. The expectations that are actually backed up by attitudinal sanctions in human communities are often misguided, reflecting prejudice, ignorance, and superstition as much as moral insight; indeed, they can operate at cross purposes to ideals of equality, insofar as there are communities in which norms of racial or gender supremacy and oppression are enforced through the local economy of disesteem and social sanction. A different way to put the point might be to say that the members of our actual communities do not have the kind of default authority that would make the commands they might direct toward us automatically binding.[35]

This difficulty might be avoided by tracing obligations, not to the actual commands of our fellow citizens, but to the fact that we all have "de jure authority" to address moral demands to other agents in our guise as representative members of the moral community.[36] This represents a shift from actual to hypothetical commands, together with the invocation of an idealized standpoint that each of us can in principle occupy for issuing commands on behalf of everyone. These modifications in the social command theory introduce some critical distance between the potentially misguided expectations of many actual communities and the genuine requirements of morality, while also giving expression to the ideal of an inclusive community of equals. But they also undermine the presuppositions that make voluntarism viable as a way of modeling practical requirements. For one thing, the notion of "authority" that results when voluntarism is revised in this way seems entirely vestigial. We are left with the idea that actions are obligatory when there are reasons for any person to address the corresponding demands to the agent;[37] but then it is these reasons, rather than any authority that might be invested in us, that are doing the real explanatory work. For another thing, this modified approach abandons an assumption that seems central to the paradigm cases of authority-based requirements, namely that the legislator should exercise its authority by issuing an actual command. Parliament may possess the de jure authority to modify the tax code in the direction of imposing higher rates on the affluent, and there might even be good reason for it to do so; but its subjects are not required to comply with such notional rates if the corresponding legislation has not actually been enacted. Merely hypothetical laws are not in fact binding on anyone.[38]

Some of these difficulties could be avoided by internalizing the relation between authority and subject, treating moral and other practical requirements as laws that agents legislate for themselves. This recognizably Kantian approach transforms voluntarism into an ethics of autonomy.[39] The moral law is binding on each of us insofar as we impose it on ourselves, through commitments that are built into the structure of free agency. It is striking that Kant in this way adapted the voluntarist model to make sense of morality as a source of nonnegotiable demands on the rational will; his interest in doing this shows the power of the voluntarist paradigm when it comes to understanding what it is for something to be a practical requirement.

It is equally striking, however, that a Kantian ethics of autonomy takes on board some very ambitious philosophical assumptions, ones that have not been defended or developed persuasively in over two centuries of work that is broadly inspired by his ethical vision. There is a need, for one thing, to show that the voluntarist model can coherently be applied in thinking about the relation that agents stand in to themselves. (What is the nature of the authority that is in play here? How can any practical law be binding on us if it is always open to us, as legislators, to modify it if we no longer wish to comply?) And there is a need, second, to demonstrate that free agents really are committed to imposing on themselves the moral law.[40] Only this will ensure that moral obligations apply universally, to all agents who are members of our notional cosmopolitan community of equals. I am not optimistic that philosophers working in this tradition will be able to vindicate these important assumptions.

Consider, finally, a perfectionist approach to basic moral requirements, one that derives them from considerations about what Philippa Foot has called "natural goodness."[41] An action is right, on this approach, if its performance is required by traits that people need in order to be good human beings, and wrong if it is incompatible with such traits. Thus, we start by thinking about the challenges that human communities typically face under the conditions that they normally inhabit, and identify a set of characteristics or virtues that members of such communities need to instantiate if they are all to do well under the conditions specified. Individuals can then be said to be good as humans if they have the traits that people generally have to have if they are to flourish under the circumstances that they typically encounter. And actions will be right or wrong, we could go on to say, if doing them is either determined or ruled out by the traits that make people good humans in this sense. Facts about natural goodness thus provide the template for understanding normative claims about individual living creatures, including claims about what it is right or wrong for those individuals to do.

This interesting approach raises a host of foundational questions. Abstracting from the details, however, we can see that part of its appeal lies in its promise to shed light on at least two of the elements in our thinking about morality that I have highlighted. The deontic character of moral considerations might be explicated in terms of the identity-based model of a practical requirement sketched quickly in section 2.1. Living things are members of a life form, whether they like it or not, and this determines standards of conduct that are not optional for them, but that flow from their essential identity. The wolf that hangs back from the pack, rather than contributing with vigor to running down the prey they are hunting together, is defective as a wolf, even if the result turns out to be advantageous for it on this occasion. Similarly, the person who acts wrongly will be failing relative to standards of attainment that are not optional for human beings, insofar as those standards are associated with the virtues that humans generally need in order to flourish under their normal conditions of life. Individual agents have to comply with the standards of virtue, we might say, on account of who they are, and those standards therefore represent practical requirements for them.[42]

The approach also renders intelligible the agent-relative character of basic moral requirements, as we ordinarily understand them. What I as an individual am required to do is determined fundamentally by the virtuous traits that I have to exhibit to count as a good human being myself. So the important thing is that I should be just and generous and reliable, not that my actions should contribute causally to the maximal instantiation of these virtues in the population at large. I must keep my own promise, even if my breaking it would lead several others in the local community I inhabit to keep promises they would otherwise have broken.

Like voluntarist accounts, however, perfectionism does less well with the cosmopolitan aspect of morality that I have maintained is central to the modern conception of it. The idea, again, was that the requirements of morality have their distinctive source in the fact that we inhabit a common world together with others who are equally real, constituting a maximally inclusive community of equals. This idea seems to drop out of the picture, however, on the perfectionist approach. Moral requirements, to the extent there are such things, trace their origin not to the direct significance of other peoples' interests for us, but to the value of individual perfection. The basic question is not how we are to negotiate life as members of a community in which other peoples' interests are no less significant than our own, but how we are to realize an ideal of human attainment in our own case.

True, the characteristics we need to exhibit in order to be good as individual human beings will include such virtues as justice and generosity, which have to do in part with how we relate to and interact with other people. Furthermore, people who have these characteristics will perform just and generous acts for their own sakes, not as a result of reflection on what it is to be good as a member of the life form to which they naturally belong. One consequence of this is that the character of the practical requirements defined by this approach is not fully salient in the deliberations of those to whom the requirements apply. We may be subject to a requirement to act in ways consistent with the virtues; but the basis of this requirement, in considerations about what it is to be good as a member of the life form to which we naturally belong, is one that will ordinarily be transparent to us in deliberation. A further consequence is that, at the level at which normative requirements are explained, the interests of other people enter as occasions for the realization of virtue, rather than direct sources of requirements on the virtuous agent. Their significance for questions about what the agent is required to do is thus mediated by the demands of human goodness, which is taken to be the ultimate source of normative requirements.

This shows itself in the fact, emphasized by Foot and other proponents of a broadly Aristotelian approach, that the virtues one has to have in order to achieve natural human goodness include traits that have nothing to do with the needs and interests of other persons, such as a hopeful outlook and an ability to accept good things in one's own life when they come one's way.[43] The sense in which one is under a requirement to adopt these attitudes, on the approach in question, is just the same as the sense in which one is required to treat people justly or with compassion; which is to say that the requirements at issue are not derived immediately from facts about our common membership in an inclusive community of equals.[44]

2.3. A Relational Approach to Moral Obligation

The remarks of the preceding section do not of course amount to a comprehensive critique of the traditional moral theories that were under discussion. My intention was instead to illustrate the specific challenges that face an account of moral obligation, and to identify the most salient weaknesses of some standard approaches to morality when it comes to meeting those challenges. For all I have said so far, however, it might be that one of the theories in question could be modified or adapted to provide an improved philosophical account of moral obligation. Alternatively, an account that seems deficient in light of one or the other of the challenges I have identified might nevertheless represent our best hope for making some sense of moral obligation. To identify the challenges that confront the project of understanding this phenomenon is not necessarily to take for granted that it will be possible to meet all of them. We might in the end conclude that the best we can do is to render intelligible some but not all of the features that we intuitively associate with the notion of moral obligation. Or we might, more radically, join Anscombe in concluding that the notion has no coherent place in a modern conception of ethics, and that we would be better off doing moral theory without it.

In the present section, however, I would like to move in a more optimistic direction, presenting in outline an approach to moral obligation that makes better sense of its central features. My point of entry will be an interesting moment in Foot's development of the natural goodness approach. In the course of sketching her version of a perfectionist theory of ethics, Foot takes up the question of our reasons to keep the promises we have made, focusing on the case mentioned in chapter 1 of Mikluko-Maklay's promise to the Malay servant. In this case, it will be recalled, the anthropologist Maklay promises the servant not to photograph him, where the servant extracted this promise from the anthropologist in the belief that his spirit would be harmed if a picture were taken of him. Foot takes it as given that the promise changes the anthropologist's normative situation, and she wonders about the nature of the reasons that it brings into existence.

Now it might have been thought that the answer to this question would be pretty straightforward for a theorist of her convictions. We need only identify some virtues—that is, traits that humans generally need in order to do well under what for them are the normal circumstances of life—that would be incompatible with breaking the promise, despite the lack of harm it would in fact cause the servant. And indeed, Foot herself mentions some such virtues in this connection, including trustworthiness and respect.[45] We could then say that a good human being, someone who exhibits such virtues as trustworthiness, will take the fact of the promise as a reason to fulfill its terms, and that this is sufficient to illuminate its normative significance.

But Foot apparently finds this answer inadequate to account for the special force of the reason that is introduced by Maklay's promissory undertaking.[46] To make sense of this aspect of the case, she suggests, we need to observe that promises exploit "a special kind of tool invented by humans for the better conduct of their lives, creating an *obligation*."[47] The idea, though underdeveloped in Foot's presentation of it, is apparently that when Maklay thinks that he should not photograph the servant, he understands the promise to have brought into existence a new and specially exigent normative fact, which we could refer to as an obligation. He has bound himself through his promise; and there are presumably further natural virtues that kick in (such as the virtue of fidelity) to explain why good human beings would not do something that goes against what they take themselves to be in this way obligated to do.

I am not sure that it is helpful to think of obligation, in the sense that is at issue here, as a "special kind of tool" that humans have invented. But Foot is certainly correct to observe that promises are generally understood to give rise to distinctive kinds of reasons, ones that are in the key of practical requirements. She also seems to me to be correct in connecting their distinctive force to the fact that they are ways of binding ourselves to do something, which bring into existence what we intuitively understand to be obligations. Indeed, these connections seem to me to point the way toward an improved solution to the general problem of understanding moral obligation. The solution will begin by taking seriously some of the distinctive features that are at work in the case of promissory duty, and treating them as paradigmatic for the more generic phenomenon of moral obligation.

Foot's basic thought seems to be that we understand ourselves to be bound or obliged when we promise to do something. The sense of obligation that is at issue in such cases, I would submit, is roughly the relational conception of normativity whose elements were sketched in chapter 1 of this book. Maklay's thought, fully spelled out, might be that he owes it to the servant to refrain from taking photographs of the servant's person, because he made a promise to the servant that he would respect the servant's wishes in this matter. There is a normative nexus, consisting of a directed duty and a corresponding claim or entitlement on the part of the Malay servant, that has been created through the promissory act, and its presence is crucial to understanding the difference that the promise makes to their relations with each other from that point on. This shows itself, for instance, in our understanding that if Maklay were to break his promise to the servant, he would not merely have acted wrongly, or displayed a deficiency that undermines his status as a good human being; more specifically, he would have wronged the servant in particular.

A directed obligation of the sort at issue in this case plainly has at least some of the features that we were looking for in an account of the normativity of the moral domain. It is, for one thing, the kind of consideration that is plausibly understood to exhibit the deontic rather than the merely aspirational form of normative significance. We might say that obligations, in the specific sense of relational or directed duties, are among the considerations that make sense to us as practical requirements in the generic sense. An action can be "to-be-done" or "not-to-be-done," just insofar as and just because it is something that we owe it to another party to do or to refrain from doing. Obligations in the relational sense are thus paradigmatically intelligible to us as practical requirements (or "obligations" of the more generic kind); this is, in large part, what makes them normative notions in the first place.

As we saw in section 2.1 above, the difference between practical requirements in the generic sense and aspirational reasons is in part a matter of differences in regard to deliberative discretion. We have the sense that many of the reasons that count for and against prospective courses of action are considerations that we have some leeway to discount in our practical thinking about what to do, whereas a similar discretion is out of place in regard to practical requirements. But the relational aspect of directed obligations helps us to make sense of this contrast. In a case with the inherently relational structure I have described, one's reasons for doing something are constitutively connected to claims to performance on the part of another person. The values in which these reasons are based are not purely monadic; they do not exclusively concern the agent, but essentially implicate the person to whom the agent is related, whose own normative situation will be altered if the agent fails to respect the value that is at issue. We might say that they are held in common by two different parties, the agent who stands under the directed duty and the claimholder to whom it is directed. But when these features are present, it seems natural that the agent would lack the unilateral discretion to discount the normative consideration that seems to be present with some other kinds of reason for action. The reason in question is part of a normative complex that does not belong to agents alone, and so it isn't for agents to determine how much weight it is to be given in their practical deliberation.[48] "Satisficing" with respect to it is not an eligible option.

A further dimension of practical requirements, I suggested earlier, is their function within deliberation as Raz-style exclusionary reasons. They are not considerations that belong in a notional ledger of pros and cons, as items that are to be weighed against other considerations of the same kind. Rather they enter the deliberative field as presumptive constraints on the agent's behavior, determining that some things are provisionally to-be-done, and that others are provisionally off the table. Practical requirements that structure deliberation in this way play a very different role from the ordinary normative reasons that count for and against prospective options that the agent might pursue, and it is a general challenge for a theory of obligation to make sense of this important dimension of them.

But the directed duties that are created by promissory exchanges, such as that of Maklay, are normative considerations that intelligibly function as presumptive constraints on agency of just this kind. Transactional duties, including those created by promises and other forms of agreement or exchange, represent what is often thought to be the original notion of obligation: an obliging of one agent by another, which brings into existence a normative debt that must be repaid.[49] The resulting obligation is something that we are aware of in deliberation, as a consideration with its own normative significance; having made a promise to do X, or signed a contract so to act, I will naturally think, going forward, that I now owe it to the other party to fulfill the commitment I have undertaken.

But it is characteristic of such *commitments* that they are properly understood to function as presumptive constraints within the agent's practical reflection about what to do. To undertake a commitment of this kind to someone is ordinarily to return a provisional answer to at least one of the questions that might be asked about how one is going to comport oneself, going forward. Having made a promise to do X, I will naturally think that I now owe it to the promisee to fulfill the promissory commitment. I will therefore take my doing X to be a presumptively fixed point in my ongoing planning about my activities, forming an intention to live up to the commitment that is in this way owed to the other party. The directed obligation is thus something that intelligibly impinges on deliberation in the way of a practical requirement; it functions to rule out certain options (at least defeasibly), and to determine that others will be performed, in virtue of the connection of those options to the claims of another individual.

Transactional duties, such as those generated through promissory exchanges, thus seem to exhibit the deontic features that we have seen to be characteristic of practical requirements. In virtue of their constitutive connection to the claims of another party, they are considerations that we don't have natural discretion to discount, and they rightly function in deliberation as presumptive constraints. Whether or not they represent the original notion of an obligation, they are certainly a natural paradigm for this distinctive phenomenon, and they are widely understood as such. This is especially the case if we assume, as I have been doing, that promissory debts are morally dispositive, representing normative commitments, rather than merely pro tanto considerations that enter into determining what we might be obligated (in some yet unspecified sense) to do. Promissory duties might be defeasible, but when they obtain, they define moral obligations that are binding on us, precisely insofar as they specify things that are owed to another party.

But what about the other features that we have seen to be characteristic of specifically moral obligations? Can we make sense of these in terms of the relational model that is exemplified in cases such as that of Maklay's promise? Consider the issue of agent-relativity. Moral obligations, I have suggested, are familiarly understood to exhibit this distinctive kind of structure, but it is a feature of them that has often been thought to be puzzling or even paradoxical. How can a concern for a basic value lead me properly to care about the instantiation of the value in my own life, without caring equally about its instantiation in the lives of others?[50] Yet this is precisely the structure of concern that seems to be determined by the ordinary understanding of moral obligations. Here we might begin by observing that this puzzling structure appears to be latent in the examples of transactional duty that we have been considering in this section. Thus, having undertaken a promissory obligation, I now owe it to the promisee that I in particular should do the thing that was promised. The promissory transaction does not generate an impersonal concern to promote the value of promissory fidelity in the larger community of moral agents, nor can it plausibly be derived from an agent-neutral concern of that kind. Intuitively, at any rate, transactional duties seem to exhibit the characteristically agent-relative pattern of concern.

Moreover, it appears that we can explain this agent-relative character straightforwardly by appeal to the relational content that we have seen to be characteristic of these obligations. The promissory transaction creates a nexus between the two parties to it, the promisor and the promisee; the former owes it to the latter to do what was promised, and the latter has a claim against the former that the promisor should so act. The obligation that someone like Maklay has undertaken in making a promise is thus one that can be honored only by remaining within the relational compass that it in this way defines—that is, by acknowledging the Malay servant's claim, and thus living up to what he owes it specifically to the servant to do. Other agents may enter into similar transactions with each other, giving rise to directed duties and corresponding claims that link them in their own normative nexus. But seeing to it that they honor the duties that they owe to each other is not something that Maklay is responsible for, either in general or in virtue of his having pledged his word to his Malay servant.

Granted, it would formally be possible to make a promise whose content was to advance some agent-neutral goal in a particular domain of action. I could promise you that I would undertake to maximize impartial welfare in my decisions about how to expend a given percentage of my net income, going forward. I might even promise you that I would do what I could to maximize the incidence of promissory fidelity among the members of my broader community. But these agent-neutral goals would be grounded in the promissory commitment that I have undertaken specifically to you, which is a commitment that I should comport myself in the way I have promised to do, by pursuing the agent-neutral goals specified in the promise. If somebody else could make it the case that those very goals would be better realized through my own personal failure to pursue them, this would not count as a way in which I had fulfilled my promissory commitment. (The situation might be different if I induced the other person to bring about this state of affairs, or accepted an unsolicited offer from the person so to act; in these scenarios, my initial act of getting the other person to intervene would count as honoring my promise to you, even if it had the effect that I would, in future, no longer be pursuing the agent-neutral goal to which I had committed myself.[51]) If we understand moral obligations along the lines of the model implicit in the promissory case, then the agent-relative character of them seems to fall out fairly directly, as a fully intelligible consequence of their inherently relational structure.[52]

Let us turn, finally, to the cosmopolitan aspect of modern morality. The idea here was that specifically moral obligations have their source in the circumstance that we inhabit an inclusive world of moral subjects who are equally real. We understand ourselves to be members of a maximally extensive community of individuals whose interests are no less significant than our own, and our moral obligations derive from this fundamental fact. Is this something we can make sense of on the relational approach to obligation that I have been exploring in this section?

The first thing to note about this question is that the paradigmatic examples of relational duties that have so far been in the foreground have features that are in tension with the cosmopolitan aspect of the moral. Transactional duties, such as Maklay's promise to the servant, rest on a causal interaction between the two parties that they bind. But it is plain that we do not interact causally in this way with all of the members of the maximally inclusive community of moral subjects. If we think of moral obligations in essentially transactional terms, then, we will clearly not be able to do justice to the inclusive aspect of morality, as I have so far presented it.

Suppose, however, that there are directed obligations that do not rest on specific exchanges or transactions with other individuals, but that specify what we owe to people just in virtue of the fact that they occupy a world in common with us, and are therefore liable to be affected in one way or another by the things that we might decide to do. Just as promisors owe it specifically to promisees to live up to the commitments they have entered into, so too might there be things that we owe to each of the other members of this maximally extended moral community, regardless of our antecedent relations to them. This would be a cosmopolitan conception of morality as an interpersonal domain of distinctively relational obligations. The cosmopolitan conception might be thought to result from generalizing the original, transactional model of an obligation to encompass all the members of an inclusive community of equals, linking them pairwise in a distinctive kind of normative nexus.

For reasons that should now be plain, an account of this kind would seem exceptionally well situated to illuminate the specific normative features of the moral to which I called attention in the preceding section. It would represent morality as a set of directed obligations, which we correctly register in deliberation as presumptive demands or requirements. Furthermore, these obligations would have an intelligibly agent-relative character, which is determined straightforwardly by their inherently relational structure. Finally, the resulting picture would offer an appealing account of the cosmopolitan aspect of morality; it would connect moral obligations constitutively to claims that others have against us, simply in virtue of the fact that we and they are members of an inclusive community of individuals whose interests are equally important.

In my view, much of the attraction of the relational interpretation, as a unified interpretation of the moral domain, lies in its promise to illuminate these basic normative features of interpersonal morality, which as we have seen are difficult to make sense of on other approaches. Of course, there is much that remains to be done before we can be confident that this relational interpretation of the moral is genuinely viable. I have so far merely invited the reader to suppose that the transactional model of obligation might be generalized to define a set of duties that are owed to anyone who might stand to be affected, in one way or another, by what we do. But there are large philosophical questions that are raised by this suggestion, which will need to be tackled before we can be confident that the cosmopolitan version of relational obligation is really defensible. We will also need to explore the first-order normative implications of understanding the domain of interpersonal morality in these relational terms. These are tasks that I take up in chapters 4 through 6 of this book. For the remainder of this chapter and the one to follow, however, I shall operate on the assumption that the generalized version of transactional obligation represents at least a possible template for understanding interpersonal morality, in order to continue to develop the theoretical advantages of this approach to interpreting the moral right.

2.4. Refining the Picture

Assume, then, that the transactional model can be generalized, so that we are linked in a normative nexus to each of the individuals who might potentially be affected by the exercise of our agency. Every one of these individuals would have moral claims against us, just insofar as they have standing as equal members of an inclusive moral community. I have so far argued that an approach along these general lines would be well suited to shed light on some of the specific features of moral obligation, illuminating the distinctive normative significance that moral considerations seem to have in the first-person perspective of deliberation. But to understand the moral in these terms, we will need to take on board some controversial and hitherto neglected commitments of the approach.

The relational account represents moral considerations as obligations in the original sense, specifying duties that are owed to the various individuals who are in a position to be affected in one way or another by what we do. According to this conception, the highest-level property of moral rightness just is the property of being owed to another party or parties, insofar as they are persons with equal standing. And to correctly identify something as morally right is to think of it as having this property, so that one conceptualizes oneself as linked to another person through a network of connected claims and directed duties.[53] Considerations of this relational kind enter the deliberative field in the guise of presumptive constraints on agency, in ways that align with our intuitive convictions about the deontic structure of the moral domain.

To take this idea seriously, however, is to attribute to moral rightness an independent normative significance for deliberation. That we owe it to other people to comply with basic moral standards of conduct is itself something that impinges on deliberation, as a consideration that needs to be taken into account and responded to. Indeed, it impinges on deliberation in the distinctive way I characterized above, as a presumptive requirement (in the generic sense). It is characteristic of the paradigm cases of directed obligation that we register them in practical thought as demands on our agency, specifying things that are "to-be-done" or "not-done" in virtue of the normative nexus that they define. This is, I have contended, the distinctive form of normative significance that directed duties have for the agents who acknowledge them in deliberative thought. The contrast is with other kinds of reason for action, such as considerations of personal enjoyment or convenience, which we register very differently in practical reflection; considerations of this kind speak in favor of our doing certain things, without presuming to exclude from the start the option of acting otherwise.

As Joseph Raz has observed, the difference in these styles of normative relation comes into clear focus in the cases in which they interact. Thus the inconvenience of going out in the rain would ordinarily count in favor of staying home, and it would normally be appropriate to take this consideration into account in just this way in one's deliberations about what to do. But if I have promised a student I would meet her at the office, the option of remaining at home is off the agenda, and the reasons of convenience that would ordinarily speak in favor of this course of action are rendered inoperative.[54] Furthermore, the consideration that operates in this way as an exclusionary constraint is the fact that I have undertaken a duty to meet the student in my office, or that I owe it to the student so to act. These are considerations that might be summarized by saying that, in virtue of my promise, meeting the student is now the right thing to do, and it would be wrong or impermissible to act other-wise.[55] I conclude that I have to meet the student, because I have in this way obligated myself to do so.

This general approach to morality is at odds with a common conception of moral rightness, as a kind of summary concept that is without independent normative significance.[56] According to this alternative conception, to judge that something is the right thing to do is to judge, very roughly, that it is what the agent ought to do, all things considered. Likewise, an action will be wrong just in case the agent ought not to do it, taking everything into account. This is the indefinable generic conception of right and wrong that we encountered at the start of section 2.2 above, which marks out actions as "to-be-done" or "not-to-be-done." Moral rightness and wrongness could then be interpreted, in these terms, as special cases of these generic summary concepts, ones that are in play when there are reasons of a moral nature that speak decisively for or against the agent's doing something. The result is a kind of buck-passing conception of moral rightness; to say that X is the morally right or wrong ac-tion is not to specify a consideration that counts in its own right as a reason for doing X, but to register the existence of other reasons for so acting that are both weighty and moral in character.[57]

Those who accept this kind of account will naturally think that it is fetish-istic to be moved to action directly by reflection on the fact that X would be the right thing to do, morally speaking.[58] The morally conscientious agent is someone who cares about, and responds immediately to, the things that tend to make actions morally right in the buck-passing sense, such as that they would alleviate someone's need or avoid unnecessary suffering or meet the expectations one has induced another person to form. To care about moral rightness, as something over and above the first-order considerations that make actions right in the first place, is to assign to a consideration the kind of significance for deliberation that it does not intrinsically possess, much as the commodity fetishist invests material objects with the social meanings that are in fact in play only as a result of their being exchanged.

Now one challenge for this summary conception of moral rightness will be to make sense of the deontic structure that seems to be characteristic of the moral realm. If there is something about moral considerations that makes them suited to enter the deliberative field as presumptive constraints on the will, this will not be the fact that the actions they recommend are morally right. That is a consideration that is, by hypothesis, without independent normative significance; as a summary or second-order concept, moral rightness is not something that we reflect on in deliberating about what to do, but expresses the initial output of deliberation, the conclusion we arrive at by reflecting on the first-order considerations that count as moral reasons in their own right. The burden of accounting for the deontic character of moral considerations will thus fall to the characterization of the reasons that we advert to when we say that an action is morally right.

For all that has been said so far, of course, one of the first-order considerations that contribute to making actions morally right in the summary or generic sense might be the fact that the agent owes it to another party to perform the action, or that the other party has a claim against the agent to such performance. So long as this is just one moral consideration among others, however, we cannot appeal to it to make sense of the idea that moral considerations in general have an inherently peremptory or demanding quality. That is, there will be no unified account of the interpersonal moral domain that itself explains why the considerations that make actions right are in the way of obligations. On the relational interpretation, by contrast, the directed character that we naturally register in moral reflection as a presumptive requirement just is the feature that we are ascribing to actions when we correctly identify them as morally right. It is thus well suited to explain this important dimension of the normativity of the moral domain.

Crucial to this account of moral obligation is the sense of oneself in deliberation as being bound to another person in a nexus of interlocking claims and directed duties. Moral reasons, on the relational conception of them, are part of a normative structure that implicates another party as well as oneself, and this is connected to the characteristic way they impinge on deliberative thought, as presumptive constraints on action and choice. As I put the point above, they belong to a normative nexus that is held in common by two different parties, and one therefore lacks the discretion characteristic of some other normative reasons to discount them unilaterally (for instance, by satisficing rather than choosing the best option, or by acting on a sufficient reason when there is more reason, on balance, to do something else).

To deliberate in these relational terms is not, I think, to fetishize a consideration that is without independent normative significance. It is an important aspect of our social relations that we are connected to other individuals through bonds of directed duty, such as those created by promises and other transactions between individuals. The relational account assumes that there are things that we in this way owe to other individuals quite generally, independently of any transactions we might have entered into with them, and just in virtue of the fact that they and we inhabit a world together. If this is right, then these general relational duties should likewise have independent significance for practical thought. True, the general relational framework of directed duties and claims is not always salient or explicit in the reflections of the agents who comply with its terms. Agents will in practice often be focused more specifically on the concrete consequences of their actions for the individuals who stand to be affected by them—for instance, on the pain or inconvenience or disappointment that might be caused by their going ahead with a course of action on which they are launched. According to the relational approach, however, thoughts of this kind will implicitly reflect, in morally conscientious agents, an awareness of their significance for directed duties and claims. One will apprehend the interests of the other individual as considerations that potentially ground claims against one to act in one way or another. The structure of one's deliberations, if it were made explicit, would thus be provided by the relational framework.

A different way to develop the idea that obligations constitutively connect us to other parties would be to interpret them in the voluntarist terms sketched earlier, as the commands of an authoritative lawgiver of some kind. According to this approach, thoughts about rightness do not have the same kind of normative significance for the authorities who impose moral requirements that they have for those on whom the requirements are imposed.[59] It is the act of demanding compliance by the authority that makes certain actions morally wrong in the first place, in the way that involves an obligation not to perform them. In imposing the requirement, then, the relevant authority cannot be understood to be responding to the independent fact that it would be morally wrong in the relevant sense to violate it. Thoughts of moral right and wrong are in this way transparent to the deliberations of the authority whose volitional acts give rise to obligations.[60] Once the relevant demands have been made, however, thoughts of moral right and wrong are available to figure in the deliberations of the agents on whom the obligations rest. They will see themselves as subject to a presumptive requirement to comply with moral standards of right conduct, just because and insofar as those standards are laid down by the voluntary acts of a suitable authority.

According to the relational alternative, by contrast, obligations are understood by the agents subject to them to constitute a nexus, not with some putative lawgiver whose commands bring them into existence in the first place, but with the specific individuals to whom they are owed. They link agents with persons who have a claim against them to performance. From the perspective of claimholders, the obligation is not something that comes into effect through a volitional act on their part. It is already there to be cognized and understood, as a requirement that is directed to them, one that goes together with a claim on their part to compliance. It is thus not transparent to the reflections of the claimholders, but instead represents for them, as for the agents, a relational consideration with independent normative significance. Just as promisors understand that they owe it to promisees to perform, so too do promisees understand themselves to have claims against promisors that they so act.

I discuss in the next chapter the distinctive form of normative significance that directed moral obligations have for the individuals to whom they are owed. Before taking up this issue, however, it is important to address a concern that probably already occurred to readers several pages ago. In developing my argument about the bearing of directed duties on deliberation, I have taken for granted our familiarity with this basic normative notion, and focused attention on features of it that suit it to figure in reflection as a basis of practical requirements. We understand ourselves to generate claims in other people when we make promises to them, and the corresponding directed duties make sense to us as considerations that enter deliberation in the guise of presumptive constraints.

But the basic schema of a directed obligation is one that has application in many different domains. There are duties and claims of private law, for instance, which may be distinguished from each other according to the different conventional systems that define them.[61] But there are relational obligations of other kinds as well, including (among others) directed duties and claims defined by the rules of various games. In the sport known in most of the world as football, for instance, there are penalties that attach to various things players might do on the field, and some of these sanctioned actions constitute fouls rather than mere infractions. Many (though not all) fouls, furthermore, have a transparently relational character, insofar as they are recognized to be offenses against an opposing player, generally involving prohibited forms of interference with the player's conduct on the field (such as tackling the player too aggressively, or otherwise impeding the player's free movement to the ball). Within the context of the game, it would be natural for players to take the rules defining such fouls as a sort of relational nexus. Conscientious players will treat these rules as presumptive constraints on their behavior, and actions that flout the rules will be understood to violate specific claims that the players hold against each other in the course of their athletic contest. Outside the context of the game, however, it is not clear that its relational requirements have much independent significance at all. This raises a natural question about the relational obligations of interpersonal morality: even if we grant that there are such requirements, how can we be confident that they represent important normative considerations, ones that conscientious agents rightly treat as presumptive constraints on their behavior? Perhaps they are no more significant to us than the rules of some random game or social practice that we do not happen to take much interest in.

There are two points to emphasize in response to this natural suggestion. The first has to do with the situations that trigger directed obligations of different kinds. I suggested that in the sports case, there are relational requirements that are partly constitutive of certain games, insofar as they are defined by the rules that make the game what it is in the first place. We might say that the rules of football (for instance) specify what the players owe to each other, just insofar as they are both engaged in a sporting contest of the relevant kind. If this much is correct, however, then it seems that it is one's role as a football player that determines whether it is correct to treat the corresponding relational requirements as presumptive constraints on one's activities. The rules do not even purport to specify what one owes to other people outside the context of the game, and so the question of whether they are important or not, independently of that context, hardly arises. But once one is out on the pitch, playing football against the members of another team, the rules assign claims that the opposing players have against one, and it would reflect a defect in one's reasoning, as a player of the game, not to treat them as constraints on one's own conduct on the field.

According to the relational approach to morality, there are claims that individuals have against us, and corresponding duties that we owe to them, just insofar as they and we are both persons, equally real. Not everyone will accept this contention, of course, and I will address various sources of skepticism about it in the chapters to follow (especially chapter 4). But let us posit, for the time being, that the relational approach is correct in its assignment of claims and directed duties to us, just in our capacity as persons. It seems to follow that we deliberate correctly, insofar as we are persons, only if we treat these person-based duties and claims as presumptive requirements, constraining our decision-making about what to do. Seen in this light, the difference between the requirements of football and moral requirements lies, in part, in the degree to which the situations with which the two systems of relational norms are bound up are escapable. It is always possible for players of football to opt out of the game, and when they do that, the constitutive rules of the game will no longer be binding on them, as practical requirements. But it is not in the same way possible for us to opt out of the situation in which we are persons whose actions potentially affect other individuals of the same kind. This situation is one that we necessarily inhabit, and so the relational obligations determined by it will figure in the deliberations of all of us as presumptive constraints, if we are well informed and deliberating correctly.[62]

A second point to emphasize concerns the positive values with which roles of various kinds may be seen to be associated. In the football case, our sense of the importance of the relational requirements constitutive of the game is connected, in part, to our appreciation of the goods that they enable. We admire football players who are able to accomplish impressive feats on the pitch in compliance with the rules of the game they are playing, without fouling their opponents in the process. Those rules impose a discipline on the activities of the players that is closely connected to whatever might be valuable in their role-based performances. This shows itself in the fact that our sense of satisfaction with a player's accomplishments would be diminished by the recognition that those accomplishments came at the expense of an overlooked violation of the rules. (Consider Luis Suárez's uncalled biting foul against Giorgio Chiellini in a decisive group match during the 2014 World Cup tournament in Brazil.)

A different example with the same structure is friendship. It seems to me plausible to suppose that there are things that we owe to other people insofar as we are their friends.[63] People who stand in this relationship, and who appreciate its normative significance, will therefore take the claims that their friends have against them as presumptive constraints on their deliberations. But the importance of these requirements is also connected to the values that compliance with them helps to make possible. Friendship is one of the profoundest goods that are achievable in a human life, and our sense of the importance of the demands of friendship is bound up with our acknowledgment of the values that are realized by honoring the claims that our friends have against us. Just as football players enjoy the distinctive values of the game only when they submit to its constitutive rules, so too are the values of friendship available only to those who recognize and honor the requirements that they owe to their friends.

In the moral case, I have not yet said anything to support the idea that there is a characteristic positive value that is enabled by compliance with the relational obligations that we owe to others, just insofar as they are persons. But the idea strikes me as deeply plausible. There is something valuable about conducting one's life on terms that honor the claims that others have against us. We can take satisfaction in the knowledge that we could look those who might be affected by our actions in the eye, and give an account of ourselves, showing that we lived up to the requirements that we owe to them in particular. We thus *recognize* them as sources of claims against us, and *acknowledge* the significance of those claims in our decisions about the conduct of our own affairs. Furthermore, our sense of the importance of such relational moral requirements is connected to our appreciation of this positive value, which we might refer to as interpersonal recognition.[64] This is a theme to which I shall return in chapters 3 and 4 below.

In the meantime, some comments about the possibility of conflicts of obligation will bring my discussion in this chapter to a conclusion. I noted above that practical requirements represent presumptive rather than unconditional constraints on the will, in recognition of the fact that circumstances can change in ways that bear normative significance. Emergencies might arise that undermine obligations that would otherwise have obtained, for instance, making it the case that we no longer owe it to someone else to do the very thing that we originally took as a constraint on our behavior. In that scenario, the reasoning internal to morality that supports the original obligation would recognize exceptions. Thus, the interests of promisees that ground entitlements to promissory fidelity are not reasonably understood to generate absolute claims to performance on the promisor's part, come what may. Or it might happen that an obligation remains in force, but comes into conflict with a different obligation whose force is also retained under the circumstances, resulting in a practical dilemma.

According to the relational interpretation, it is possible, for all that has been said so far, that a dilemma of this kind might arise within morality. Moral obligations are directed duties that correspond to claims on the part of individuals against the agent to performance. A conflict within the domain of interpersonal morality in this sense would emerge if there were a situation in which there is no way for an agent to live up to what is owed to one individual without violating the claims that some second individual has against that agent.[65] But this is at least a coherent possibility. Insofar as the duties in question can be traced to the claims of different individuals, it makes sense that what one needs to do in order to live up to one such claim might preclude the action that is required to honor the other claim. The two obligations would be owed to different persons, each of whom might be entitled to complain if one fails to fulfill one's obligation to them, even if in doing this one is living up to one's obligation to someone else.

But what about apparent conflicts between morality and other forms of obligation? As I noted above, there are relational requirements of different kinds, associated with discrete normative domains, such as those defined by various private law systems, as well as by conventions, practices, and games of various sorts. I think it is plausible to assume that the relations between many of these systems are ones of hierarchical subordination rather than potential direct conflict.[66] The intuitive thought here is that directed obligations often function as presumptive constraints in a domain-specific way, and that their force as practical requirements does not extend outside the relevant domain. This prevents them from conflicting directly with the more fundamental requirements that structure and have priority over them. In the game case, for instance, the relational duties of football properly structure one's activities on the pitch, in the situation in which one functions as a player of the game. But this role is normally understood to be subordinate to one's standing as a person who interacts with other individuals, equally real. In a situation in which the relational duties of football appear to conflict with those of morality, it is therefore natural to conclude that the former are no longer fully in force. Thus, if you and I are on opposing teams, and the only way you can prevent me from being hurt by the bomb that has been tossed onto the field is to tackle me from behind without the ball, this is clearly what you owe it to me to do. The fact that you would be fouling me is no longer a pertinent consideration in this context.

A different case that is interesting to consider concerns political obligations. The idea that there are obligations of this kind, such as an obligation to obey the laws of the political communities of which we are members, is not uncontroversial. But to the extent the idea is plausible, the broadly relational model might provide a promising way to understand these obligations.[67] Political associations involve distinctive forms of interpersonal relationship that can be non-instrumentally valuable, and under these conditions we might well owe it to the other individuals to whom we are so related to comply with the legislative commitments that we have undertaken together. But these obligations, to the extent they obtain at all, are naturally understood to be subordinate to the more basic requirements of morality. We might put this by saying that our membership in a given political community is valuable only insofar as the terms of association for the community meet some threshold of basic moral acceptability. The result would be that there are independent normative requirements associated with political membership, but not ones that are liable to conflict fundamentally with the requirements of interpersonal morality.

But this does not mean that conflicts between moral and other obligations are impossible. Some directed duties, for instance, are associated with relationships that are fundamental to the meaning of our lives, relationships whose value does not derive from the interpersonal moral values of mutual recognition and regard. There are things that I owe to other individuals insofar as I love them, and stand to them in a relationship of friendship or attachment.[68] Insofar as these directed duties have a source in values that are independent from those at the heart of morality, they might sometimes diverge from moral requirements. Nor does it seem plausible to insist that the requirements of such special relationships always give way to moral requirements when the two of them come into conflict. There might be a certain sensitivity to moral demands that is built into most reasonable conceptions of friendship and love;[69] in contrast to the case of political membership, however, it is doubtful that relationships of love and attachment can be valuable only to the extent they are conducted on basically moral terms. So some potential for conflict may go together with our involvement in these relationships.

And there are other possibilities for conflict, as well. I noted in section 2.1 above that there are different models available for understanding the phenomenon of a practical requirement, beyond the relational model that is implicit in the conception of morality as a set of directed obligations. These models, despite their limitations, have at least some application within the terms that they lay out. Thus, a consideration that is anchored firmly in core features of our identity, such that our identity will be threatened or undermined if the consideration is not acted on, is one that it would make sense for us to treat as a presumptive constraint on our planning agency. If my standing as an artist would be betrayed by my failure to take advantage of an important opportunity, this might be something that does not merely count in favor of my so acting, but requires or demands it.

Practical requirements of these various kinds would have sources that are distinct from that of moral obligations, which according to the relational account define what we owe to others just insofar as they are persons who are equally real. But insofar as these independent requirements are also fundamental, the possibility cannot be ruled out that they might sometimes come into intractable conflict with our moral duties. Bernard Williams's probing critical reflections about impersonal morality in its various forms often center around conflicts of this general kind: between, for instance, an imagined Gauguin's artistic commitments and the moral requirements that are owed to his family, or between our moral responsibilities to strangers and what we owe to the people to whom we are connected by ties of love and affection.[70]

Conflicts of both of these two general kinds—those within morality, involving moral duties owed to different individuals; and those between morality and other sources of practical requirement—raise interesting issues, which are beyond the scope of the present discussion. For now, I would merely observe that nothing in the argument of this chapter precludes the possibility that there are conflicting obligations of either type. On the contrary, the framework I have offered for understanding moral obligation seems to bring with it opportunities for conflicts of both kinds potentially to emerge in the course of living a human life. Insofar as moral obligations represent duties that are owed to individuals, there might be a conflict within morality between duties that are owed to two different parties. And insofar as there is a plurality of models for making sense of something as a practical requirement, the obligations of morality might potentially come into conflict with requirements that have a distinct source, for instance in features of our practical identity or in the demands of the special relationships we stand in to those to whom we are attached.

It is sometimes assumed that a vindication of morality must show that it is not merely a source of obligations, but that its obligations are overriding or supreme, such as to trump any of the normative considerations that might potentially come into conflict with them. It might be nice if there were a philosophical demonstration that this is the case, but it seems to me too much to expect from a theory of moral obligation that it should necessarily secure the supremacy of moral obligations in this ambitious sense. Instead, I have concentrated on a preliminary but to my mind more important task, of explaining why moral considerations should have the distinctive normative force of obligations. As we have seen, considerations of this kind bind the will in the way of practical constraints wherever they remain in force, even if they might sometimes come into conflict with competing practical requirements.[71] The relational interpretation promises to make sense of this aspect of the morality of right and wrong, and this is already an important consideration in its favor.

3

Morality as a Social Phenomenon

IN THE PRECEDING CHAPTER I looked at the normative significance of moral rightness for the agent. I argued, specifically, that moral considerations present themselves as practical requirements of a special kind, and that the relational approach to morality is well positioned to illuminate this dimension of it.

In this chapter, I shift my focus from the agent to those potentially affected by what the agent does. A leading idea here will be that interpersonal morality apparently has normative significance not only for the agent, but for other parties as well, and that it is an important but neglected task for moral theory to make sense of this aspect of it. Moral standards of right and wrong purport to define constraints on agency; but they also purport to provide a basis for interpersonal accountability relations between individuals, articulating what we can expect of each other as each of us pursues our private ends. Disregard of such interpersonal expectations by an agent thus has normative implications for other parties, giving them reason to adjust their attitudes and behavior in response, in the characteristic register of blame.

My main aims in this chapter are as follows. First, I hope to work out the basic idea sketched hastily above, that requirements of moral right and wrong have direct normative significance for other parties besides the agent subject to them. A nondebunking account of them should establish that they are suited by their nature to structure relations of accountability, and that disregard of them by an agent gives others reasons to react in distinctive ways. Second, I shall argue that it is a signal advantage of the relational account of rightness that it provides a satisfying response to this desideratum. According to the relational account, moral rightness is to be understood in terms of directed obligations that are connected to the claims of other parties. But people

66

who have claims against the agent to compliance with obligations also have reasons to hold the agent accountable for such compliance, and to blame the agent when the obligations are flouted. Finally, I shall identify further elements in our practices of interpersonal accountability that make sense only if the moral norms on which they are based represent relational obligations. In these ways, relational moral obligations are uniquely well suited to provide a normative basis for our social practices of accountability.

The argument of the chapter can be understood as having two complementary phases, which move in different directions between modern conceptions of interpersonal morality and our accountability practices. Phase one, which occupies the first two sections of the chapter, begins with the modern concept of the morally right, arguing that it purports to have normative significance for other parties besides the agent, and that the relational interpretation alone is able to make sense of this dimension of it. Especially important here is the idea that a conception of moral rightness should provide a plausible normative basis for accountability relations, including reactive and other forms of blame. In the second phase, which takes up sections 3.3–3.4, I take a closer look at some of our accountability practices, and argue that they have features that make sense only if the moral norms with which they are connected have a relational structure. Central to this phase of the argument will be the specific reactions characteristic of blame, and the related practices of apology, forgiveness, and moral repair. Taken together, the two phases make the case that interpersonal morality is an inherently social phenomenon, in ways that become fully intelligible only on the relational conception of it.

3.1. The Interpersonal Significance of Moral Right and Wrong

In the preceding chapter, I suggested that morality seems to have normative significance in the first-person perspective of agency. That a course of action would be morally wrong is not merely an interesting theoretical fact about it, but something that makes demands on the rational will. Indeed, I suggested that moral considerations of this kind present themselves to us not simply as reasons for action, but as obligations, and that it is an important task for an account of morality to make sense of its characteristically deontic form of deliberative significance.

But what is the status of this claim about the apparent normative significance of morality for agents? Does it follow a priori that if X is the right thing

for me to do, then X is something that I am obligated to do? Or is the normative standing of moral considerations as obligations a merely contingent fact
about them, one that isn't guaranteed, for instance, by the correct application
of the concepts involved in moral judgment? The issues here are delicate ones.

On the one hand, it is certainly part of our modern understanding of morality that it constitutes a domain of practical requirements. Thus we typically
cite moral considerations in discussion with other people, as factors that are
of peremptory normative significance, requiring or ruling out options that
are under active consideration. We raise our children to treat moral considerations in this way, for example. Furthermore, many of us structure our
(adult) deliberations on the supposition that moral considerations have this
kind of importance, taking facts about rightness and moral value to enter into
our deliberations in the way of presumptive constraints. These considerations
suggest to me that it belongs to the modern concept of morality that conclusions about what it is right or impermissible to do are imbued with the normative significance of obligations. This is what I meant, in section 2.2 above,
in saying that deontic structure is one of the features that characterize the
modern concept of morality, a feature that specific conceptions of moral
rightness are answerable to. On the other hand, there has to be room for the
skeptical position that coherently questions whether people are really obligated to comply with the standards that define what is morally right and
wrong. The skeptical position might be mistaken as a matter of fact, but it isn't
merely confused; one can grant that it would be wrong to do X, and yet without contradiction deny that this is a reason against acting in that way, never
mind a practical requirement.

The best way to do justice to these twin pressures, it seems to me, is to take
an element of revisionism to be endemic to the skeptical position. Skeptics,
insofar as they deny that moral rightness represents a source of obligations,
are asserting the falsity of one of the platitudes that help to fix the modern
concept of the morally right.[1] They are thus denying that there is anything in
the world that completely answers to this moral concept. It doesn't follow,
however, that the position they are adopting is merely confused or incoherent.
In saying that people are not in fact required to comply with the standards of
moral rightness, they can be interpreted as suggesting that the properties in
the world that most closely approximate to our concept of the morally right
are not properties that have this kind of normative significance. Morality cannot, as a result, be everything that it represents itself as being, insofar as one

of the platitudes that help to fix the modern concept turns out to be false as a matter of fact. But this strikes me as a plausible thing to say about the kind of skepticism I have been considering. It is a modestly revisionist position, denying something that strikes us as partly constitutive of the modern concept of the moral in the first place, namely the direct significance of the high-level properties it describes as presumptive normative constraints on agency.[2]

I now want to suggest that it is an additional element in the modern understanding of morality that the obligations of moral right and wrong have normative significance for parties other than the agent immediately subject to them. They provide, in particular, a reasonable basis for responsibility relations between individuals, who hold each other accountable for their compliance or lack of compliance with moral obligations. This is a further feature of the modern concept of morality that a substantive conception of it is answerable to. I referred in chapter 1 to the domain of interpersonal morality, suggesting that it collects a set of requirements that is intermediate between the narrow domain of moral rights and the broader class of reasons and values that provide potential bases for assessing exertions of the rational will. But morality in this intermediate sense is interpersonal not merely in virtue of representing obligations that derive from our relations to other people, but also in virtue of collecting considerations that have normative significance *for* other people. A nonskeptical account of morality must make sense of the interpersonal dimension of it, no less than its deontic significance from the first-person standpoint of deliberation about what to do.

There are two closely linked aspects of responsibility that I would particularly wish to emphasize in this connection. The first is the general stance that we adopt toward people when we are prepared to hold them to account for what they do. P. F. Strawson famously adverted to this stance when he contrasted the attitude of "participation or involvement in a human relationship" with a different, objective attitude that may be adopted toward other people.[3] In viewing people objectively, we step back from the expectations that define our ordinary social relationships, and regard them dispassionately, as individuals to be studied or manipulated or cured or understood. Strawson himself did not believe it was possible to sustain an attitude of objectivity in this sense across the board, toward all of the people we interact with as we go about our lives. But it is available to us in the specialized contexts defined by professional activities and roles, such as those of the therapist or the anthropological researcher, and also as an occasional "refuge from the strains of involvement."[4]

The participant attitude, by contrast, is one that we take up toward people by default, and it involves the attribution to them of responsibility for what they do.

Let us call the stance through which responsibility is in this way ascribed to people that of interpersonal accountability. For present purposes, it is not important to take a stand on Strawson's claim that interpersonal accountability relations in this sense represent our default mode of interacting with people.[5] But the contrast with objectivity brings out that accountability has distinctive features that it is open to us to suspend, for strategic or professional or other purposes, at least for limited periods of time. How might these distinctive features best be understood? A promising framework for thinking about them, I believe, is to understand them in terms of demands or expectations.[6] To stand in relations of interpersonal accountability with others is not to be accepting of or indifferent to their conduct, whatever its shape or character, but to hold them to certain standards for comporting themselves. It is to expect or to demand that they should comply with those standards, in a sense that (as Strawson observed) is reasonably familiar to all of us who have been participants in ordinary relationships with other human beings.

To hold people to demands and expectations, in the manner characteristic of accountability, is a way of addressing those demands and expectations to other parties.[7] This stance is connected in turn to distinctive ways of reacting when the demands and expectations at issue are flouted. This brings me to the second aspect of responsibility that I wish to highlight. Those who stand in relations of interpersonal accountability with other people are typically prone to respond to infractions of the relevant expectations with responses that are in the general key of blame. Blame is a complex phenomenon that will probably always elude definitive philosophical analysis; it is simply too protean and multidimensional.[8] I myself favor an approach to it that is indebted to Strawson's work in emphasizing the reactive sentiments, including preeminently resentment, guilt, and indignation, but that can also encompass other, related forms of angry disapprobation.[9] Attitudinal reactions of these kinds are paradigmatic and salient examples of blame, even if we wish to concede that blame can take other forms as well.

Reactive blame, as we might call it, insofar as it is emotionally inflected, reflects the fact that the person subject to it has internalized a concern for the expectations or demands that somebody has flouted. When we blame in this way, we reveal that it is not a matter of indifference to us whether agents comply with those standards, but that it matters to us; reactive anger is a way of being exercised about someone's behavior and attitudes, and it reflects the fact that we are invested in certain basic standards, as ones that govern the person whom we blame. That said, we should allow that blame might take other, less paradigmatically angry forms as well. These extend from expressions of disapproval to comparatively cool modifications of one's relationship with another agent in response to that agent's violation of demands or expectations, such as withdrawal and avoidance.[10] For purposes of discussion in what follows, however, I shall focus primarily on the paradigm form of reactive blame, while also noting the adjustments that might be required in my position in order to accommodate some of the other forms that blame is able to assume.

We have, then, the general stance of interpersonal accountability, whereby we hold people to demands or expectations, as well as specific reactions in the key of blame, to which interpersonal accountability disposes us when those demands and expectations are flouted. The suggestion I would now like to explore is that moral rightness is normative not only for individual agents (insofar as it represents for them a source of practical requirements), but also for these accountability practices, which involve individuals other than the agent.

My basic thought here is that standards of moral rightness are intrinsically suited to figure in an interpersonal practice of accountability. That is, it should make sense, in virtue of the nature of moral obligations, that people hold each other to them, in the way that is characteristically connected with reactive blame. Such obligations thus provide a reasonable basis for social relations that are structured in terms of the addressing of demands or expectations to another party. Furthermore, and relatedly, it should follow from an account of moral rightness that people who act with disregard for the requirements of the moral right thereby give others at least pro tanto reasons for the reactive attitudes involved in blame.

These suggestions reflect a conception of morality as a phenomenon with an essentially social function. Moral obligations, as we have seen, purport to have direct significance for individual agents, providing them with compelling reasons for action that shape their deliberations about what to do. But they are not merely considerations that have this kind of normative importance in the context of first-personal deliberation. They also have an essential role to play in providing the basis for a shared social life, via their role in a practice of interpersonal accountability. This may be thought of as a further element in the characteristically modern concept of morality that I adverted to at the start of the current section.[11]

A reflection of this aspect of interpersonal morality is the thought that we can understand a community's morality by identifying the things that attract reactive attitudes within the community, eliciting responses of angry disapprobation. *Our morality*, in this familiar sense, just is that set of standards that we address to each other in an interpersonal practice of holding one another to account. This is not to say that we are infallible about what morality requires of us. We might attach opprobrium to the wrong things, blaming people when they engage in eccentric sexual practices with other consenting adults, for instance, and failing to get exercised at all when they turn their backs on the basic human needs of vulnerable members our community. We could express this possibility by saying that our moral standards are mistaken or misguided in cases of this kind, and this tells us something about the modern understanding of morality: namely, that we think of morality as a set of standards that function to regulate our responsibility relations with each other, giving people reasons for reactive and other forms of blame when they are violated.

This is an initial statement of my main idea about the interpersonal dimension of the morally right. But the idea requires further clarification and development. I have suggested that there are two ways in which moral rightness seems normative for practices of accountability. First, standards of moral rightness are ones that are intrinsically suited to function as expectations or demands in an interpersonal practice of accountability, and to be addressed by agents to each other within such a practice. Second, violations of these standards provide other parties with reasons for reactive and other forms of blame. But these two aspects are closely connected, and tracing the links between them will help us to understand better the apparent normative significance of moral obligations for the reactions of others.

I said that moral rightness delivers standards that are suited by their nature to define the expectations to which we hold each other within a practice of accountability. This means that it is at least pro tanto reasonable to address those standards to other parties in the ways characteristic of interpersonal accountability. Whether this stance is reasonable on balance arguably depends on ancillary factors, independent of the content or nature of moral rightness, that ultimately bear on the assessment of the stance. For instance, skeptics about moral responsibility argue that it is never ultimately justifiable to hold people to account for their actions, because the conditions of responsible moral agency cannot be satisfied in a world of natural causal processes, or perhaps because the notion of moral responsibility is itself incoherent (so that it would lack application in any possible world we might try to imagine). These arguments raise very large issues that, though interesting and important, are well beyond the scope of my discussion in this book. Abstracting from global concerns of this kind, however, we can say that standards of moral rightness are ones that it is reasonable to hold people accountable for complying with. That is, assuming that it can ever be reasonable in our world to address demands or expectations to others in a practice of interpersonal accountability, it is reasonable to grant standards of moral rightness this distinctive role. If it would be morally wrong for people to do something—say, breaking their word for reasons of trivial personal convenience—then it is the sort of thing that it is, to that extent at least, reasonable for other parties to expect them not to do.

But when, exactly, is this condition of pro tanto reasonableness satisfied? A plausible answer, in my view, is that it is satisfied, in the first instance, just in case and just because the flouting of the moral standard would give other parties reasons to adopt reactions in the general key of blame. The stance of interpersonal accountability involves a preparedness to blame people when they fail to live up to the expectations to which we hold them in our interactions with them. So standards of moral rightness are suited by their nature to figure in this stance when they are such that their violation gives people reasons for reactive and other forms of blame. It is their potential provision of reasons for blame of this kind that is the primary form of normative significance that moral obligations have for the attitudes and actions of other parties. The view I am developing, then, is that it is part of the modern concept of morality that standards of moral rightness have this kind of significance for blame, and that it is to that extent reasonable to hold others accountable for complying with them.

More precisely, what provide others with reasons to blame an agent are not facts about the violation of moral standards by the agent, but attitudes of disregard on the part of the agent toward the standards. It is possible to act impermissibly, in a suitably objective sense, even if one is reasonably conscientious about one's moral obligations.[12] Having promised to accompany you to the gym to try out one of their Pilates classes, something you are reluctant to do on your own, I will count as acting wrongly if I fail to show up at the appointed time and place. This will be true even if I made scrupulous efforts to see to it that I kept the promise as I planned my activities in the interim. Perhaps I entered the appointment carefully into the Google calendar that I use to keep track of my life, but the entry ends up getting shifted to a different day on account of a malicious cyberattack on the Google servers. Or perhaps, though the calendar does not malfunction, the subway train I board on my way to the promised appointment does, trapping me short of my destination with no hope of timely egress.

Moral standards define obligations or practical requirements, and as we saw in the previous chapter, agents respond correctly to them when they form intentions to comply with them, treating them as presumptive constraints on their ongoing activities. From the perspective of other parties, then, what it is reasonable to expect or demand of people is only that they will make a conscientious effort to live up to the requirements of the moral right, acknowledging and striving to realize their deliberative role as presumptive constraints. We cannot reasonably expect perfect compliance with the letter of the moral law, insofar as innocent epistemic and other limitations can sometimes lead agents astray even when their attitudinal responses to their moral obligations are beyond reproach. Reasons for blame are provided, accordingly, not by actions of agents that are objectively wrong or impermissible,[13] but by actions that reflect a disregard for the standards of the moral right. It is the flouting of moral obligations—construed broadly, to include the negligent failure to comply with them—that gives others reasons for the reactions characteristic of blame, not their mere violation by the agent. Conversely, if agents make a conscientious effort to comply with moral obligations, this ensures a degree of normative protection from the responsibility-attributing reactions of other parties. Other people might still get angry with agents who act in this way, but such reactions would not be warranted, precisely insofar as the actions to which they respond do not reflect attitudes of disregard for moral standards.[14]

On the general approach to blame that I find most promising, the reasons primarily involved here are reasons for attitudes. The paradigmatic forms of blame are reactions in the general range of angry disapprobation, including most saliently the reactive emotions of resentment, indignation, and guilt. So the reasons that are provided by the disregard of moral requirements are reasons for reactive attitudes of these kinds.[15] But reasons for action may also be in play as well. For one thing, as I noted earlier in this section, there are non-emotional reactions that may legitimately be regarded as forms of blame in at least an extended sense, including the expression of moral disapproval, as well as such actions as avoidance and withdrawal from trust-based interactions with the wrongdoer. For another thing, there are secondary reasons for action associated with the general stance that I have called interpersonal accountability. This stance is, in the first instance, a complex of attitudes through which we can be said to hold other people to expectations, including dispositions to reactive and other forms of blame upon the flouting of those expectations, and acknowledgment of the legitimate reasons for those attitudes that such deliberate immorality provides. But someone who has these attitudes can reflect on them, and take further measures in regard to them as a result of such reflection.

Our susceptibility to reactive emotions is a refinement of basic psychological mechanisms that function socially to encourage compliance with social norms. We are, as Rousseau was acutely aware, deeply social creatures, and it matters to us profoundly how we are thought of by our fellows, in particular whether people hold attitudes of angry disapproval toward us on account of what we do. We care about such attitudes not merely because it is disagreeable to experience them, but because we do not wish to inhabit a social world in which such attitudes are harbored toward us, regardless of whether they are expressed to or experienced by us. But our reflective awareness of our participation in this economy of esteem and disesteem constitutes a point of entry for larger practical questions about how we wish to comport ourselves in relation to it, going forward.

If we are moved by the global skepticism about moral responsibility mentioned earlier in this section, for instance, then we might conclude that it is not reasonable on balance to continue to subject individuals to the psychological sanctions that have historically helped to ensure compliance with basic social norms of conduct. (We might be led to this conclusion by the thought that it is unfair to subject people to such sanctions under conditions of general determinism.[16]) If, on the other hand, we are not moved by such skeptical worries, then we may be happy to accede to our participation in the economy of esteem and disesteem through which social norms are traditionally enforced. This would be to acknowledge and act on reasons for affirming the legitimacy of our own tendency to hold others morally to account, and for cultivating a similar disposition in our children, as a way of bringing them to appreciate the importance of social norms and to care about whether they are adhered to.[17]

To sum up, moral rightness appears to be a source of accountability-related reasons of various kinds, including reasons to expect people to comply with the demands that define what it is right and wrong to do; reasons to respond to the disregard of such expectations with reactive and other forms of blame; and reasons to participate knowingly in the economy of social esteem and disesteem that helps to enforce compliance with requirements of the moral right. As I noted, it seems to be part of our modern understanding of interpersonal morality that it has these kinds of normative significance for our accountability practices, just as it provides individuals with obligations that regulate their deliberations in the way of presumptive constraints on agency.

Note, however, that this conceptual point about interpersonal morality should not be taken to entail that moral standards are in fact reasons for such accountability practices. There is room for a focused skepticism about this aspect of morality that is analogous to the skepticism about moral obligations discussed earlier in this section. This view would hold that the willful or negligent violation of moral standards is not after all something that we have even pro tanto reason to respond to with reactive or other forms of blame. That is, even if we abstract from more global concerns about the concept of responsible agency or about the prospects for its realization in the natural world, we might conclude that attitudes of disregard for moral standards do not in fact provide others with good reasons for angry disapprobation. If I am right, then this debunking position, just like the corresponding skepticism about moral obligations discussed above, would involve some element of revisionism about morality. It would maintain, for instance, that our modern concept of moral rightness or permissibility is not fully realized in the world as we find it, precisely insofar as the standards that determine rightness and permissibility do not appropriately regulate our accountability relations with each other. Our feeling that this outcome would involve a degree of revisionism, however, is a reflection of the basic idea that a normative connection to responsibility relations is built into the modern idea of moral rightness and permissibility.

3.2. Individualistic and Relational Conceptions of the Moral Right

Some moral theories are individualistic; they conceive moral standards primarily as helping to define an ideal of individual achievement, or as articulating the obligations of agents who are not understood to stand in normative relations with other parties.

Consider, for instance, the perfectionist theory of Philippa Foot, discussed in chapter 2, which conceives moral (or better, ethical) standards as means to the realization of an ideal of natural goodness, and as deriving their significance primarily from this function.[18] Such an approach is individualistic, insofar as its locus is the individual agent's relation to an ideal of personal attainment. Whether a given person acts rightly is entirely a question of whether the action reflects traits that human beings need in order to flourish under conditions that are natural to them; it does not in general depend on the claims or entitlements of other parties. But many other modern theories seem to be individualistic in the same sense. Utilitarianism, for instance, conceives of moral standards in maximizing terms, telling individuals that it is wrong to act in ways that are suboptimal in their effects on the interests of sentient beings. Utilitarian rightness depends in part on how other individuals react causally to the things that an agent might do, but it does not depend on any normative relations that the agent stands in to those individuals.

Individualistic approaches of this kind appear to leave it mysterious why attitudes of disregard for the standards of the moral right should provide others with a normative basis for relations of interpersonal accountability. For example, utilitarians often hold that lifestyles of bourgeois consumption are morally objectionable in a world in which there are vast numbers of people living in conditions of extreme need. So long as these conditions persist, individual expenditures on consumer goods will be hard to justify in utilitarian terms, insofar as greater utility would be achieved by donating the funds at issue to an organization such as Doctors without Borders or GiveDirectly. But it is another matter entirely whether we should blame individuals when they display attitudes of disregard toward this moral consideration.

On the utilitarian approach, blame should be treated like any other intervention into the causal order, and assessed by reference to its likely effects on the welfare of those affected by it. Thus, it is sometimes argued that it would be wrong to blame affluent individuals when they fail to organize their personal lives according to the principles of utilitarian consumption. Doing so might just discourage and demoralize them, making it clear how onerous morality would be if they actually took it seriously as a basis for ordering their lives, with the effect that those who are blamed would do even less to contribute to improving the conditions of the many millions of people whose lives are characterized by deprivation and disease.[19] For these same reasons, it might conceivably be for the best not to encourage children to internalize the kind of emotional commitment to utilitarian standards that would render them disposed to react to deliberate moral infractions with such sentiments as resentment and indignation.[20] The question of the attitudes of an individual toward moral standards seems to be completely independent from the question of whether those same attitudes provide others with a normative basis for interpersonal accountability relations.[21]

Against this, it might be said that it is open to utilitarians to distinguish more carefully between the attitudinal and the behavioral dimensions of blame. Actions that serve to sanction people for their moral lapses are certainly, on the utilitarian view, to be assessed with an eye to their consequences for human welfare. But the reactive attitudes that register blame emotionally, such as resentment and indignation, might be taken to function differently, answering to considerations that render them intrinsically warranted or fitting. I do not believe that this move will save the utilitarian, however. As I shall argue in more detail in sections 3.3 and 3.4 below, the considerations that we understand to provide reasons for attitudinal blame are not captured by individualistic conceptions of the right such as utilitarianism. Individuals who fall short of the conduct prescribed by the principle of utility, or who do not strive to act in accordance with that principle, may be going astray relative to normative standards that in some sense apply to them. But it is not at all clear why this should be thought to render warranted focused reactive attitudes such as resentment or indignation on the part of other people, any more than it provides a basis for the behavioral expressions of blame.

Individualist approaches such as utilitarianism thus seem to deny the element in the modern concept of morality that I have been at pains to explicate in this chapter. According to that concept, standards of moral right and wrong are such that the agent's attitudes toward them have direct normative significance for the responsibility reactions of others. Moral standards must be ones that it is reasonable to hold people accountable for complying with, in the ways that characteristically involve a susceptibility to blame. There must be something about them that gives an agent's attitudes toward them a special normative significance for our responsibility reactions, protecting from opprobrium those who conscientiously strive to comply with them, and rendering those who are indifferent to them specially vulnerable to reactive and other forms of blame. Utilitarian and perfectionistic theories seem deficient when viewed in this light. They take moral requirements to derive from an individual's relation to impersonal value or to an ideal of human attainment. But there is nothing in the nature of such requirements that would seem to explain why our attitudes toward them necessarily have normative significance for accountability relations. Why should other people become exercised by the fact that you are indifferent to standards of human perfection in the conduct of your affairs, or that you do not fully live up to the rigorous demands made on you by an ideal of impersonal value? An individualistic theory might turn out to be correct at the end of the day. If the argument of the preceding section is sound, however, it will follow that such theories are revisionist in at least some measure, denying an interpersonal dimension of morality that seems to us to be essential to it.[22]

In response, it might be suggested that there are individualistic theories that do not leave it a contingent matter whether we have reason to respond to deliberate wrongdoing with reactive and other forms of blame. Consider a version of perfectionism that holds that it is a virtue, part of the ideal of a flourishing human life, for agents to internalize the kind of concern for moral standards that makes them prone to blaming reactions when people flout those standards. On a theory of this kind, morality itself would enjoin us to respond with something like blame to instances of deliberate wrongdoing, and it would therefore seem that there is a nonaccidental connection between such behavior and the responsibility reactions.

A theory of this kind would not really do justice, however, to the aspect of morality described in section 3.1. There are two aspects to the problem. First, on the perfectionist account, what makes actions wrong, in general terms, is that performing them would be incompatible with virtue. This is an individualistic approach, as I noted above, which holds that the rightness and wrongness of actions are matters of the agent's relation to an ideal of human perfection. But there is nothing in this general way of thinking about morality that explains why an agent's attitudes toward rightness and wrongness should *themselves* provide a normative basis for the responsibility reactions. It is only when we supplement the general account with a specific, substantive theory of virtue that we introduce a reason for people to adopt blaming responses toward episodes of deliberate wrongdoing.

Second, the reason that is introduced by the substantive theory of virtue seems to be a reason of the wrong kind. I should react to deliberate wrongdoing on the part of others, according to the perfectionist theory, because a failure to do so would instantiate a vice on my part. My reason for blaming, in other words, is provided by considerations having to do with my own relation to an ideal of human attainment.[23] According to the view I have been developing, by contrast, what provides me with a reason for the responsibility reactions is, in the first instance, the attitudes of the person whom I would blame. It is because that person has acted with indifference or contempt toward moral standards that I have reason to hold the person responsible.[24] This is precisely the normative connection between rightness and responsibility that I have been developing, and it points toward an essentially interpersonal dimension of morality. Insofar as the perfectionist theory under consideration remains individualistic, it continues to have a revisionistic character, even if it yields the conclusion that morality gives us a reason of some kind to blame others when they flout moral standards.[25]

Consider next the divine command theory.[26] This approach, like other versions of voluntarism, is not individualistic, insofar as it understands moral rightness by appeal to the normative relations that agents stand in to figures who have authority over them. But its non-individualistic character does not shed light on the aspect of morality that is currently under investigation. According to the divine command theory, there may be things that it would be morally good to do, independently of whether we are commanded by God to do them. But we stand under obligations to act in these ways only in virtue of the fact that God lays down a requirement on us so to act. God is thus the source of the moral obligations that are binding on us, and we owe it to God to act in accordance with those obligations.[27] As we saw in the preceding chapter, an approach along these lines might go some way toward explaining the significance of obligations in the first-personal perspective of deliberation, their standing as genuine requirements that make claims on the agent's will. But it does not offer an illuminating account of the social dimension of moral obligations, where this is taken to involve their suitability to structure an interpersonal practice of mutual accountability.

To stand in relations of accountability to another person, or to address moral demands to the person, is, on the account sketched in section 3.1, to hold the person to the demands in the ways constitutively connected to broadly reactive attitudes. So the question is whether it is reasonable to hold people to demands in this reactive way if those demands derive from the commands of a benevolent and omnipotent deity. I think there is a real question whether it is. The worry, in a nutshell, is that it isn't really anyone's business whether other people live up to the requirements that are owed by them, individually, to God. It is between them and the deity, as we might put it, and hence not something that the rest of us have good reason to get exercised about, in the ways characteristic of interpersonal accountability.

Granted, many of the divine commandments may prescribe behaviors that affect other persons in our local or less local community, insofar as they include demands to act charitably or with justice (for instance). Those who are members of our social world are in this way apt to be affected, in one way or another, by our compliance or lack of compliance with the requirements that God imposes on us. But this is completely incidental to the status of the requirements as genuine obligations. As was noted in the preceding chapter, God could in the very same sense lay down requirements on us that have nothing to do with our relations to other people, such as dietary restrictions on the consumption of flora and fauna of various kinds. The account of moral

rightness on offer thus leaves it mysterious why things that are morally required are for that very reason also things that it is reasonable to address to the
agents whom the requirements regulate, in the way characteristic of a practice
of mutual accountability.

As with the individualist theories considered earlier, it would be possible
to make substantive additions to the divine command theory that could help
shed light on why it is reasonable for people to hold one another to the moral
requirements commanded by God. For instance, we might, once again, appeal
to a specific theory of virtue, one that has it that virtuous agents adopt the
stance of holding each other to moral requirements, as a basis for relations of
accountability. This might be a good disposition for individuals to cultivate
and acquire, for instance, insofar as its presence in a community helps the
members of the community to live up to the demands that God has addressed
to them individually. Or perhaps it is a further divine commandment that each
of us should cultivate a disposition to reactive moral address with regard to
the other requirements that God has imposed on us; we would then owe it to
God, so to speak, to treat those requirements as a basis for a practice of mutual
accountability.

But these would be ancillary stipulations, going beyond the account of
moral rightness itself, which identify reasons for holding people to moral obligations that are potentially of the wrong kind. The stipulations are no more
successful within this framework than in the case of the individualistic theories
canvased above. The core account of moral obligations latent in this version
of voluntarism traces them to the relation that individuals stand in to the deity,
insofar as they are addressees of divine commandments. Nothing in this core
account, however, explains why moral obligations, so understood, should also
function as the basis of a practice of essentially interpersonal accountability.

Let us turn, finally, to a different non-individualist approach, namely the
relational account that is my main topic in this book. According to the relational approach, moral rightness essentially defines a set of requirements that
are owed to other individuals in particular, where those individuals have claims
against the agent to compliance with the requirements that are directed to
them. I now wish to argue that an account of this kind is peculiarly well suited
to make sense of the social aspect of moral requirements, their status as considerations that appropriately structure relations of mutual accountability.

Thus, suppose that you owe it to me morally to keep the promise you made
to me, or to refrain from bodily trespass as you encounter me in the street.
According to the relational account, these requirements essentially concern

our relations to each other, and they are connected constitutively to claims that I have against you to compliance with them. Insofar as I have a claim against you to compliance, however, it would seem perfectly reasonable for me to hold you to the requirements in the way that we have seen to be characteristic of interpersonal accountability. Indeed, moral requirements of this kind seem tailor-made, in virtue of their relational structure, to be requirements that function as a basis for a practice of accountability to other parties.

Note, for one thing, that it is a noncontingent feature of relational requirements of this kind that they have significance for another party. They are owed to other individuals, to whom the agent is, as Gary Watson has put it, "beholden."[28] But if a requirement that you are under is in this way directed to me, then it is necessarily not a matter of indifference to me whether you make a conscientious effort to comply with it. Rather it is my business, in virtue of the relational structure that makes the requirement obligatory in the first place. As a claimholder, it is thus fully reasonable that I should take an interest in whether the requirements that are owed to me are lived up to and taken seriously by those who stand under them. And holding someone to the requirement, in the spirit of interpersonal accountability, is the natural way of doing this.

Consider, next, what happens if a directed moral requirement is flouted. The agent who failed to take it seriously will have shown a certain disregard for the values at the heart of morality. But moral obligations, on the relational account of them, are essentially connected to individual claims; so disregard for such requirements is eo ipso disregard for the person to whom the requirements are owed. There are, more specifically, two distinct forms that such disregard for persons could take. First, agents who flout a directed requirement could acknowledge the persons to whom it is owed as the bearers of claims, but fail to take the claims seriously in their deliberations about what to do. Second, the immoral agents could treat the persons to whom the requirement is owed as if they didn't hold claims to performance in the first place. In the first case, the agents are disregarding the other parties by neglecting to honor the claims the parties hold against them; in the second case, disregard of the other parties takes the more basic form of failing to take seriously their standing as bearers of claims.

But showing disregard for other parties, in either of these ways, is precisely the kind of stance that would seem to provide a reason for the characteristic reactions of blame. In failing to take the moral requirement seriously, you have not merely fallen short of some personal code of conduct that pertains to you alone (or to your relation to the divinity). You have displayed indifference to or contempt for another person, as someone whose interests undergird claims the latter holds against you, and this is the primary normative basis of the reactive attitudes. Thus resentment, which we may take to be a paradigm of reactive blame, is constitutively a response to the fact not just that something bad has happened in a person's immediate environs, but that—to recall an expression introduced in chapter 1—the subject of the attitude has suffered a specifically moral injury through the actions of another party. It in this way presupposes a relational understanding of the requirements of the moral right that give it content.

The point here is a deceptively simple one, but it is of great significance for understanding the connection between moral rightness and interpersonal accountability. It is something of a commonplace in the literature on responsibility to characterize blame, at least in its paradigmatic forms, as a response not merely to actions that are morally wrong, but to actions that wrong another party. Thus, Miranda Fricker writes of what she calls "communicative blame" that it is "a cognitively loaded moral emotion," whose content involves "a perception of a wrong one suffers at the hands of another."[29] Similarly, Gary Watson writes of moral norms that "those who violate these norms wrong others, which explains the distinctive significance for interpersonal relations these standards possess."[30] Another example is provided by Pamela Hieronymi, who observes that "your resentment of my impatience marks the fact that you have been wronged by someone, the quality of whose will matters."[31]

These remarks are offered by the quoted philosophers without much explicit defense; they are apparently regarded as sufficiently plausible that it can be taken for granted that the reader will assent to them as soon as they are formulated. But it is worth dwelling at least briefly on these ways of speaking, for they point toward two connected truths about responsibility and blame that are of profound importance for the argument of this chapter. First, the characteristic occasion for blame is the fact that one party has acted in a way that wrongs another; this is the circumstance that we intuitively understand to provide people with reasons for reactive and other forms of blame. Second, those reactions themselves incorporate an appreciation of the fact that their target has done something to wrong another party. Reactive blame is cognitively structured, and its content is naturally cashed out in terms of essentially relational norms; as Fricker puts it, resentment incorporates "a perception of a wrong one suffers at the hands of another." It is not merely the fact that agents have acted wrongly, but that they have wronged somebody, that is both the reason for blame and its cognitive focus.[32]

Note, however, that both of these points presuppose something that was emphasized in section 1.1 above. This is that the relational conception of a wrong or a moral injury is an attitude-dependent one. The kind of wrong or injury that constitutes an occasion for blame, and that figures in the content of accountability-ascribing attitudes, is not an objective violation of a moral obligation, but involves an attitude of disregard for the obligation on the agent's part. To return to the example from section 3.1 above, I do not wrong you if I fail to show up to the Pilates class on account of a malicious attack on the server that maintains my calendar or a breakdown on the train I am taking to get to the class. In cases such as these, I might be said to have violated the duty I owed to you, but I didn't flout the duty, and it is only in cases that involve something like flouting or neglecting a duty that I can be said to have wronged you, or caused you a moral injury. But in fact, this is precisely the kind of connection between obligation and reasons for blame that we were trying to make sense of. We wished to understand how an attitude of disregard for moral requirements could itself constitute a pro tanto reason for reactive and other forms of blame. The answer is that it does this if the requirements themselves are connected to claims held against the agent by another party, as they essentially are on the relational account.

A similar line of thought is implicit, I think, in Strawson's highly influential account of our interpersonal accountability practices. As noted in the preceding section, Strawson favors an approach to these practices that emphasizes the reactive attitudes, a paradigm of which is resentment. He notes, further, that the occasion for resentment is an "offense" or "injury" to one party by another,[33] and that offenses or injuries in the relevant sense are in turn connected to the "quality of the will" of the offending party. Thus the reactive attitudes "are essentially natural human reactions to the good will or ill will or indifference of others towards us, as displayed in *their* attitudes and actions."[34] Finally, Strawson emphasizes the connection between these reactions to ill will and the notion of a demand, observing that such sentiments as resentment reflect demands or expectations to which we hold people in our ongoing interactions with them.[35] Let us call these three elements in his position injury, quality of will, and demand.

Strawson does not himself advocate explicitly for a relational interpretation of the demands or expectations characteristic of the participant standpoint.

But it seems to me that a relational account of this kind represents the natural tendency of his position; it is the interpretation that makes best sense of the connections he posits between the elements of injury, quality of will, and demand. Thus, Strawson assumes that the demands to which we hold each other in practice are such that disregard of them will itself involve an attitude of disregard for or indifference toward another person, constituting thereby an offense or injury against that person. As we have seen, however, the relational interpretation of demands is best equipped to make sense of these connections. On that interpretation, moral demands are constitutively connected to claims that other individuals have against the agent to compliance with them. So disregard for relational demands will essentially involve disregard for those individuals (in the form, specifically, either of disregard for their claims, or of disregard for their standing as bearers of claims). This in turn is the sort of "quality of will" that we intuitively understand to constitute a kind of offense or moral injury against claimholders, providing them with a normative basis for resentment.[36]

The ideas that I have been developing in this section, concerning the normative significance for other parties of the violation of relational moral requirements, are connected to the positive value that is enabled through compliance with such requirements. In section 2.4 above, I referred in this connection to the value of interpersonal recognition, which is realized when we conduct ourselves on terms that fully acknowledge and do justice to the claims that other parties hold against us, simply as persons. When we satisfy this condition, we will be in a position to give an account of ourselves to each of the individuals who may have been affected by our conduct, one that shows us to have honored the obligations that are owed to them in particular. Interpersonal recognition, construed in this way, is the converse of the situation we find ourselves in when we flout or neglect the requirements of relational morality. Disregarding such requirements, I have suggested, amounts to disregarding the claims that someone else holds against us, which in turn is a form of disregard for them as a person. By the same token, however, conscientious regard for the directed obligations that are owed to others is a way of acknowledging their claims against one, and so displaying recognition for their standing as morally significant persons.

I have argued, further, that disregarding the claims of others renders one vulnerable to the negative reactions characteristic of blame, providing others with a normative basis for these reactions. If this is right, however, then instantiating the positive value of interpersonal recognition in one's relations to others should ensure a measure of protection from these unwelcome reactions. Of course, other parties might subject us to opprobrium and blame even when we have not done anything that would genuinely warrant these responses. People are sometimes irrational, petty, and vindictive, and nothing we might do can guarantee that we will never be the target of negative attitudes that are untethered from any normative basis in the facts about our relations to them. But there is a melancholic satisfaction to be taken, even here, in the knowledge that these reactions are not in fact fitting responses to our behavior.

Interpersonal recognition is achieved when we act in a way that deprives others of a warrant to resent our treatment of them. In acknowledging the significance of their claims against us, as constraints on our decision-making, we also acknowledge their moral standing as individuals whose interests matter equally. Doing this does not ensure that we will live in harmony with the actual individuals who share our social world, but it represents a valuable contribution to the normative basis of such a community.[37]

3.3. The Relational Structure of Interpersonal Accountability

Proponents of utilitarianism (or other consequentialist views) may be tempted to respond to the argument of the preceding section that their theory, too, can make sense of the role of moral requirements as bases for a practice of interpersonal accountability. The crux, as we have seen, is to explain why disregard for moral requirements should itself provide other parties with reasons for reactive and other forms of blame. The utilitarian understands the standards of the moral right to require that we maximize the impartial good, taking equally into account the interests of all those potentially affected by our actions. But then it might seem that to disregard moral requirements, so understood, is to fail to regard the interests of some person or persons as worthy of equal consideration. And this failure of regard, it might be argued, is something that could provide a normative basis for the blaming reactions that are characteristic of interpersonal accountability.

The inference involved in this argument, however, seems questionable. One potential problem is that it appears possible to disregard standards of consequentialist rightness without formally denying the equal standing of those affected by our actions. Climate change skeptics, for instance, might insist that there is no moral requirement for members of affluent societies to reduce the carbon emissions associated with their activities, not because they deny that peoples' interests ultimately count equally, but because they deny the consensus of scientists about human contributions to whatever changes in global temperature might be occurring. Consequentialist rightness requires individuals to maximize the impartial good, and this involves both a willingness to treat peoples' interests equally, and a willingness to reason soundly about the causal effects of the various actions that it is open to one to perform.

Against this, it might be replied that one does not really count as having disregarded the consequentialist standards if one's failure to meet their terms results from nonculpable forms of mistaken causal reasoning. In the preceding section, I suggested that disregard for relational moral requirements involves a failure to make a conscientious effort to comply with them, or a failure to take them seriously in one's deliberations. But there need be no failure of these kinds, in relation to consequentialist standards, if agents who fall short of them do so through innocent mistakes in reasoning about the effects of the actions that it is open to them to perform.[38]

There is a different and more serious difficulty for the consequentialist account of the social dimension of morality, which was mentioned briefly in section 3.2 above. Consequentialists will ultimately condone actions through which accountability is interpersonally expressed only if those actions contribute to the overall maximization of the good. As we saw, however, there are many cases in which it seems dubious that it would be for the best to subject individuals to blame when they fall short of the standards of the consequentialist right. Consider the many people who continue to spend discretionary resources on indulgences for themselves and their friends and family members, rather than contributing those resources to alleviating the plight of strangers who are much worse off than they are. Such agents might be failing to count the interests of all people equally, in the way consequentialist rightness would require. But it would arguably be suboptimal to blame them under these circumstances, since that would lead them to dismiss moral requirements altogether rather than to do what they can to comply with them.

In response, the consequentialist might maintain that disregard of the relevant standards of right conduct is at least a pro tanto reason for reactive and other forms of blame, even if it might not be warranted on balance to subject agents to those reactions whenever they flout consequentialist requirements. The pro tanto reason for blame, it might be said, just is the failure of equal consideration that is implicit when agents disregard, in the relevant sense, consequentialist standards of rightness. But even this residual connection between consequentialist rightness and accountability seems to me questionable. As I noted in section 2.2 above, consequentialism offers a particular interpretation of the cosmopolitan ideal latent in modern approaches to morality, according to which we operate as agents in a world that includes others who are equally real, and whose interests matter equally for moral thought. The consequentialist interpretation of rightness tells us to attach equal weight to the interests of each person in maximizing the good, and it is an appealing feature of that interpretation that it gives expression to the more fundamental ideal of the equal standing of persons within moral reflection.

Note, however, that it is no part of the consequentialist conception that individuals have *claims* against us, as agents, that we should in this way attach equal weight to their interests. Consequentialism is an individualistic account of rightness, in the terms of the preceding section, which articulates requirements of right conduct in abstraction from assumptions about the normative relations that the agent stands in to other parties. Within this individualist context, however, it is not at all clear that a failure to attach equal weight to someone's interests is an attitude that provides that person with even a pro tanto reason for reactive and other forms of blame. Such a failure may represent a criticizable defect on the agent's part, relative to an applicable norm of individual attainment, one that involves a flaw in reasoning about the interests of another person. But it is not something that could be said to *wrong* the person whose interests are at issue, or otherwise to constitute something like a moral injury to that person.

Insofar as we intuitively think of a failure to attach equal significance to someone's interests as a basis for blame, I submit that we are taking for granted the relational framework that was shown above to be implicit in our ordinary understanding of the circumstances that warrant blame. That is, not only are we assuming that individuals are required to attach equal importance to the interests of others, by attempting to maximize the impartial good in their actions (something that is controversial in itself, as an interpretation of the more basic ideal of the equal moral standing of persons). We are assuming, more specifically, that they owe it to each other to deliberate about action in this way. This is the framework of normative relations that would make the disregard of consequentialist standards something that provides a pro tanto normative basis for accountability reactions. But this relational framework is foreign to the consequentialist approach to moral rightness.

These remarks reinforce the point made in the preceding section, which is that we commonly (if implicitly) understand the circumstances that occasion reactive blame in relational terms, as actions that wrong another party. I now want to argue that there are additional features of our practices of interpersonal accountability that are essentially positional, and that their positional aspect equally presupposes a relational account of the requirements that underlie those practices. These features are apology, forgiveness, and repair; let us take them up in turn.

It is part of our common moral understanding that wrongdoing calls for a distinctive kind of response on the part of the agent who flouts moral requirements. Specifically, it calls for acknowledgment of wrongdoing and apology. In saying that these responses are called for, I am saying, in part, that there will be a compelling basis for others to blame the agent at least as long as these responses are not forthcoming. Just as wrongdoing provides a normative basis for reactive and other forms of blame, so too do these reactions give agents a reason to acknowledge their wrongdoing and to apologize for their trespass against moral requirements. Indeed, it is not a stretch to suppose that responses of this kind are morally obligatory on the part of agents who have acted impermissibly. To think this is the case is to suppose that there is a secondary obligation that applies when people have flouted a primary moral obligation, the content of which is that the agents who have acted wrongly should acknowledge their moral failing and apologize for what they have done.[39]

It is a striking fact about our accountability practices, however, that our understanding of these secondary obligations is itself relational. A natural way to express the secondary obligations would be to say that wrongdoers owe an apology to those they have wronged through their actions. That is, there is another party who is uniquely positioned to be the recipient of the agent's acknowledgment of wrongdoing and apology, and the duty to respond in these ways is directed to that party in particular. Thus, suppose that Nora and Sebastian are playing with Legos, and that in a fit of envy and frustration Nora smashes the elaborate castle that Sebastian has been working on for the past half hour. Nora might confess what she has done to the supervising parental authority, and say that she is sorry for her action. But it would be perfectly natural for the parent to respond by telling Nora that she needs to apologize to *Sebastian* for destroying the structure he was working on (and to add, perhaps, that she needs to do this *nicely*). That is, we induct people into our accountability practices by encouraging them to appreciate that these agential responses to wrongdoing are owed to another party in particular. They cannot be discharged by directing an apology to just anyone.

Furthermore, it is equally implicit in those practices that the party to whom acknowledgment and apology are in this way owed is the person who was originally wronged by the impermissible actions that now call for apology. Nora owes Sebastian an apology for her willful action, because it was Sebastian who was wronged by that action in the first place. He had a claim against her not to treat him in that way, which was flouted by what she did. Apology and acknowledgment are thus doubly relational. Not only do we understand the secondary obligations of apology to be directed to another party; our understanding of their direction presupposes that the primary obligations whose violation gives rise to them are themselves directed to the same party. There is a positional aspect to our practices of apology and acknowledgment that makes sense only against the background of a deeply relational interpretation of basic moral requirements.

Consider next forgiveness. This is a stance that is normally adopted after the point in time at which the agent of wrongdoing has apologized and acknowledged moral fault. It is a complicated business, involving on the one hand the tacit recognition that the agent acted in a way that makes reactive blame fitting, but forswearing, on the other hand, the reaction that would in this way be warranted. There are difficult questions raised by forgiveness about how these different aspects of it can be combined, and also about the conditions that paradigmatically occasion it and the purposes that it serves.[40] I would like to set these interesting questions to side for the moment, however, in order to focus on a more elementary point about forgiveness. This is that we commonly understand it to be, like apology, a profoundly positional phenomenon.

Forgiveness may be understood to involve the exercise of a kind of normative authority. In bestowing forgiveness, we step back reflectively from the reactive blame that we understand to be rendered fitting by what an agent has done to us, and disavow that reaction, going forward, as a significant factor in our continuing relations with the agent. To forgive is not necessarily to overcome all resentment in one's feelings about the wrongdoer, but to adopt a distinctive stance toward such attitudes, forswearing them as attitudes that should be accorded importance in one's ongoing relations to the agent of wrongful action. The individual who bestows forgiveness is someone who is authorized to adopt this kind of reflective stance, and who has a measure of discretion about when and in what ways to make use of this authority. Thus, even after the wrongdoer has acknowledged moral fault and issued a remorseful apology, it is not the case that forgiveness can be demanded as a matter of right or entitlement. Apology and acknowledgment of fault do not, after all, undo the fact of moral injury, which continues to represent a consideration that would render reactive blame fitting or warranted. Those who are authorized to bestow forgiveness thus have some leeway to decide for themselves whether and under what circumstances it will be forthcoming.

Note, however, that the authority that is thus presupposed by forgiveness is the proprietary possession of only some individuals, who stand in a distinctive relation to the wrongdoing that might be forgiven. Thus, it is not the case that just anyone is empowered to forgive a wrongdoer's moral transgressions. Just as apologies are owed specifically to those who have been wronged by what the agent did, so too are those individuals alone authorized to bestow forgiveness on the wrongdoer.[41] Once again, we see that there is a positional aspect to our practices of interpersonal accountability, which presupposes that the norms that structure those practices are relational in their content. Third parties lack the authority to bestow forgiveness for actions that flout moral requirements, precisely insofar as they have not themselves been wronged by those actions. The authority to forgive is a retrospective residue of the claim that was disregarded through the wrongdoer's action. It is only those to whom compliance with moral requirements was originally owed who are empowered to forgive wrongdoers for their transgressions.

Indeed, it seems to me that forgiveness would not really make sense, as a distinctive practice, in the context of an individualistic interpretation of moral obligations. One might attempt to emulate that practice within an individualistic framework by stipulating (say) that those individuals should be viewed as authorized to bestow forgiveness who have been harmed, in a nonmoral sense, through actions that flout nonrelational standards of conduct. The positional element in forgiveness would be operationalized, according to this interpretation, through the causal relation between an action that is individualistically defective and harm caused by that action to another party (or parties). But the resulting account seems implausible.

I have suggested that the power to forgive is a form of normative authority or entitlement, which the individuals who are so empowered have discretion to exercise or not, as they see fit. But it is mysterious why standing in a merely causal relation of harm to an act that is personally deficient should ground a normative status of this kind. The point is not the metaethical one that normative statuses cannot be based or grounded in nonnormative facts, for at the end of the day, even a robustly realist conception of the normative should allow that there are systematic relations between the normative and the nonnormative.[42] The point, rather, is that the individualistic account does not identify a convincing basis of any kind for the normative status involved in forgiveness. The causal connection between individually deficient conduct and harm to another party isolates a contingent effect of wrongdoing, rather than something that is essential to it. But our conception of people as having authority to forgive is not hostage to whether they happen to have been harmed on balance by the wrongful conduct of another party. Rather, it is of a piece with our sense that they have suffered a distinctively moral injury through such conduct, where this in turn presupposes that they have a claim against the party not to have acted in that way. As I put it above, the authority to forgive is a residue of the claim that was originally flouted through the wrongful action that is a candidate for forgiveness.[43] Severed from the context of this kind of normative relation between the agent of wrongful action and the person whom it wrongs, it seems that the essentially positional notion of the authority to forgive would be out of place.

Consider, finally, the phenomenon of moral repair. It is customary to think that the person who transgresses against moral requirements is under a duty not only to acknowledge wrongdoing and to offer an apology, but also to do what is possible to make amends. Like apology and forgiveness, this element in our accountability practices is deeply positional. The obligation that the wrongdoer is under to make amends is owed to one individual (or set of individuals) in particular; this is, as in the case of apology, the individual who was wronged by the agent's action in the first place. We thus encounter, once again, a structure that is doubly relational, with a directed secondary obligation that is parasitic on our understanding that the action that gave rise to it involved the flouting of a primary obligation that was likewise relational.

Here, more plausibly perhaps than in the cases of apology and forgiveness, we can offer a nonrelational reconstruction of our practice that at least makes partial sense of it. In this spirit, it might be suggested that the duty to make amends can be explained as an equitable way of allocating the costs incurred through an individual act of wrongdoing. Insofar as such acts cause adverse effects for other persons, there is a need to make up for them, so far as it is possible to do so, and the costs of satisfying this need seem most fairly assigned to the individuals whose actions gave rise to it in the first place.

But this quasi-economic way of thinking about repair neglects an important dimension of our accountability practices. Those who flout relational moral requirements show disregard for the individuals to whom they are owed; they thereby impair the relationships they stand in to the persons whom they wrong, and this is a reasonable basis for the secondary obligation to make amends that is also directed to those individuals. The quasi-economic inter- pretation of repair, by contrast, does not really make compelling sense of the directed character of the duty that it defines. It may be equitable for the social cost of redress to be assigned to the agents whose voluntary violation of indi- vidualistic requirements caused the damage that now requires compensation. But it does not follow from this observation that the duty to provide redress should be owed by the agents to the parties who were harmed. To render intel- ligible this aspect of the practice of repair, we need to embed it within an es- sentially relational framework, tracing the original wrongs that give rise to the duty of repair to the disregard of the claims held by other individuals against the agents who acted wrongly. It is because those agents have impaired their relationships to the claimholders, through actions that wrong those persons in particular, that the secondary obligation of repair is owed to the same par- ties. Once again, the secondary duties can be understood as retrospective resi- dues of the claims that were originally flouted.

This way of speaking is reminiscent of a formulation that Arthur Ripstein has used to characterize the duty of remedy in the private law of torts. That duty, Ripstein says, needs to be understood to reflect the fundamental idea that the right or entitlement flouted through the tortious action "survives its own violation."[44] The duty of redress on the part of the tortfeasor should be conceptualized in relation to this persisting entitlement, as a duty owed to the plaintiff to enforce the entitlement that lives on after the original tor- tious action. But this characterization of the normative situation, while sug- gestive, seems to me ultimately somewhat misleading, both in application to the private law of torts and in extended application to the generalized moral case.

On the one hand, there is a perfectly trivial sense in which an entitlement or claim, as a normative notion, survives its own violation. That is, the fact that the claim was not honored does not entail or bring it about that the claim was not after all in place; this shows itself in the fact that we understand the wrong- ful action, retrospectively, precisely to be one that wronged the claimholder. On the other hand, once a claim has in this way been flouted, it is no longer open to us to enforce or uphold it. There is no undoing the past, and if the wrongful action flouted a claim that was held against the agent, then the ques- tion of enforcing that very claim is now moot. The object of remedy can only be to make it, so far as it is in our power to do so, "as if" the violation had not occurred, typically by compensating the wronged party for losses or harm suffered as a result.

My suggestion is that the secondary obligation to bring this state of affairs about should be understood as a residue of the original claim that was flouted. It is a residue of that claim in the specific sense that the relational structure of the secondary obligation derives from the relational structure of the primary wrong that gives rise to it, in particular from the fact that the primary wrong flouted a claim of the party to whom remedy is now owed.[45] What's done is done, and it is no longer open to anyone to honor or enforce the specific claim that was violated through the original wrongful action. But because that claim was flouted, the wrongdoer now owes it to the bearer of the claim to acknowledge wrongdoing, apologize, and (so far as possible) make amends.

A final point to emphasize about our accountability practices is that they have a constructive function that comes into clear focus when we appreciate the relational content of the moral norms that structure them. When reactive blame is considered in isolation, it can easily appear to be a punitive response that we would perhaps be better off without. But it is in fact one element within an ordered temporal sequence that gains significance from the relational norms that link it to other elements in the sequence. The immediate context of blame is the normative nexus between agents and the parties who have moral claims against them. The action that occasions blame is one that involves disregard for such claims, which to that extent reflects a deficient way of relating to the claimholder (a failure of what I have called interpersonal recognition).[46] In particular, it involves a failure to acknowledge the significance of the other parties' claims against one in one's deliberations about what to do, which may reflect a deeper failure to acknowledge the other parties as individuals with moral standing in the first place. Treating people in this way ruptures one's interpersonal relations with them, and this aspect of wrongdoing structures and renders intelligible the further reactions that it sets in motion. Reactive blame is rendered fitting by a failure of interpersonal recognition of this kind, and it in turn calls out for distinctive responses on the part of the wrongdoer, generating directed obligations of acknowledgment, apology, and repair that potentially culminate in the bestowal of forgiveness.

Seen in this light, blame appears to be a focused response to a rupture that has affected one's relationship to another party. It is occasioned by a failure on the agent's part to relate to the claimholder on a basis of interpersonal recognition. And it is embedded within a network of secondary obligations and entitlements that serve to repair the rupture and to reorient the parties toward the norms that properly govern their interactions with each other.[47] The result, if all goes well, is to restore the value of interpersonal recognition that was damaged through the original act of wrongdoing.

3.4. The Relational Content of Blame

In the final section of this chapter, I would like to discuss the content of the reactions through which we characteristically hold people accountable for their actions. I have already noted that we customarily understand blame to incorporate an understanding of the relational requirements that structure our practices of interpersonal accountability. The aim of the present section will be to develop this point in greater detail, and to reflect on its implications for the relational account of morality.

It will be helpful to begin by contrasting the relational interpretation with a different approach that attributes to moral requirements a significantly social dimension. This is what I earlier called the social command theory, a version of voluntarism that explains moral obligations by appeal to the commands that are actually laid on agents by the members of the societies in which they live.[48] As we saw in chapter 2, voluntarist views in general connect obligations to the relationship that obtains between the agent and another party. But the relationship that matters is not that between a claimholder and a person against whom claims are held, but the relationship that is created when an authority addresses directives to a subject.

Like all versions of voluntarism, the social command theory grounds moral obligations in an antecedent interaction between different parties; in this case, it is the interaction through which commands are addressed by the members of a single society to each other. I argued in section 2.2 above that this kind of approach will be too crude to leave us with a plausible account of error with respect to moral obligation. From the fact that the members of a given community fail to exert pressure on each other to comply with a candidate requirement, it does not follow that the requirement does not represent a genuine moral obligation. Even if we abstract from this difficulty, however, I now want to argue that the social command theory distorts rather than illuminates the normative features of the obligations that are at issue.

Thus, if obligations are created by the commands of another party, their normative significance for the agent who is subject to them should derive from the relationship the subject stands in to the authority who issues the command. But this seems false to our intuitive understanding of the reasons at the heart of morality. As an agent, my obligations to fulfill my promises and to respect the bodily integrity of other persons seem to derive from the interests of those who stand to be affected in one way or another by the things that I might do—from the promisee's interest in assurance, for example, or the interest of a potential victim in freedom from pain. This is connected to the point that honoring moral obligations involves a form of interpersonal recognition, through which one acknowledges the standing of other individuals as sources of claims. But the social command theory shifts the agent's focus in a different direction, toward the authority who issues the command in the first place. This seems to give agents the wrong kind of reason for complying with the requirements of morality.

If social commands take the form of exertions of social pressure (through blame and other expressions of opprobrium), agents will naturally think that their ultimate reason for complying with obligations is that doing so is necessary to avoid these sanctions.[49] True, voluntarists typically claim that commands generate obligations only when there is independent reason for agents to do the things that are commanded.[50] So the social command theory needn't deny that there are reasons for acting in conformity with moral obligations that are more directly connected to the interests of those who might be affected by the agent's behavior. Still, their status as obligations derives from the fact that directives have been addressed to the agent, through (for instance) the generation of social pressure by other members of the moral community. It follows that their distinctive normative significance, as obligations, is a function of the subject's relation to those who exert social pressure, which distorts rather than illuminates their reason-giving force. Voluntarists in this way substitute for the relation between agents and those who have claims against them the relation between agents and those who address commands to them.[51]

Social command theories also offer a distorted account of the reasons to which authorities are responding when they address demands to the agents who are thereby subject to them. Insofar as it is the actual addressing of the demand that creates the obligation in the first place, we cannot say that the authority's reason for addressing the demand is that it captures something the agent is morally obligated to do. Considerations of this kind are, as we saw in chapter 2, transparent to the reflections of the authorities whose commands give rise to obligations, on the general voluntarist approach. But the fact that the agent is under a moral obligation is, as it seems to me, the most natural reason for holding agents to a social demand that they should act in accordance with it. Nor is this problem avoided by those variants of the social command theory that appeal not to the actual demands people address to each other, but to the demands that it would be appropriate for them to address to each other.[52] The right kind of reason for addressing a demand of the relevant kind to someone, through the application of social pressure, is that the addressee is under a moral obligation to comply with it. But this consideration isn't yet available at this point in the voluntarist story, insofar as obligations are created by the existence of other kinds of reasons for addressing demands toward the agents whose actions they regulate.[53]

These problems are entirely avoided by the relational account of morality that I have been developing. Its notion of obligation is that of a complex of directed duties and claims, and these are considerations that are available to enter into the deliberations of both agents and the persons who have claims against them. As I noted in section 2.4, the existence of a nexus of this kind is naturally taken to have normative significance for both of the parties who are implicated in it. It enters into the reflections of the agent as a presumptive constraint on behavior, one that is connected in the right way to the interests of the people potentially affected by that behavior. A relational obligation is essentially one that is directed to another individual, who has a claim against the agent to performance. So in understanding themselves to be under moral obligations, on this way of conceptualizing them, agents are thinking of the implications of their actions for the interests of other individuals, and acknowledging the standing of other individuals as sources of claims against them. By contrast with the voluntarist approach, this traces the normative significance of moral obligations to the right source, and connects compliance with such obligations to an attractive positive ideal of interpersonal recognition.

The relational interpretation also gives the notion of moral obligation work to do in the perspective of the members of a society who hold each other morally to account. In adopting this stance toward each other, people are exerting a kind of social pressure that helps to constitute them as members of a common moral community. Our reasons for participating in this interpersonal practice, however, derive from the independent fact that there are complexes of directed obligations and claims in place that antecedently connect us to others in a normative nexus. We understand that there are things that others owe it to us to do, and this makes it reasonable for us to take a special interest in whether they live up to the relational standards that specify these obligations, holding them accountable with respect to the obligations. Similarly, disregard for these relational standards provides a normative basis for reactive and other forms of blame, insofar as it amounts to disregard for claims we have against agents to compliance with those standards. It is because there are things that people owe it to us to do that we hold them to account when they fail to live up to their obligations and claims. The reasons to which our accountability practices are responsive are therefore reasons of the right kind, stemming from facts about the moral obligations and claims that link people to each other in a normative nexus.

These remarks help to fill in the picture that was drawn very swiftly at the end of chapter 2, of moral obligations as considerations that have normative significance for two different parties. In conclusion, I now want to look more closely at the attitudes on the part of claimholders that are rendered appropriate by the obtaining of directed moral obligations. I have characterized these attitudes so far in terms of interpersonal accountability. They involve a stance of holding agents to moral demands in a way that confers on them responsibility with respect to the demands, and that is connected with distinctive responses of moral blame on occasions when the demands are breached. The general idea, then, is that directed obligations make it fitting for claimholders in particular to adopt this array of characteristically accountability-conferring stances toward the agents who are under moral obligations.

If this is right, however, then we should expect our interpersonal accountability practices to prioritize the relationship between agents who are subject to moral requirements and the claimholders to whom those obligations are owed. Claimholders, after all, are in a privileged position by comparison with the other people who might be affected by the agent's actions. If A flouts a duty that is owed to B, then it is B in particular who is wronged or has suffered a moral injury, and B would seem to have a specific grievance or complaint about what A has done that is not shared with other parties. This is connected to the idea that it is B, in the first instance, who has an immediate reason to respond to A's action with blame. Our accountability practices should reflect these facts about the claimholder's privileged normative position in the wake of wrongdoing; or at least this is how they should look if I am right in suggesting that they are structured through relational moral norms.

One might express the point in terms of an analogy between moral responsibility and the law. There are two legal paradigms to which we could appeal in thinking about our interpersonal practices of moral accountability. One of these is the criminal law, where agents of the state are authorized, on behalf of the community for which they work, to bring charges against defendants for violations of relevant statutes. The other paradigm is private law, where standing is assigned to individual claimholders who may sue for damages, on their own behalf, that result from actions that wrong them in particular. If we think in terms of the criminal law model, then the paradigmatic expression of moral blame should be a stance that is taken up on behalf of the larger community of moral persons, and that it is in principle open to anybody to adopt. To blame another, on this conception, is to assert moral demands impersonally as a representative person, acting out of the interest that we all have that relations between us should be conducted on a moral basis.[54] On the private law model, by contrast, the paradigmatic expression of blame is the interpersonal assertion of claims that one holds in one's own person in cases where those claims have been disregarded. In these terms, the hypothesis expressed earlier would be that the private law model should more closely reflect our moral practices of accountability if I am right to contend that they are structured through essentially relational requirements.

But this hypothesis seems consistent with a plausible independent analysis of our accountability practices. Thus, the reactive attitudes that are widely taken to be paradigmatic forms of moral blame in fact have a content that reflects the privileged position of claimholders. The primary reactive attitude is perhaps resentment, and as noted in section 3.2, this is an emotion that it is open to people to feel only on occasions when they believe themselves to have been wronged in some way. You can't really resent the morally problematic thing someone has done, however reprehensible it might be, if you don't understand the action to be one that violated some specific claim that you had against the agent not to do it. Resentment is thus the accountability-ascribing attitude that is rendered distinctively appropriate on the part of claimholders when agents flout their claims. It precisely reflects a claimholder's privileged complaint about what the agent has done, in a way that mirrors the positional conception of standing within private law.

To privilege resentment in this way in an account of interpersonal accountability, however, is not to hold that blame is available only to the party whose claims have been flouted. What we should expect, rather, is that other forms of blame, such as those available to third parties or to agents who hold themselves to account, are parasitic on our understanding of the reasons that those who are wronged have for resenting what was done to them. But this corresponds well to common ways of conceptualizing the more extended forms of reactive blame. Thus indignation is plausibly characterized by P. F. Strawson as the "vicarious analogue" of resentment; it is an attitude that we typically feel on behalf of the person who has been wronged, and it in this way seems to presuppose that the action we are objecting to violated a claim that was held by another party.[55] The angry disapprobation we experience in a case of this kind rests on the attribution to the claimholder of a privileged basis for complaint against the agent, one that would render resentment fitting on the claimholder's part. Third parties do not always have a good reason for reactive blame in response to wrongdoing; but when they do, it is natural to understand their indignation as derivative from the complaints that wrongful action generates in the person whom it wrongs.

On the criminal law model, by contrast, we would expect an impersonal form of indignation to represent the primary expression of moral blame. An impersonal conception of blame, in the relevant sense, would be based in interests we all share in the maintenance of a well-ordered moral community, rather than in the claims of individuals that might provide a privileged basis for them to object to wrongdoing on their own behalf. As we saw earlier in this section, however, an impersonal conception of this kind has difficulty understanding the reactions that it defines as responses to the flouting of obligations that are antecedently intelligible. The natural development of this approach is a kind of social voluntarism that sees the assertion of moral demands, by the representative moral person, as the original source of moral obligations, rather than a response to their violation. On the private law model, by contrast, the directed duties that give claimholders a privileged basis for complaint also define a notion of obligation that is available to figure in the thoughts characteristic of third-party blame. Indignation is about the flouting of obligations, precisely insofar as it is a vicarious reaction that is parasitic on the standing of claimholders to object on their own behalf to what was done to them.

It is a further reflection of the applicability of the private law model that indignation does not go together with the special authority to forswear blame that we have seen to be characteristic of resentment. Special contexts aside, third parties do not really have the normative standing to forgive the wrongdoer whom they might blame; this is among the positional features of forgiveness that, as I have argued, presuppose the relational approach to the requirements that structure our accountability practices. But it is unclear why there should be this asymmetry in normative power if third-party indignation, on behalf of the moral community, is the paradigmatic expression of blame. Within the criminal law model, there is room for those who blame on behalf of the moral community to overcome their angry reactions. But this will have the character of mercy or compassion rather than forgiveness, which is available only to a person who is understood to have a privileged basis for complaint about what the wrongdoer did.[56] The relational interpretation of indignation, as an essentially vicarious attitude that is adopted on behalf of someone who has the primary standing to blame, better accommodates these aspects of interpersonal accountability.

Consider next self-blame, the canonical expression of which is guilt. One salient feature of this reaction is that it reflects an understanding of oneself as not only deficient, relative to an ideal of personal attainment, but as having violated obligations or practical requirements that are binding on one.[57] As we saw in the preceding chapter, however, the relational interpretation of moral rightness provides a natural account of its standing as a source of practical requirements of this kind. Our sense of ourselves as having flouted requirements in these cases might well be understood to reflect our recognition that we owed it to another party to comply with them. In the same spirit, guilt is often said to involve the awareness on the part of agents who have done something wrong that they have caused a rupture or break in a valuable relationship that they stand in to another party.[58] This seems to correspond intuitively to the idea that the moral requirements the guilty agent is understood to violate are ones that are owed to another individual in particular. The rupture one has brought about, we might say, is precisely the fact that one has acted in a way that gives the other party a privileged complaint, something that would make it fitting for that party to resent one for what one has done.

Guilt and indignation, on this plausible way of thinking about them, incorporate an implicitly relational understanding of the moral requirements that help to fix their contents. Once we appreciate this point, however, then the possibility opens up of extending reactive blame even further, to cases involving parties who may not be in a position to assert claims or to understand when they have been flouted in their own case. It is natural to suppose that young infants, for instance, or adults who are severely mentally impaired, have claims just like the rest of us do to be treated with consideration and due regard—this despite the fact that they may not be in a position to hold other people to the demand that their claims be acknowledged and respected, or even to understand very clearly when these standards have not been met. Although it is a more controversial position, one might finally want to broaden the class of moral claimholders further to include nonrational animals, at least if they have a developed capacity for pain and suffering and reasonably complex interests.[59]

Claims, we have been assuming, have normative significance for the claim-holder; but in cases of all these kinds, claimholders are not actually in a position to adjust their attitudes in response to the specific recognition that reasons for such an adjustment are in place. Here, it seems to me, the notion of a vicarious reactive attitude has a further potential application. A third party, acting as it were as a trustee for the claimholder, can assert a claim on behalf of the injured party through attitudes such as indignation, which incorporate an understanding of the action that is blamed as wronging the injured claim-holder.[60] In doing this, we are incorporating the individuals in question into our practices of interpersonal accountability, insofar as we are asserting claims on their behalf that they are not in a position to assert themselves. This is a perfectly coherent move, it seems to me, involving a distinctive deployment of the capacity for vicarious blame that is already available to third parties in cases in which the individuals who were wronged are able, in principle, to assert claims for themselves.

To this point, I have mainly focused on the reactive forms of blame, arguing that the paradigmatic instances of angry disapprobation are naturally understood to involve an implicitly relational conception of the wrongs to which they are a response. It is worth adding, however, that the paradigmatic nonreactive forms of blame similarly seem to rest on a relational conception of those wrongs. T. M. Scanlon, for instance, has influentially argued that blame should primarily be understood to involve the adjustment of one's intentions in response to reasons for such adjustments that are provided by the attitudes of another party.[61] Scanlon argues, more specifically, that attitudes of disregard for moral standards typically impair the agent's relations to other persons, and that the impairment of a relationship gives the other parties to it reasons to modify their behavior in response, including reasons to avoid the agent, to withdraw from trust-based interactions with the agent, and so forth. These are reasons that one might act on even in the absence of the attitudes of angry disapprobation characteristic of reactive blame.

I think Scanlon's talk of the impairment of relationships in this context is potentially misleading, since it suggests that nonreactive blame is available only to parties who already stand in an ongoing historical relationship with each other, one that is eligible to be impaired by the attitudes of the parties to it.[62] Abstracting from this issue, however, I am prepared to acknowledge that there is a characteristic syndrome of behavioral responses to wrongdoing that might be understood as an extended form of blame. Note, however, that these nonreactive instances of blame make sense only insofar as they are responses to the flouting of essentially relational requirements.

We have reason to withdraw from interactions with other people who act wrongly, because their doing so reflects attitudes of disregard for us and for the claims we have against them. Such attitudes may not impair a relationship between us that exists antecedently; but they are certainly attitudes that have personal significance for us, on account of the fact that they are attitudes of targeted disregard. The syndrome of withdrawal, retrenchment, and avoidance behaviors is a warranted response to actions that reflect negative qualities of will toward us. As I have argued, however, the flouting or neglect of moral requirements will have this character only if we understand those requirements in relational terms. It simply doesn't make sense to respond to wrongdoing with nonreactive blame except insofar as it expresses attitudes of ill will toward us in particular, in ways that rest on a relational understanding of the norms against which the wrongdoer has offended.[63] This is a further reason for thinking that our accountability practices should be understood in terms of the private law model sketched above.

In his classic paper "The Nature and Value of Rights," Joel Feinberg invited us to think about "Nowheresville," a hypothetical community whose members possess all of the familiar moral notions except that of a right.[64] In discussing the elements that would need to be added to introduce rights or claims into this community, Feinberg identifies as crucial a "performative" sense of asserting a claim, which he understands as a "rule-governed activity" that is "public, familiar, and open to our observation."[65] His ultimate suggestion is that rights just are considerations that can validly be put forward as claims in this performative sense, and that they acquire their meaning and interpersonal significance from their relation to this practice. We can understand this as an argument that starts from the notion of a moral right or claim, and works backward to identify the forms of social interaction that are necessary to make sense of these normative notions.

In this chapter, I have mounted a complementary argument that locates relational moral notions within the distinctive practice of interpersonal accountability, understood as a practice that is organized around reactive and other forms of blame. My starting suggestion, put forward in section 3.1, was that it is a constraint on a nondebunking interpretation of morality that it should make sense of the idea that moral norms are distinctively suited to structure interpersonal accountability relations of this kind, so that disregard for them would provide a normative basis for the various manifestations of blame. The first phase of my argument, completed in section 3.2, established that the relational interpretation of morality is tailor-made to meet this constraint, insofar as it connects moral obligations constitutively to the claims that individuals have against them. It in this way does justice to our understanding that morality is an inherently social phenomenon.

In the argument's second phase, I showed that our interpersonal practice of holding people accountable for complying with moral requirements itself presupposes a relational understanding of them, as obligations that are owed to individuals who have claims against us to their compliance. This idea was developed in sections 3.3 and 3.4, which explored the positional character of the interlocking elements that together make up our practice of accountability, as well as the relational content of reactive and other forms of blame. Seen in this light, the practice of accountability may be understood to involve the assertion of essentially interpersonal claims (to echo Feinberg's language), together with focused responses on the part of wrongdoers to such assertions. If the relational account is rejected, then we shall have to conclude that morality is not everything that it seems to be, insofar as standards of rightness will not provide a normative basis for relations of interpersonal accountability; and those practices, for their part, will similarly be called into question, insofar as their content and structure show them to be organized around inherently relational norms.

4

Relational Requirements without Relational Foundations

IN *ETHICS AND THE LIMITS OF PHILOSOPHY*, Bernard Williams writes, "There is an everyday notion of obligation, as one consideration among others, and it is ethically useful." He also writes, "It is a mistake of morality to try to make everything into obligations."[1] These remarks bear on the relational interpretation of morality that I have been developing in this book. The obligations in the everyday sense to which Williams refers include a range of apparent duties, but the most familiar of them are the obligations created by promises.[2] These are obligations that are owed to another person, which we register in reflection as presumptive constraints on our ongoing planning about what to do. The relational interpretation does indeed try "to make everything into obligations" in this core sense. As noted in section 2.3 above, it understands modern morality to consist of a set of directed obligations that derive from our membership in a notional community of moral equals, and that are owed specifically to the individual members of this community. Actions are morally right, on the resulting approach, just in case they are ones that others have a claim against us to perform, and the set of potential claimholders in this sense is maximally inclusive.

Williams had reasons of his own for thinking that it is a mistake for morality to make everything into obligations in the "everyday" sense. I do not propose to go into those reasons here, at least not directly. But I think there are some important concerns that are at least related to Williams's skepticism about whether it is really plausible to extend the original notion of directed obligation to the entirety of the moral domain, as the relational interpretation proposes to do. I develop these concerns in the first two sections of this chapter, observing that some of the most salient examples of relational requirements grow out of nonnormative relations or interactions between the individuals who are bound by them, and that morality first emerged in human development as a device to facilitate cooperation in contexts of this kind.

These observations raise the natural question whether the relational model can be extended into a general framework for thinking about moral obligation, even outside of contexts of personal interaction and in-group cooperation. I argue that any account of interpersonal morality will involve some degree of abstraction and extension as we adapt moral resources to do justice to the modern idea that we are members of an extensive community of moral equals. Drawing on the relational model for this purpose has the signal advantage that it enables us to understand interpersonal morality as a source of obligations that also have direct significance for our accountability practices. Philosophers have offered some general arguments against extending the relational morality in this way, but I show that those arguments do not succeed. Morality may be understood as a set of self-standing relational obligations, ones that can link individuals who are not already connected through ties of history or causality or cultural practice.

Only once we recognize that moral obligations take this form do some of their presuppositions and consequences come into clear focus. I argue in section 4.3 that these include an anti-individualism about normativity. On many popular approaches, reasons for action and for attitudes are thought to be contingent on subjective facts about the states and capacities of the person to whom they apply. This kind of individualism, I suggest, is hard to square with the idea that there is a genuine moral nexus that links agents and claimholders through directed requirements and their corresponding claims. But it is equally hard to reconcile with the central features of interpersonal morality that the relational account seems well designed to accommodate.

The self-standing character of the moral nexus raises a further question about the agent-relative character of the duties that it defines. A natural strategy for explaining the agent-relative structure of moral requirements appeals to the nonnormative patterns of historical interaction on which they are based; but on the approach I am sketching, many directed moral obligations obtain independently of any such relational basis. In section 4.4, I suggest that the agent-relative character of moral obligations is explained, at the deepest level, by the relational character of the claims with which they are connected, and that this explanation carries over to cases in which there is no antecedent relationship between the parties. I also argue that there is a positive personal value that is realized through compliance with relational moral requirements, which is connected to, though distinct from, the value of mutual recognition.

4.1. Obligations and Relationships

The paradigm cases of directed or relational obligation that have so far been considered are ones that have a transactional character. The central example has been that of promissory obligation, which arises through a concrete, datable interaction between the parties whom it binds. The promisor undertakes an obligation by making a representation of some kind about what will happen in the future, one that is registered by the promisee, and that thereby gives rise to a new directed duty. Promisors come in this way to owe it to promisees to fulfill the expectations that they have attempted to raise, and these directed duties correspond to claims on the promisees' part to such fulfillment.

The relational obligation, in this paradigm case, thus derives from a social exchange between the parties that can rightly be regarded as its basis. If we wish to extend this relational model to the whole of the moral domain, however, we will have to construe it as applying in cases where the moral nexus is not similarly grounded in a prior transaction or interaction between the parties that it links. According to the modern understanding of it that I sketched in chapter 2, morality consists in a set of directed duties that derive from the fact that we inhabit a world in common with other agents whose interests also matter, and matter equally. Its requirements correspond to claims that people have against us, just insofar as they are persons or agents. The class of people to whom moral duties are owed, then, will include vast numbers of individuals whom we have never even met, and with whom we therefore cannot have engaged in a transaction or exchange. The random person I encounter on the public sidewalk with a gouty toe is someone who has a moral claim against me, on this conception, that I not act in ways that aggravate her suffering. So do the inhabitants of a remote foreign region whose territory I am flying over as I contemplate jettisoning some excess cargo or waste. The question is whether there can be a relational nexus of this kind that is not grounded in a prior relationship between the parties, such as the transactional relationship that gives rise to a standard promissory duty.

The case of promissory obligation raises complications, however, that the discussion so far has glossed over. A brief review of some of these complications will help us to understand better why it might seem a mistake to try to generalize the relational model to the entirety of the moral domain.

According to a common and to my mind plausible way of thinking about them, promises function to generate expectations about the behavior of promisors via the awareness of the parties to them that a distinctively moral obligation has been incurred. That is, the promissory transaction generates a moral obligation, and the promisee's assurance that promisor will perform is parasitic on the understanding that an obligation of this kind now exists, and that the promisor is morally conscientious.[3] There are, to be sure, puzzles that this way of thinking about promising tends to generate. A particular difficulty confronts those who believe that the moral obligations involved in promissory exchange derive from more general principles of assurance, pertaining to cases in which people have come to rely on us to do something as a result of our having deliberately led them to expect that we will so act. For if promises give rise to assurance on the part of the promisee that the promisor will perform via the promisee's awareness that a moral obligation has been incurred, it seems the obligation cannot derive from the fact of the promisee's assurance. The approach appears to be circular, presupposing the existence of the moral obligation in its account of the state of mind on the part of the promisee that is supposed to give rise to the obligation in the first place.[4]

Putting this difficulty to the side, the moralized approach to promises assumes that promissory obligation is a special case of moral obligation. That is, there are general moral obligations that we stand under, specified by principles such as those of assurance and of fairness (pertaining to our responsibility to contribute our fair share to sustaining useful social practices from which we have ourselves benefited). These obligations apply to us when we deliberately raise expectations in other people about what we are going to do or exploit valuable social conventions to advance our ends. Making promises turns out to be a way—though not, perhaps, the only way—of incurring obligations of these more generic kinds; and the obligations that are generated are therefore distinctively moral in character.

According to a different and less moralized conception, promissory obligation is sui generis. That is, promises give rise to obligations, but it is not characteristic of those obligations that they are distinctively moral. They are, as we might put it, practice-based obligations, whose nature is connected with and defined by the specific social conventions with which promising is bound up.

Proponents of this conception may agree that promises function to generate expectations on the part of promisees through their awareness that the promisor has incurred an obligation in virtue of the promissory exchange. But they will deny that morality has anything essential to do with the obligation that is involved in this process. Promising is, on this way of thinking about it, a social practice that confers on its participants a sui generis normative power, and that thereby subserves their normative interest in being able to generate new directed claims and obligations.[5] There might be, and presumably there generally are, distinctively moral reasons why people ought to keep their promises, and these may even be sufficient to ground moral obligations in many cases. These moral considerations supervene, however, on a prior and independent set of practice-based obligations and claims, which represent the primary level on which promissory obligation operates.

But what story can we tell about the directional features that intuitively seem to characterize promissory obligations? How can we make sense of the relational character of such obligations? On the nonmoralized account sketched above, as I understand it, the relational features will be traced to the structure of the social practice that is said to confer normative powers on those who participate in it.[6] That is, the practice just is one in which promises give rise to obligations that are understood to be owed specifically to the promisee, who has a practice-based claim against the promisor to fulfillment of the obligation that the promise generates. The practice represents, in the phrase of Michael Thompson, a self-standing order of right, which defines the manifold of persons who participate in it as potential parties to relational requirements of the now familiar kind.[7]

According to the moralized approach, by contrast, the relational obligations that promises create are specifically moral obligations. So if we are to make sense of them as directed obligations, owed specifically to the promisee, we will need a way of understanding how moral requirements can have this kind of character. Here, I think, it is tempting to suppose that what makes a relational moral obligation possible will be something about the antecedent relationship that the parties to the obligation stand in. One possibility would be to interpret morality as a self-standing social practice that can inscribe directed obligations and claims, in a way that parallels the practice of promising. Moral principles, such as those of assurance and fairness, might be construed as norms that some historically situated group of people already implicitly internalizes and accepts, perhaps in the style of a Humean convention. In that case, promisor and promisee will already be linked with each other, prior to entering into their promissory agreement, through their joint participation in the social practice of morality, which makes them both members of the same Thompson-style manifold of persons, and therefore potential parties to relational bonds that are constituted through this practice.

This strategy falls back on the practice-based account of directional obligation, and simply applies it to morality itself, construing the moral domain as a distinctive set of conventional arrangements. One curious result of this approach will be that there are two separate practice-based obligations that can be brought into existence through promises: a specifically promissory obligation that is prior to and independent of morality, and a separate and equally practice-based moral obligation that piggybacks on the first. A second consequence of the approach is that morality comes to have a somewhat provincial character; it will represent a set of conventional norms or understandings that implicitly regulate the interactions of a group of people in the way of a social convention, rather than universal requirements that stem from the fact that there are other persons or agents in the world who are equally real, and whose interests matter to practical thought (even if they are not participants in our social practices or conventions in particular).[8]

A different way to make sense of the directed moral obligation in the promising case would point to the transaction between the parties that the promise itself represents. According to this line of thought, there might well be universal moral obligations that are not based in the norms that are shared by the participants in a common social practice. All the same, morality can generate directed obligations only as a result of a specific causal interaction or exchange between the parties who are thereby linked to each other, such as the issuing of a promise that is registered as such by the promisee. The role of the transaction, on this approach, is to render intelligible the idea that there is something specific that one of the parties owes it to the other to do, morally speaking. There is a pattern of causal interaction between promisor and promisee that brings into existence the nested set of duties and claims characteristic of relational normativity, and that is necessary for a specific normative nexus of this kind to obtain.

Normatively significant patterns of causal interaction might also be present in other cases, such as those that link the parties to a relationship between friends or family members, and they can similarly give rise to directed moral obligations and claims in those cases as well. Thus, it is natural to suppose that friends and romantic partners have special moral obligations to each other, and corresponding claims against each other, in virtue of the relationships that they stand in to each other, which among other things involve extended patterns of historical interaction.[9] And there are still other forms of historical relationship that involve less deep and extended patterns of interaction, such as those that arise when one person invests trust in another or makes a significant sacrifice to benefit the other in some way. In these cases, too, it is natural to suppose that there are directed moral obligations in play, including obligations of gratitude, reciprocity, and loyalty.

On this way of thinking about things, individual persons or agents can in principle be potential parties to directed moral duties to each other, just in virtue of their common standing as persons or agents. There is no need for them to share some antecedent basis, such as participation in a common social practice, in order for them to be members of the same manifold of persons, and hence eligible to have moral claims against each other. But actual duties and claims of this kind can arise only through particular interactions between individuals, which generate patterns of causal influence that provide a concrete basis for the relational nexus that comes to bind them to each other. Duties that we owe to each other, as Joseph Raz has written, thus seem to "presuppose some kind of personal relationship."[10]

Both of the views sketched above pose a challenge to the relational account of morality that I have been attempting to explicate. Either there are relational obligations of morality, but only ones that extend to participants in a common social practice or convention; the result would be that there is nothing that we owe, morally, to outsiders to our own social practices who nevertheless stand to be affected by what we do (such as the inhabitants of the region we are flying over as we contemplate jettisoning our aircraft's waste). Or there are universal moral requirements, but ones that acquire a specifically relational character only in cases in which there is a prior interaction between the parties that grounds the moral obligation through which they are yoked together. Here, too, we will have no moral obligations that are owed specifically to individuals who could be disadvantaged by our actions, but without our having previously interacted with them in one way or another (such as the unfortunate stranger on the sidewalk who is suffering from gout). On either view, it will be, as Williams suggested, a mistake to interpret interpersonal morality as a unified domain of directed obligations.

To understand morality in this way is to extend the relational paradigm from core cases in which it familiarly operates, such as the obligations created by promises and family relationships, to cases that are perhaps less naturally interpreted in relational terms. This extension will involve the application of the relational model to situations that lack some of the features that are present in the core cases, and it is fair to ask whether the model remains tenable when it is applied in this way. Can there be directed obligations and claims between individuals who are not antecedently related to each other, via bonds of friendship or personal history or participation in common institutions or conventional practices? And can there be specific obligations that are owed to other people that do not track and supervene upon antecedent patterns of causal interaction?

These skeptical questions grow out of reflection on some of the central cases of directed moral obligations; but a similar line of thought is encouraged by reflection on the natural history of morality. Consider, for instance, Michael Tomasello's interesting account of the evolution of our moral capacities.[11] This account posits several distinct sources of moral agency that come to the fore sequentially, in response to the distinctive challenges that our ancestors encountered in different phases in the development of the species. There is, first, a prosocial tendency to sympathy and helping behavior, especially toward kin and friends, that is essentially continuous with similar tendencies in the great apes. Second, Tomasello identifies a distinct capacity for a kind of "second-personal" morality that emerged when our ancestors were forced to enter into collaborative foraging activities with other individuals. This involves a capacity to see oneself as engaged in a joint project together with other individuals, to understand oneself as subject to role requirements that are defined by the collaborative project, and to feel a sense of commitment to the individuals with whom one is engaged in a joint pursuit. Finally, Tomasello posits a move from interpersonal to objective morality, which involves a "scaling up from collaboration to culture";[12] here humans develop a sense of themselves as members of larger collectives or tribal units, and see themselves as subject to objective requirements that are partly constitutive of the groups with which they are identified.

On Tomasello's account, then, human morality involves distinctive patterns of thought and motivation, ones that are responsive to the forms of interdependence characteristic of our species life. A similar idea figures in the developmental story that Joshua Greene has recently presented.[13] Greene argues that morality can be understood, in the first instance, as a set of emotional dispositions that evolved to solve the problem of coordination within groups. Tendencies such as empathy, family attachment, gratitude, anger, and the other moral emotions implement different but complementary strategies for avoiding the familiar dilemmas of cooperation between individuals who interact with each other within a common social framework. These emotional dispositions involve swift and unreflective, "System 1"–level action tendencies that are effective under the circumstances for which they evolved, enabling us reliably to avoid mutually destructive conflict within our local communities.[14] But these same tendencies promote a sense of tribal belonging and a correlative awareness of our differences from other tribal groups.

The evolutionary solution to the problem of cooperation within groups thus leads to a new problem of competition between groups, each of whose members is prone to favor other in-group individuals. Tribal membership is constituted in part through shared moral understandings, which help group members to navigate their local world, but which also put them at odds with members of other groups, organized as they are around different thick conceptions of right and wrong. The most pressing moral problems of the present age are raised by these intergroup conflicts. To resolve them, we need to develop a new "metamorality" that will be capable of universalistic application, and that may command the assent of individuals who belong to different moral tribes. Greene goes on to argue that solving this problem must fall to our reflective "System 2" processes, and that its terms are set by some version of utilitarian moral reasoning.

These two historical narratives differ on several important points. Greene, for instance, questions the authority of the emotionally tinged reactions that tend to enable cooperation within groups, which he thinks should not be viewed as reliable guides for reflection about the intergroup conflicts that loom so large today.[15] Tomasello, by contrast, tends to grant the continuing legitimacy of the "second-personal" morality that enables cooperation between individuals in contexts of joint agency, suggesting that it is supplemented rather than supplanted by the forms of reasoning that enable more cosmopolitan forms of cultural life.[16] Abstracting from these differences, however, both accounts emphasize the role that morality initially plays in facilitating mutually beneficial collaboration between people who stand in close, face-to-face relations with each other. From the standpoint of the natural history of the species, this appears to be the primal scene for many of the forms of reasoning and emotional response that we continue to recognize as characteristically moral.

At the same time, these developmental accounts raise an important question: what moral resources can we draw upon as we extend our horizon, as we must do, to encompass our relations to persons with whom we have not interacted in an "up close and personal" manner? For Tomasello, this extension involves the development of new forms of moral reasoning that are centered around objective norms, and that rest on our conception of ourselves as members of larger (but still parochial) groups. But this enrichment of our moral resources does not yet get us all the way to a genuinely universal framework for thinking about what to do (for instance, in cases of intergroup conflict). Greene is especially concerned about this problem. To cope with it, he contends that we need to leave behind the emotional tendencies that evolved to regulate our in-group relations, and deploy the reflective resources of utilitarian metamorality.

The challenge, in the present context, is this. Relational moral requirements, as I have explicated them, seem tailor-made for the kinds of face-to-face encounters that shaped the earliest stages in the evolution of human morality. As I argued in the last chapter, they are also closely associated with the reactive attitudes that might have evolved to help us cooperate with members of our own groups. Thus, our paradigms of directed obligation, such as those generated by promises, are cases that rest on concrete interactions between two individuals, and that give rise to resentment and reactive blame when the obligations in question are flouted. Perhaps it is reasonable to grant the legitimacy of the relational model in application to cases of this kind.[17] But there is a question about whether the model can be generalized into a plausible account of modern, universalistic morality in its entirety. It cannot be taken for granted that patterns of reasoning and emotional response that are suited to contexts of close interpersonal interaction will be adequate for thinking about our responsibilities in more impersonal contexts, where we are called on to consider the implications of our conduct for people to whom we are not antecedently related in any particular way. Moral principles that function well in situations structured by close interpersonal exchange might simply not be up to the task of regulating our actions in other situations.

This line of inquiry dovetails with the questions posed earlier in this section, on the basis of reflection on the mechanics of promissory obligation. In this paradigm case, it seems that directed obligations are anchored in something that antecedently links to each other the parties whom they bind. This might be a Humean convention in which the two parties both participate (something that would connect them as members of the same tribal or cultural in-group); or it might be a personal transaction between them (the result of a face-to-face interaction on some particular occasion). But it is then natural to wonder whether this feature of the promissory case represents something that is essential to directed obligation more generally, as Raz for instance has suggested that it is. Can there be directed obligations that float free from the personal relationships and social bonds that link us antecedently to other individuals, and that might be understood to underwrite the assignment to those individuals of specific claims against us?

4.2. Self-Standing Relational Requirements

The questions posed at the end of the preceding section will to some extent occupy us throughout the remainder of this book. The main aim will be to articulate and defend the assumptions that need to be taken on board when the relational model is expanded into a comprehensive interpretation of the domain of modern interpersonal morality, and to consider whether it provides an illuminating framework for thinking about first-order moral issues. I shall try to identify the most important theoretical commitments of this approach, and I shall explore its implications for several challenging questions within normative ethics.

Throughout this discussion, however, it will be important to bear in mind the conclusions established in chapters 2 and 3 of this book. I argued there that the relational approach is unique in its ability to make sense of central features of interpersonal morality, understood as a distinctive and internally unified normative domain. In particular, the approach explains the idea that moral considerations have the force of obligations, ones that have their source in the equal standing of an inclusive domain of persons. It also renders intelligible the social significance of moral requirements, their standing as a basis for relations of interpersonal accountability. These are core elements in our modern conception of the moral realm, and it is a great attraction of the relational model that it promises to illuminate them. The presumptive rationale for trying to "make everything into obligations" in the relational sense is the promise it holds of enabling us to understand interpersonal morality as a unified set of considerations that reflect the equal standing of persons, and that are intelligible both as defeasible constraints on the will and as a basis for relations of accountability.

Against this background, it strikes me as natural to turn the questions posed in the preceding section around. Why should we *not* interpret the domain of interpersonal morality as having an implicitly relational structure? Understanding it in this way will, to be sure, involve an extension of the relational model from the contexts in which we first encounter it in practice to situations that are somewhat different in character. But any attempt to make sense of morality, as we typically understand it today, will involve some extension of this kind. A suitably modern conception of the moral must be cosmopolitan in spirit, acknowledging what I referred to in chapter 1 as the postulate of equal standing. The basic moral insight of modernity is that we are all persons, equally real, and that there is an important class of interpersonal requirements that stem directly from this important fact. But doing justice to this cosmopolitan insight necessarily requires an exercise of reflective adaptation, through which more primitive moral commitments are modified to reflect the fact that we belong to a maximally inclusive community of moral equals. We must move beyond the parochial and limited parameters within which we initially learn to operate with moral concepts in both our individual development and in the natural history of the species.

Utilitarians such as Greene and Peter Singer, for instance, emphasize the need to extend natural empathy to encompass the entire domain of sentient creatures, through the exercise of System 2 capacities for critical reflection.[18] But prosocial empathy is only one among several tendencies that have emerged in our evolutionary history to promote moral behaviors and to facilitate cooperation. There is, in addition, the ability to see oneself as subject to directional requirements that specify duties that are owed to other individuals. This is an ability that plausibly emerges in situations that involve close interpersonal contact, including contexts in which we are trying to do things together with other people. But these abilities too are capable of being extended to encompass a much broader domain of individuals. We can come, through reflection, to see others as having claims against us, just insofar as they are persons who are equally real, and regardless of whether we are already connected to them through personal relationships or shared social practices of some kind. Similarly, though we initially understand ourselves to owe specific debts to people with whom we have already interacted in some way, it is perfectly coherent to think that there might also be debts we owe to others, just insofar as they are persons, equally real. Understanding interpersonal morality along these lines has the signal advantage that it enables us to make sense of it as a domain of practical requirements, ones that are at the same time suited to structure relations of interpersonal accountability; this was the argument of chapters 2 and 3 above.

As I noted earlier in this book, the postulate of equal standing is often thought to favor broadly consequentialist accounts of morality, which treat the interests of each as equally important in the determination of what it is morally right to do. Approaches such as those of Greene and Singer draw much of their appeal from the straightforward expression they give to the commitment to equality that is implicit in universal morality. But there are other interpretations of this commitment that are at least as appealing, and that can be detached from the specifically consequentialist interpretation of the requirements of the moral right.

Consider Samuel Scheffler's compelling suggestion that the value of equality in the context of political life should be seen as a special case of a more general value, that of an egalitarian relationship.[19] The hallmark of such a relationship, on Scheffler's account, is that the parties to it acknowledge an egalitarian deliberative constraint; they take the interests of the different parties to the relationship to be equally significant to their deliberations within the context of the relationship.[20] To conduct a relationship on these terms is not to be antecedently committed to realizing any particular pattern of outcomes (such as ones that equalize the welfare level of all parties to the relationship), but to participate in an ongoing interpersonal practice whereby the equal standing of the parties is reciprocally acknowledged. Scheffler believes that this egalitarian ideal can be realized in personal relationships of different kinds, including not only those between members of the same political community, but also the relationships between friends or family members or life partners. An egalitarian political practice will make different demands on members from the demands that egalitarianism makes on friends and intimates; but these differences will reflect differences in the character of the relationships that are to be conducted on a basis of equality, not differences in the ideal of equality that applies to them.[21]

Scheffler himself associates the egalitarian deliberative constraint with valuable relationships that have an ongoing, historical character, such as those between friends or between the members of a common political community. The assumption seems to be that egalitarian commitments get a grip on agents only in the context of existing relationships that are valuable along other dimensions.[22] But while relationships of this kind might provide our initial exposure to the egalitarian deliberative constraint, the relational value that they instantiate is one that potentially has application outside the context of such relationships.

Thus, we can see ourselves as having directed obligations that are owed to individuals with whom we have not yet interacted at all, just in virtue of the fact that they stand to be affected in one way or another by the things we might do. As I have argued in chapter 2, directed obligations of this kind make sense to us as practical requirements, that is, considerations that intelligibly function as presumptive constraints on an agent's deliberations. The constraints, moreover, appear to operationalize a commitment to equality, insofar as they acknowledge the standing of persons as equally worthy of moral consideration. The interests of others count equally, in this context, not as considerations that are to be assigned equal weight in assessing the consequences of actions that the agent might perform, but as potential bases of moral claims that are held against the agent. The generalized relational model of obligation in this way seems to exemplify Scheffler's egalitarian deliberative constraint in its most abstract form. It enables us to understand interpersonal morality as a set of cosmopolitan obligations that potentially ground accountability relations with anyone, realizing a practice of equality distinct from, though structurally similar to, the egalitarian practices that Scheffler situates within thicker human relationships.[23] This is an additional respect in which it is attractive to understand morality as an extension of the relational model of interpersonal obligation that is familiar to us from situations of face-to-face interaction with other people.

According to the resulting interpretation of interpersonal morality, specific causal interactions with other people might affect what we owe to them, but they do not represent general preconditions for the possibility of directed moral duties and claims. If I have induced other people to form expectations about my future behavior, or benefited specifically from their significant efforts to help me out of a bind, then I will have obligations to them, of fidelity or gratitude, that would not otherwise obtain. It does not follow, however, that there is nothing that I owe to people with whom I have not previously interacted in these or other ways, or to whom I am not antecedently linked through shared relationships or practices of some kind. It might be a condition for the obtaining of directed moral obligations and claims that the parties connected by them are not causally isolated from each other, so that there is at least the possibility that one of them would be affected significantly by something that the other might do. Thus, it is arguable that there is nothing that we owe to the rational denizens of distant galaxies, assuming there are such beings, at least until such time as we are able to have a discernible impact on them through exertions of our individual and collective agency; this is an issue to which I shall return in chapter 5 below. But this condition, of course, does not require that we should already have interacted with those to whom moral duties are owed. The strangers whom I encounter on my travels have basic moral claims against me, even if we are meeting for the first time, insofar as they are in a position to be harmed and benefited in specific ways by various actions that it is open to me to perform. My sense of myself as owing them consideration is a particular way of articulating the idea that they and I are moral equals.

Given the coherence and initial attraction of this way of understanding interpersonal morality, are there general theoretical considerations that would stand in the way of it? Michael Thompson has argued that there are. As noted earlier, he takes relational or "bipolar" requirements to define an order of right that potentially links individuals within the manifold of persons to which it applies. But he contends that there is an explanatory challenge we face in making sense of how individuals can belong to one and the same manifold of persons, a challenge that universalistic conceptions of relational morality may not be able to meet.[24]

Thompson illustrates the general problem by asking us to consider members of two different tribes, the Lombards and the Schlombards, whose systems of personal private law include directed requirements with the same content, and who encounter each other for the first time at a remote location in the Alps.[25] Thompson suggests that these individuals, taking each other to belong to the same tribe, might endeavor to enter into a contract with each other, concluding their attempted agreement with the ritual mixture of song and dance that is called for under the terms of their respective private law regimes. But this exercise will not succeed in generating contractual obligations that are genuinely owed to each other, since there is no single order of right through which the parties to the putative contract are linked. As Thompson writes, "They are like ships passing in a juridical night."[26]

On Thompson's view, it seems, there are two conditions that have to be satisfied in order for individuals to belong to the same manifold of persons under a common order of right. First, it must be the case that the individuals can come nonaccidentally to have thoughts about directed duties and correlative claims that are shifted into the same normative "gear," invoking the very order of right that they both fall under.[27] If they encounter each other on a remote highway for the first time, and swerve in their automotive trajectories so as not to cause harm to each other, this must normally be because they understand themselves to have valid claims against each other, and corresponding directed duties, that are of the same normative kind. Second, Thompson suggests that a system of nonaccidentally convergent relational thoughts is possible only if there is something else that the bearers of those thoughts have in common, which gives their shared dyadic thoughts a "foothold" or represents their "common source."[28]

Appealing to these conditions, Thompson goes on to argue that it will be very challenging to make sense of the kind of cosmopolitan order of relational right that I have been trying to sketch in this book.[29] The common source for convergent bipolar thoughts about morality might be sought in shared Humean conventions or (along Aristotelian lines) in a common human nature that binds the individual bearers of such thoughts. But then it will be lacking in full universality, failing to apply to agents who do not participate in our natural life form or share in our conventional arrangements.[30] A more abstract conception of the manifold of persons could perhaps be constructed on Kantian grounds, by appeal to the shared principles of pure practical reason that we might take to be latent in any exercise of concept-governed self-determination, construed as a kind of "intelligible cause" of such agency. But Thompson views this as an "alarming" metaphysical commitment, one that it is difficult for even a mildly naturalistic conception of ethics to maintain.[31] Without it, the allegedly universal manifold of persons who are united under common moral norms will lack the kind of shared basis that it requires.

But both of Thompson's conditions strike me as questionable.[32] First, I do not see that it is built into the notion of an order of relational right that the individuals to whom it applies should be capable of converging nonaccidentally on thoughts about it. Doubts about this assumption are already raised by some examples that Thompson himself considers, such as duties that we owe to infants or to members of our species who are mentally infirm.[33] It isn't obvious to me that directed obligations in these cases are unintelligible unless we can see the inability of the claimholders to grasp thoughts about them as accidental, in some sense. More fundamentally, however, it seems at least conceivable that there might be things that we owe to individuals who are not capable of entertaining normative thoughts of any sort, not even when they come to exhibit the full spectrum of capabilities that is normal for adult members of the species to which they belong. Our dogs and cats, for instance, might have claims against us that we look after their basic animal needs, and provide them with a comfortable and secure environment in which to live in accordance with their nature.

Thompson concedes that there might be prohibitions on how we may treat individuals of this kind, things that it would be wrong for us to do to them.[34] But he maintains that we cannot wrong them, insofar as they lack in principle the capacity for normative judgments about the relational order of right that allegedly links us to them. But in the present context this assumption seems to me question-begging. There is nothing incoherent about the idea of a manifold of persons that tolerates at least some internal asymmetries, insofar as it assigns claims to individuals within the manifold who are not capable of asserting those claims on their own behalf, and who also do not stand under directed duties toward other members of the manifold. But if this idea is not incoherent, then Thompson's first condition must be rejected. It is not an a priori constraint on an order of right that the manifold of persons who stand under it must normally or nonaccidentally share thoughts about the bipolar norms that link them with each other.

Even if I am wrong about this, however, it would not be enough to motivate Thompson's second condition. He contends that individual members of a manifold can converge in bipolar thoughts about its requirements only if there is something else that binds them to each other, and that makes possible this alignment in their normative attitudes. But this seems deeply implausible.

Return to Thompson's case of the Lombards and Schlombards. Individual members of these two tribes are, let us assume, capable of nonaccidentally entertaining bipolar thoughts about the private-law orders that prevail in their respective tribal societies. They can thus think about themselves as having contractual claims against other members of their tribe, as well as obligations that are owed to such individuals; this much Thompson himself clearly accepts. But if these resources are available to them, it seems they can easily, through a modest exercise of abstraction, step back from their tribal identity and think of themselves as individuals who are capable of bipolar normative thoughts of one kind or another. This in turn will open the way to their understanding themselves to be members of a larger manifold of persons whose defining feature is the capacity for bipolar normative judgment. They can then ask themselves about the directed duties and claims that link them to each other, just insofar as they are each members of this manifold. They would thus arrive at convergent judgments about what they owe to each other not as Lombards or Schlombards, but simply as individuals who are competent with bipolar concepts.[35] (This is true even if their reflections lead to the conclusion that there is nothing they owe to each other in their common capacity as persons capable of bipolar thought; this negative conclusion would still be a judgment about the abstract order of moral right.) This is precisely the kind of reflective extension of our relational normative concepts that I envisaged at the start of the present section, whereby relational requirements that are originally brought to bear in face-to-face or tribal encounters come to be applied more universally to a much broader class of individual persons.

Against this, it might be suggested that the postulated abstract competence with bipolar normative concepts is something that the individual members of the larger manifold have in common, and that might therefore represent a "source" or "foothold" for the convergence in judgment that I have described. But to interpret Thompson's second condition in this way would render it empty. As he understands the condition, it pushes us toward seeing the members of a manifold of persons as bearing substantive connections with each other that are independent from the bipolar norms that purport to link them. Examples include the historical and causal ties that bind together the individuals who participate in and benefit from a Humean convention or practice, or their joint membership in an Aristotelian natural life form, or their shared connection to pure practical reason, understood as a kind of intelligible cause. But individuals who exhibit competence with bipolar normative competence need not share any substantive connections of these kinds. They hold a property in common, but this represents a merely logical relation between them, not a thick social or natural-historical or metaphysical relationship that has independent explanatory significance (for instance, as something that might make sense of the fact that their bipolar thoughts nonaccidentally converge in their content).

A different basis for skepticism about the possibility of universalistic relational morality is suggested by some reflections of Margaret Gilbert's on the nature of obligation.[36] Gilbert notes that obligations, in a core sense, should be understood in what I have called relational terms, as owed to another party who has a special claim against the agent to compliance. In a case with this structure (involving, for instance, an obligation generated through a promissory exchange), the behavior called for is not the exclusive possession of the agent's, but belongs in some sense to both parties whom the directed obligation links. This is connected to the important fact that the party to whom the obligation is owed has special standing to complain in case the obligation should be flouted. The challenge for an account of obligation, in general terms, is to make sense of this kind of directionality. Gilbert argues that this challenge can easily be met if we understand directed obligations to be constitutively connected with the structure of joint commitments among different parties to do something together; and she suggests that it will be very difficult to meet the challenge outside of these kinds of contexts.[37] The upshot would be that directed obligations will not be possible for agents who are not already linked to each other through ties of shared agency.

A particular focus in Gilbert's development of this position is the idea that directed obligations render the actions they prescribe the joint possession of the parties to them.[38] I emphasized a similar point in section 2.3 above, noting that relational norms belong to the different parties that are connected through them, and that this helps us to see why agents lack unilateral discretion to fall short of the obligations that they define; this is among the features of these norms that suit them for the deliberative role of practical requirements. Gilbert argues that this joint ownership condition is fully intelligible in the context of shared agency. For if two parties are jointly committed to doing something together, then it is already the case that they see their individual activities as belonging to both of them, insofar as they are actions done in accordance with a commitment jointly undertaken by them. As Gilbert at one point writes, "Any one party of the joint commitment can appropriately say of the other's conforming actions: 'They are mine—in my capacity as co-creator of the commitment.'"[39] She further suggests that to be the owner of an action in this sense just is to be the person to whom its performance is owed.[40] So the relational structure of directed obligation goes together with the nature of joint commitment, and appears difficult to make sense of outside of this context.

Note that this account, if plausible, would potentially place surprisingly strict constraints on the applicability of directed obligations. Thus, even within the kind of close social contexts in which we encounter other people on a face-to-face basis, there are many such encounters that do not appear to rest on or involve a structure of Gilbert-style joint commitment. It seems that I owe it to the gout-afflicted stranger I encounter on the sidewalk not to step on her toe, and I would similarly be understood to owe a debt of gratitude to the stranger who made a significant personal sacrifice to help me change my flat tire in the rain. In these cases, it is far from obvious that there is any joint commitment that links the parties who are bound to each other through relational requirements and claims; and yet we intuitively feel that there is enough in the interaction between the parties to give rise to such a relational nexus.[41]

But Gilbert's argument for embedding relational obligations within contexts of joint commitment does not in any case succeed. One difficulty is that the argument does not elucidate the directionality that is characteristic of relational obligation. If Olive and Roger are jointly committed to doing something that requires Olive to fly to Chicago, then it seems that each of them, in their "capacity as co-creator of the commitment," can regard Olive's going to Chicago as his or her own, insofar as this is part of something larger that they have undertaken together. This joint commitment sense of ownership is equally available to both of the individuals who are implicated in the commitment, including Olive (who can also regard the action as her own in a different, individualistic sense). Now Gilbert claims that being the owner of an action in the joint commitment sense is necessary and sufficient for being the person to whom the action is owed, which would have the consequence that Olive owes it to herself, as well as to Roger, to fly to Chicago. But this seems wrong. If Olive owes it to Roger to fly to Chicago, then it is Roger, and not she herself, who has a claim against her to this action, and who would have special standing to complain should she fail to carry it out.

More fundamentally, Gilbert's argument appears to equivocate on the notion of joint ownership. The sense in which Roger owns Olive's action in a case of directed obligation is fundamentally normative. The action belongs to him just insofar as he has a claim or entitlement against Olive to her performing it; and what Roger shares with Olive, strictly speaking, is not the action of hers that fulfills her duty, but the normative complex of obligations and claims that links them to each other. In this, the situation is precisely analogous to that obtaining with literal property relations. To own a given physical object (the green Ford that is parked a few streets down, say), is not to have the object in my physical possession at a given point in time, but to have a claim or entitlement to determine what is done with it. This normative claim is shared in common with other parties, insofar as it is constitutively connected with obligations on their part to refrain from making use of the car without my consent; it exists only as part of a Hohfeldian normative complex that includes those obligations.

Against this background, Gilbert's appeal to joint commitment appears to be a non sequitur. Olive and Roger, in virtue of their joint commitment, might each be able to view Olive's trip to Chicago as his or her own, in the sense of being something that they have both undertaken.[42] But our quarry was the different, normative sense of ownership at issue when we say that Roger has an entitlement or claim to Olive's action. This normative relation is not captured by appeal to the very different sense of shared ownership at stake in cases of joint commitment. For the same reasons, we could not elucidate the normative relation of property ownership by appeal to the distinct relation of physical possession; a given car can be mine, insofar as I am physically occupying and operating it on the roadway, without belonging to me in the sense of my having a property right to it. But if this is correct, then shared ownership of the kind at issue in joint commitment would appear, absent further argument, to be neither necessary nor sufficient for directed obligation.[43] There would then be no principled obstacle to thinking of universal morality in relational terms, as a set of directed obligations and claims that can link individuals who are in no sense bound up in shared commitments of any kind.

The moral nexus, understood in this way, represents what we might call a *self-standing domain* of relational requirements and claims. This is to say that it is not grounded in prior relationships or interactions between the parties that it links. In this, it differs from some other examples of relational requirements, such as those that arguably connect friends or family members to each other. But as I noted above, interpersonal morality *must* differ from other normative domains on any interpretation, relational or otherwise, that aims to make sense of it as a coherent set of requirements that reflect the equal standing of all. Nor have we encountered compelling principled reasons for thinking that the relational paradigm cannot be extended in this way.

Philosophers attracted to a broadly relational approach to morality tend to gloss over its standing as a self-standing normative domain. Thus, it is sometimes said that moral duties are grounded in an abstract relationship we stand in to those who have claims against us that is analogous to the special relationships we stand in to friends and colleagues and members of a family group, a relationship we might call "fellow humanity."[44] But the analogy is specious. The familiar relationships that we recognize as sources of special obligations have a historical and social reality, consisting in patterns of causal interaction that are psychologically salient for those caught up in them. The relationship of fellow humanity, by contrast, involves joint instantiation by different individuals of a morally significant property, such as the capacity for reason or for principled self-determination. This is, as I remarked above, a merely logical relationship. To say that moral obligations are owed to those to whom we are related as fellow humans is merely to designate the maximally inclusive manifold of individuals who potentially have moral claims against us, and against whom we ourselves have claims. It does not serve to specify some antecedent relationship that might provide a "foothold" or "common source" (to use Thompson's helpful expressions) for the normative nexus that interpersonal morality defines.[45]

4.3. Anti-Individualism about the Normative

I have been suggesting that it is open to us to interpret interpersonal morality as a self-standing domain of relational requirements. Requirements of this sort are not grounded in any independent relationship that might obtain between the individuals to whom they apply, and it is therefore possible that they might regulate our interactions with any agent who has moral standing, including individuals we have never before encountered. But the resulting relational interpretation of interpersonal morality has some significant normative implications that we now need to consider.

In chapters 2 and 3 of this book, I argued that considerations of moral rightness, interpreted in relational terms, have normative significance for two different parties. For the agent, they are considerations that are registered in reflection as presumptive constraints on the will, defining normative requirements that ordinarily have to be complied with. For the claimholder, they have a different kind of normative significance, representing considerations that make it fitting to hold the agent to the directed obligation that is owed to the claimholder, in the way that is characteristic of relations of interpersonal accountability. Relational moral requirements thus provide a kind of normative scaffold for the interactions between the two parties that are distinctively connected through them. It is in this sense that, as noted in the preceding section, they are held in common by the individuals whom they link.

This relational theory of morality, however, interacts in interesting ways with the general theory of normativity. In particular, it looks as if there might be some tension between the idea that there are moral obligations, on the one hand, and some popular approaches to practical normativity on the other. Many of the most influential accounts of reasons for action are broadly individualistic; they affirm that questions about what a given person has reason to do depend, in some way or other, on facts about the subjective attitudes of that individual in particular. Thus, Humeans of a fairly familiar kind hold that what an agent has reason to do is a function, in part, of the agent's desires or wants, broadly construed. On this kind of approach, facts about an individual's motivational profile are either reason-giving in themselves, or they are understood as states that condition the reason-giving force of other facts about the agent's situation.[46] Similarly, constructivists about normativity claim that normative principles of all kinds are binding for an agent in virtue of the agent's individual attitudes, which commit the agent to treating some considerations rather than others as reasons for action and for other attitudes.[47]

If we understand practical reasons in these recognizably individualist terms, however, it becomes very difficult to make sense of the kind of normative nexus that I have taken moral obligations to represent. The basic idea, as I just noted, is that the obtaining of a directed moral obligation—its being the case that A owes it morally to B to act in a certain way, or that B has a moral claim against A that A so act—should have normative significance for two distinct agents. The directed obligation represents a presumptive constraint on the deliberations of A about what to do, as well as a consideration that makes it fitting or appropriate for B to adopt a distinctive practical stance toward A, holding A to account with regard to the obligation. According to the individualist approach to normativity, however, whether reasons of these kinds exist for A and B will depend on facts about their different psychological profiles, facts that go beyond the obtaining of the directed obligation itself, and that are liable to vary independently of each other. Under these philosophical assumptions, it is hard to see how a genuine moral nexus of the kind we have been discussing could really obtain.

The facts, whatever they are, that suffice to determine that A has reason to comply with a directed obligation that is owed to B should also suffice to establish that B has reason to adopt toward A an accountability-conferring stance with regard to the obligation, and vice-versa. But individualism does not appear to deliver this result. The facts that go into determining that the obligation is a presumptive normative constraint on A's exertions of agency include facts about A's attitudinal profile; but no set of facts of this kind could, on individualist assumptions, determine what stances B has reason to adopt toward A. A and B might come to develop attitudes that fortuitously align with each other, ensuring that, at least as long as the alignment persists, the directed obligation is a source of reasons for each of them. But this is not the kind of normative nexus that we take moral obligations to constitute. The obtaining of the directed obligation should *itself* provide the parties that it implicates with reasons to adopt the attitudes toward it that are appropriate to their different positions. Its normative significance for the two people who are bound by it should not depend on the fortuitous alignment of factors extraneous to it.

One response to this might be to observe that on any plausible account of normativity, there are going to be some subjective conditions on one's reasons, if only constraints of an epistemic nature. Thus, whether B has reason to adopt toward A a responsibility-conferring attitude has to depend, in some measure, on information about A that is at least accessible to B. It would hardly be fitting for B to blame A, for instance, unless B has reason to believe that A has done something to flout duties that A owed to B, and this will be a matter of B's subjective epistemic situation. By the same token, A can be said to have flouted an obligation owed to B only if A had reason to believe that the obligation obtains and that the action in question would violate it. But this observation does not defuse the apparent tension between individualist accounts of normativity and robustly relational accounts of the moral right.

The normative significance of a directed obligation for the two parties who are connected by it is filtered, we may concede, by facts about the individual epistemic situation of each of them. But the role of these epistemic filters is to make accessible to the two parties a normative nexus that obtains independently of whether they are in a position to grasp it.[48] It is in this way only shallowly conditioned by subjective facts about the parties' epistemic situation. Individualist accounts, by contrast, posit deeper subjective conditions on normativity. In different ways, Humeans and constructivists both want to say that considerations are made normative for a given agent by facts about that agent's attitudinal profile, which function not to make accessible to the agent reason-giving considerations that independently obtain, but to constitute them as reasons for the agent in the first place.[49] This is the kind of position that seems difficult to reconcile with the relational conception of normativity, which takes directed moral obligations and claims to provide reasons for two different persons who may have never so much as met each other before, and whose attitudinal profiles will therefore not antecedently be coordinated in any way.

Individualist approaches differ, among other things, on the scope of coverage they aspire to achieve. Constructivism, as I understand it, is at least sometimes put forward as a general account of normativity in any domain,[50] but other versions of individualism are less ambitious. Humeans, for instance, typically take reasons for action to be constituted by motivating attitudes of the agents to whom they apply, but they don't, or needn't, affirm that reasons for other kinds of attitudes, such as beliefs and emotions, have similar subjective conditions. A more restricted position of this kind might apply, at most, only to one side of the alleged moral nexus.

Directed obligations represent presumptive constraints on the agency of the person who stands under them; but for the person to whom they are owed, their normative significance is at least partly of a different nature. They are reasons, in the first instance, not for actions on the claimholder's part, but for emotional attitudes, including centrally those through which accountability is conferred on the agent who is subject to the obligation. Reasons of this kind are considerations that make reactive and other forms of blame fitting or warranted, in response to the flouting of a valid moral obligation on the agent's part. But the Humean about reasons need not maintain that reasons of this kind are subjectively conditioned by the claimholder's motivational profile. The Humean account of reasons for action therefore does not require us to think that a directed obligation can be in place only if the attitudinal profiles of both parties to the moral nexus align in a nonfortuitous way. It is enough for agents to have the attitudes that render the obligation normatively binding for them. Once this condition is satisfied, the Humean might say, there is a claim in place that the other party holds against the agent. This in turn means that the agent's disregard of the obligation amounts to a disregard of another person's claim, which is sufficient to render fitting reactive and other forms of blame by the claimholder.

This might appear to diminish somewhat the tension between Humean individualism concerning reasons for action and the relational account of morality. But the appearance is misleading. As noted in section 3.1 above, the social dimension of morality is complex; it is a matter not merely of reasons for accountability-conferring attitudes on the part of those affected by an immoral agent's behavior, but of their having accountability-related reasons for action as well. The attitudes and actions characteristic of blame represent elements in an economy of social esteem and disesteem that serves to structure our social relations and to incentivize and reinforce compliance with basic moral standards. But it is open to us to step back from our participation in this system, and to reflect on whether it is reasonable for us to accede in the reactions and behaviors to which it disposes us. In doing this, we pose for ourselves a question about our reasons for action, asking (inter alia) whether we should continue to contribute normally to the economy of esteem and disesteem, or should instead attempt to withdraw from it, ignoring or disregarding our blame reactions in our interpersonal relations with other persons. Reasons for action are also at issue when it comes to nonreactive forms of blame, including such behaviors as avoidance of the wrongdoer, withdrawal from trust-based relationships with the wrongdoer, and so on.

The normative significance of relational norms for claimholders, then, is at least partly a matter of their providing the claimholder with reasons for action of this kind. These reasons may in some sense be derivative from the reasons for reactive blame that the flouting of relational obligations represents. It is the fact that such wrongdoing renders resentment and other reactive attitudes fitting that gives us pro tanto reason to accede to our participation in the economy of esteem and disesteem, and to adjust our behavior toward the wrongdoer in ways that express the reactive emotions that are appropriate under these conditions. That is why I said above that the normative significance of directed obligations for claimholders is "in the first instance" a function of reasons for attitudes rather than for actions. But reasons for action are secondarily also in play. To the extent that this is the case, a Humean individualism about such reasons will still seem at odds with the relational account of the moral that I have been trying to develop in this book.

To this, the individualist about the normative will naturally respond: so much the worse for the relational approach. Most radically, one could appeal to this kind of individualism to argue for a skeptical take on relational accounts of normativity in any domain. According to this form of skepticism, the appearance that there is ever a genuine normative nexus of the sort we have been discussing is an illusion. At bottom, there are just the reasons that people who are differently situated have for doing and feeling different things. Sometimes these individual reasons fortuitously align, in ways that might lead us to think that there is a normative connection that links two people with each other, as in cases of an ordinary promissory exchange. But strictly speaking there is no such connection; that is, the reasons of the two parties to the exchange are not constitutively tied to each other, so that it would be possible, in principle, for the promise-given reasons of one party to change, without changes either in the nature of the promise, the reasons of the other party, or the epistemic situation that the parties both find themselves in.[51]

A different position that retains a commitment to individualism about reasons might hold that there can be a normative nexus, but only under conditions in which there is an antecedent meeting of the minds by the parties that it links. According to this position, it is open to individuals to make it the case that they have reasons for action and attitudes that are constitutively connected to the reasons of another party. They can, for instance, undertake to do something together with the other party, forming a joint commitment that shapes the normative situation of each of them, going forward. Or they could enter into some other kind of transaction that binds them to each other, creating reasons that hang together in the right way (for instance, through participation in a common practice or convention).

Under these conditions, the individualist might concede that a normative nexus can come to exist. But the relevant conditions would precisely not be in place in all of the cases to which relational moral norms would seem to extend. As we saw in section 4.2, cosmopolitan moral requirements, when interpreted in relational terms, represent self-standing normative structures that need not be grounded in any antecedent relational interaction or connection to the parties that they link. But individualism apparently entails that there could be no self-standing normative structures of this kind, even if it does not necessarily rule out the very possibility of a distinctively relational requirement. On the present interpretation, individualism precisely requires that a relational nexus of directed obligations and corresponding claims be based in some antecedent relation between the parties to it, one that ensures the presence in them of the individual conditions that reasons for actions and attitudes presuppose. Individualism, on this interpretation, could therefore be understood as a form of revisionism about relational moral requirements.

As should be clear by now, I myself favor the idea that directed moral requirements and claims constitute a self-standing normative domain, one that is not grounded in any antecedent relation or connection between the parties that fall under its manifold. But I concede that this position will be difficult to sustain if one accepts an individualist account of normativity (in either a global or a more qualified formulation). If they are willing to countenance them at all, individualists will grant that there can be relational requirements and claims only in circumstances in which there is an independent connection between the parties who are thus related. The result would be a restriction in the class of situations in which genuinely directed moral requirements and claims could be in place. But that is only to be expected: insofar as the relational interpretation of normativity has metaethical presuppositions, it will be hostage to metaethical fortune.

There is obviously not the space here to undertake an independent assessment of individualism about the normative. But there are three points that may be worth emphasizing in this connection, at least very briefly. The first has to do with the modern, cosmopolitan conception of morality that I have invoked at various points in my discussion. So far, I have mainly emphasized the idea that this conception aspires to acknowledge the maximally inclusive character of the community of agents whose interests count for moral reflection. The suggestion is that we inhabit a world together with others who are equally real, and that moral obligations must be traced directly to the equal standing of the members of this inclusive notional community. This aspect of universalistic morality is straightforwardly accommodated on the relational approach, insofar as it treats moral obligations as connected to claims that others have against us, just insofar as they are members of this inclusive manifold of equals.

But it is also part of the modern conception of morality that its obligations are universal in a different sense: they not only reflect the equal standing of all persons, but they are binding on all individuals who are equipped with normal capacities for moral agency. Morality is in this way a source of requirements for everyone. But this is an aspect of the modern conception that will be difficult for individualists to make sense of, quite independently of whether moral requirements are interpreted in relational or in nonrelational terms. On individualist views, reasons of various kinds are a function of the subjective attitudes of the agent whose actions they would regulate, including their desires and dispositions or their beliefs about what there is reason to do. But it is a philosophical challenge to establish that all agents have the subjective attitudes that would secure for them compelling reason to comply with moral requirements, compatibly with individualistic assumptions. The most promising strategy for securing this result might be the familiar Kantian suggestion that the commitment to comply with the moral law is somehow built into the structure of agency, so that it can be regarded as an element in the subjective outlook of all individuals who are capable of self-determination.[52] But the prospects for successfully executing this strategy are not, in my opinion, terribly bright. The upshot is that individualism about the normative seems difficult to reconcile with the modern conception of universalistic morality on any interpretation of it, relational or nonrelational.

A second point worthy of notice in this connection is that our accountability practices seem to incorporate a commitment to anti-individualism about moral reasons. I noted in the chapter 3 that these practices have a relational deep structure; they involve responses to wrongdoing that are ordinarily occasioned by a disregard for relational claims, and this is reflected in their cognitive content as well. Resentment, for instance, both is, and is understood to be, a response to actions that wrong the person subject to it. What makes this reactive attitude fitting, then, are facts about the willful violation of claims on the part of an agent. But from the standpoint of a participant in the practice of interpersonal accountability, the kind of subjective conditions that standardly figure in individualist accounts of the normative do not enter into it at all.

To be sure, resentment and other reactive forms of blame do attribute to the agent who is their target attitudes of some kind or other, specifically including attitudes of disregard for another person's moral claims against them. But reactive blame will typically be warranted on the claimholder's part so long as this condition is satisfied. It is not necessary, in addition, to establish the presence in the agent of the kinds of motivational and belief states that individualists take to be conditions of reasons for action.[53] If A is normatively competent, as we might put it, then it would be fitting for B to blame A when A acts with contempt for or indifference to B's claims. This is true, regardless of whether A's desiderative profile includes an attitude of concern to respect the moral requirements that are intuitively associated with those claims, and regardless of whether A's normative beliefs commit A to accepting the validity of those requirements. In this way, our practices of interpersonal accountability seem to reflect a pragmatic rejection of individualistic assumptions about normativity. Individualism is in tension not merely with the relational interpretation of morality, but with the participant understanding of our familiar reactions to moral infractions. This is perhaps not surprising if, as I argued in the preceding chapter, our practices of interpersonal accountability are themselves structured around relational moral norms.

The third and final point I wish to emphasize about individualism concerns obligation. As noted earlier, the normative phenomena that individualists most saliently take to have implicit subjective conditions are reasons for action rather than for other attitudes. Thus, Humeans typically contend that one can have reason to pursue a given goal only if one has a desire (broadly construed) that suitably aligns with such a pursuit (for example, a desire either to achieve the goal directly, or for something else that would be advanced by its realization). As was emphasized in chapter 2, however, the normative significance of moral considerations for the agent consists in the provision of obligations, rather than merely aspirational reasons for action. That it would be morally wrong to do X is not just a consideration that counts against doing it, but one that enters the deliberative field as a presumptive constraint on one's agency (of the form: whatever else you do, don't do X!). But obligations or practical requirements, in this sense, do not appear to be the sorts of normative phenomena that are naturally thought of as grounded in or conditioned by an agent's desires. Indeed, in our developmental experience, our initial encounter with practical requirements is likely to be in contexts in which they are precisely at odds with our desires. We come to understand what it is to be under an obligation by seeing that obligations constrain us even when we do not feel like complying with them. Obligations thus do not seem to be auspicious candidates for treatment in standard Humean terms.

As I observed in section 2.1, there are individualistic approaches that provide at least potential models for understanding practical requirements. Identity-based accounts, for instance, trace obligations to features of one's practical outlook that are constitutively bound up with one's conception of who one is. These features might well include aspects of one's desiderative or motivational profile, such as the care one has for another person whom one loves. But this strategy seems unpromising when it comes to making sense of the kinds of moral obligations that have been at the center of discussion in the present chapter.

Consider, for instance, the transactional obligations that are generated by promises and agreements between two parties. I suggested earlier that individualists might concede that relational obligations can be in place in such cases, insofar as their transactional character makes for a meeting of the minds between the parties to them. But further reflection raises doubts about whether relational models aptly apply even to cases of this kind. Most significantly, there is a temporal dimension to such transactional cases that seems fundamentally at odds with individualistic approaches. Let us grant that the promissory exchange brings together the attitudes of promisor and promisee at the point in time when the transaction between them is entered into, mobilizing in them some identity-based concern to take the promise seriously. The promise, once it has been made, generates an obligation that remains in force, going forward, until its terms have been discharged. But there is nothing in the promissory exchange that will guarantee the persistence of the subjective attitudes it relies on into the future. The promisor, having entered into the promissory undertaking with a sincere concern to honor it, might lose interest in it over time, coming to care much more vividly about other things. The traditional individualist about reasons for action should say that the promisor's obligation to fulfill the terms of the promise will change with time, in accordance with these changes in the promisor's motivational profile. But this is completely at variance with our understanding of how promissory obligation works.

In sum, standard individualist stories about the normative seem peculiarly ill-equipped to deal with central features of the modern conception of morality. They have difficulty making sense of the universal applicability of moral requirements, of the conditions that warrant reactions of interpersonal accountability, and of the status of moral considerations as obligations, and not merely as aspirational reasons for action. Individualism about normativity may be in tension with the relational approach I have been developing, but this is because it is more fundamentally in tension with basic aspects of morality that the relational approach helps to illuminate.

For my part, I do not believe that individualism about the normative is an independently plausible position to take. But that is not a view that can be defended here. It is enough, for present purposes, to observe that those who are committed to individualism will find it a struggle to make sense of many aspects of the moral domain. These include, most saliently, the very features of modern morality that the relational approach seems especially well equipped to help us understand.[54]

4.4. Agent-Relativity and Morality as an Ideal

In chapter 2, I suggested that it is part of our conventional understanding of moral obligation that it involves constraints on behavior that are agent-relative in character. The moral prohibition on duplicity or deceit does not give us the objective of reducing the incidence of these forms of conduct in the population at large, but enjoins us not to act in these ways ourselves. I suggested, furthermore, that the relational notion of a directed obligation promises to illuminate this feature in our conventional understanding of morality. The idea was that the paradigm examples of directed obligation, such as the obligations that are created by promises, are intuitively understood to be in the way of agent-relative constraints, and that this feature of them is connected to the directed character of the obligations at issue. Having made a promise that I would do something, I owe it to the promisee that I should myself do the very thing (whatever it was) that I promised to do. This obligation is neither equivalent to, nor derivable from, an agent-neutral commitment to promote the general goal of promissory compliance in the local or global community.

In light of the discussion in the present chapter, however, it might be wondered whether this argument trades on an aspect of the paradigm examples that does not generalize to all of the cases that fall under the universal moral nexus. Promissory obligation, as we have seen, involves a specific transaction between the two parties that it links, and this seems to have a bearing on its agent-relative character. By making a promise to someone, I establish a relationship with the promisee that grounds a directed duty, owed specifically to the promisee, that I should fulfill my promise. The promissory transaction thus connects me with the promisee in a way that renders intelligible my agent-relative duty to satisfy the terms of the promise.

Something similar is true of other cases in which directed duties arise from causal or historical interactions between the parties that they link. If I have benefited in particular from the costly assistance of a stranger, I owe my benefactor a duty of gratitude, one that can be complied with by reciprocating in some fashion for the efforts that were undertaken on my behalf. I would not count as fulfilling this obligation if I were merely to promote the general objective of rewarding benefactors for the sacrifices they have made on behalf of people in need of assistance; rather I must do something to express gratitude toward the specific individual who has benefited me. Similarly, the directed duties that derive from the special relationships we stand in to friends and family members have an agent-relative character that is appropriate to the historical connection between two people that relationships of this kind essentially involve. Friends owe each other duties of loyalty that they would not discharge by promoting the general value of friendship in the community at large, but that require them to stand by each other in moments of anxiety and need.

It is natural to associate directed obligations with the valuable forms of interpersonal relationship that are enabled by them. T. M. Scanlon, for instance, traces the reason-giving force of moral requirements to the value of what he calls mutual recognition.[55] His idea is that a contractualist interpretation of moral requirements enables us to see how compliance with them makes possible a distinctively valuable form of relationship, whereby the parties acknowledge each other as sources of claims against each other. Though it requires qualification and development, I find this to be a deeply suggestive proposal, and I shall return to it later in this section. In the meantime, I note that Scanlon's idea seems to have natural application to the kinds of examples we have just been discussing, where directed requirements are grounded in an antecedent relationship between the parties that are connected through them. The promisor has already entered into a relationship of some kind with the promisee through the making of the promise, defining them both as parties to a single normative nexus. Compliance with the requirements and claims that constitute this nexus enables them to conduct this existing relationship in a distinctively valuable way, on a basis of mutual recognition or regard.

Similar remarks apply to the other cases we have discussed, involving the relationships between benefactor and beneficiary and between friends or members of a close family. Directed obligations grow out of the antecedent relationships that are in place in these cases, and by fulfilling those obligations the parties are able to structure their ongoing relationship with each other in a valuable way. The agent-relative character of the requirements that are here in place seems connected to the fact that there is an existing relationship between the agents who are subject to them, one that can be managed better or worse, where compliance with the requirements is a condition for conducting them well. By flouting the terms of their agreements, promisors impair their own relationship with promisees. Doing this might, in the philosopher's familiar scenario, bring it about that five other promissory relationships are not similarly impaired; but insofar as the promisor is not a party to *those* ongoing relationships, this consideration lacks the significance for the promisor's deliberations that the impairment of his or her own relationships clearly has.

When we turn to the self-standing relational requirements that also seem to be a part of a cosmopolitan conception of morality, however, things seem otherwise. Here there is no antecedent, nonnormative relationship or interaction between the parties to the moral nexus that is the basis for its linkage of obligations and claims. It is therefore not the case that the parties are already connected to each other through an ongoing relationship that, whether they like it or not, it is up to them to conduct better or worse. In this general situation, I might well be invested in the value of relationships of mutual recognition. But why should this concern take a distinctively agent-relative form? Why should I be concerned that I myself stand in relationships of this kind with people I have not yet met or interacted with, rather than being concerned that valuable relationships of the same kind should generally be promoted in the larger social world? Why should I refrain from stepping on the gouty toe of the stranger if—as philosophers have the power to arrange—by doing so I can bring it about that five other agents respect the bodily interests of gout-stricken strangers that they will encounter sometime in the future?

In considering this question, we cannot appeal to the fact that I am already party to an ongoing relationship with the person whose gouty toe is vulnerable to being affected by the personal trajectory of my body. In the cases at issue, there is no such relationship to appeal to, and so it isn't a matter of conducting better or worse a relationship in which I am already implicated. To render intelligible the agent-relative character of our moral concerns in such situations, we therefore need to draw on considerations of some other kind.

But an alternative basis for understanding the agent-relativity of moral requirements is provided by the relational interpretation I have been developing. In the preceding discussion, it was assumed that agents have a legitimate interest in conducting the relationships in which they are already implicated on the best possible terms. Being a participant in an ongoing relationship of this kind is a consideration that can make sense of a person's concern for the terms on which that relationship in particular is conducted. But a distinct consideration that might ground such a concern is a person's standing as the targeted object of a moral claim. On the relational approach, individuals can have claims specifically against us, regardless of whether we already stand in nonnormative relationships of any particular kind with them. In respecting those claims against us, we relate to their bearers in a way that acknowledges the significance of their interests for our agency, and that ensures that there will be no basis for their resenting what we have done. This is something that might reasonably matter to us even if we have not antecedently interacted with them at all.

Consider again the case in which five gout victims' claims will be respected by others if we ourselves flout the claim of a sixth. This is a situation in which it makes all the difference against whom the various claims are held. The single victim has a claim on us in particular, and so it is naturally important to us to conduct ourselves in a way that respects that claim, going forward. That five other agents will flout claims that different strangers have against them is not in the same way important *for us*, since it is not a consideration that directly affects the question of how we relate to those who have claims against us. The intellectual temptation to suppose that we might appropriately honor claims by promoting their maximal satisfaction in the population at large rests on a neglect of their relational structure; they are directed at specific individuals, and it matters to our thinking about a given claim whether we are the person against whom it is held. Indeed, it seems plausible that this same feature is what ultimately accounts for the agent-relativity of directed obligations even in the cases in which there is an antecedent relationship between the parties whom they link. The relationship between the promisor and the promisee matters in thinking about what the former must do, because it gives rise to a claim on the part of the promisee against the promisor in particular. It is true that the two parties are already implicated in a historical relationship, but this is significant for our understanding of the promisor's obligations only insofar as it bears on the question of the promisee's claims against the promisor.

This way of thinking about morality might seem to invite the charge of moral self-indulgence. The complaint would be that conscientious moral agents should not be prissily concerned with their own moral purity, but should care in the first instance about how others fare who are apt to be affected by what they do. If there are five moral claims that can be honored as a result of an action of mine that violates the claims of a sixth, then that is a small price to pay to ensure a better outcome for the larger universe of moral claimholders.

This complaint rests on a flawed conception of moral self-indulgence, however. As Bernard Williams argued long ago, there is such a thing as moral self-indulgence, understood as a defective form of moral motivation. It involves a reflexive concern for the virtues that are expressed in the actions that one performs, rather than for the first-order reasons to which those virtues themselves are properly responsive.[56] Understood in these terms, however, moral self-indulgence is a hazard to which agents are potentially subject according to any account of what morality requires of us, including nonrelational accounts such as utilitarianism. To act out of a concern for how one stands with regard to the claims of other people is not to betray an objectionable obsession with one's own moral virtue, as opposed to a concern for the legitimate interests of other agents. Rather, it reflects a proper concern for those interests, understood as considerations that ground inherently relational duties. Persons who are unwilling to violate a claim held against them in order to bring about a reduction in the overall number of claims-violations are responding directly to the deeply relational structure of moral obligations. Of course, it is a matter of philosophical controversy whether the obligations of impartial morality are inherently relational in their structure. If they are, however, then a concern for how one stands in regard to others need not betray a preoccupation for one's own virtue as opposed to the claims of others. Concerns about moral self-indulgence therefore do not represent an independent basis for objecting to the relational story I have been telling.

Let us now return to the idea that compliance with directed moral obligations makes it possible for us to stand in relations of mutual recognition. I noted earlier that this idea has natural application in cases in which there is an ongoing relationship between the parties who are connected by moral requirements and claims. The concern, in this context, is to conduct a relationship one is already implicated in on a basis of mutual recognition. But what about the situations we have just been discussing, in which directed moral requirements apply to people who do not already stand in any significant interpersonal relationship? In honoring the claims that others have against us in these situations, our concern is not to continue an ongoing relationship in accordance with the relational standards that connect the parties to it. It is, rather, to ensure that we relate to anyone who might be affected by our actions in accordance with such standards. If people we have never met before have claims against us, as I have argued that they can, then we will rightly strive to conduct our planning agency on a basis of respect for those claims, treating them as presumptive constraints on our activities. To do this is, among other things, to show a concern for how one relates to the bearer of the claim.

I have elsewhere suggested that moral requirements should be understood to be relationship constituting, not relationship based; they make possible valuable forms of interpersonal relationship, even if they are not grounded in some antecedent pattern of interaction between the parties related through them.[57] But talk about "mutual recognition" is somewhat misleading in this context, taken as a characterization of the value that is realized through compliance with moral norms. If we interpret such talk in literal terms, it would appear to presuppose moral reciprocity. Two individuals would be party to a relationship of mutual recognition, on this literal interpretation, just in case each of them acknowledges and accords the claims that the other holds against them. The reciprocal element in mutual recognition is an important respect in which it resembles a different relational value that is sometimes mentioned in this connection, as an analogy or model for the value realized through compliance with moral requirements. This is the value of friendship, which figured in my discussion of the positive moral ideal of interpersonal recognition in section 2.4 above. But if mutual recognition involves something like the kind of reciprocity characteristic of friendship, it is also, for that very reason, an ideal that does not literally apply to many of our relationships within the manifold of moral persons.

The problem is that people have moral claims against us, on any plausible construal of relational morality, even when they do not show respect or concern for our moral claims against them. There are things that it is clearly impermissible for me to do to other people, even if they are out to kill me or to subordinate me completely to their will. (Force may plausibly be used to defend myself against such assaults, for instance, but only to a degree that is both necessary and proportionate, given the nature of the threat that is posed.) Under these circumstances, there is no prospect of realizing the literal value of mutual recognition in my interactions with those who have set themselves against me. They have, through their actions, already seen to it that this reciprocal value cannot be achieved, regardless of what I might do to them. And yet, as I just noted, they continue to have moral claims against me. It follows that the concern that leads me to honor those claims cannot be a concern for mutual recognition, construed in the literal way that would require the different parties to a relationship to honor the claims that each has against the others.

Interpersonal morality, on the relational interpretation of it, includes principles that apply to everyone, and that define obligations that are owed potentially to each member of the extensive manifold of persons that it defines. General compliance with such principles would bring about a situation in which all individuals conduct their affairs on a basis of equality, acknowledging that the interests of members of this extensive manifold count equally, and honoring the claims that others have against them in virtue of their equal standing within the manifold. Acknowledging and honoring other persons' claims is a way of recognizing them as bearers of moral claims. So each person's recognition of others will be reciprocated, under conditions of general compliance with relational moral principles, through a similar attitude of recognition on the part of those who have claims against that person. This idealized situation might aptly be described as one of mutual recognition or regard.[58]

Each of us, as individuals, is powerless to bring about this idealized condition through our own efforts alone. It requires the collaborative agency of others, something over which we do not exercise control. What is in our power is to do our part in the scheme of interlocking ends that is represented by a situation of literal mutual recognition. The concern to act in this way, however, is not derivative from a concern for the value of the condition that would be realized if everyone else were doing his or her part, as well. If it were, then the concern would presumably dissipate as soon as it becomes clear to us that the specific claimholders we are interacting with do not respect our claims against them. Situations of this kind make it clear that the fundamental value that is realized through moral agency is not derivative from the collaborative good of mutual regard. It is an independent value that involves a distinctive way of relating to others, on a basis of what I have called interpersonal recognition. Those who realize this value in their actions acknowledge the moral claims that other individuals have against them, and honor those claims in their decisions about how to comport themselves in the world. They do this, moreover, in the understanding that their recognitional stance remains valuable even if it is not literally reciprocated.

It is sometimes said that morality enables us each to live in harmony with our fellows, and that it in this way contributes to the quality of our own lives.[59] The point is suggestive, but also somewhat misleading, for reasons that dovetail with the concerns about mutual recognition discussed above. Other people have claims against us even when they do not acknowledge our claims against them, and respecting their claims under these conditions will not bring about a condition of mutual recognition. But neither will it achieve social harmony, necessarily. On the contrary, especially under the conditions of entrenched inequality that prevail in most societies, standing up for the claims of some will likely put us in opposition to others, including most notably the powerful and the privileged. A morally decent life is often one that stirs up controversy and conflict, posing awkward questions to the complacent and challenging the conventional wisdom about social arrangements. To the extent this is the case, acknowledgment of the moral claims of others will not promote harmony with our fellows, any more than it will ensure a situation of literally reciprocated recognition and regard. This is an important respect in which relational moral values are different from those involved in relationships of friendship or personal attachment.

The personal value that is realized through deliberate compliance with relational moral requirements is more subtle than these conventional formulations might suggest, though it is no less important for that. It is the value that is achieved when we have done what we could to honor the claims that other individuals hold against us, regardless of whether they have shown a similar regard for our claims against them. To satisfy this condition is to adopt a special sort of attitude toward people, relating to them (as I put the point above) in a way that seems distinctively worth caring about. This is a claim about intrinsic value and, as with other such claims, it does not admit of proof or demonstration. I cannot establish the goodness of the attitude of interpersonal recognition by deriving it from premises that are independently more compelling, for example. The best that can be done is to try to articulate the aspects of this stance that make it valuable, in the hopes that others will concur in recognizing the value once its good-making features have thus been laid bare.[60]

There are different strands that could be emphasized in the attempt to articulate more specifically what is valuable about interpersonal recognition. We might start with Scheffler's idea, discussed in section 4.2 above, that there is an egalitarian form of relationship that we intuitively recognize to be valuable across a wide range of contexts. I have repeatedly referred to the postulate of equal standing that is a hallmark of modern, cosmopolitan thinking about the moral realm. We feel that it would be absurd to deny that the interests of each individual are neither more nor less important than the interests of any other. It matters to us that we should do justice to this desideratum in the conduct of our lives, and a plausible way of understanding this concern is in deliberative terms. Morality, on the relational interpretation of it, attributes equal importance to the interests of each individual as potential bases of claims that are held against others. So to make a conscientious effort to comply with its requirements is, in effect, to deliberate about conduct that might affect other people on a basis of equality with them, something we moderns rightly care about.

Granted, the ideal of relational equality plays out differently in the moral context than it does within the ongoing thick relationships that are Scheffler's primary concern. A relationship such as friendship operationalizes the egalitarian deliberative constraint through the acknowledgment by both parties that their interests are equally important. Interpersonal recognition, however, insofar as it remains valuable even when it is not literally reciprocated, lacks this element of mutual acknowledgment. But this difference between the cases undermines neither our conviction of the importance of unreciprocated recognition nor our sense that it is a special case of a generic value that is also realized in the context of ongoing relationships between individuals. Important here is the idea, explicated above, that the principles through which we realize interpersonal recognition are the very principles that would make possible a relationship of genuinely mutual recognition, one in which the egalitarian deliberative constraint is reciprocally satisfied.

A distinct strand that might be emphasized by way of articulating the value of interpersonal recognition is that it affects concretely one's relationships with other people, going forward, even in cases in which it is not fully reciprocated. By honoring the claims that others have against us, we ensure that those affected by our conduct will not have a legitimate complaint to bring against us on the basis of it. We will have done them no moral injury or wrong, and we will in this way ensure some degree of protection from their justified resentment. This is connected to another consideration that I mentioned earlier in connection with the value of interpersonal recognition, that of justifiability to others.[61] When we conscientiously comply with relational moral requirements, we can in principle appeal to the requirements to justify our conduct to each of the persons it affects, showing in this way that we have lived up to the obligations that we owe specifically to them, and that we have honored the claims they hold against us. We could look them in the eye and give an account of ourselves specifically to them, if called on to do so. People intuitively feel that it matters whether they are able to relate to others on this kind of basis, and this reflects the widespread conviction that interpersonal recognition is a valuable way of conducting oneself.

Taking these discrete strands together, it seems to me highly plausible to suppose that our own lives go better to the extent we satisfy the condition of interpersonal recognition in which these strands are interwoven. If, as I have argued, there are directed obligations that we owe to others, just insofar as they are persons who are equally real, then people who acknowledge those considerations as presumptive constraints on their agency will be deliberating correctly. They will be, in this respect at least, good practical reasoners. But this fails to capture the significant positive contribution that acknowledgment of moral obligations has on the agent; in acknowledging the claims that others have against us, we thereby relate to them on a distinctive basis, what I have called interpersonal recognition, which has a value that goes beyond its contribution to making us generically good practical reasoners. It is a noteworthy if underappreciated feature of interpersonal moral standards, on my interpretation of them, that compliance with them has this positive effect on agents and the lives that they lead.

Now, to focus primarily on this aspect of relational morality in deliberating about what to do would perhaps betray an objectionable self-concern, something in the ballpark of moral self-indulgence. The attention of conscientious moral agents should ordinarily be directed to the claims that others have against them, as considerations that constrain their deliberations about what to do in the way we have seen to be characteristic of practical requirements. To act out of consideration for such claims just is to deliberate in a way that acknowledges the equal standing of all. But the discussion in the preceding paragraphs suggests that compliance with this egalitarian deliberative constraint will bring it about, as a kind of secondary effect, that our own lives are made better as well. They will have been conducted on a basis of interpersonal recognition, reflecting a commitment to the equal importance of others that immunizes us from legitimate complaints about the effects of our conduct on them, and that makes it possible to give a compelling account of ourselves to them.

There is a role for considerations of this kind to play in thoughtful agents' awareness of the values realized through their agency, a role that will be salient in contexts of what we might call eudaimonistic reflection.[62] This is the kind of reflection we engage in when we think about what it is for our own lives to go well, identifying things that make them meaningful or worthwhile from our own point of view. This is a context, as it seems to me, in which the intrinsic value of interpersonal recognition might have a constructive role to play. The case of friendship, though disanalogous with interpersonal recognition in some respects, may help to illustrate the point.[63] To be a friend is, in the first instance, to acknowledge the special reasons and requirements that apply to us in virtue of standing in this relationship to another person. It is, for instance, to take another person to have claims against us just in virtue of being our friend, and to strive to honor and respect those claims. Attitudes of this kind track and respond to reasons that people have in virtue of standing in the relationship of friendship to others. But we also understand the relationship that is partly constituted by these kinds of recognitional attitudes to be valuable in itself, in ways that go beyond their value as generically correct responses to reasons. The relationship of friendship of which they are a part is among the things whose presence in our lives can contribute to making them meaningful and worth living, from our own point of view—for instance, as things that we take particular pride or satisfaction in, when we look back in reflection on how things have gone for us; or as personal values that give us reason to carry on in life in the first place.

It has been suggested that the value of relationships such as friendship can help us to understand the "reason-giving force" of the considerations associated with them.[64] This suggestion is initially somewhat puzzling, since true friends do not generally act, in the first instance, out of a concern to have the goods of friendship in their lives, but out of a concern for their friends. But the eudaimonistic significance of valuable relationships of this kind has an indirect role to play in bolstering our conviction that the considerations associated with them are serious reasons for action. Friends have claims against each other, just in virtue of standing in this relationship to each other; we might say that it is constitutive of friendship that these relational obligations obtain and are honored. As was noted in section 2.4, however, our sense that the normative constraints at issue are significant is connected to our understanding that the form of relationship in which they are implicated is independently valuable, something that we have reason to care about when we think about what it is for our own lives to go well.

As I have emphasized above, interpersonal recognition is different from friendship in lacking the element of mutuality. It is a way of relating to people rather than a full-fledged relationship with them, one that retains its value even under conditions in which it is not reciprocated by the individual who is its object. If this claim is plausible, however, then we should acknowledge that interpersonal recognition has a role to play in eudaimonistic reflection that is similar to the role played in this context by thick relationships such as friendship. Agents who have these attitudes are not merely reasoning correctly about what they are obligated to do; they are also realizing other values that people should care about when they survey their lives retrospectively or make provision for the future. Indeed, the fact that interpersonal recognition is valuable in this way helps to reassure us that the moral requirements to which it responds are genuine constraints on our conduct, and not merely arbitrary demands associated with an alien and questionable system of values. It is a significant contribution of the relational approach that it helps us to appreciate this eudaimonistic dimension of interpersonal morality, isolating a significant respect in which our own lives go better when we comply with its requirements.

5

From Interests to Claims

TO THIS POINT I have marshaled some considerations in favor of thinking about the moral domain in relational terms. Doing so, I have suggested, offers us the best hope of making sense of the characteristic normative features of morality, as it is conceived in the modern period. These features include, above all, the significance of morality for both individual deliberation and our social relations with each other. I have also discussed in general terms some of the challenges that are posed to the project of extending the relational model from the social contexts in which we first learn to operate with it to the entirety of the moral domain. Construed as a cosmopolitan framework for thinking about moral issues, the relational interpretation takes morality to consist in a set of self-standing obligations, which are not grounded in any antecedent relation in which agents stand to those who have claims against them. These obligations define duties that are owed to others, just insofar as they are persons with moral standing (in some still unspecified sense).

The present chapter takes up questions about the range and the internal structure of relational morality, understood along these general lines. I start (in section 5.1) with the question of what exactly it is to be a person with moral standing, in the sense relevant to the modern conception of morality. I suggest that it makes sense to proceed in two stages. We should start by thinking about the inclusive manifold of persons that modern morality defines as the set of persons who are capable of reciprocally recognizing the claims that they have against each other. Even here, as we shall see, there are grey areas that challenge our understanding of the extension of the moral nexus. But relational moral norms are capable, at least in principle, of playing both of their characteristic normative roles within the context of interactions between individuals who are equally capable of bipolar thought. We can then, in a second stage, consider extensions of the manifold of moral persons to include individuals who might be bearers of moral claims against others, even if they are not capable of honoring such claims themselves.

I turn next to the role of individual interests within a relational conception of the moral. As we saw in chapter 1, individual interests are to be distinguished from moral claims (just as the notion of a harm to someone's interests is different from the normative notion of a moral injury). But at the same time, interests seem to have direct relevance to the moral claims that are held by individuals, as I also suggested in chapter 1. I explore this issue in section 5.2. Taking as a point of reference some discussions of interests in relation both to rights and to remedies in private law, I argue that we should reject theories that attempt to reduce relational normative notions to nonrelational interests. (In this respect, too, the moral nexus should be understood as a domain of self-standing relational norms.) But there is nevertheless reason to think that the interests of individuals are relevant to questions about their claims. The basic idea, I suggest, is that there is nothing that we owe to members of the inclusive manifold of moral persons if their interests do not stand to be affected, in one way or another, by our agency.

If the argument of section 5.2 is on the right lines, it follows that the task of moral deliberation could be characterized in the following terms: how do we get from premises about the personal interests of individuals to conclusions about their moral claims? I discuss moral reasoning, so construed, in sections 5.3 and 5.4. I argue, in section 5.3, that we need to distinguish moral reasoning, in this sense, from practical deliberation of a more generic kind. I also consider the role of specifically normative interests in relation to moral claims, as well as the connections between interests and moral wrongs and the role of deontic considerations in thinking about our moral obligations *sans phrase*.

In section 5.4, I take up the question of the nature of the moral reasoning that gets us from interests to claims. I suggest that there may be no general procedure that will be followed implicitly in all cases of correct moral reasoning; the result would be an intuitionistic interpretation of relational morality. But nonintuitionistic interpretations are possible, as well. I consider, in this connection, T. M. Scanlon's moral contractualism, arguing that it can be understood as a theory of relational morality, describing a general schema for moving from personal interests to claims; I also argue that this is fundamental to its philosophical appeal.

5.1. Defining the Manifold: Who Are the Claimholders?

I have made repeated reference to the modern understanding of interpersonal morality in this book, noting that it operates with a maximally inclusive conception of the individuals who count for moral thought. According to this conception, it is a basic desideratum for morality that we inhabit a world together with other persons who are "equally real" (to recall Thomas Nagel's vivid expression), and whose interests are no less important than our own. I have also suggested, in section 4.3, that it is a distinct aspiration of universalistic conceptions of morality to identify obligations that are binding on a maximally extensive group of agents.

Translating these ideas into relational terms, the basic issue is about the domain of individuals who are linked through directed moral obligations and the claims that correspond to them. I have suggested that moral obligations, according to the relational conception of them, concern the claims that people have against us, just insofar as they are persons, equally real. But what, more precisely, is the definition of "person" for these purposes, construed as individuals who bear moral claims? And what is the extension of the class of agents on whom directed moral obligations are binding? In the idiom introduced by Michael Thompson, these are questions about the manifold of persons who are yoked together in the abstract and inclusive order of moral right, understood in relational terms.[1]

In section 4.2, I argued that there is nothing that would block, in principle, our understanding the manifold of moral persons as including (at a minimum) all individuals capable of bipolar thought. In particular, we can make sense of the idea that members of such a manifold might converge in thoughts about the abstract moral norms that link them to each other, even if they are not antecedently connected through bonds of history or culture or species nature or metaphysical substance.[2] Thompson is skeptical about this possibility. But I argued, against him, that it merely requires a modest form of abstraction, whereby individuals who are capable of thoughts about a conventional order of bipolar right—such as Roman private law—step back from it in reflection, and conceive of themselves as individuals who are competent with some kind of bipolar thought or other. They then have a concept that can be applied generally to define a more extensive class of moral persons, and to pose questions about what each member of this extensive class owes to the others, just insofar as they are individuals equipped with the capacities for bipolar thought. This is a path along which individuals who are not antecedently connected to each other might come to converge on thoughts about an abstract order of moral right that links them in a normative nexus of directed obligations and corresponding claims.

This strikes me as a natural place to begin when thinking about the manifold of moral persons under a relational conception of morality. That is, the minimal interpretation of the domain of persons over which cosmopolitan moral norms extend should be understood to include all individuals capable of thoughts about relational requirements of one kind or another. The rationale for this baseline interpretation of the manifold of moral persons is connected to the distinctive kind of normative significance that we have seen morality to have, both for agents and for other parties.

For agents, moral norms define practical requirements, which are registered in deliberation as presumptive constraints on agency. The relational approach makes sense of this dimension of the moral by interpreting morality as a set of directed obligations, defining things that we owe it to each other to do. The idea is that directed obligations of this kind are tailor-made to function as presumptive constraints on agency; they represent the original intuitive notion of an obligation, and are rightly understood to be considerations that define limits on our activities. They will be able to play this deliberative role, however, only for agents who possess the basic capacity to grasp bipolar normative thoughts about what one party owes to another. Furthermore, reflective agents who meet this basic condition would also seem capable in principle of grasping bipolar thoughts specifically about the moral obligations that they owe to other people. Thus, suppose I am right about the minimal exercise in abstraction involved in conceiving of oneself as a member of the class of individuals capable of bipolar thought. Then thoughts of what the members of this class owe to each other should be accessible to any individuals who belong to it, so long as they possess the capacities for reflection that are involved in elementary abstraction. These considerations make it reasonable to assume that relational moral obligations are binding, at a minimum, on all agents capable of entertaining relational normative thoughts.

The normative significance of moral obligations for other parties, I have suggested, lies in the provision of a normative basis for relations of interpersonal accountability. My argument has been that relational moral requirements are uniquely suited to this dimension of the moral. Insofar as such requirements connect to the claims of other parties, their violation would wrong the bearer of those claims, providing them with reasons for reactive and other forms of blame. As claimholders, however, individuals will be capable of responding to such reasons only to the extent that they have the capacity for bipolar normative thoughts. They must be able to see themselves as holding claims against other parties, and to understand the actions of those parties as ones that are not merely wrong, but that wrong them. Furthermore, for reasons just canvased, reflective agents who are capable of grasping some bipolar normative thoughts or other should also be able, through minimal abstraction, to think of themselves as members of a manifold that includes all individuals capable of bipolar thought, and to entertain thoughts about what each owes the others in this capacity. This suggests that we should assume the class of bearers of moral claims to include, at a minimum, all individuals who are competent with the basic conceptual elements of relational normativity. For that is the class of individuals who will be able, at least in principle, to respond directly to the accountability-related reasons that are provided by the flouting of moral claims.

Nearly all biological human beings, I will assume, fall within the manifold of moral persons, understood along these lines. At least this will be the case as long as we take facility with some bipolar normative concepts or other to be a fairly universal accomplishment among adult members of our species in the contemporary world. I shall provisionally operate on the assumption that this is the case, while allowing that the assumption is subject to empirical investigation that could potentially put pressure on it. Even with this assumption in place, however, it will be noted that there are some individual humans who do not satisfy the minimal conditions I have articulated for inclusion in the manifold of moral persons. Infants and young children, for instance, do not yet have competence with relational moral concepts. And yet, on any plausible conception of morality, they are individuals whose interests should count for moral reflection, and who are bearers of claims against us. Similar remarks apply to the elderly and others who, through illness or infirmity, have lost the facility with bipolar moral thoughts that they once exhibited.

Here, it seems to me, it is natural to take account of the temporal dimension of the lives that are in question. Infancy and adult infirmity do not designate classes of persons, but phases in the lives of individuals who, in their prime, normally exhibit some reasonable degree of facility with thoughts about what people owe to each other. Individuals who satisfy this condition can plausibly be assigned moral claims, and these claims, once assigned, could include claims to moral consideration even during phases when the claimholders are not (yet) able to assert the claims on their own behalf. Thus, to take a sadly topical example, adults might naturally feel resentful about how they were treated as children by the caregivers and mentors who subjected them to sex-

ual and other forms of abuse long ago. Similarly, with adults who have become
mentally infirm, we can intelligibly ask how they would have felt about the way
they are now being treated (in the assisted living facility to which they have
been sent, say) if they were fully aware of what was happening to them. In these
cases, we are dealing with individuals who satisfy the basic conditions for inclusion in the core manifold of moral persons at some point in their lives; this
seems sufficient to undergird the assignment to them of moral claims against
others in the manifold at the points in time when their capacities for relational
moral thought are attenuated or not yet developed.

There are two features of these examples that are worth pausing to emphasize. First, the treatment of them I have just proposed involves the assignment
of claims to persons who, at the time when the claims are operative, may not
be under any corresponding moral obligations toward others. This seems to
me uncontroversially true of cases that involve early infancy, before capacities
for coherent agency are even developed, and for later phases in a person's life
when such capacities may have largely dissipated. It would be absurd to say
that there are things that we owe to other people when we have lost our powers
of deliberation and choice, or at a period in our development before those
powers have even emerged.[3] This shows the coherence of postulating asymmetries within a manifold of moral persons: there can be individuals who, at
a given point in time, have moral claims against the rest of us, even if they do
not at that time have obligations that they owe to us.

Another thing to note about these examples is that they are prime candidates for the application of the kinds of vicarious reactive thoughts that were
discussed in section 3.4 above. Claimholders in the examples just considered
are not able to assert their moral claims on their own behalf. But at the time
when such claims may be flouted, it is open to the rest of us, acting on behalf
of the bearers of the claims, to assert the claims for them, subjecting the wrongdoers to indignation and other forms of blame. This is an important resource
that is made available by the relational account of the significance that obligations have for interpersonal practices of accountability. Applied to the recent
examples, we might think of the vicarious assertion of claims to be on behalf
of persons who are not yet, or who are no longer, able to assert claims for
themselves. But this resource, once it is available to us, could also be brought
to bear on other kinds of cases, in reference to claims assigned to individuals
who are never able to assert them for themselves.[4]

One example of this kind involves individual members of our species who,
through illness or genetic misfortune, will never be able to develop normal
adult capacities for bipolar or other forms of normative thought. We might

think of children who contract a disease that will kill them before their capacities for speech and thought can be developed very far, or people with intellectual disabilities that would merit clinical classification as severe or profound. In these cases, individuals clearly have moral claims against us, and yet there may be no time in their life at which they are able cogently to assert the claims they have on their own behalf. In including such people in the manifold of moral persons, we might plausibly be understood to be taking implicit account of their species nature. They belong to a biological kind whose members normally develop capacities for bipolar normative thought, and the conditions that prevent the emergence of such capacities in these individuals should therefore be understood in relation to these norms, as conditions that damage them or impede their natural development.[5] The vicarious assertion of claims on their behalf is a way of acknowledging this aspect of their situation. As individual human beings, they have a nature that non-arbitrarily situates them within the domain of moral claimholders, and our reactive responses to mistreatment of such individuals serve to acknowledge their standing as bearers of claims against others.

Here we extend the manifold of moral persons to include members of our species who will never acquire the capacities for bipolar thought that would equip them for relations of mutual recognition with other members of the manifold. But other kinds of extension are possible as well. Note, for one thing, that facility at bipolar thought is something that could be detached from membership in the human species. It is conceivable that there are rational creatures of one kind or another who are not human beings, but who nevertheless are able to entertain thoughts about what one individual owes to others. If there are such creatures, then it seems to me that they are straightforwardly eligible for membership in the manifold of moral persons, whatever else might be true about their species nature. They are both subject to moral obligations themselves, and bearers of claims against other members of the manifold. (For reasons that will become clear later in the present chapter, however, the nature of their claims against the rest of us will depend at least in part on the interests that can be assigned to individual members of this hypothetical kind.) We should also be prepared to include in the moral manifold artificial persons whose capacities for collective agency incorporate mechanisms for recognizing and responding to relational requirements. There are basic expectations that universities and private corporations owe it to their employees to live up to, for instance, something that becomes clear when we think about the resentment that people are naturally prone to when they are the targets of open harassment or mobbing in the workplace. And there are duties that run in the other direction as well: one might naturally feel one owes a debt of gratitude to one's employer if the company or institution has gone to great lengths to accommodate a personal crisis one was going through at home.

But what about further extensions, beyond the class of individual or collective agents (of whatever species) who are competent at bipolar normative thought? Let us start with the agential pole of the moral nexus: the class of individuals who are subject to moral obligations. Is it reasonable to think that this class extends beyond the class of individuals capable of relational normative judgment? This seems doubtful to me. The characteristic normative significance of directed duties, as we have seen, is that of practical requirements, which are registered in deliberation as presumptive constraints on agency. But an individual who is not capable of grasping bipolar normative thoughts will eo ipso be insensitive to the very thing that warrants this deliberative response to them. It doesn't seem reasonable to me to suppose that obligations are binding on a creature who is in this way unable to appreciate their characteristic form of normative significance. I suggested in section 4.3 above that practical requirements are not among the normative phenomena that are auspiciously understood to be conditioned by the subjective desires of the agent who stands under them. But it does seem to be a condition for standing under a practical requirement that one should be capable of appreciating that feature of it that suits it to figure as a presumptive constraint on one's agency. In the case at issue, the relevant feature is one's owing it to another party to do something; but this is precisely the kind of thought that is available only to those who have the capacity for bipolar thought.

A different route to this conclusion proceeds by reflection on the claims that correspond to directed obligations. When agents are subject to such obligations, there are individuals who have claims against them to compliance with the obligations, and who are eligible to be wronged by them in cases of noncompliance. But is it so much as possible to be wronged by the actions of an agent who is not competent to grasp thoughts about relational obligations? This seems doubtful to me. In section 1.1, I suggested that there is an attitudinal component to moral wrongs that is often neglected in discussions of them. To wrong people is, at least in part, to act with disregard for the claims that they have against one; this in turn involves a recognitional failure to acknowledge either the significance of their claims or their standing as individuals who are bearers of claims. But I don't believe one can act with the attitude of disregard for the claims of others if one lacks the competence to grasp the relational concept of a claim in the first place. An agent who is incapable of bipolar thought might be oblivious to the claims of others, but to be oblivious in this way is not to act with disregard for the claims that one fails to register. But if there is nothing an agent could do that would count as wronging another person, then it seems to me doubtful that that person really has claims against the agent, which is to say that the corresponding directed obligations are not really binding on the agent in the first place.

Philosophers sometimes maintain that blame can be a warranted response even in cases of actions done by agents who lack fully developed capacities for moral understanding and self-control.[6] This may or may not be correct.[7] But it seems to me that there is an agential capacity that represents a minimal necessary condition for warranted blame, which is elementary competence with concepts of relational obligation. Someone who lacks the capacity for bipolar thought will not so much as be capable of wronging other people; but as I argued in chapter 3, reactive and other forms of blame are precisely responses that are rendered fitting by the fact that one party has wronged another.

These considerations lead me to conclude that the manifold of agents who are bound by moral obligations extends only to individuals capable of bipolar normative thought. But what about the other pole of the moral nexus, that is, the potential claimholders? Here, it seems to me, things look different. We have already seen that our conception of the moral domain tolerates coherent asymmetries, cases in which we assign claims to an individual who is not at the time of the assignment subject to reciprocal obligations. Once this possibility is acknowledged, however, it seems very natural to entertain further extensions of the moral manifold, to include claimholders who are at no point in their normal existence capable of the forms of normative thought that would render them subject to relational obligations.

Plausible candidates for claimholders who do not stand under reciprocal moral obligations are many of the higher animals, insofar as they exhibit the following characteristics: (a) a conscious point of view on the world; (b) individual interests that are registered by the individual who has them, for example in a susceptibility to pain and pleasure; and (c) some capacity for structured protest against treatment that is inimical to the individual's interests, or otherwise unwelcome. The latter feature in particular seems to me interesting and significant, insofar as it enables us to understand our vicarious assertion of claims on behalf of the individual animal as continuous with more primitive (albeit nonnormative) reactions that it is capable of on its own behalf. In this

way, we can see the animal as incipiently in touch with the normative significance that claims have for those who bear them. They may not grasp that others wrong them, but they reliably track and recoil against the very actions of
others that constitute wrongs against them.[8]

Having noted the plausibility of extending the manifold of moral persons
in this way, however, I shall not further defend such an extension in this book.
Controversy about the exact scope of morality is endemic, and it exceeds the
remit of my discussion to attempt to resolve such controversy here. My main
point, at present, is just that debates about this issue can cogently be situated
within the framework of the relational approach, as debates about the manifold of moral persons to whom moral claims might be assigned, even if such
claimholders do not stand under reciprocal moral obligations themselves.

Once we distinguish between the two poles of the moral nexus in this way,
further questions can be asked about the connections between them. One
such question concerns the possibility that the moral domain has a partially
reflexive structure, so that there are claims that members of the domain have
against themselves, and directed obligations that correspond to those claims.
There are certainly cases where it is natural to suppose that morality imposes
obligations whose basis lies solely in the effects of actions on the agents who
perform them. Perhaps the most compelling examples come from the general
area of so-called prudence: there is the imperfect duty to develop one's talents
and make something of one's life; and the related duty to make adequate provision, to the extent it is open to one to do so, for the needs one will encounter
after one's working life is over.

These putative self-regarding obligations are ordinarily described in a way
that suggests directedness, insofar as we talk about them conventionally as
duties *to* oneself. We owe it to ourselves, it is natural to suppose, to develop
our talents and to make provision for our old age. Furthermore, we owe this
to ourselves, just insofar as we are members of the manifold of moral persons,
which makes it plausible to understand these duties as continuous with other
moral obligations.[9] At the same time, there are also features of the cases that
make these natural assumptions somewhat puzzling.[10] Most significantly, the
actions and omissions that would count as violations of the duties involve
voluntary activities of the very person who allegedly holds the claim that the
duties should be complied with. In engaging voluntarily in those activities,
aren't agents consenting freely to the things that are done to them? And doesn't
this kind of consent serve to waive any claim they might have had that they
themselves should have acted otherwise?

In thinking about these questions, it seems to me helpful to recall the temporal dimension of human life that was discussed earlier in this section. Thus, it is not at all unintelligible that you might look back on your earlier self, from the perspective of a later phase of life, with a feeling of personal grievance, and even resentment, about how you then comported yourself. Perhaps you squandered important opportunities, with the result that you are now in a much worse position than you otherwise would have found yourself in. The fact that the things you earlier did or omitted to do were voluntary seems irrelevant to the intelligibility of this later complaint. To make sense of this, we need to suppose that the perspective from which you might press a complaint on your own behalf against the earlier actions is not the perspective from which those actions may have been performed, but one that takes into account the broader arc of your life and the effects of your actions throughout its different phases. The grievance you have against your earlier self, at the later point in time, is based in the interests you have as a person whose life unfolds in time.

Such interests might in principle equally ground complaints about things that you do in your youth that are excessively deferential to the needs you will have toward the end of your expected natural lifespan. There is perhaps more room in such situations for the thought that your voluntary sacrifices amount to waivers of any claims you have against yourself, since the interests that are relevant to the claims are ones that are likely to be salient at the time when the voluntary actions are undertaken. But here, too, the complaint might sometimes get a foothold: it makes sense to think that you owe it to yourself to get out and enjoy your youth rather than spending all your days and nights in the library or the office, assiduously preparing for a future that might never even arrive.

5.2. Interests, Claims, and Moral Wrongs

In chapter 1, I noted that interests are distinct from moral claims. That this is the case is established by the familiar example of third-party beneficiaries from a promissory transaction. It might well advance the third party's interests if A keeps the promise that was made to B, but it doesn't follow from this that the third party has a claim against A to keep the promise. The claim, if there is one, is held by B, the promisee, and it seems that it is B alone who is eligible to be wronged by A through the breach of the promissory obligation.[11]

Even if interests and moral claims are distinct notions, it is tempting to suppose that there is some connection between them. In section 1.1, I hazarded a conjecture about how these notions might be connected; the suggestion was that moral claims, in the sense relevant to the relational approach, must be anchored somehow in the (nonnormative) interests of individual claimholders. In the present section, I wish to return to this conjecture, and to marshal some considerations in support of it. The leading idea will be that there is nothing specific that I owe to particular members of the extensive manifold of moral persons if it is not the case that the interests of those individuals stand to be affected, in one way or another, by exertions of my agency. In developing this idea, I shall also address the question of the kind of interests that matter to questions about the specific moral claims we have against each other.

The first thing I wish to emphasize is that it is no part of my project to propose that directed moral duties and their correlative claims can be analyzed in terms of nonrelational notions, including the notion of an individual interest. There is a lively debate about the nature of rights, for instance, which divides the landscape of theoretical options into "will" and "interest" theories. This debate is often understood to be one in which it is taken for granted that there are obligations or duties under different systems of norms, construed (for instance) as things that people ought all things considered to do, within those systems. Only some of these obligations have direction, in the sense of being owed to another party (in the way that corresponds to a right on the other party's part to performance). The question, then, is what needs to be added to a generic obligation to make it one that is directed to another party, and to entitle us to say that that party has a corresponding claim right?[12]

Proponents of the will theory appeal in this connection to some notion of normative discretion on the part of an individual who is the beneficiary of the dutiful action, including a power to enforce the obligation, as well as the power to waive it (or to waive the duty to compensate in case of nonperformance). A theory of this kind is often attributed to H. L. A. Hart, who characterizes the bearer of rights as a "small scale sovereign."[13] Interest theorists, by contrast, interpret directed obligations as ones that in some sense serve to benefit another individual in particular, who can be taken to be the bearer of a claim right to performance on the agent's part.[14] There are familiar cases that are standardly recognized to present challenges to each approach, raising doubts about their extensional adequacy. For the will theory, these include rights that we intuitively think of as being inalienable (such as the right not to be enslaved), as well as duties that are owed to persons who are not competent to exercise discretion as to their performance. For interest theories, challenges are posed by cases, such as that of the third-party beneficiary to a promise, in which individuals stand to benefit from dutiful actions without intuitively having a right that they be performed. There are also cases in which we assign rights to individuals who will not themselves benefit on balance if the corresponding duties are carried out (such as the legal right of parents to receive support payments for their children). Taking these challenges as a starting point, philosophers have gone on to propose other theories of rights that distinguish in different ways between the directed and the nondirected duties, and that are designed to cope better with the problem cases.[15]

But the relational account I am developing is not meant to be a competing theory within the parameters of this debate, for several reasons. First, analyses of rights and directed duties are often meant to apply to any domain in which these notions might gain application, including legal, institutional, and even sporting rights (such as those assigned to players by the rules of the game of rugby). But I am primarily attempting to elucidate a distinctively moral notion, one that helps to define the subject matter of interpersonal morality. Second, as I noted in chapter 1, relational moral duties do not, as I understand them, correspond to assignable rights on the part of other individuals, but are connected instead to a more general notion of a relational claim. Finally, and perhaps most significantly, I do not take it as given that there is a well-understood notion of a generic moral obligation that admits of both directed and nondirected variants (so that there is a theoretical challenge we face of identifying the further factor that will distinguish the directed from the nondirected moral duties). Rather, I appeal to the relational model of directed duties and corresponding claims to make sense of the standing of morality as a source of obligations in the most basic sense, construed as considerations that enter deliberation in the guise of presumptive constraints.

The appeal to interests as bases of claims, then, should not be understood as a variant of the interest theory of directed obligations. In particular, I am not maintaining that individual interests represent differentia that might help us to distinguish the directed from the nondirected moral obligations. Nor do I propose some other kind of theory that might aspire to reduce moral claims and the directed duties corresponding to them to individual interests. One might attempt to justify a given assignment of claims and directed duties to individuals, for instance, by an argument in the style of indirect consequentialism, to the effect that the basic interests of those individuals would best be served, on balance, by the proposed assignment. This and other approaches exhibit familiarly reductionist ambitions, insofar as they attempt to elucidate the relational notions of a directed duty and a claim through a stretch of normative argument or conceptual analysis that appeals exclusively to nonrelational elements, such as those of an individual interest. But my approach to relational moral obligation does not share this reductionist aspiration. I am content to take the notion of a relational normative nexus as a kind of theoretical primitive, and to see how far we can understand impartial morality as a domain that is structured in terms of a determinate relational nexus of this irreducible kind.[16]

The thesis I have put forward about the connection between moral claims and individual interests is meant to be internal to the order of moral right that is structured in relational terms. Even if claims cannot be reduced to individual interests, it might still be the case that one can have a moral claim against other agents that they should act in a certain way only if one's interests stand to be affected by what they do. This is the basic idea that I should like to pursue in what follows.

The intuitive idea behind it is this. Let us suppose, in accordance with the argument of section 5.1, that the inclusive manifold of persons who are potentially linked by directed moral duties and claims includes, at a minimum, all individuals who are capable of bipolar normative thought. It seems deeply implausible, even with this assumption in place, that there is anything in particular that I owe morally to many of the people in this extensive class. For all I know, there may be contemporary moral persons in the relevant sense who inhabit solar systems light years away from ours, and who are not liable to be affected, in one way or another, by anything that I might or might not do. My firm conviction, about such a case, is that such beings would have no specific moral claims against me, even if they are members of the moral community in the relevant sense (and so potential bearers of claims against me, as well as directed duties toward me). A perhaps even clearer example of the same point concerns our relations to other moral persons on our planet who were alive generations before us, and who therefore do not stand to be affected causally by how we conduct our lives in the here and now.

My reference to interests as bases for moral claims is, in the first instance, meant to be a placeholder to mark the class of effects that an agent's actions have to be capable of having on another party in order for that party to have a specific claim against the agent under the order of moral right that unites them. The suggestion, in these terms, is that even if A and B are both moral persons in the relevant sense, A can have a specific claim against B only if A's interests would be affected negatively by B's failure to honor the claim. This condition is not satisfied in the examples given above, of individuals competent at bipolar normative thought who are extremely remote from us in place or time, and who are therefore beyond our sphere of causal influence. Note, however, that this condition might well be asymmetrical in the relations between any two given individuals. Perhaps we are unable to affect the interests of the denizens of the remote planet, but they might have science-fiction style technologies that would enable them to affect our interests. The point is even clearer in cases that involve temporal distance. There is generally little that we can do to affect the interests of our remoter ancestors.[17] But it is open to the members of each generation to do things that could potentially have a significant impact on the interests of their descendants. They might, for instance, heedlessly damage the planet's environment or climate in ways that will foreseeably inflict serious hardship on members of future generations.

That is the basic intuitive thought. To make it more precise, however, we need to say more about the conception of an individual interest that it operates with. It is a familiar point that the notion of an interest ranges extremely widely. On one end of the spectrum of cases to which it might apply, it is connected closely with what we might think of as individual well-being. One's interests, in this very narrow sense, are those aspects of one's life that are directly relevant to the question of whether one is faring well or badly. These include both subjective elements, such as freedom from pain, a sense of satisfaction or enjoyment in one's activities, and so on, as well as more objective elements, including one's physical and mental health and good functioning. On the opposite end of the spectrum, interests might be construed to include virtually anything that an individual takes an interest in. If you care that progress should be made in reducing the incidence of malaria in tropical countries, then the success or failure of efforts in this direction would count as affecting your interests in the expansive sense, even if you are not yourself at any risk of contracting this disease.

The notion of an interest that seems intuitively relevant to questions about moral claims is intermediate between these two extremes. To begin, it is not to be equated with the expansive concept of an individual interest, for the reason that the expansive interpretation does not track the distinction that is our target. The idea is that another individual in the manifold of moral persons cannot have a specific claim against me unless that individual is apt to be affected in one way or another by what I might do. But if I can affect another person, in the relevant sense, simply by affecting things that he or she happens to take an interest in, then the set of moral claims that we potentially have against each other threatens to expand much more widely than is plausible. Thus, the denizens of the distant planet to which I earlier referred might take an interest in the flourishing of all members of the manifold of moral persons, wherever they might happen to reside. It would then follow that we could affect their interests, in the expansive sense, by acting in ways that enhance or reduce the well-being of the contemporary human beings who inhabit our own planet. But this is not the kind of effect that seems plausibly to ground a claim on the part of the extraterrestrials to our treating our fellow humans better rather than worse; this is not something that we owe specifically to them.

At the same time, the narrow conception of an interest also seems inadequate to the purposes at hand. That this is the case was already made apparent by the discussion of Mikluko-Maklay's promise in chapter 1. In that example, Maklay's Malay servant wishes to be assured that the anthropologist will not photograph him, believing that it would damage his spirit if this were done, and Maklay provides the sought-after assurance by promising that he will not take a picture of the servant. The servant now has a promissory claim against the anthropologist that he not be photographed by the anthropologist. And yet that claim cannot be based in the servant's concern for his own well-being, since it would not cause the servant any real physical or spiritual harm if (for instance) Maklay were secretly to take a picture of him while he was napping. In discussing this example in section 1.1, I suggested that there are interests of the servant's that nevertheless seem relevant to the assignment to him of a promissory claim. These include the servant's interest in autonomy—in determining for himself what uses are to be made of his person and his body—as well as distinct interests he has in obtaining assurance from other people that they will act in ways that respect such concerns as these. But what makes these interests potentially relevant to the assignment of claims to individuals, when the expansive conception of what an individual might take an interest in is not?

An important feature of the autonomy and assurance interests, it seems to me, is that they are personal interests in a reasonably familiar sense. They are interests one has in how one's own life goes, identifying things one cares about for one's own sake, so to speak. Thus, the uses that are made of one's own person and one's bodily image, and whether these uses accord with one's wishes regarding them, are aspects of one's personal biography. So too is the fact that one has obtained assurance from another individual that a certain use would not be made of one's bodily image. It has an effect on the character and quality of one's own life (or at least a stretch of it) if one can "rest assured" that one's wishes in these matters will be respected. These are aspects of one's own biography, even if they are not things that directly affect one's physical or mental well-being in the narrow sense. In taking an interest in such questions, the servant is betraying a concern for what happens to him, and for the potential effects of others' actions on how his own life goes. This is the kind of interest, it seems to me, that intuitively bears on the question of whether an individual can have a moral claim against another agent. In order for there to be something in particular that I owe to another moral person, there must be some difference that my actions might possibly make to what happens in that person's life, some effect I might have on aspects of that person's own life that matter to him or her.

The basic idea, then, is that moral claims must be based in some way on the personal interests of the claimholder. This is not to say that moral claims are reducible to the personal interests of claimholders or that these notions are otherwise equivalent to each other. As we have already seen, one can have all manner of personal interests regarding the character of one's own life that do not give rise to corresponding moral claims. The case of the third-party beneficiary is a salient example of this kind, though there are many others as well. It follows that to have a specific claim against someone that he or she should do X is not merely to have a personal interest regarding one's own life that would be affected adversely if the person were to fail to do X.

What we can perhaps say is the following. Your having a personal interest that stands to be affected adversely by something an agent might do or refrain from doing raises the question of whether the agent owes it to you to avoid affecting you in this way. This is why the moral persons whose lives are completely outside the scope of our causal influence do not have specific moral claims against us; insofar as their personal interests cannot in any case be affected by our actions, the question of what in particular we might owe it to them to do does not even arise. Nor is this thought at odds with the thesis, emphasized in chapter 4, that the moral nexus, properly construed, represents a domain of self-standing normative requirements. The present thought is not that a specific complex of moral duties and claims must be based on an antecedent causal relation that the parties stand in to each other. It is, rather, that such a complex presupposes that the claimholder's personal interests are liable to be affected, in one way or another, by exertions of the other party's agency. This is a condition that can be satisfied even in reference to two individuals who have not previously interacted in any way at all: consider, again, the gout-afflicted stranger I encounter on my path along the sidewalk as I walk to work.

Furthermore, in those cases in which individuals have specific moral claims against us, we can justify the claims, at least in part, by reference to personal interests of theirs that underlie them. Our sense that they have a moral claim against us to do X, and that we owe it to them to honor this claim by X-ing, is illuminated by understanding the ways in which a failure to do X would have an adverse impact on some personal interest of theirs. That interest will figure saliently, for instance, in a specifically moral argument for the conclusion that we are under a duty to do X that is directed to them.[18] A natural line of thought here is that a duty is directed to another party only if the considerations that go into establishing the duty center around that party, and it is personal interests of the putative claimholder that will be prominent within such a person-involving justification. Moral claims will be grounded in a personal interest of the claimholder, then, in a justificatory rather than a metaphysical or an analytical sense.

This idea about the justificatory basis of moral claims in personal interests connects to the relational moral ideal that was discussed in section 4.4 above. I have described that ideal as realizing the value of interpersonal recognition, which involves two components: acknowledgment of the standing of other persons, as individuals to whom consideration is owed; and the ability to justify oneself specifically to those individuals, insofar as they might be affected by the things we do. But both of these aspects of interpersonal recognition seem helpfully developed by appeal to the personal interests of claimholders. The consideration we owe to moral persons is plausibly understood as recognition of them as individuals who take an interest in how their own lives might go. We show due regard for them as such individuals, insofar as we appreciate the ways in which their personal interests might give rise to claims against us, and conscientiously strive to respect those claims as constraints on our own behavior. Similarly, we can justify ourselves specifically to other individuals when we take their personal interests into account as potential bases for objecting to things we might do, and respect the claims of theirs that are based in such personal interests. These aspects of interpersonal recognition help us to understand why the ideal makes no specific demands on us in cases in which other moral persons lie completely outside the causal range of our agency. When this condition is satisfied (and we are aware that it is satisfied), then anything we might do will be capable of being justified to the other parties by reference to their personal interests, and hence compatible with due regard for them as individuals who bear such interests.

If interpersonal recognition in this way privileges the personal interests of claimholders, however, it does not follow that the bearers of claims will necessarily follow suit in their decision-making about their own lives. There are many other-regarding and impersonal things that individuals might care about, representing interests in the expansive sense noted above. Among these are some things that they may attach greater importance to than they do to the personal interests that matter to relational morality. And even within the class of personal interests, those that end up giving rise to relational moral claims might not always be the ones that matter most from the perspective of the bearer of the interests. Thus, it seems we have moral claims of some kind to assistance in meeting our basic human needs, but not necessarily to aid in pursuing our personal ambitions; this is true, even if we are ourselves willing to sacrifice some of those same needs in order better to advance our aspirational ends (our project of base jumping from alpine cliffs, for instance, or of obtaining publicity for the cause of eradicating malaria).

This is a familiar point that pertains in some version or other to many different conceptions of the moral realm.[19] In application to the relational approach, it suggests that the underlying concern for the effects of our actions on other individuals reflects priorities that sometimes diverge from the priorities of the individuals in question. This can seem paradoxical, but it is perhaps only to be expected, given the special features to which a conception of interpersonal morality is answerable. The perspective from which we engage in reflection about what we owe to other moral persons, construed as individuals whose interests are of equal importance, will of necessity define a distinctive standpoint of deliberation. In particular, the significance that is attached to personal interests within such reflection is different from the significance we attach to the same interests when we set priorities for our own lives. It is morally permissible for us to sacrifice some of our basic needs in pursuit of our aspirational ends, even if we cannot demand that others should be conscripted into these pursuits on our behalf.

In section 1.1, I noted that philosophers sometimes appeal to normative interests to make sense of moral claims. In discussing the case of Maklay's promissory obligation, for instance, it has been suggested that the servant's claim against the anthropologist must be grounded in some interest of this kind, since by hypothesis the violation of the promise would not in fact harm the servant or make him worse off than he otherwise would have been.[20]

Against this suggestion, I have noted that there are personal interests of the servant's that are nonnormative in their content, and that might help us to make sense of the promissory claim in this case, including autonomy interests and interests in assurance.

Having said that, however, I do not wish to deny that interests with normative content are ever relevant to the justification of moral claims. Some of our personal interests, about how our own lives go, are also normative interests, and these can have a bearing on questions of what we are owed by others. We have a personal interest, for instance, in being treated fairly, and this might be the basis for a moral claim we have not to be singled out arbitrarily in decisions about who among us will bear the burdens necessary to advance a common aim. Maybe one member of the commune needs to stay home to look after the kids and the dog over the weekend while the others participate in a project-related retreat, and everyone is equally disinclined to take on this responsibility. In this context, it would be wrong for the majority in the commune to assign this task to the person who happens to be out shopping for that evening's meal; the person who had in this way come to have the assignment could rightly complain, on her own behalf, that the others had not treated her fairly.[21] (A better procedure would be to ensure that members take turns at doing the burdensome tasks of this kind that regularly come up, or to draw lots if such situations rarely arise.)

5.3. Moral Justification and Moral Reasoning: From Interests to Claims

There is, however, one kind of appeal to normative interests that strikes me as problematic in the context of justifying moral claims. This is the strategy that would justify the assignment of a claim to an individual by appeal to the interest that the individual has in being the bearer of just such a claim. Normative interests of this kind count as personal interests in the sense I have distinguished. They are interests specifically in the character of one's own life, insofar as they reflect a concern not that a given claim should generally obtain among the members of the broader community of moral agents, but that one should oneself have the claim in question. Furthermore, normative interests with this content are sometimes mentioned as considerations that could potentially justify the assignment of claims to the individual who has the interest. Thus, Joseph Raz has written that "[s]ome rights may be based on an interest in having those same rights." This suggestion has been taken up in recent work on the nature and sources of promissory obligation, specifically to account for cases such as Maklay's, where breach of the promise would allegedly constitute a "bare wrong" that doesn't harm any nonnormative interest of the promisee.[22]

Let us call the personal interests that feature in this approach "claim interests," since they are not merely interests with some normative content or other, but interests in having a specific moral claim against other people. I believe that people do have such claim interests, and there may be conceptions of practical justification within which they have an important role to play.[23] I also believe there is a different but related normative interest that is significant in view of the relational conception of morality. This is the personal interest we have, not in bearing some particular moral claim or other, but in being a member of the manifold of moral persons, in the sense of being an individual to whom moral claims are in general attributable. To be a person in this sense is to have a valuable interpersonal status, one that might be described—using a suggestive, if also somewhat imprecise term—as inviolability.[24] It is a systemic feature of the relational conception, insofar as one of its distinctive aspects is the assignment of claims to individuals, that it confers on them this significant interpersonal status. It thereby speaks to the interest we all have in being persons to whom moral claims are in principle assignable.

But the relational conception of morality leaves little scope for claims that are justified directly by reference to the distinct interest an individual might have in bearing those very claims (to echo Raz's formulation). Within the relational conception, I have suggested that moral claims must be based somehow in personal interests of the individual to whom they are assigned. The reasoning that explains why a given claim obtains must make reference to the personal interests of the individual who is its bearer. Only an argument of this kind will be equipped to make sense of the idea that the corresponding duty is owed specifically to that individual. Note, however, that the moral claim that is assigned to the individual is a claim, held against the agent, that the agent should comply with the corresponding duty. This is what the agent owes it to the claimholder to do. Note, further, that the flouting of the duty by the agent would not merely be wrong, but something that wrongs the claimholder in particular, leaving the latter with a privileged basis for complaint. This is the specifically interpersonal dimension of relational morality that was discussed extensively in chapter 3 above.

It is a reasonable expectation on moral justification that the considerations that explain why a moral claim is assigned to a given individual should illuminate these further relational features of the assignment, as well. They should

explain why it is important to the claimholder that the agent should conscientiously strive to live up to the duty that is owed to him or her, and also why the
flouting of the duty should leave him or her with a privileged basis for complaint about the agent's conduct. But these expectations will not be satisfied
by moral justifications, within the relational framework, that appeal directly
to claim interests.

To make the problem concrete, let's return to the example of promissory
obligation. We are looking for a moral argument in support of the conclusion
that promisors generally owe a duty of promissory fidelity specifically to promisees. For the purposes of discussion, we may grant here that individuals in the
situation of promisees typically have interests in bearing claims against promisors to performance. Can we appeal to these claim interests of promisees to
support their having such relational claims to promissory performance, in fact?

The first thing to observe is that an argument with only these elements
would be excessively short-winded. A successful justification of moral claims
will have to take into account *some* considerations beyond the personal interests of the putative claimholder; this is a general feature of relational justification, to which I return below, and does not pertain exclusively to arguments
in which claim interests figure centrally. Moreover, the additional considerations that are adduced within a complete justification need to be such as to
neutralize the danger of rampant bootstrapping that is posed by the strategy
of appealing to claim interests. After all, it is not in general plausible to suppose
that we have moral claims whenever we have an interest in bearing such claims.
I may have an interest in its being the case that members of my local community owe me one-tenth of their net income; and yet it hardly follows from my
having this interest that I have a genuine moral claim against them that they
should surrender this percentage of their income to me every month.

Having raised these general difficulties, however, I shall now set them aside,
assuming that there will be a way to supplement the appeal to claim interests
within moral argument, so that moral claims are not assigned to individuals
too promiscuously. Still, within such supplemented moral justifications, it
remains the case that the personal interests of an individual must elucidate
the assignment of a moral claim to that individual, providing a basis for that
assignment. And I now wish to argue that claim interests are ill suited to play
this role.

Claim interests might help us to make sense of the fact that an individual is
the bearer of a normative claim, considered just in itself. They are, after all,
personal interests that individuals have in possessing such a claim, so they are

interests of the individuals that would be advanced if the claim were in fact assigned to them. But these interests do not illuminate the further relational features that go into having a moral claim. The claim interests of individuals will be fully satisfied when the claims are assigned to them, for they are personal interests in the obtaining of just that normative state of affairs. But those claims, once assigned, will continue to obtain, regardless of whether the agents against whom they are held fulfill the duties that are owed to the individuals who bear the claims. Insofar as this is the case, however, we cannot appeal to claim interests to make sense of the importance to claimholders of agents fulfilling the duties that are owed to them; nor can we understand in these terms why claimholders have a privileged basis for complaint about such nonperformance. These elements of the specific moral nexus that obtains are not illuminated by the appeal to claim interests; the interest in having a specific claim, once it is isolated, is not affected in any way by facts about whether the claim in question is honored or flouted.[25]

True, it would be possible to appeal in this context to generic second-order interests that individuals might have in the satisfaction of their moral claims. If there are such generic interests, then they could conceivably figure in a two-stage procedure of moral argument. In the first stage, claim interests would be cited to justify the assignment of claims to specific individuals. And once those claims are assigned, it could be argued, in a second stage, that the individuals' generic interest in the satisfaction of their claims serves to illuminate the other features of the moral nexus that require explanation. The generic interest could help us to understand the importance individuals attach to having agents honor the duties that are owed to them; and it could potentially provide, as well, a basis for the privileged complaint that claimholders have when they are wronged.

But there is something unsatisfying about a story along these lines. For one thing, the account it proposes of the structure of our personal interests seems implausible. The suggestion is that the primary interest of individuals that figures within at least some moral arguments is the normative interest they have in the assignment of a given claim to them. Their interest in fulfillment of claims, according to the picture, is derivative from this primary interest, and enters the account only after the moral claim has been assigned. But this seems to reverse the order of priority between our normative and our nonnormative concerns. We care that our claims should be honored, because we care about the things that ground those claims in the first place (such as our bodily integrity, our capacity to shape our lives through our own agency, our ability to trust those we interact with, etc.). For another thing, the second-order interests that the two-stage strategy relies on seem too generic to capture the specific moral complaint that individuals have when their claims are disregarded. That complaint is not that the agent has flouted some claim or other, but that the agent's action shows a lack of consideration for the first-order interest at stake in the assignment of the particular claim that is at issue.

For these reasons, I am skeptical about direct appeals to claim interests within the framework of the relational conception. As I remarked above, the personal interests of ours that justify the assignment of a moral claim to us should also help us to understand why we care about whether the claim is honored, and what our privileged complaint is against those who flout the claim. For instance, a personal interest in autonomy or in assurance might justify the assignment to promisees of claims against promisors to performance. But the very same considerations seem to make sense of the interest promisees take in having promisors honor the duties that are owed to them, as well as the specific complaint they have against promisors when they fail to do so. In disregarding the promissory obligation, delinquent promisors are disregarding the very interests of promisees that ground the directed obligation in the first place; this contributes to our understanding of how the different parts of the specific nexus created by the claim and the corresponding duty fit tightly together.

I use the expression "disregard" in this connection advisedly. The personal interests in which moral claims are based provide a basis for complaint by the claimholder in cases of wrongful action. But the complaint is not simply that the interests in question were not satisfied. To see this, return to a case introduced in section 3.1 above, in which I promise to meet you at the Pilates class, but end up failing to be there on account of a malfunction in the service that maintains my online calendar, or a breakdown on the subway I am using to get to the class. Your claim against me that I should keep my promise might be based in part in your personal interest in being able to rely on me to accompany you to the class, and in the case at issue, this interest is not in fact satisfied. But this alone does not give you an entitlement to resent me for my failure to show up to the class as promised.

Though your interest was not satisfied in this case, I nevertheless gave it full and appropriate consideration in my deliberations about what to do, treating the obligation to which it gave rise as a presumptive constraint on my activities (by entering the commitment conscientiously into my calendar, scheduling other activities around it, taking appropriate precautions to get to the appointed place on time, etc.). The most we can reasonably expect of people is that they show due regard for our claims and for the personal interests of ours that are their basis. This is connected to a point I have made repeatedly, which is that only when this attitudinal condition is not met can we be said to have been wronged by the actions of another party, or to have suffered a specifically moral injury.

To have due regard for the moral claims that others have against us, we must first be able to identify what those claims are. There is a distinctively moral form of reasoning or reflection that is suited to this purpose, which involves, on the general approach I have been sketching, a characteristic movement of thought, taking us from personal interests to the assignment of moral claims. There are many different ways in which the options for action that it is open to us to choose might affect, both positively and negatively, the personal interests of other parties. Identifying these effects perhaps serves to define a class of people who might well have specific moral claims against us, raising the question, as I put it earlier, of what in particular we owe it to them to do. But to answer this question, we need to go further, singling out within this class the individual or individuals to whom specific moral duties are owed, and specifying the content of those duties. This is the general shape of the problem that must be solved through moral deliberation, on the relational interpretation of it.

In chapter 2, I suggested that directed moral obligations intelligibly enter the deliberative field as presumptive constraints on the agent's deliberations about what to do. The idea there was that, once a moral obligation has been identified, it represents a consideration with independent normative significance for the agent whom it binds, one that reasonably functions as a defeasible constraint on the agent's ongoing deliberations. In the present section, however, I have been addressing the prior question of how agents arrive at moral conclusions about what it is they owe it to others to do. This is a task for what we might reasonably call specifically moral deliberation, and my present point is that it requires the agent to solve a general problem, of moving from interests to claims.

Theorists of Hohfeldian claim rights sometimes represent rights not merely as inputs into deliberative reflection of the generic kind, but as inputs into moral deliberation in particular. The idea, it seems, is that there can be genuine moral rights that are nevertheless permissibly infringed by the agents against whom they are held.[26] Thus, the promisee has a moral right that the promisor should do the thing that was promised, but there are circumstances in which it would seem morally permissible for the promisor to fail to perform. A family emergency might develop, for instance, that the promisor could not have been expected to anticipate at the time when the promise was made. Or a person might have a property right against unauthorized trespass on the premises of her business, which it might nevertheless be morally permissible for someone to infringe on a particular occasion (imagine a different emergency situation in which the survivors of an aviation disaster will die if they do not get access to the canned foods that are stored on the property in question).

On this way of thinking about them, rights do not represent the output of specifically moral deliberation, but are rather considerations that are to be taken into account within reflection about what it is morally permissible or required to do. This shows itself in the fact that establishing that someone has a right against the agent that the agent act in a certain way does not yet settle the question of whether the agent is morally obligated to act in that way; the agent may be under a duty of some kind, owed to the right-holder, to respect the right, but it might nevertheless be morally permissible for the agent to infringe it. To determine whether this is the case or not, further considerations will need to be taken into account, in particular considerations that go beyond facts about the moral rights and directed duties of various parties to the situation.

This is one important respect in which the connected notions of a moral claim and a directed obligation that I have been developing differ from familiar Hohfeldian conceptions of moral rights (at least on standard interpretations of them). For essentially the same reasons, they also appear to differ from prima facie moral duties of the kind introduced by W. D. Ross, which are likewise meant to be taken into account directly within moral reflection.[27] Prima facie duties, in Ross's sense, identify considerations that count in favor of conclusions about what it would be right or wrong for a person to do. So in any given situation, prima facie duties of this kind need to be weighed against other prima facie duties to arrive at conclusions about the agent's duties *sans phrase*. There is a prima facie duty of promissory fidelity, but also a similar duty to assist family members in emergencies, and it is a task for moral thought to determine which of these prevails in the circumstance.

On closer inspection, however, the language of prima facie duties may be misleading in this connection. It suggests that the considerations that are taken into account, within the reflection that goes to determining one's obligations *sans phrase*, are themselves deontic in character. But this is in fact questionable. The considerations that determine what one is obligated to do, in any given situation, are not themselves plausibly understood as duties in any sense. For Ross, it is the fact that you have promised to do something, not the fact that keeping your promise is a prima facie duty, that seems to have basic significance for normative thought; that is what counts in favor of conclusions about your duties *sans phrase*, and similarly for other kinds of prima facie duty (such as the fact that you have an opportunity to provide a concrete benefit to another person).[28] Once we appreciate this point, we see that duty itself arguably does not function as a contributory normative concept in Ross's philosophy. That, moreover, is as it should be, for it is not really clear that it is intelligible to posit a specifically deontic concept that contributes, as such, to determining one's duty in a final or unqualified sense.[29]

The only way to make this work, it seems to me, is to define a technical notion of duty that is then treated as a special kind of reason for action, one that might be weighed against other reasons in determining what the agent ought to do. This might be the best way to make sense of the Hohfeldian conception, at the end of the day. Hohfeld-style claim rights correspond, as we have seen, to directed obligations, which are owed to the bearer of the rights. I noted above that deontic complexes of this kind are sometimes thought to figure as inputs into specifically moral deliberation, where it is a matter of deciding what it is morally permissible or required to do. But it is not clear what the notion of moral requirement might be that directed obligations are supposed to contribute to determining. (Thus it cannot be the relational notion of a directed obligation, for that is the consideration that is meant to be doing the contributory work.) A better way to develop the position might be to think of rights and the directed duties correlative to them as ordinary reasons, which contribute to determining not what it is morally required for the agent to do, but what the agent ought on balance to do. This is a coherent way of thinking about the deliberative role of directed obligations and claims, but it is one that ultimately dispenses with the notion of a practical requirement that was at the center of my discussion in chapter 2 (as central to our conception of interpersonal morality). There is no consideration, on this picture, that intelligibly functions within deliberation as a presumptive constraint on agency, but merely a class of specifically moral reasons that are to be weighed in the balance against reasons of other kinds.

As I hope is clear by now, claims and directed obligations in the sense at issue in the relational account function very differently. As we saw in chapter 2, they represent deontic inputs to generic deliberation about what an agent is to do, entering such reflection in the guise of presumptive constraints on agency, to which conscientious agents respond by forming intentions to comply with them. On this conception, directed obligations and claims figure neither as ordinary reasons that are to be weighed against reasons of other kinds within generic practical deliberation, nor as considerations that contribute to determining what one is morally required to do. Rather, they represent the most fundamental notion of a moral obligation, and hence are outputs or conclusions of the specifically moral reflection through which agents determine what it is permissible or impermissible for them to do. That is, to establish that A has a claim against B that B do X just is to establish that B is under a moral obligation to do X, in the basic sense of "obligation" that is relevant to moral reflection. There is no room, within this conception, for judging that a moral claim and a corresponding directed obligation obtain, but thinking that it would nevertheless be permissible for the agent to flout the obligation or to infringe the claim. An action is morally permissible, in the pertinent sense, just in case it would violate none of the directed moral obligations that the agent owes it to various individuals to comply with.[30] And if an action is obligatory in the same sense, then that already decides the question of whether it is something the agent is under a practical requirement to do.

This means, to return to the cases that were mentioned above, that the promisee does not really have a claim against the promisor to performance in the situation in which a previously unanticipated family emergency has arisen, on the conception of claims that I have been developing. Nor does the landowner have a moral claim against the survivors of the crash that they should not trespass on the commercial property. Ordinarily, promises and property ownership go together with claims against other individuals, but the obtaining of these claims is conditioned by certain factual circumstances that are not always and everywhere satisfied.[31] When the relevant conditions are not satisfied, it is not that the claim persists, but that it becomes morally permissible for agents to infringe it; nor is there a prima facie duty that is outweighed by a conflicting moral duty of the same kind. Rather, the original claim and the duty that went along with it are altogether extinguished.[32]

To say that the original moral duties and claims are extinguished, of course, is not to say that there are no residual duties and claims that may apply in situations of this kind. In the case involving the unanticipated family emergency, for instance, there are presumably fallback duties and claims that obtain in virtue of the original promise, such as a claim against the promisor to a timely warning about promisor's inability to perform (if the circumstances allow for this), and a claim to compensation for losses that are suffered as a result of relying on the promisor to do what was promised.[33] Similar things might be said about the case involving justified trespass on someone's property, where there is ordinarily a fallback obligation to compensate the owner of the property for any losses or damages pursuant to one's unauthorized use, and to provide an explanation of the circumstances that gave rise to it in the first place.[34] But these fallback duties and claims likewise represent outputs of moral reflection rather than moral considerations that could conceivably be outweighed or permissibly infringed.

It might be thought that we need a notion of duties or claims as inputs to moral reflection if we are to do justice to these aspects of the moral situation. The fallback duties and claims obtain just because, and just insofar as, the situation is one in which there is a claim or prima facie duty that has been infringed or outweighed by a competing moral consideration. The fallback duties and claims might be described as normative residues of the original duties and claims; but this way of speaking presupposes that those elements in the situation live on, only in a way that is overshadowed by other aspects of the situation.[35] Similarly, it appears to be an advantage of Ross's theory of prima facie duties that it acknowledges the possibility of deontological constraints on agency that are nevertheless not absolute.[36] The fact that you are under a prima facie duty to keep your promise means that you are not permitted to break it in order to produce a modestly better outcome, though there are other circumstances, such as a family emergency, in which conflicting prima facie duties will prevail.

But these considerations do not require us to think of duties and claims as contributory inputs into moral reflection. Note, for one thing, that for Ross himself, deontic notions of this kind may not represent elements that contribute to determining what we are morally required or permitted to do. As we saw above, it is not the fact that one is under a prima facie duty that apparently goes to determining one's duty *sans phrase*, but rather the presence of the nondeontic considerations that are collected by the prima facie duty, such as the fact that one has made a promise to do something, or that one is presented with a concrete opportunity to benefit another individual. Even on this kind of view, then, one would expect the work of explaining fallback obligations to be discharged by the very same nondeontic considerations that contribute to determining one's original obligations in the cases in which they obtain. The fallback obligations are not, after all, well characterized as normative residues of genuine duties that have somehow been overridden or superseded.

This is consistent with the relational approach to these matters that I myself would favor, which similarly makes sense of fallback obligations by appeal to the nondeontic considerations that help to determine all moral obligations, in the most basic sense. Conclusions about directed moral duties and claims, on the conception of them I have been developing, are supported in the first instance by appeal to personal interests of the individual to whom the claims are assigned. But those interests may persist, even under circumstances in which they do not suffice to ground moral claims on the part of their bearer, and we can explain in terms of them the features of the moral landscape here in question. Thus, in the promising case, it is, for instance, the promisee's interest in reliance or assurance that helps to explain the function of the promise as a restriction on the promisor's acting to promote the good. But those same interests will explain why promisees have claims to timely warning and to compensation in cases where they are not sufficient to ground a claim to promissory fidelity.[37] There is no need to appeal to specifically deontic notions, such as an infringeable right or claim, to make sense of the existence of non-absolute constraints and of residual duties of warning and compensation.[38]

A final point to emphasize in this connection is that there is room, within the conception of morality I have been developing, for a range of first-order views about the kinds of change in circumstance that can suffice to extinguish a defeasible moral obligation. In the promising case, I have repeatedly made reference to unanticipated emergencies as paradigmatic for this phenomenon. But the references have been meant to be illustrative rather than exhaustive, providing especially clear examples of the way in which new developments can undermine presumptive promissory commitments. For all I have said, there might be a range of non-emergency changes in circumstance that are equally capable of making it the case that the promisor is no longer strictly obligated to do the thing that was promised.

In most emergencies, the changes in circumstance that undermine the original promissory commitment are ones that ground a new moral obligation (for example, to rescue someone who is in acute distress when one is uniquely positioned to do so at little danger to oneself). But perhaps there are other cases in which this feature is not present: consider promisors who encounter an unanticipated opportunity to do something supererogatory, but also very important, such as donating a kidney or risking their lives to save the victims of a shipwreck in very stormy seas.[39] In a different kind of case, a promise that is understood by the parties to it to be of fairly minor significance might no longer be morally binding if keeping it would prevent the promisor from taking advantage of a surprising opportunity to pursue a personal goal. (Suppose you have promised to return someone's library book by the end of the day, but on the way to doing so you receive a call from an old friend who is in town on the same day, and who reports that she would be delighted to get together with you if you can drop what you are doing and come right over to her hotel.)

These cases raise interesting practical questions about the precise contours of the moral obligations that are introduced by promissory transactions, questions that I do not propose to answer here. It suffices, for the present, to note that the relational conception of moral obligations I have been defending leaves room for a variety of positions about the ways in which new circumstances can interact with promissory commitments to undermine their moral status. We do not need to think of directed obligations and the claims that correspond to them as inputs into moral deliberation in order to accommodate this range of first-order views.

5.4. A Theory of Relational Morality?

With these points of clarification in place, we may now return to the question of the nature of moral deliberation. I have just suggested that such deliberation will issue in verdicts about the obtaining of directed obligations. And I suggested, earlier in the preceding section, that the general task of arriving at such conclusions involves a movement in thought from personal interests to claims. The justification for assigning a moral claim to a given individual will be one in which the personal interests of that individual figure centrally, and we can understand moral reasoning to involve the articulation of these interest-centered justifications.

To say this is of course not to attribute to moral deliberation a necessary role in relation to exertions of human agency. In particular, it is decidedly not to say that agents must always engage in an episode of self-conscious moral reflection before they can begin to make up their minds about what to do. There are many situations in which well-habituated persons will simply know immediately, without any prior episode of moral thought, that there are certain moral duties that they owe to other individuals. In other situations, agents might be disposed to structure their deliberations so that actions that are incompatible with moral claims against them are not even taken to be among the alternatives that are theoretically available, so that they are excluded from consideration without the agents needing to think that they would be morally

wrong.[40] In situations of both kinds, agents will in effect have solved the problem of responding to moral claims without needing to engage in any discursive
thought about how to identify such claims, given the array of divergent interests that might be affected by the things it is open to them to do.

Even in cases such as this, however, there is a theoretical question that could
be asked, about how the moral claims that the agents succeed in responding
to are to be justified. In other, harder cases, some reflection may be required
beforehand on the part of agents to figure out what exactly it is that they owe
it to other people to do, reflection that might reasonably be characterized as
reasoning or deliberation of a specifically moral kind. Is there anything that
can be said, in perfectly general terms, about how we are to go about solving
the problem of justifying valid claims in moral reasoning of this kind?

The preceding discussion has already brought to light several abstract desiderata that bear on such moral justification. First, justifications of this kind
will be ones in which the personal interests of prospective claimholders figure
prominently, as considerations that provide a basis for the moral claims that
are assigned to them; this is the main point that was emphasized in the preceding section. Second, as was also noted in that section, moral reflection cannot
restrict itself to considering the personal interests of prospective claimholders
on their own. A course of reasoning that took this shape would be too one-
sided to yield plausible conclusions about what we morally owe to each other,
neglecting other important moral considerations (including the effects of prospective actions on the personal interests of the agents who might be required
to perform them). Finally, I have suggested at several different points in this
book that it is an important element in modern conceptions of morality that
it should be suitably cosmopolitan. This means, in the present context, that
the procedure of moral discovery or reasoning that it defines should be one
that operationalizes a commitment to the equal standing of all individuals who
are within the manifold of moral persons. It should justify moral claims by
appeal to the personal interests of prospective claimholders, but in a way that
gives equal consideration to the interests of all who might be affected by the
actions that are up for moral assessment. This is the feature of relational morality that enables us to understand it as a source of *egalitarian* deliberative constraints of the kind discussed in section 4.2 above.

But is there anything we can say, more specifically, about how these abstract
desiderata are to be negotiated in moral thought? There are, I think, certain
plausible negative conclusions that can be drawn about reasoning of this kind
by any theorist of relational morality. One way, for instance, to meet the second

and third abstract desiderata I outlined above would be through a process of cost-benefit analysis, in which the personal interests of different parties would be balanced against each other with the aim of maximizing their impartial satisfaction. But reasoning of this kind would not do justice to the first desideratum. That is, it would not be a way of taking personal interests equally into account *as* potential bases of moral claims, which as we have seen are considerations that function as presumptive constraints within deliberation and as a basis of accountability relations between individuals.[41] Beyond such negative conclusions, however, it is not obvious that anything more positive can be said about the general processes through which moral claims are identified in moral thought. That is, we might insist that, though there are determinate solutions to the problem of moving from personal interests to claims in a way that gives them equal consideration, and though moral reasoning is the process of thought through which we identify such solutions, there is no single template that is followed by agents when they engage in this kind of thought.

The resulting position might be thought of as a relational version of intuitionism. It would hold that there are truths about what it is morally right or obligatory to do in particular circumstances of action, but that there is no single procedure of reasoning through which these truths are apprehended; we grasp them, instead, through capacities for rational intuition. The difference from other forms of intuitionism in ethics is that the conclusions that are grasped through unsystematizable intuition are not monadic conclusions about moral right and wrong, but conclusions specifically about what we owe it to each other morally to do.[42] In any given case, the relational intuitionist will say, there is a route that will get us from the personal interests of people potentially affected by our actions to the assignment of moral claims to particular individuals, as people to whom specific duties are owed. Furthermore, it is characteristic of relational moral thought that the personal interests of claimholders will justify, in some sense, our assigning claims to them. But there is nothing illuminating to be said, in general terms, about how moral justification of this kind will proceed in all cases to which it might pertain.[43] The problem is one that is solved, instead, through the application of particularistic judgment to the materials at hand.

A different position would hold that we can characterize, in general terms, the processes through which agents identify claims in moral reasoning that takes appropriately into account the personal interests bearing on moral judgment. There are various forms that a position of this kind could conceivably take, but I would like to focus on moral contractualism, in the form put forward by T. M. Scanlon; a considerable part of the appeal of contractualism as a moral theory, it seems to me, lies in its ability to illuminate the general structure of reasoning about essentially relational moral duties and claims.[44] In the remainder of this section, I shall develop this suggestion. In particular, I wish to highlight the implicitly relational features of moral contractualism, and to show that it offers an illuminating account of the structure of moral reasoning about directed duties and claims. I shall argue, further, that moral contractualism can also be understood as a philosophical account of relational morality in the form I have been concerned to explicate in this book.

Moral reasoning, on the contractualist conception of it, is reasoning about the justifiability of actions to the various people potentially affected by them. An action counts as justifiable to each such person if it is permitted by principles for the general regulation of behavior that nobody could reasonably reject. So in moral reasoning, we are attempting to identify principles for the general regulation of behavior that would permit us to act in certain ways, and considering the objections that could be brought against these principles from the perspective of the people variously affected by the actions they allow.

Scanlon suggests, specifically, that we are to consider the objections that representative people would have on their own behalf to the principles that are up for assessment; we might think of these as objections that are grounded in personal interests of such people, in the sense identified in section 5.2.[45] The potential objections of each affected person are to be taken equally into account, and considered in fundamentally the same way, as bases for rejecting principles that would permit or require various forms of behavior. In this respect, contractualist reasoning does justice to the impartiality of morality, its aspiration to treat equally the interests of each member of a maximally inclusive manifold of moral persons. Of course, for reasons we have already canvased, the objections that individuals have to prospective principles are cheap: there are virtually countless ways in which our actions might bear on the interests of those who are within our causal orbit, and there are correspondingly many objections that could be brought against nearly any principle for the general regulation of behavior we might consider. So long as we restrict ourselves to considering such objections on their own, then, we are going to be stymied, left with the impression that nothing we might do can be justified to others.

Contractualism overcomes this problem by adopting an essentially comparative perspective. The question of justifiability to others is not decided simply by identifying objections that various representative people might have to principles that would permit actions we are thinking about performing. Rather, we are to ask whether those objections are such that it would be reasonable for the people who have them to reject the principles. And to determine whether it would in this way be reasonable to reject a principle that permits a given way of acting, we need to compare the strongest objections that people might have to it with the strongest objections that others would have to principles that would prohibit the same actions. Thus, promisors have personal interest-based objections to principles that require them to keep their promises. But promisees have weightier objections on their own behalf to principles that permit promisors to fail to perform (in the absence of special circumstances that could not have been anticipated at the time when the promise was made). By keeping their promises, then, promisors ordinarily ensure that their behavior is justifiable to those who stand to be affected by it. There is no valid complaint that could be brought against them for so acting, given the powerful objection that promisees in particular would have had if they had done otherwise.

This account of moral reasoning can be understood to describe a kind of schema for effecting the transition from interests to moral claims. We consider the personal interests of a representative individual as potential bases for objecting to principles that would permit the agent to act in certain ways, comparing them to the objections to alternative principles that are grounded in the personal interests of other individuals. This way of thinking does justice to the three abstract desiderata for relational deliberation that were identified earlier. Personal interests of affected parties enter such deliberation as bases for objecting to principles, and hence as potential grounds of moral claims. They do this, furthermore, in a comparative procedure that assigns each person's interests equal significance, but without collapsing into consequentialist maximizing or cost-benefit analysis. The outcome of this contractualist procedure of justification can be understood to involve the assignment of a claim to one or more of the parties who stand to be affected by the action that is up for assessment.

This isn't something that Scanlon himself is very explicit about, but it represents an important structural feature of the procedure of justification that his contractualism describes. An individual has a claim against the agent that the agent should comply with a candidate moral principle, just in case the personal interests of that individual make it reasonable for someone in his or her position to reject alternative principles for the general regulation of behavior (that is, principles that would permit the agent to act otherwise).[46] In virtue of having this kind of objection to principles that would permit the agent to do X, the claimholder would have a specific kind of grievance or complaint if the agent should so act, one that is not shared by people whose interests might differently be affected by the action. We could say, similarly, that the agent *owes it* to the claimholder to refrain from doing X, and that flouting this directed requirement would *wrong* the claimholder in particular. The elements in the relational conception of moral requirements thus seem to fall out of the contractualist way of thinking about their derivation.

To make this more concrete, let's return to the example of promissory obligation and the third-party beneficiary, in the variant where the third party would benefit accidentally from the promisor's fulfillment of the promissory commitment (rather than being the intended beneficiary of it).[47] The challenge here is to make sense of the intuitive thought that promissory fidelity is something that is owed to the promisee rather than to the accidental beneficiary; within contractualist reasoning, this difference will have to be traced to differences in the objections the two parties have to principles that permit promisors to flout the promissory agreements they have voluntarily entered into.

Promisees, it seems, have perfectly reasonable objections to such principles, even once account is taken of the objections that promisors have to principles that require them to perform. Principles of the latter kind bind promisors to doing things that they might sometimes prefer not to do when the time comes; but these commitments can already be anticipated when promises are undertaken, and promisors who prefer not to be subject to them have the option of refraining from undertaking the promise in the first place. Promisees, by contrast, have powerful interests in reliance that give them a basis for rejecting principles permitting promisors to defect from their promissory commitments under ordinary circumstances. These are the interests that generally lead promisors to offer promissory assurance in the first place, and once such an offer has been made and accepted, it seems perfectly reasonable for the promisee to insist that it be honored. These considerations help us to make sense of the idea that promisees have a claim against promisors to performance, and that breaking the promise would wrong the promisee in particular. These relational features can be traced to the role that is played by personal interests of promisees in reasoning about principles for the general regulation of behavior that nobody could reasonably reject.

Consider next the situation of the accidental beneficiary of the promise. People in this position also, it seems, have an objection to principles that permit promisors not to perform under the circumstances in question. There is, by hypothesis, some interest of theirs that would be affected adversely if the promisor were not to perform, and this grounds a complaint that they have, on their own behalf, to such behavior. Note, however, that there are some noteworthy respects in which their objection to promissory infidelity differs from the objection of the promisee. For one thing, it is inessential to the complaint of the accidental beneficiaries that the harm that should befall them comes about through the violation of a promise, which is a deliberate attempt on the promisor's part to induce someone else to rely on the assurance the promisor has offered. Their objection, strictly speaking, is a more generic complaint about principles that permit agents to act in any way that would be disadvantageous to prospective beneficiaries' basic interests.

Now there are versions of such a generic complaint that ground reasonable objections to principles that permit the agent to perform the harmful action. If you have promised a friend that you would stay away from a gallery opening she was hoping to attend, and you know, in addition, that your attendance would induce a deranged art critic to attack random bystanders at the opening, then you should probably stay away, even if your friend has released you from the promise. But the third party objections in this case would not be to your failure to honor a promissory undertaking, but to your acting with disregard for their physical well-being; the same objections would be in place even if no promise had ever been made to avoid the reception at the gallery. By the same token, if the third party objections to your attendance are merely that, having heard that you would not be going, they would like to be able to rely on you to stay away, that would ordinarily not be sufficient on its own to make your attendance morally impermissible. Considered as a general basis for social life, principles that required agents not to enter public spaces whenever third parties might have an unforeseeable interest in relying on them so to act would be virtually paralyzing, and agents would have powerful objections to such principles on their own behalf.[48]

The upshot is that accidental beneficiaries might or might not have reasonable objections to principles that permit agents to act in ways that flout promises they have made. But their objections, when they obtain, are independent of the fact that a promise has been undertaken. This distinguishes their complaints from the positional objections of promisees, and enables us to see why promissory fidelity is not owed to parties who fortuitously stand to benefit from it.

It has been argued, by Margaret Gilbert, that no appeal to impartial moral principles can explain the directional character of promissory obligations that has been at issue in this discussion.[49] Gilbert focuses especially on the "special standing" that promisees have to issue a rebuke against promisors in case they fail to live up to their promissory obligations.[50] The gist of her argument is that moralistic accounts of promissory duty, including that offered by Scanlon, are not adequate to make sense of this feature of them, which is deeply connected to their character as directed obligations. Moralistic accounts such as Scanlon's identify impartial principles that govern cases of this kind, which specify conditions in which agents act wrongly in violating promises that they have made. But Gilbert argues that acting wrongly in this sense cannot give promisees special standing to rebuke the agent for so acting; either nobody has standing to object when such impartial principles are flouted, or everybody does. Nor can special standing to complain be explained by appeal to the content of the impartial principles that might be brought to bear in these cases.[51]

Gilbert considers, in this connection, the idea that impartial principles of promissory fidelity might imbue promisees with the ability to release promisors from their commitments. Scanlon's own favored principle of fidelity includes a clause that achieves this effect, and it connects to something that is often associated with moral rights or claims. Thus, as we saw earlier, theorists such as Hart tend to emphasize the role of moral claims as conferring on their bearers normative powers, making them "small scale sovereigns" with respect to the domain of actions that is defined by the duties that are owed to them. In the promissory case, the conferral of such a power on the claimholder suggests the further idea that promises function to effect a transfer of rights from the promisor to the promisee.

But Gilbert contends that having the ability to neuter the promissory commitment through consent is not sufficient to make it the case that the promisee has special standing to rebuke the promisor in the case of nonperformance.[52] She offers, in support of this idea, an example in which Jane promises Diana that she will stay with Timmy unless Timmy consents to Jane's leaving. Here, we have a promissory commitment that is conditional on Timmy's consent. But it doesn't follow that the obligation is owed to Timmy, or that Timmy has a right or claim to performance. We would not say, for instance, that Timmy has special standing to rebuke Diana in case of nonperformance, and for the same reason we should not think of him as having the genuine normative power to release her from her (conditional) obligation. These deeply relational ideas are not operationalized simply through the inclusion in impartial moral principles of clauses that render promissory obligations conditional on the will of some other party.

These points are well taken, I think. But they neglect the deeper feature of Scanlon-style contractualism that gives the moral principles it delivers a relational character. This, as we saw above, is the role of personal interests in grounding reasonable objections to principles that would permit agents to act in certain ways. Promisees have claims against promisors to fulfill their promissory commitments, because it would be reasonable for them in particular to object, on their own behalf, to principles that permit promisors to defect from their promises (without special justification or prior consent). Their objection to such principles is, in itself, an objection to acts that violate promises made to them, one that is not shared by other individuals in the situation at hand. It is in this way a consequence of the contractualist procedure of justification that it grants to certain individuals "special standing" to complain about behavior that violates moral principles (or to "rebuke" such agents, in Gilbert's preferred expression). These same aspects of contractualist reasoning enable us to see those individuals as, in effect, the bearers of claims against the agent to compliance with the principles, and as the persons to whom such compliance is owed.[53]

Scanlon initially presented his theory as an account of what it is for actions to be right or wrong, in a narrow sense that we associate with morality.[54] As I noted in section 2.2, however, he has more recently backed away from this characterization, preferring to say that contractualism identifies a high-level property that *makes* actions right or wrong, in the generic sense of being to-be-done or not-to-be-done.[55] The newer formulation seems to me apt, insofar as it captures the idea, defended in chapter 2, that the relational property identified by contractualism has a distinctive kind of normative significance in the deliberation of agents, that of a practical requirement or a presumptive constraint on behavior. Scanlon also seems to me correct in thinking that this way of understanding contractualism helps us to understand how it represents an alternative to other standard moral theories, such as consequentialism, perfectionism, and divine command accounts. These approaches can all be understood, in part, as attempts to identify a high-level property or properties that have the distinctive significance for deliberation of practical requirements; and indeed, this is how I treated them in section 2.2.

But this way of thinking about contractualism does not preclude our also thinking of it as an account of *what it is* for actions to be right or wrong, in a sense different from that of being generically to-be-done or not-to-be-done. And I think there is considerable merit in this characterization as well, which corresponds to Scanlon's original way of presenting his theory. As I noted in chapters 2 and 3, we have a (perhaps indeterminate) concept of the morally right or wrong, which is understood to involve a set of objections to actions that connect to the interests of other individuals, and that have normative significance not only for agents, but also for those who are affected by their actions. Competing moral theories can be understood as filling in this abstract concept of the moral in different ways, offering alternative conceptions of what it is for something to be morally right or wrong.[56]

I have proposed that we understand the relational approach as a substantive conception of the morally right and wrong in roughly this sense. To be morally right, according to this conception, is to be something that we owe it to others to do, just insofar as they are moral persons, where these directed obligations connect to claims on their part to our compliance. I have argued that it is a signal advantage of this conception that it can help us to understand how the property of moral rightness makes actions to-be-done, in the generic sense, defining a class of practical requirements on the will. It also helps us to make sense of the characteristic interpersonal significance of the morally right and wrong, the way in which disregard for these considerations provides others with grounds for reactive and other forms of blame. Scanlon's contractualism can be understood as a further theoretical specification of this normatively significant property. To be something that we owe it to others to do, just insofar as they are persons who have corresponding claims against us, is on his account to be required by principles for the general regulation of behavior that nobody could reasonably reject.[57]

Scanlon represents contractualism as a theory of "what we owe to each other," and this characterization seems to me deeply appropriate to the relational structure that is implicit in his account of moral reasoning. It is true that he does not say very much about the possession by individuals of moral rights or claims, nor does he tend to emphasize the related idea that others are wronged by actions that flout moral obligations.[58] He appears to reject the view that these structural features of a moral conception have much explanatory work to do in helping us to understand why particular actions are morally right or wrong (a point on which I am in full agreement with him).[59] Still, it is significant that these relational features fall out of his account, which specifies principles in a way that implicitly assigns claims to particular individuals who stand to be wronged when the principles are flouted, and who will then have a privileged basis for complaint about such behavior. Moreover, if the argument of this book is correct, then the possession of these features by his account is essential to its overall plausibility as a moral theory. For these are precisely the aspects of contractualism that enable it to shed light on the characteristic normative significance of moral rightness, both for agents and for those affected by what they do.

It is important to observe, however, that the relational structure of contractualism is connected to Scanlon's original account of the nature of the objections to candidate principles that are admissible within deliberation about the morality of right and wrong. As I noted above, these are objections that individuals would have on their own behalf to principles that would permit actions that affect them in various ways. Objections of this kind are based in what I earlier called the personal interests of individuals, and we can therefore follow Scanlon in calling them personal objections. It is this aspect of contractualism that makes it appropriate to characterize it as a schema for moving from personal interests to moral claims. It is a schema I will often invoke, for ease of exposition, in discussing the derivation of specific moral duties and claims in the following chapter—though it should be kept in mind that there are also intuitionistic variants of the relational approach that dispense with the idea that there is an informative general template for moral reasoning.

It is sometimes objected that it is too restrictive to incorporate an "individualist" restriction into our account of the nature of contractualist reasoning. Thus Derek Parfit and others have contended that contractualist reasoning should not confine itself to considering objections that are based on the personal interests of individuals, but must also take into account impersonal and impartial reasons that people might have for accepting or rejecting candidate moral principles: reasons, that is, that do not have to do with how their own lives will go under the principles in question, but with their effects on the well-being of humans and other sentient creatures more generally.[60] On this way of thinking, we might all have reasons to accept principles under which things go better in the aggregate for people, even if there are no individuals who would have an objection on their own behalf to principles that would permit agents to act otherwise. Interpreted in this way, contractualist reasoning does not move from individuals' personal interests to moral claims, but from impersonal values that people might take an interest in to conclusions about what is morally required.

Debate about this issue typically focuses on the first-order normative consequences of the different interpretations of contractualism that are at issue.[61] Parfit, for instance, highlights a range of situations in which aggregative considerations appear to matter to moral thought, arguing that we can do justice to them only if we abandon the individualist restriction within our account of how moral principles are arrived at. This argument raises some important issues, to which I shall return in chapter 6. But it is also important to note that the individualist restriction is integral to the relational structure of contractualist reasoning. It is the idea that individuals have personal objections to principles that permit agents to treat them in certain ways that allows us to assign specific moral claims to them, and to suppose that they have a privileged grievance or ground for complaint when moral requirements are flouted (including grounds for resenting the actions that wrong them). Similarly, it is because of the individualist restriction that contractualism connects morality to the idea of justifiability to others, and thereby to the value of interpersonal recognition. I can justify my action specifically to each of the people affected by it if there is no reasonable basis for objecting to it in its effects on their interests in particular.

In his official response to Parfit's reflections about this issue, Scanlon showed himself to be surprisingly open to modifying the individualist restriction in order to accommodate the intuitions that Parfit was attempting to marshal.[62] More recently, he has proposed a different way of developing the contractualist method of reasoning to better cope with at least some cases in which aggregative considerations appear relevant to moral thought.[63] Start with the assumption that individuals can reasonably reject candidate principles only if those individuals have objections to the principles on their own behalf. Scanlon notes that within a framework that accepts this individualist assumption, there is room to take into account other kinds of consideration as well when thinking about whether it is reasonable, *on balance*, for individuals to reject a given principle.

Thus, consider a case in which the personal objections of individuals to the alternative principles are entirely symmetrical, so that they cancel each other out, considered one by one, but in which there are more individuals with objections of the relevant kind to the one principle than to the other. An example, to which I shall return in section 6.3 below, is a rescue case in which you can either save the single individual on Rock 1, or several individuals on Rock 2, but you cannot rescue all of the people in distress. Each of the prospective rescuees has a comparable objection, on his or her own behalf, to a principle that requires you to save the people on the other rock. But Scanlon notes that it does not follow from this that you are not required to save the people on Rock 2. Perhaps it would be unreasonable for the Rock 1 person to reject a principle that prescribes this course of action, given the greater number of individuals who stand to enjoy symmetrical benefits from the acceptance of that principle.

This understanding of contractualist reasoning seems to me closer to the spirit of Scanlon's original position than Parfit's direct appeal to impersonal and impartial reasons. The question at the center of this modified approach is what principles it would be reasonable *for an individual* to reject, where aggregative considerations are allowed to bear on this question as a kind of tie-breaker in cases in which the personal objections of those affected by the alternatives cancel each other out, taken one by one. Scanlon is right that it is not built into the notion of reasonable rejectability that it should not have some limited sensitivity to the number of people who are liable to be affected in the same way if a given principle were accepted and generally followed.

Having said that, I worry that the resulting interpretation still attenuates the specifically interpersonal dimension of contractualism that I have been at pains to emphasize in this section, even if it does this less dramatically than the wholesale abandonment of the individualist restriction. We were looking for an interpretation of moral reasoning that would elucidate the idea that moral obligations are owed to particular individuals, who have claims against the agent to compliance with the principles that determine them. Those elements are most firmly in place if what resolves the question of whether a given individual can reasonably reject a principle are the comprehensive implications of the principle for the life of that very individual, as compared to the similar effects of the alternative principles on the lives of other individuals. The people on Rock 2 might have an objection to principles that permit you to save the single person on Rock 1, but it is not an objection they have on their own behalf, grounded in personal interests in how their own lives might go under such principles. For that reason, it does not intuitively undergird the assignment to each of them of a specific claim against you that he or she, rather than the Rock 1 person, should be saved.[64] Nor does it shed light on the idea that they would each be wronged if you were to go to Rock 1, or that doing so would involve a failure to recognize them in particular as sources of claims.

Parfit, for his part, asserts that he is interested in an interpretation of contractualism that explains why actions that are wrong in the generic and "indefinable" sense of being not-to-be-done are also wrong in several ancillary senses: being, for instance, actions that cannot be justified to others, or actions that would make reactive emotions appropriate on the part of those affected by them.[65] But these further senses of wrongness are parts of a relational conception of the moral that is ultimately sacrificed when the individualist restriction is abandoned or relaxed. Furthermore, the features they involve are crucial to the appeal of contractualism, construed as a substantive conception of morality that will make sense of its distinctive normative features. We can allow impersonal objections to candidate principles within contractualist reasoning, or concede that questions of reasonable rejectability are sensitive to the number of persons who have personal objections of a similar kind. Alternatively, we can hang onto the attractive idea that contractualist reasoning functions to assign moral claims to individuals. But I do not believe we can do both. And if we sacrifice the relational character of contractualism, we will lose, as well, the very features that make it so powerful as a theoretical account of the domain of interpersonal morality.

6

Some Practical Consequences

IN THIS CHAPTER I TURN to the implications of relational morality for some first-order questions about what it is right and wrong to do. According to the relational approach, actions are obligatory or morally right just in case there are individuals who have claims against the agent to their performance. But there are a variety of particular duties that seem difficult to wedge into this framework. These include, for instance, cases in which directed obligations do not seem to correspond to any assignable Hohfeld-style rights, such as duties of gratitude and of mutual aid. Another class of potential problem cases are those in which morality apparently requires us to take into account the aggregate effects of our agency on the many people who might be affected by it, rather than considering its bearing on the personal interests of individuals, one by one.

The field of first-order normative ethics is exceedingly capacious, and I can obviously only scratch the surface of it in the space of a single chapter. Even the central example to which I have repeatedly returned in this book, that of promissory obligation, raises issues that I have hardly begun to address, and that will also not be resolved in the present chapter (concerning, for instance, the precise nature of the personal interests that ground promisees' claims to promissory fidelity). My larger aim in this book is to make a case for the fruitfulness of understanding moral requirements in relational terms. To this end, it is not necessary to resolve specific questions about what exactly we owe it to other people to do, morally speaking; nor do we need to clarify the justifications that figure within moral reflection in all cases. The hope, rather, is that readers can be persuaded to agree that first-order moral questions are aptly characterized in relational terms, as questions about the claims that individuals hold against each other, just insofar as they are each members of the manifold of moral persons. For this purpose, however, it will be necessary to say something, at least in general terms, about the kinds of moral issues that have seemed especially resistant to treatment within a relational framework.

I begin by discussing some of the cases in which it seems most intuitive to think of moral duties in directed terms, as owed to other persons. These cases turn out to be surprisingly disparate in character, raising the question of whether they have any important features in common that might preclude the extension of the model of directed obligation to the entirety of the moral domain. One feature I focus on is the foreseeability of a specific individual as the person to whom duties of these disparate kinds might be directed. This leads me to consider some cases in which it has been alleged that others can be wronged by our actions, even though the individuals who are wronged are not discernible as claimholders by us in advance of acting. I suggest that cases of this kind, to the extent they are agreed to be plausible as cases of moral wrongs, can be understood to involve secondary claims, which are parasitic on the first-order claims held by discernible individuals.

Secondary moral claims such as these, if there really are such, would diverge in certain ways from familiar Hohfeldian claim rights. Other cases in which the moral claims posited by relational morality differ from assignable moral rights include cases of imperfect moral duty, such as duties of gratitude and mutual aid. I discuss these examples in section 6.2, suggesting that we can make sense of them within a broadly relational framework if we adapt the notion of a moral claim in ways that seem to me independently defensible (if also, perhaps, somewhat surprising).

In the final two sections of the chapter, I discuss some cases that are widely taken to be especially challenging for relational conceptions. These are cases that involve the non-identity problem, where the assignment of claims to individuals has the paradoxical consequence that the individuals would not have existed had the claims been honored, and cases, such as those involving rescue situations, in which the number of people who might be affected by our actions seems to matter to moral thought. Cases of both kinds have generated a very large literature, and I have no expectation of being able to do justice to them here. My very limited aim will be, instead, to point out that the most important of the non-identity cases can in fact be accommodated in relational terms, and to sketch an overlooked way in which the numbers might count within a conception of moral deliberation that is focused on the claims of individuals.

I concede, however, that there may be some cases involving aggregation that cannot be accommodated neatly within a relational framework. In section 6.4, I propose that we understand cases of this kind to elicit normative intuitions about the extramoral significance of human life and well-being. Considerations of this kind may have an important role to play in certain deliberative contexts, where legitimate authorities have decisions to make about the allocation of resources under conditions of scarcity, but this is compatible with their lacking the same kind of significance in contexts of individual deliberation. I conclude by suggesting that if well-being has independent significance for individual deliberation, it is not as a consideration that outweighs the duties of relational morality, but as a potential source of independent requirements that might conceivably conflict with what we are morally obligated to do.

6.1. Foreseeability, Claims, and Wrongs

In section 4.1 above, I noted that directed obligations are often understood by philosophers to arise out of historical relationships between the parties that they link. Joseph Raz, for instance, has suggested that there are three kinds of personal relationship that can generate a directed duty between two people: commitments or undertakings by one party toward another; thick social ties, such as those that connect friends and family members; and the relationships that underlie debts of gratitude.[1] About directed obligations of these kinds, he also observes that some of them do not correspond to anything we would intuitively think of as a right on the part of the person to whom they are directed; and that we cannot, in any case, understand all of morality to consist of such obligations. This first of these two further claims seems to me correct, though I reject the second of them.

Before getting to these issues, however, it will be well to look more closely at some of the cases in which Raz takes personal relationships to give rise to directed obligations. For they are surprisingly disparate in character. One subclass of cases involves interactions that can be understood to give rise to literal or metaphorical debts of some kind. There is, for instance, the kind of undertaking whereby people accept a benefit from another party in exchange for a commitment to provide a benefit to that party at a later time. Think of a commercial transaction, such as the consumer contract that gives you a television set now on the condition that you make monthly installment payments to the store over the next three years. In this kind of case, one has incurred through the transaction a financial debt that one owes it to the other party to repay, in accordance with the contractual terms. With debts of gratitude, we have something similar, only the debt to be repaid is generally figurative rather than literal, and the terms of repayment leave more to the discretion of the indebted party (a point to which I return in the following section). In these kinds of cases, the personal relationship that gives rise to the directed obligation is one that confers a benefit or advantage on the agent who stands under it, and the feeling that the agent owes something to the other party goes together with an awareness of a kind of imbalance between them that needs to be righted.

Some of the debts that give rise to directed duties are incurred voluntarily, including the transactional ones that involve commercial and other forms of contracts or commitments. But others are not, including many debts of gratitude, which result from kindnesses or advantages bestowed on a person who has not necessarily done anything to bring them about. This is clear, too, in at least some cases involving social ties, such as those that link the members of biological families. Children obviously do not get to choose their parents, and yet they are generally understood to have obligations of various kinds that are owed to them. These directed obligations might be understood, at least in part, as a special case of debts of gratitude, insofar as children have generally benefited extensively from the exertions that their parents undertook to raise them.[2] Here, as in other such cases, the sense of obligation to the parents might be traced to the positive effects that one has enjoyed as a result of the historical relationship, which somehow need to be repaid, even if they were not voluntarily incurred.

But this feature, too, is not essential to Raz's examples of familiar directed duties. In other cases that involve close social ties, it is implausible to suppose that the sense of a duty owed to the other party has much if anything to do with an awareness of oneself as having enjoyed a benefit that needs to be repaid. Friendship, for instance, typically does not have this character. To be sure, it represents a great good for the parties to it; but the good is one that is symmetrically enjoyed by both of them, rather than involving an imbalance of burdens and benefits that somehow requires to be righted, going forward. And yet friends are naturally understood as having special obligations that are owed to each other. A similar point might be made about the relationship in which parents stand to their children. Naturally this is a tremendously valuable form of human relationship, representing one of the great goods of which humans are capable; and people who have relationships of this kind clearly owe various duties of care and concern to their children. But it would be odd to theorize these directed duties as involving the enjoyment of benefits that now stands to be paid back to the party who has bestowed it.[3] The debt model, in either its voluntary or its nonvoluntary variants, simply doesn't apply to cases such as these. Nor is it a felicitous template for understanding promissory obligation, which is another Raz-style undertaking that is conventionally understood to give rise to a directed duty. Promisors bind themselves to promisees by giving them their word, but these commitments are in force regardless of whether there is an asymmetry of benefits and burdens between the parties that requires to be rebalanced.[4]

Raz's examples are all cases in which directed duties are generated by historical relationships between the parties to them. But as we have just seen, it is difficult to discern any significant feature that they might be understood to have in common, beyond their being cases in which directed duties are relationship based. The most we could say, perhaps, is the following. First, the diverse historical relationships at issue in these cases all serve the function of rendering discernible the particular claimholder to whom the directed duty is owed. For instance, out of all the countless friendships that exist in the world, the duties that I owe as a friend are directed to the specific person with whom I have interacted in a relationship of this general kind. The relationship thus helps to individuate the claimholder, making foreseeable to agents the persons to whom they are linked in a specific relational nexus.

Second, in each of the cases considered so far, it seems there is a valuable relationship of some kind that is in play. In many cases, the valuable relationships in question are the very ones that play the individuating role. This is the pattern we see in the examples involving friendship and family relationships, where ties of love that are immensely important in human life also serve to pick out the specific individuals to whom directed obligations are owed. But the pattern does not extend to all of the Raz-style examples. The consumer contract that is entered into when the purchaser of a good commits to making future payments to the seller helps to individuate them, as parties who are connected to each other by a specific directed duty and claim. But the contractual relationship is not itself necessarily valuable; on the contrary, as noted above, it is tempting to think of it as involving a worrisome imbalance between the linked parties that requires being restored to equilibrium. The valuable relationship in this case, and in many other cases of promissory commitment, is one that is enabled through compliance by the agent with the terms of the directed obligation. This behavior serves to right the imbalance between the parties that is created by the original commitment, or to enable promisors to realize in their relations to promisees the value of interpersonal recognition discussed in section 4.4 above.

Once we are clear about these points, however, then it looks as if the role of personal relationships as a basis for directed duties is dispensable. There has to be something, perhaps, that renders claimholders discernible by the agents against whom their claims are held. It is also plausible to suppose that compliance with the relational duty that is owed to those individuals should realize a valuable way of relating to them. But these conditions can be satisfied even in cases in which there is no antecedent relationship at all between the parties. This brings us back to a theme from chapter 4, where I argued that morality might be understood to consist in a set of self-standing relational requirements. Thus, consider the case of a face-to-face encounter with an individual whom you have never met before, but who stands to be affected significantly by something it is open to you to do. (To return to a recurring example, perhaps she is lying on the sidewalk with an obvious case of gout, and your continuing trajectory would cause a painful encounter with her outstretched foot.) Here it is clear enough from the situation which individual might be understood to have a claim against you not to cause her easily avoidable distress. It also seems that acknowledgment of this claim against you would enable you to relate to the individual in a valuable way, on a basis of what I have called interpersonal recognition. So it appears that there is no obstacle in the way of extending the relational model of moral obligations and claims to a situation of this kind, despite the absence of any antecedent relationship between you and the individual to whom the duty is directed. You owe it to the stranger on the sidewalk to avoid a painful encounter with her diseased appendage, and this thought is fully available to you in the situation I have described.

There are, of course, plenty of cases in which our actions have significant effects on individuals who are not foreseeable in advance of our performing them. Cases of this description figure prominently in a novel interpretation that Nicolas Cornell has recently advanced of the notion of a moral wrong.[5] Cornell holds that there are two ways in which people could be wronged morally by the actions of another party. They might, first, have rights that are infringed through the party's actions. Or they might, second, be affected adversely by actions of the party that infringe somebody else's rights. In cases of the latter kind, there will be a moral wrong that does not itself violate the claims of the persons who are wronged, and that therefore cannot be understood to involve attitudes of disregard for those persons' claims or for the interests that underlie them. Cases of this kind would thus fail to fit the schema

I have offered in this book for understanding the idea of a wrong or a moral injury, which connects these notions closely to that of a claim.

Cornell's argument for his conclusion is driven by consideration of a range of more and less familiar cases, which he believes elicit the firm intuition that people are often wronged by actions that do not infringe rights of theirs in particular. There is, for instance, the case of the third-party beneficiary to a promissory transaction (where, in at least one common variant, A promises B that A would look after B's mother, C). Cornell agrees with H. L. A. Hart and others that it is B rather than C who holds a moral claim against A to promissory fidelity in a case of this kind;[6] but he thinks that C would be wronged by A's action if A were to fail to honor the promise that was owed to B (thereby violating B's right). Another example with this alleged structure is the well-known case of *Palsgraf v. Long Island Railroad Co.* Here the employees of the railroad negligently rush a passenger onto the carriage of a moving train, dislodging the passenger's luggage in the process, which happens to have contained some fireworks; as a result of the mishap, the fireworks explode, causing a scale to topple over and injure Mrs. Palsgraf, who was standing in a different area of the platform. The New York Court of Appeals ruled that the railroad company was not liable for the harm to Palsgraf, who had no right against them to protection from harms that were not foreseeable. But Cornell thinks Palsgraf was nevertheless clearly wronged by the actions of the company's employees, insofar as these caused her significant harm. And similar conclusions may be reached about a range of other cases in which adverse consequences accrue to individuals as a result of actions that violate the claims of another party, including harms caused by overheard lies or negative effects that fall to family members of individuals whose rights have been infringed (such as the parents of a child killed in a car accident involving a drunk driver).

I do not myself share Cornell's intuitions about many of his cases. In most of them, the details that would make it plausible that a third party is wronged through the agent's action would also provide a basis for an antecedent claim or right that is assignable to that individual. If A's promise to B induces C to rely on A to provide the assistance that C needs, and this effect could be anticipated by A at the time the promise was made, then it seems to me pretty clear that C has a claim against A to such assistance, even if C was not the addressee of A's promise. Similarly, if people make misleading statements about matters of general interest in a public setting, they may negligently violate a duty of due care to ensure that others in causal range of them do not form false beliefs based on their behavior and speech. In virtue of occupying the same public space with the speaker, those whose beliefs are apt to be influenced by the speaker's utterances are foreseeable as potential claimholders, even if they are not the immediate object of the speaker's attention at the time when the deceptive statements were put forward.[7]

Furthermore, it seems to me that we all have claims against other people that they should not act to harm those we love, or subject them to significant and avoidable risk of harm. We may not be known specifically by the wrongdoers in cases of this kind. But insofar as the immediate victims of their actions can be discerned by wrongdoers, they have cognitive access as well to these additional claimholders. It is well known, after all, that each individual is connected to other persons through chains of love and affection, and that their personal interests will also be damaged if the individual to whom they are attached is harmed by the malicious or reckless conduct of the wrongdoer. These effects on friends and family give them a reasonable basis for complaint about the things that are done to those to whom they are attached. In *Palsgraf*, on the other hand, it may be more difficult to assign a clear claim to the person who suffered an injury as a result of the wrongful conduct. Here, the individual who was harmed by the railroad employees' conduct was really not foreseeable in advance by them, in part because they had no reason to believe that the luggage contained explosives that might pose a danger to passengers waiting innocently on other parts of the platform. But then, the court that decided the case seemed to agree that there was no clear wrong to the injured party under the civil law of tort.[8]

Having made these observations, I do not wish to insist that Cornell is incorrect in his verdicts about at least some of the cases he discusses. There is a rigorist tradition, to which he alludes, of thinking that people can rightly be held to account for the harmful consequences that flow from the wrongful actions that they perform.[9] If holding morally accountable is an ex post response to actions that wrong another party, as I suggested it is in chapter 3, then this might entail that the parties who are harmed in such cases are also morally wronged. Note, however, that by Cornell's own reckoning, the wrongful actions that harm third parties count as wrongs to those parties only if they violate *somebody's* rights or claims.[10] This strikes me as a significant concession, pointing toward a different account from the one he favors of what might be going on in cases with the structure he describes.

People who flout their relational moral duties disregard, in the first instance, the claims that are held against them by the people to whom the duties are owed. In doing this, however, they can also be said to have shown neglect for the social dimension of their agency, including its bearing on the personal interests of those who stand to be affected by it. But we all have a stake in people taking seriously this dimension of their conduct. One way to articulate this thought within a relational conception of morality would be to assume that we each have secondary claims not to be harmed as a result of conduct that flouts, in a primary sense, the moral claims of other parties. These secondary claims will be apt to proliferate rampantly in any given case, and in a way that is not foreseeable by agents, insofar as there are any number of unpredictable harmful consequences that could potentially befall third parties as a result of wrongful exercises of their agency. But the proliferation of claimholders is not a problem, in itself (as we shall see in more detail in section 6.2). As for foreseeability, that too does not seem to be an obstacle to the assignment of secondary claims in these cases, insofar as that assignment is parasitic on the assignment of primary claims to parties who *are* foreseeable by the agent. Agents might owe it to individuals in the larger community to protect them from the harmful consequences that could result when they flout the primary moral claims that others hold against them. The way to live up to these secondary responsibilities would be to honor the primary claims of other parties, and this is something that it is anyway reasonable to expect them to do.

Though I do not wish to take a stand on the plausibility of this general picture here, it seems to me a promising way to accommodate the intuitions Cornell is trying to marshal within a thoroughly relational conception of moral wrongs. There are clearly personal interests that each of us has in not being harmed or affected adversely as a result of the agency of other persons. And these interests might well ground secondary claims that we have against agents, which piggyback on the primary moral claims of other parties, and which find expression in complaints we have against agents in cases in which we are harmed through their neglect of the primary duties that they owe to others. To put this reasoning in contractualist terms, people who stand to be harmed by actions that wrong another party have an objection, based in a personal interest of theirs, to principles that permit such actions. What counterobjections might agents bring on their behalf to principles that prohibit such actions? They are, by hypothesis, already morally impermissible, which means that the agent's objection to a prohibition on them is weaker than the objections of those in the position of the primary claimholder. It follows that it isn't intolerably burdensome on people in the agent's position to expect that they should refrain from the actions that are in question. But then, it would also not seem unreasonable for people who are adversely af-

fected by such actions to object, on their own behalf, to the agent's performing them.

In neglecting or disregarding the primary claims that others have against
them, agents could be said to be thereby disregarding the secondary interests
that unforeseeable third parties have in not being subjected to avoidable
harms. As agents, we cannot completely immunize people against the harmful
effects that might befall them through our actions. But it is in our power to see
to it that we honor their primary claims against us; and it is a coherent further
thought that we might also owe it to members of the larger community of
moral persons to protect them from the adverse consequences that sometimes
result when we flout these foreseeable primary responsibilities.[11]

Secondary claims of the kind just described, if there are such, would not be
a hugely important part of the moral landscape. But my present point is that
they are at least intelligible within the kind of relational framework I have been
developing. If it is accepted that these secondary claims exist, however, they
would be unlike familiar Hohfeld-style rights, in at least some respects.

It is sometimes said that rights of this kind need to be "enforceable," and
that enforceability in turn presupposes that there are agents to whom the corresponding directed duty can clearly be assigned.[12] I am not entirely sure what
exactly "enforceability" is supposed to come to in this connection, or whether
it legitimately applies to all cases of moral rights (in contrast to what we might
call juridical or political rights).[13] It does not seem to me to be a general condition on the intelligibility of moral rights that it be permissible for the bearer
of them to use physical coercion to ensure that they are honored. Promisees,
for instance, cannot in this way force promisors to uphold their promissory
commitments. But perhaps the internalization of claims as a basis for accountability relations, including subjection to reactive and other forms of blame,
could be understood as a form of enforceability appropriate to moral rights. It
might then be maintained that moral rights should at least be enforceable in
this manner. But I have argued that this kind of enforceability condition is
satisfied by any moral consideration that rises to the status of a claim, including the secondary claims characterized above. This shows itself in the fact
that it would be fitting for the bearers of the claims, if there are such, to resent
the agents who flout them by engaging in wrongful conduct that ends up
harming them.

But there are other features of Hohfeld-style rights that seem to be missing
in these cases. One of these is that the class of secondary claimholders can be
identified only ex post, after the wrongful action has been performed. What
they allegedly have is a claim not to be harmed through wrongful agency,

rather than a claim not to be exposed to the risk of harm; but we cannot tell whether wrongful conduct will in fact harm a third party in unforeseeable ways until it has taken place. This makes it virtually impossible to identify in advance specific agents to whom the corresponding obligations not to harm might be attached.[14] This connects to the fact that the claims in question are not able to function, in the deliberation of agents, as considerations with independent normative significance; their relevance to deliberation, as noted earlier, is inherited from that of the primary rights on which they are parasitic. There are potential moral considerations here with an implicitly relational structure, but they differ in this way from paradigm cases of moral rights.

Another feature that we associate with the familiar examples of rights is ex ante determinacy in regard to the behavior to which the right-holder is entitled. Our basic defensive liberty rights, for instance, include fairly determinate claims against others, specifiable in advance, not to initiate intentional bodily contact without our consent (barring special circumstances), not to impede our free movement through public spaces, and so on. And promisees' moral rights against promisors include the claim against them (again, barring special circumstances) to see to it that the specific terms of the promise are upheld. Where ex ante determinacy of this kind, as to the specific behavior that is expected of an agent, is not in place, I think we would be reluctant to understand the situation as involving an assignable moral right. This may be a further respect in which secondary moral claims do not resemble standard cases of assignable moral rights, insofar as there is no way to specify determinate standards of ex ante conduct to which they allegedly connect. Finally, rights are generally understood to be considerations that connect to behavior that specifically affects the bearer of the alleged right. Thus, suppose an agent is under a duty to do something that won't (as it happens) affect me at all, and that isn't intended to affect me. I might conceivably take an interest, of a suitably nonpersonal kind, in whether the duty is fulfilled. But it would strike us as odd to say that I have a right against the agent so to act. Rights are intuitively assignable to individuals, it seems, only in cases in which the determinate actions to which those individuals are entitled are ones that would promote their personal interests in some way.

According to a relational conception, however, it seems there will be some primary moral claims that do not have these salient characteristics that we associate with moral rights. I turn to some important examples of this kind in the following section.

6.2. Claims without Rights: Imperfect Moral Duties

In the section 5.3 above, I noted one important difference between moral claims, as I would propose that they be understood, and Hohfeldian moral rights. Moral claim rights are often taken to be considerations that we reflect on within moral deliberations, and that we might permissibly infringe. By contrast, the relational interpretation takes moral deliberation to culminate in the assignment to individuals of moral claims. In this section I want to consider some specific moral claims that we would ordinarily be reluctant to classify as rights. These are claims that correlate with so-called imperfect moral duties. Ultimately it seems to me fairly unimportant whether we designate these claims as rights, or call them something else instead. But the features of them that lead us to reject the talk of rights in this context might also suggest that the moral considerations in question cannot be accommodated within the kind of relational view I have been developing in this book. So it is important to take a closer look at their nature and structure.

Suppose that another person does you a kindness, at significant personal cost—say, stopping at the side of a dark and lonely road to help you fix a flat tire, with the result that she gets home very late, very hungry, and needing a shower. The act of benefiting you is normally understood to involve a change in your moral relations, bringing it about that you now stand under a moral duty of gratitude. This way of speaking is perfectly natural, but it lacks at least some of the elements that we tend to associate with directed obligation. In particular, we would normally balk at assigning to the benefactor a moral right to your gratitude for the kindness that was bestowed on you.

Another case of this general kind involves duties of mutual aid. We all have moral obligations to assist those who are in serious distress, even at some significant sacrifice. But there are of course many different potential beneficiaries in the world, and it is not remotely the case that we can personally do anything to assist more than a small number of them. We intuitively have significant discretion, as it were, to determine for ourselves how we will live up to the requirements of mutual aid. Under these moral conditions, we would ordinarily not want to say that any of the potential beneficiaries of our efforts has a specific moral right against us to our help, despite the fact that we have an obligation (perhaps a very weighty one) to contribute to relieving the acute needs of people in their position.

The general question that is raised by such cases is whether they can be made sense of within the framework of the relational interpretation of morality that I have been developing in this book. There are moral obligations here, but apparently nothing in the way of assignable moral rights. Can we nevertheless understand the obligations to be directed to specific claimholders, in accordance with the schema of relational morality that I have been presenting?

Let's start with gratitude. It is natural to think that debts of gratitude are owed by beneficiaries to those who have bestowed benefits on them. Indeed, as noted in section 6.1, Raz cites cases of this kind as among the salient examples of personal relationships that can give rise to directed duties. But Raz also agrees with my observation that benefactors would not ordinarily be understood to have a moral right to the gratitude that beneficiaries are under a duty to display. What might lie behind the reluctance to assign rights to benefactors, especially given the fact that the obligation seems to be one that is owed to them in some way? One consideration might be alienability. Many moral rights can be waived by the person who is their bearer, through the right-holder's consent to the actions that would ordinarily count as infringements. I can waive my right against you that you not trespass on my property or body by inviting you into my home, or by consenting to the surgical procedure whereby you would remove the mole on my chin. But the benefactor cannot in the same way waive the obligation on the part of the beneficiary to reciprocate with gratitude for the kindness that was done. This consideration is inconclusive, however, since it is controversial (to say the least) to suppose that alienability is built into the idea of a moral right. There is certainly no incoherence in supposing that some basic rights, such as the right not to be enslaved by another person, cannot be alienated by any voluntary exertion of the right-holder's will.[15]

In most cases of this kind, the reason why the right will be inalienable is that it is grounded in personal interests on the part of the right-holder that are especially important, perhaps on account of their connection to the right-holder's moral standing. But nothing like this seems to be the case with duties of gratitude. So that is one feature of gratitude that we need to make sense of. Another is the discretion that beneficiaries seem to have to determine for themselves how they are to fulfill the duties they undertake by accepting another person's generously bestowed benefits. This latter feature seems especially important to the question of the assignment of rights to the benefactor. As we saw in the preceding section, rights seem to be most clearly in place in situations where there is a specific category of performance that the right-holder has a claim against other people to engage in. Thus rights to property or bodily integrity involve claims against other people that they not engage in unauthorized trespass, and promissory rights involve claims against promisors to keep their word. But there is nothing so specific in play in the gratitude case; it isn't as if the benefactor can insist, say, that the person benefited should take her out to dinner at a nice restaurant on a day of her choosing, even if a performance of that kind would count as satisfying the beneficiary's duty of gratitude.[16]

It would take us too far afield to attempt a complete explanation of the importance of agential discretion in the case of gratitude. But a plausible account might begin by emphasizing the function of these duties in restoring an element of equality into the relationship between the benefactor and the beneficiary.[17] As I noted in the preceding section, directed duties that involve literal and figurative debts to another individual are cases in which there is often an imbalance between the parties that is restored to equilibrium through the discharging of the duty. This is obvious in cases involving literal financial debts, but it also seems present in cases of merely metaphorical debts.

In the gratitude case, the figurative debt is a matter, in part, of the receipt by the beneficiary of some concrete advantage that has been bestowed by the benefactor. If this were all that the imbalance involves, however, then the debt of gratitude that restores equilibrium should be comparatively straightforward to calculate, and the role of discretion on the part of the benefactor would remain mysterious. But there is a distinct element to the imbalance created by the benefactor's act that hasn't yet been acknowledged, involving the beneficiary's dependency on the agency of the benefactor.[18] In our original example involving the flat tire, the benefactor's act of generosity, though it confers a clear benefit on you, also takes something away from you, namely, your active role in shaping the relationship with the benefactor on common terms. What is needed, then, is not merely a repayment of the positive benefit, but a mechanism of repayment that also corrects the disequilibrium of dependency and agency that has emerged between the parties. By undertaking to reciprocate for the favor that was bestowed, beneficiaries assert agential control as partners to the relationships in which they stand to their benefactors, something that is not really possible so long as gratitude is not displayed or performed. But if gratitude is a mechanism for effecting the transition from dependency to agency, it makes sense that beneficiaries should have wide latitude to determine for themselves the specific form that their gratitude will assume. It also makes sense that benefactors should lack discretion to waive the duty of gratitude that is in place, since their doing so would only serve to exacerbate the dependency that the duty of gratitude is meant to help overcome.

Even if we do not speak of a right to gratitude in these cases, however, it nevertheless seems to me that there is a residual claim that is in place, one that corresponds to the familiar idea that the duty is owed by beneficiaries to their benefactors. The claim is not to any specific action on the part of the beneficiaries of the kind that, on its own, would be understood to discharge their debts. It is, rather, a claim that the beneficiaries should exercise their discretion to do something to restore the agential imbalance that has emerged, by reciprocating in some way for the kindness that was originally done to them. A moral consideration of this kind, insofar as it makes essential reference to the discretion of the beneficiary, lacks the determinacy characteristic of cases involving standard moral rights. But it includes the other elements that are familiar to us from the relational framework. It corresponds to a duty that is understood to be directed to the benefactor, and to the extent that this is the case, we can understand it as a claim held by the benefactor against the beneficiary. This shows itself, further, in the fact that a failure to discharge the debt of gratitude that is held by the beneficiary would not merely be wrong, but something that wrongs the benefactor in particular. It would reflect the kind of disregard for claims that gives rise to a grievance or moral injury, understood as a privileged basis for reactive and other forms of blame.

I would note, however, that the benefactor might not be the only moral claimholder in cases of this general kind. Benefactors have specific interests in conducting relationships with others on a basis of agential equality; to put things in contractualist terms, this gives them a reasonable ground for objecting to principles for the regulation of behavior that permit beneficiaries to refrain from reciprocating for benefits received. But beneficiaries, too, have a strong personal interest in conducting relationships on this basis, one that might ground a reasonable objection on their own behalf to the same principles. This suggests that beneficiaries might owe the debt of gratitude not only to their benefactors, but also to themselves, and that they have a claim against themselves to live up to the debt, one that runs in parallel to the claims that are held by their benefactors. Among other things, this would help to make sense of the feeling that gratitude can intelligibly lead beneficiaries to bestow benefits on people other than their immediate benefactors (for instance, in cases in which there is no longer anything that can be done to reciprocate for the favor that was done to them).[19] A consequence of this way of thinking would be that beneficiaries who fail to discharge their debts of gratitude would not merely have wronged their benefactors, but also themselves, giving them a retrospective grievance about their own past conduct. We might express this aspect of the situation by saying that they failed to take advantage of an opportunity that was open to them, at the earlier time, to restore agential equality to a personal relationship to which they were a party. As with the secondary claims considered in section 6.1 above, this may not be the most important dimension of cases involving debts of gratitude. But it is something that is intelligible within the relational framework, and that helps us to make sense of features of these cases that might otherwise seem puzzling.

Turn next to the case of mutual aid. Here, too, though there are duties that we stand under to help people who are in severe distress, we are reluctant to suppose that any specific individual has a claim against us to such assistance. And here too, our reluctance to ascribe rights to potential beneficiaries seems to go along with the discretion that agents are understood to have to determine for themselves how the duty is carried out. It is noteworthy, however, that agential discretion goes much farther in the case of mutual aid than in that of gratitude. With gratitude, as we noted above, there is a specific individual, the benefactor, to whom the duty of gratitude is at least partially owed. But with mutual aid, by contrast, agents have extensive discretion to decide for themselves which of many potential beneficiaries they will in fact end up assisting. They could choose to provide aid to the impoverished and vulnerable individuals in remote countries that the Against Malaria Foundation is targeting through its efforts to distribute insecticidal nets; or they could help people in their immediate community who receive the support of a local food and housing organization. If we are to bring such duties within the ambit of the relational approach, then, we will need to reconcile this extensive discretion with the idea that the duties in question are nevertheless owed to some particular individuals, who can be understood in turn to have a claim, if not a specific moral right, to the agent's compliance.

In setting the problem up in these terms, I am taking for granted what I believe to be our common-sense way of thinking about moral duties of mutual aid, as the paradigm case of imperfect duties to others. But this aspect of the conventional wisdom about them might be questioned. Adherents of the Effective Altruism movement, in particular, are inclined to challenge the idea that there is genuine agential discretion in cases of this kind to pursue projects of mutual aid that are less than optimal in their expected effects on the welfare of those who might benefit from them.[20] There is of course much to be said for developing a critical understanding of the effectiveness of various aid programs and development efforts that it is open to both individuals and governments to support. Research into this question might help us to appreciate that some options are not above the threshold of effectiveness that would make it reasonable to include them in the set of charitable alternatives that we have discretion to pursue. To the extent the proponents of Effective Altruism deny that we have this discretion, however, it seems to me that they are simply shoehorning this aspect of our moral thinking—the part concerned with beneficence, as we might put it—into an essentially consequentialist mold. If we are not under a standing requirement to maximize the impartial good, then there is no reason to question whether we have agential discretion to pursue suboptimal projects in fulfillment of our imperfect duty of mutual aid.[21]

So my question is, how should we understand the discretionary duty of mutual aid within the framework of relational morality? Here is one possible answer. That agents are under such duties at all presumably reflects the fact that there are powerful objections that certain people have on their own behalf to principles that permit affluent agents to do little or nothing to assist those who are in extreme need. True, agents have objections in their own person to principles that require them to assist others in need. The most compelling of these stem from the requirements of living a recognizably individual human life; we have attachments to persons and projects that structure our activities at the most fundamental level, and that make it impossible to think of ourselves simply as conduits for the promotion of impersonal value.[22]

But of course those who are in a situation of acute need have even more powerful objections to principles that permit affluent agents to do little or nothing for people in their position. Thinking about the situation in these incipiently relational terms, it is plausible to suppose that acceptable principles would require that level of sacrifice from the affluent that would be sufficient to alleviate the acute need and dependency of the most vulnerable, if the principles in question were generally internalized and complied with by those in a position to help, while granting such agents discretion to decide for themselves, compatibly with their own projects and commitments, how exactly they will contribute.[23] The role of agential discretion, in this context, would be to reconcile, as far as possible, the positive demands of beneficence with the need that individuals have to live a distinctive human life, one that reflects their own personal projects and interests. (Note that for all I have said so far, the resulting duties of mutual aid might be as demanding as you please; it is a further first-order question, to which I do not propose to enter here, precisely how onerous it would be for any given individual to live up to the moral requirements of mutual aid in a given case.[24])

If this is the right way of thinking about mutual aid, however, then it seems we have a way of identifying the parties to whom the duties are owed. They would include all of those with acute needs who are in the class of potential beneficiaries of a given agent's beneficent efforts.[25] These are the people who have objections on their own behalf to principles that would permit agents to do little or nothing. We might therefore wish to say that agents owe it to all of the individuals in this class that they should live up to the principles of mutual aid that it would be unreasonable for anyone to reject; by the same token, each of these individuals has a claim against agents that they should comply with the principles in question.

These moral claims admittedly have some unusual features. For one thing, they are not claims that can be waived or alienated voluntarily by the persons who individually hold them. This seems to reflect the fact that each of the individual claimholders is a member of a class of potential beneficiaries of aid that includes many other individuals who are equally in a position of acute need; no one of them is authorized to waive entitlements that in any given case are liable to benefit other members in the class. This points to a further feature of the claims at issue that is even more peculiar. Not only are they not claims to any specific kind of performance on the part of the agent against whom they are held, since agents have wide discretion to determine for themselves which kinds of contribution they are going to make to alleviating the distress of those who are in dire need. They are not even claims that agents should do anything to help the claimholder in particular, since they could fully be discharged through discretionary efforts that end up assisting completely different members of the class of potential beneficiaries.

These peculiarities make it especially inapt to speak of assignable moral rights to assistance in cases of mutual aid. But it seems to me that moral claims, and the corresponding directed duties, may nevertheless intelligibly be ascribed to the parties in these cases, and that it can be illuminating to think in these terms. Affluent agents owe it to each of the individuals in the class of potential beneficiaries to do their fair share to provide needed assistance. And each of those individuals in turn has claims against individual affluent agents that they should so contribute. We are perhaps accustomed to thinking of moral claims as demands, compliance with which would redound to the benefit of the claimholder in particular, but I don't see this as something that is built into the very meaning of a claim. A reflection of the relational structure implicit even in cases such as this one is the naturalness of the idea that affluent agents who do little or nothing to help out will be unable to justify their conduct to any of the individuals who are in the class of potential beneficiaries. Those individuals may accordingly be thought to have suffered a wrong or a moral injury, in virtue of the agent's small but not insignificant role in a collective failure to avert the humanitarian disaster that has overwhelmed them.

This relational interpretation of duties of mutual aid focuses in the first instance, in ways characteristic of moral contractualism, on the situation of full compliance. The primary task for moral reasoning is to assess the comparative strength of individual objections to candidate principles, supposing the principles in question to be generally internalized and complied with by agents as a basis for their common social life together. This leaves open the different, but important question of what we as individuals are obligated to do under circumstances of merely partial compliance, including circumstances in which we ourselves have complied with the general demands of mutual aid, but many other people in a comparable position to us are doing little or nothing to help.

It is a striking fact about such situations that further incremental contributions by us, beyond what would be required from each if all were doing their fair share, would make a significant difference to the life prospects of some actual individuals who are subject to acute need. But do prospective beneficiaries have moral claims against us to go above and beyond in this way, given that many others in a comparable position to help out are doing so little? There are at least some considerations that seem to speak against this conclusion.[26] If there are moral claims in play here, they would seem primarily to be held against the other individuals who are currently doing nothing. Those individuals need to step up to the plate and contribute their fair share to the collective project of alleviating the acute distress of the most vulnerable among us. This seems to be reflected in the emotional reactions that it would be natural for individuals in the class of potential beneficiaries to experience under the circumstances of partial compliance that I have described. They certainly have a grievance in this situation, something that would provide grounds for resentment and other forms of blame. But it strikes me as odd to suppose that these reactions should be directed at individuals who are already doing their fair share when there are so many in a similar position to help who are doing nothing, and when it is also the case that contributions by those agents would suffice to address the basic needs of the claimholders.[27]

Against this, it will be objected that there are plenty of situations in nonideal theory in which people might have claims against us to emergency assistance, even though the emergency obtains only because of wrongs that have been committed by other agents, who are therefore already available to serve as objects of opprobrium. Think of the waves of desperate refugees currently fleeing the violent conflicts in Syria, Iraq, and other areas in the Middle East and North Africa. It seems to me correct to view their needs as creating salient opportunities for acts of mutual aid on our part; we may even have special responsibilities to help out in this situation, in virtue of our historical complicity in the political and economic conditions that generated the conflicts from which the refugees are now fleeing. Still, if we are already contributing our fair share to addressing the basic human needs of these vulnerable populations, there is a real question of whether we owe it to them to do more when so many others in our position are doing nothing.

There are admittedly some circumstances in which our moral responsibilities to help other people in need are not well conceived in terms of fair share contributions. Consider those familiar situations in which already conscientious individuals come across others in peril who can be rescued only by those on the immediate scene, where the rescue could be carried out at comparatively little cost to such proximate agents. The fact that individuals in this position have already contributed their general fair share to projects of mutual aid does not seem to release them from a responsibility to save imperiled strangers if they are now in a position to do so. Indeed, this conclusion appears to hold, even if there are other agents around who are equally in a position to rescue the imperiled strangers, and even if those agents have not yet done their fair share to contribute to mutual aid efforts over time.[28]

Examples such as this suggest that there may be separate principles that govern our ongoing contributions to collective efforts at mutual aid, and our duties in emergency situations that require a spontaneous response from individuals on the scene.[29] The latter rescue situations seem to make demands on us that are fairly insensitive to questions about whether we have been doing our fair share to support ongoing programs to address the basic human needs of the most vulnerable. But the principles that govern these contexts define obligations that seem comparatively easy to understand in relational terms. There are specific individuals who have assignable claims against us to assistance, and who also stand to benefit directly if we honor those claims. Furthermore, the duties that we are under in these contexts do not grant us the kind of discretionary leeway characteristic of paradigm imperfect obligations. It is natural to conclude about these duties that they are owed to the imperiled individuals whose emergency plight we happen to be in a position to remedy.

But what about the situation of partial compliance with requirements governing our ongoing collective efforts of mutual aid, where we have already done our fair share, but many others in our position have done nothing? I admit that even here, there is residual pressure to think that already compliant individuals should do still more. After all, each incremental further contribution, beyond those they have already made, will cost them so little, and benefit others so much![30] I continue to think it is at least relevant to these contexts that there are many in a position to make the same additional contribution to the collective project who have not yet done so; given this aspect of the situation, it isn't obvious that reactive and other forms of blame are rightly directed by the potential beneficiaries to the parties who have already contributed their fair share. But this is a question on which there is room for disagreement within the relational framework. Perhaps those in the position of potential beneficiaries have reasonable objections to principles for partial compliance contexts that permit compliant agents to make no further contributions. If so, the resulting, more demanding duties will still be directed in character, despite the discretion they seem to leave to the already compliant agents about how they are to be satisfied, and despite the fact that those to whom they are owed might not benefit directly from the actions the duties lead those agents to perform.

6.3. Numbers and Non-Identity

In this section, I shall address two classes of moral obligations that have seemed especially difficult to make sense of in terms of the claims of individuals. These are cases that involve the so-called non-identity problem, and cases in which the number of people who might benefit from our actions apparently has a direct bearing on what we ought morally to do. Each kind of case has attracted a vast and sophisticated literature, and there is no prospect of doing full justice to the issues within the brief compass that remains to me. My aim will be instead to highlight some resources of the relational approach, drawing on the preceding discussion, that seem to me to have been neglected in other treatments of these issues.

The non-identity problem arises in situations, involving our relations to future generations, that have the following two features: what we do (individually, or together with others) will foreseeably have a significant effect on the well-being of the people who will be alive in the future; but which particular individuals then exist will itself depend on how we now comport ourselves.[31]

Thus in cases involving resource depletion and global climate change, our current complacent behavior might be modestly beneficial to those who are currently alive, insofar as it frees up resources for present consumption that enhance our immediate well-being. But that same behavior will seriously degrade the natural environment that future generations of human beings will inhabit, in ways that can easily be predicted to have devastating consequences for the quality of the lives those future people will be able to lead. At the same time, it is also plausible to suppose that the significant changes in current lifestyles that would be necessary to avert these environmental effects would also make a difference to the identities of the people who will be alive in the future. The future individuals who will have to cope with the effects of our current complacent behavior would by and large not come into existence in the first place under a more environmentally responsible present regime, since identity, dependent as it is on genetic origins, is highly sensitive to even minor counterfactual perturbations in the behavioral patterns of ancestral generations.

The relational approach, as I have developed it, holds that the class of potential moral claimholders against us includes all of the people whose personal interests are apt to be affected, in one way or another, by the things that we do. This class clearly includes people who do not yet exist, but whose life circumstances stand to be shaped decisively by the behaviors that we and others of our generation choose to engage in. The personal interests of those future people provide grounds for objecting strongly to principles that would permit us to act in ways that predictably degrade the life circumstances they will be forced to cope with.[32] But what exactly is the nature of those objections? Given the non-identity problem, it cannot be that we will have made them worse off than they otherwise would have been, since general compliance with alternative principles would have had the effect that those individuals never came to exist in the first place. It is tempting to infer that the moral objection to our current complacent behavior reflects an impersonal concern for the overall quality of the lives that are led by people in the future,[33] rather than a specific concern about what we owe to each of the individuals who will then be alive.

This inference is too quick, however. It is true that the objections of future individuals to our complacent behavior cannot be couched in terms of a comparative conception of harm; they cannot complain that we have made them, as individuals, worse off than they otherwise would have been, since by hypothesis the behaviors determined by the general acceptance of alternative principles would have prevented them from coming into existence. But they also have noncomparative interests in obtaining those basic resources and opportunities that we all understand to be necessary for a flourishing human life, including adequate supplies of food and water and shelter, access to a basic education, freedom from constant social insecurity and displacement, and so on.

The pressing moral importance of issues such as global climate change and environmental degradation, it seems to me, stems from the thought that these behaviors are likely to lead to natural and social catastrophes for the members of future generations, affecting the noncomparative personal interests of those individuals in securing access to the necessities of a decent human life. By contrast, the noncomparative interests of the different people who would come to exist under a regime of responsible environmental and climatological stewardship do not ground a symmetrical objection to our behavior under that alternative regime. Under these conditions, it seems to me that the future people who will have to cope with our current complacent environmental and climate policies could be said to have moral claims against us as individuals, grounded in objections that can be lodged on their own behalf, to our current behaviors. This, despite their inability plausibly to claim that we have made them worse off than they otherwise would have been. It is the combination of a noncomparative conception of individual interests with an essentially comparative method of moral reasoning that yields relational resources for articulating our moral intuitions about cases of this kind.

The noncomparative notion of individual interests is not an innovation of mine; on the contrary, it is familiar from philosophical discussions of the non-identity problem.[34] I emphasize its availability, however, because it enables us to understand, in relational terms, the most important contemporary cases that involve the non-identity problem. These are cases in which our collective behavior can be anticipated to have catastrophic effects on the actual individuals who will exist in the future, and in which alternative courses of action are available to us that would not have similar effects on the different future people who would exist if we chose them.

Consider, for instance, Derek Parfit's recent critical discussion of contractualism and the non-identity problem, the burden of which is to show that contractualists must abandon the individualist restriction if they wish to develop plausible treatments of cases in which this problem arises.[35] Parfit's argument is advanced through the consideration of a series of highly artificial examples in which we are asked to choose between different distributions of a medical or other good across future populations. The moral urgency of his discussion of such cases, however, derives largely from frequent references to the important issues of global warming and environmental degradation. A characteristic passage is the following: "What now matters most is that we rich people give up some of our luxuries, ceasing to overheat the Earth's atmosphere, and taking care of this planet in other ways, so that it continues to support intelligent life."[36] But as I have just explained, there are compelling ways of making sense of the serious moral concerns about these issues within the framework of the individualist restriction, so long as we operate with the noncomparative conception of harm and personal interests whose plausibility Parfit himself seems to acknowledge, and so long as we combine this conception with an essentially comparative procedure of moral reasoning.[37]

There are, of course, many different kinds of situation that involve the nonidentity problem. One class of cases involves procreative decisions. Consider, for instance, an adult who confronts a choice between the following three options: (1) not having a child; (2) conceiving child A, who will live a life of moderate happiness; (3) conceiving a different child B, who will live a life that is very happy.[38] It certainly seems permissible for the adult to choose the first option in this scenario, electing to remain childless rather than become a parent. But if she decides to bring a child into the world, some philosophers are convinced that it would be morally wrong for her to conceive child A rather than child B. Indeed, Parfit has argued that it would be just as wrong to choose (2) over (3) in a case of this kind as it would be to make the same choice in a different case in which the individuals conceived in (2) and (3) would be the same person, someone who would be made worse off by the choice of (2) over (3).[39] If this is correct, then it is an intuition that would seem difficult to make sense of in terms of the relational approach I have been advocating. After all, the familiar reasoning goes, child A cannot have an objection on her own behalf to the adult's choosing option (2), given that the life she is given in that scenario is one of moderate happiness, and that she would not even have existed if (3) had been chosen instead.

But this conclusion may again be too hasty. In standard presentations of cases of this general kind, it is stipulated that the reason why A's life would achieve only a moderate level of happiness is that it would subject A to a serious "handicap," albeit a handicap that is compatible with A's having a life that is well worth living. But to bring it about that someone comes into existence with a handicap or a serious congenital ailment is arguably to bring it about that she will be harmed, in the noncomparative sense mentioned above. Our conception of a condition as a handicap or a congenital ailment presupposes a conception of the things that human individuals generally need in order to flourish, defining a noncomparative sense in which they have an interest in obtaining those very things in their lives. This noncomparative interest, in turn, might plausibly ground an objection, on A's own behalf, to course of action (2), which foreseeably brings A into existence with the handicap in question. (Note that here, as in other cases with this structure, to have an individual complaint about the actions of an agent is not necessarily to prefer on balance that the agent should have acted otherwise.[40]) Options (1) and (3), by contrast, will not result in the existence of any new individual with a comparable objection. This seems to me sufficient to make sense of the intuition that there is a moral objection, couched in relational terms, to the agent's doing (2) when options (1) and (3) are also available.

But suppose we modify the example, so that A and B have the same overall level of welfare as in the original scenarios brought about by actions (2) and (3), but it is not the case that A suffers from a handicap or a congenital ailment. It just happens that we can know in advance that unimpaired agent A will lead a life that is less happy overall than the life that would be led by B. In the vast recent literature on so-called population ethics, there is some tendency simply to assume that there must be a moral objection to bringing about future people whose welfare level is suboptimal (compared with the welfare of the different individuals who would come into existence if we acted otherwise).[41] As Parfit wrote in his original discussion of these issues, "If in either of two possible outcomes the same number of people would ever live, it would be worse if those who live are worse off, or have a lower quality of life, than those who would have lived."[42] But if we accept this idea, it will be very tempting to conclude that it would be wrong for an individual to bring about the outcome that is in this way impersonally worse when alternatives are available to the agent that would have brought into existence a population of different individuals with a higher quality of life.[43]

This moral verdict, to be sure, cannot be accommodated within the framework of the relational account I have been developing in this book. But I think we should be deeply suspicious about the assumption that the verdict is an important datum for an account of interpersonal morality to accommodate. As many have observed, future individuals are not well thought of as vessels to be filled by us with happiness or well-being, and it is a serious distortion of our individual obligations to think that we have a duty to see to it that future populations exist that are as happy as it is possible for such populations to be.[44] Our obligations in this area are better thought of as duties to ensure that humanity can continue under conditions that are conducive to the flourishing of future individuals, and these are duties that the relational account can comprehend.[45] There may well be some cases of collective or administrative agency in which aggregative considerations of impersonal well-being have direct relevance to questions about how those in a position of authority ought to act. I believe that many of the artificial cases that exercise Parfit can be understood in these terms, as cases that mobilize intuitions about administrative or bureaucratic rationality. But this is a point that I shall set aside for the time being, returning to it in section 6.4 below.

In the meantime, I would like to take up, with similar briskness, the hoary question of whether the numbers count for moral deliberation. For ease of exposition, I shall concentrate on the very simple case already introduced in section 5.4 above, in which you are in a position to rescue some survivors of a shipwreck, at little risk to yourself, who are stranded on two different rocks. On Rock 1 there is a single survivor, while there are several on Rock 2, and it is clear that you cannot make it to both rocks to save everyone before the tide comes in and sweeps people away. Working within a relational framework that considers only the objections that individuals have on their own behalf to principles that would permit treating them in various ways, it appears that we cannot explain why it might be morally wrong to go to Rock 1 when it was also open to you to go to Rock 2, saving more.[46]

The first thing to note about cases of this kind is that it is open to a relational theorist to deny that there is a specifically moral objection to saving fewer rather than more.[47] It would be wrong to save no one when you can rescue some at little risk to yourself, but we might bite the bullet and accept the conclusion that it is a matter of indifference to individual morality how many you save, precisely because you owe it to nobody in particular that more rather than fewer should be rescued. Furthermore, someone who takes this line could add that there might be compelling nonmoral reasons that speak in favor of going to Rock 2, where the greater number of survivors have sought temporary refuge.[48] Given that there is no individual who has a moral claim against you to go to either rock, appreciation for the impersonal value of human life might provide a consideration, ancillary to relational morality, in favor of saving the greater number.[49] On this approach, there is no moral obligation in the sense that is connected to individual moral claims to save more rather than fewer, but doing so is nevertheless something the rescuer has reason to do, in a more generic sense that does not ground a practical requirement or connect specifically to the claims that provide others with a basis for interpersonal accountability.

This is an important line of thought, and I want to come back to it in the following section. Before doing so, however, I wish to dwell a bit more on the case of the shipwrecked passengers on the two rocks. Is it really correct to think that there is no relational objection, couched in terms of the personal interests of the individuals whose lives are at stake, to saving the Rock 1 person rather than the several who are on Rock 2? Perhaps not. Remember that we are looking for principles for the general regulation of behavior that will be acceptable to everyone, and considering the consequences for individuals of adoption of the principles in question as a basis for social life. As we have seen, once a rescue situation has arisen, there will be particular individuals on the two rocks who are in a position to be assisted, and who will have precisely symmetrical individual objections to principles that permit the rescuer to save those on the other rock.

As noted in the previous section, however, we need perfectly general principles for dealing with situations of immediate rescue, where individuals find themselves uniquely positioned to avert human catastrophe through their direct efforts on the scene (acting either alone, or in concert with others who happen to be on the scene as well). Each of us, deliberating in abstraction from knowledge about which particular rescue situations of this kind might emerge, would seem to have personal reasons to reject some general principles for the behavior of rescuers in favor of others. In particular, it seems that we each have compelling objections on our own behalf to principles that permit rescuers to save fewer rather than more, at least when it is open to them to do so at comparably minor cost to themselves. The basic idea is that our own ex ante likelihood of being saved will be highest if rescuers are in general required to save as many as they are safely able to assist.

To think in these terms is to suppose that we are all liable to require the assistance of direct rescuers from time to time as we make our way through life, and that the shipwrecks and other events that make necessary assistance of this kind function as a kind of natural lottery, distributing individuals randomly across the various positions occupied by rescuees. True, the individual who ends up on Rock 1 in our particular rescue case would be relieved if you followed the policy of rescuing fewer that she herself had ex ante reason to reject. But this does not undermine the force of the ex ante objection to the general policy permitting rescuers to save fewer rather than more. As we have already seen, the later objections of the individuals on the two different rocks have already been determined to be inconclusive, insofar as they are countered by precisely symmetrical objections that can then be brought by other individuals to alternative principles.[50] The idea is that, in this dialectical context, the fact that we all have ex ante personal reasons to reject principles permitting rescuers to save fewer might make it reasonable for each of us to reject such principles, as a general basis for regulating our interactions with each other.[51]

But what if there are individuals who know in advance that they are likely to end up in the smaller group when they need the assistance of rescuers?[52] Such individuals, it seems, would have ex ante personal reasons to reject principles that require rescuers to save more rather than fewer. And their individual objections would neutralize the ex ante objections that each of the rest of us has to principles that permit rescuers to save fewer. There are two different scenarios that need to be distinguished here. First, individuals might know in advance that they will reliably find themselves in the smaller groups of people who need assistance in emergencies, because they choose to engage in risky activities that can be anticipated to have this consequence. (Perhaps they always swim out to remote areas that are far from the crowds, drawn in part to solitude and danger.) Under this scenario, the ex ante objections that the individuals would have to principles that require rescuers to save more rather than fewer seem undermined by the fact that their propensity to end up in the smaller group is the result of their own voluntary behavior. If they are concerned to increase their ex ante likelihood of being rescued in the event of an emergency, there is a way for them to do this compatibly with general policies for rescue situations that ensure that the ex ante interests of other agents are catered to as well.

Consider, next, agents who know in advance that they are likely to find themselves in smaller groups of potential rescuees through no fault of their own. Maybe they have grown up in comparatively remote and unpopulated regions of countries that are prone to earthquakes and tsunamis. Such agents would seem to have objections to principles that require rescuers to save more that are not in the same way undermined by their responsibility for the feature of their situation that generates those objections. The question to ask here is whether there are alternative policies, short of the adoption of general principles for rescue situations that would disadvantage others, that would address the special vulnerability of people in these remote regions. Perhaps we could make resources available to reduce their reliance on rescuers in the situations of danger that can be anticipated periodically to arise, by (for instance) securely depositing copious rations and emergency supplies in the remote villages. As long as measures of this kind are available, it would arguably be unreasonable for residents of such regions to reject principles requiring rescuers to save more rather than fewer, given the strong ex ante objections others have to alternative rescue principles.

This has necessarily been an abbreviated discussion of a complicated issue, but perhaps enough has been said to identify a potential relational objection to saving the single person on Rock 1 rather than the several on Rock 2. The argument to this conclusion rests on the assumption that rescue situations can reasonably be regarded ex ante as natural randomizing events, distributing people with equal likelihood across the different positions occupied by the actual individuals who need to be rescued.[53] Given that there is generally no independent reason to reject this assumption on epistemic or metaphysical grounds, it strikes me as a defensible way of thinking about emergency situations in advance of their occurrence. The assumption can be thought to express an attitude of solidarity with other individuals, the idea that it is part of the common human predicament that we require emergency assistance from time to time. But this strikes me as a reasonable way of proceeding when we reflect on what we owe to each other in situations of this kind.

Suppose, in the light of this discussion, that you go to Rock 1 rather than Rock 2, saving fewer when it was open to you to save more at no further risk. On the relational view, as we have seen, actions that flout moral principles are not merely wrong; they wrong some individual or individuals in particular, reflecting an attitude of disregard for those individuals' moral claims. But whose claims have been disregarded in this case? The individual objection that has been articulated to principles that would permit your behavior is not one that is specific to the individuals in the larger group; rather it is an ex ante objection that each of us has to the adoption of such principles, including the actual individuals who find themselves on both of the two rocks. So which individual or individuals have been wronged?[54]

As we saw in section 5.4, people are wronged by an action when it affects personal interests of theirs that would make it reasonable to reject principles permitting actions of the relevant kind. To take a simple example, we all have reasonable objections to principles for the general regulation of behavior that permit people to kill us for professional or private advantage, objections that are grounded in our basic personal interest in remaining alive. But in any particular case of impermissible killing, it is the individual whose interest in life is actually disregarded who will be wronged by the killer's act: that is, the person who is killed. In the rescue case, I said that we all have reasonable ex ante objections to principles that permit rescuers to save fewer rather than more. In any given emergency situation, then, it will be the individuals who get caught up in it whose interests in being saved are actually at stake. So all of them may be said to have been wronged by rescuers when they omit to save as many lives as they are safely able to rescue.

This includes the Rock 2 people, of course, who have specifically been disadvantaged by your going to Rock 1. But the surprising thing is that it also includes the person on Rock 1. This person, after all, had an identical ex ante objection to giving rescuers permission to save fewer rather than more, despite the fact that it worked out all right for her in the end. Thus the Rock 1 person might reason, "It was antecedently more likely that I would be saved if you had gone to Rock 2 rather than Rock 1. If you had been appropriately concerned about my interests, this is therefore the action that would have been selected. That I ended up benefiting from your choice to go to Rock 1 is a kind of moral accident, from which it does not follow that you showed the kind of regard for my interests that makes your action justifiable specifically to me."[55]

The situation of this person might be compared to that of a promisee who ends up benefiting in a fluky and unpredictable way from a promisor's flouting of a promissory obligation (perhaps you miss your flight when I fail to take you to the airport as I promised to do, but the flight you were hoping to catch goes down in flames). In both cases, the persons who are affected will probably be unable to regret the agent's action when they look back on it in reflection. But it might nevertheless be the case that the action wronged them, and gave them a basis for resentment about it, insofar as it displayed a disregard for their specific interests. This is in many respects an eccentric position to be in; but in this as in some of the non-identity cases described earlier, the attitudes I have described nevertheless seem perfectly coherent.[56] That they are provides some support for the suggestion I have been developing in this section, that there is a personal objection to principles permitting rescuers to save fewer rather than more.

The appeal to ex ante objections that agents have on their own behalf, once it is admitted within relational reasoning about what it is permissible to do, has potential application in some other contexts that have attracted the attention of moral philosophers. I shall conclude this section by mentioning, briefly, one such context, and will mention another at the start of the section to follow. Consider, then, emergency rescue situations in which it is a question, not of saving more rather than fewer, but of saving some in ways that bring it about that others are harmed. There is a vast literature that has explored this context by considering variations on cases involving runaway trolleys that are on course to kill people on the track ahead.[57] One of the more robust intuitions that people have about variants of these cases is that it is permissible, if you are the driver of the trolley, to shunt it onto a siding where it will kill one person rather than to allow it to continue on its present course, killing five (where it is assumed that these are the only options open to you). Killing five is worse than killing one, as it is sometimes said, and this principle seems to explain our judgment about the permissibility of the driver's action in this case.

The principle, thus stated, is about the comparative badness of actions, and it is not immediately obvious how to translate that verdict into a principle about the duties that are owed to the various individuals who are apt to be affected in the context described.[58] But the preceding discussion suggests a possible solution to this translation problem. Discussing the rescue situation that involved people stranded on different rocks, it was suggested that everyone might have an ex ante objection to principles that permit rescuers in such situations to save fewer rather than more. Each of us has a personal interest in increasing the likelihood that we will be saved if we should find ourselves needing to be rescued, and this gives us a compelling basis for rejecting principles that permit rescuers to save fewer when more can be saved by them at little cost to themselves. But a similar line of argument appears to apply to the trolley context we have just described. Viewing ourselves as individuals who, given the vagaries of human life, are occasionally liable to find ourselves in harm's way, it seems we would each have compelling personal reasons for authorizing agents in the trolley driver's position to see to it that fewer rather than more are killed as a result of their activity. If this is right, then we might conclude that the driver owes it to all six of the people on the main track and the siding to divert the trolley, so that only one rather than five end up losing their lives.

This is only a crude first stab at formulating a relational principle to deal with cases in which it seems permissible to harm some in order to save others. Refinements will be necessary to deal even with the simple variant of a trolley case that has been considered so far. Thus, while it seems intuitive to say that killing five is worse than killing one, a principle corresponding to this thought will not by itself be adequate to deal with the driver's situation. As F. M. Kamm has observed, it does not seem permissible for the driver to stop the trolley from killing the five who are in its path by pressing a button that (say) causes someone currently out of harm's way to be catapulted onto the track, killing that person but arresting the further progress of the trolley toward the five.[59] In this scenario, the driver kills one, and that by hypothesis is better than killing five, and yet the action the driver performs seems wrong. Indeed, it wrongs the sixth person, somehow, and in a way that is similar to the wrong that would be committed if a bystander (rather than the driver) were to stop the trolley by pushing someone off of a bridge onto the track.[60]

It might be hoped, further, that the refinements necessary to make sense of these verdicts will also assist us with other variants of the trolley problem, including that of the bystander at the switch, whose options are to do nothing and allow five to be killed by the runaway trolley, or to activate the switch, shunting the trolley onto the siding where it will kill one. Many people have the intuition that it would be permissible for the bystander to cause the trolley to divert to the siding in this scenario, even though she would be killing one rather than allowing five to die.[61] But this description applies equally to the situation of the person who pushes someone off a bridge onto the track in front of the trolley, something that, as noted above, it does not seem permissible to do.

I do not wish to enter into a discussion of these and other variants of trolley cases at this time, something that would take us into thickets from which we might never emerge. But I would contend, without further argument, that the relational approach appears to provide a fruitful framework for considering these issues. On the one hand, we seem to have compelling ex ante objections to principles that permit agents to kill more through their actions when there are options available to them that would result in fewer being killed. Similar objections potentially extend to "disaster mitigation" principles that permit agents to allow more to be killed when they could act to avert that outcome, albeit with the result that some smaller number of other persons will come to grief. On the other hand, each of us also has powerful objections to principles that permit agents to co-opt us into their life-saving projects, for instance by using us instrumentally to rescue others when we were not otherwise in harm's way at all.[62] It is not entirely clear that principles are available that will be adequate to all of the intricate variations of trolley scenarios that ingenious philosophers might succeed in devising. There would then be indeterminacies within the morality of what we owe to each other, questions concerning the claims individuals have against us to which there is no satisfactory answer.[63] But to the extent the trolley problem(s) admit of a solution, it is one that can plausibly be understood in the relational terms I have been sketching.

6.4. Extramoral Concern for Moral Persons

Another context to which ex ante individual objections may be relevant involves risk. In real life (as opposed to the life of philosophers' examples), many of the choices that in fact confront agents, especially public officials who are called on to make decisions about social policies, have a significant risk dimension. It is not that we must choose between options that will each impose known harms on known individuals; more commonly, our options involve subjecting populations of individuals to risks of harm, together with benefits that are themselves more or less probable. In many cases of this kind, it is intuitively permissible to choose policies that will involve a miniscule risk of very serious harm if the prospective benefits are sufficiently great. This remains the case, even if there is an alternative policy available that will achieve the same benefit while exposing nobody to a comparable risk.

Think of a vaccine that would immunize the children to whom it is administered against a lethal disease, but where it is known be ineffective in 0.1 percent of cases; and suppose there is an alternative vaccine that would immunize all of those to whom it is administered, though it would also be certain to impose on each of them a very serious harm (resulting, say, in a paralyzed limb). Most of us would think it right to choose the first vaccine, despite the risk that it carries of death in a small percentage of cases. But this can seem puzzling in a relational context that focuses on the personal objections that individuals have to principles that would permit the actions under consideration. If the population is sufficiently large, it is a statistical certainty that there are children who will die under the first vaccine regime who would merely suffer a paralyzed limb under the second. We therefore know in advance that there will be individuals who will have powerful ex post objections to principles that would permit such a regime. And similar arguments would appear to tell against many risky policy decisions that seem intuitively acceptable in their moral implications.[64]

Persuasive arguments have recently been mounted, however, for the conclusion that contractualists should focus on the ex ante objections of individuals exposed to risky policies in situations of this kind.[65] If it is genuinely unknown in advance which individuals would be harmed by the first vaccination regime, then it is plausible to think of it in analogy to a single-person case. If you faced a choice for your child between a vaccine that is 99.9 percent effective against a fatal disease, and a vaccine that is 100 percent effective, but also certain to cause paralysis in a limb, you would be right to opt for the first on the child's behalf. What matters for the personal interests of the child are the *prospects* that each vaccine would afford the child, where these reflect both the worst-case outcomes and the likelihood that they will occur. Those are the considerations that seem relevant at the time the vaccine must be administered, which is the perspective that matters for assessment of its permissibility. Of course, if one were to choose this vaccine for one's child, and the vaccine turned out to be ineffective in this particular case, one would no doubt have regrets about one's decision, and even wish on balance that one had done otherwise. But from this it does not follow that it was not the right thing to do at the time.[66] And by parity of reasoning, the fact that it is statistically certain that some children will die if the first vaccine is administered to a sufficiently large population does not entail that they were wronged by the policy that led to their death, so long as the prospects that were afforded to them individually by the policy were sufficiently favorable.

But it is not clear that all cases involving risk can be dealt with by appeal to ex ante individual objections of this kind. Johann Frick, who favors the ex ante contractualist approach to risk sketched above, also thinks that there are situations for which it does not yield a satisfactory treatment. Consider the following case that he describes:

> *Miners (1 vs. 100)*: Gareth, a miner, is trapped in a collapsed shaft. If we do not save him, he is virtually certain to die within days. However, a rescue will be costly. Suppose we must choose between the following two options:
>
> - Rescue: Spend all our available funds to rescue Gareth.
> - Prevention: Spend our available funds to improve safety at this mine, reducing the risk of future accidents. If we choose this option, the risk of death for each of the other 100 people working at this mine of dying in a future accident will be reduced from 3 percent to 1 percent. We expect that this will save two lives (though we cannot know whose). However, Gareth will die.[67]

Frick says that this case, which involves trade-offs between identified and merely statistical lives, is well handled by ex ante contractualism. The one hundred miners each have personal objections to principles that permit Rescue, insofar as it modestly worsens their prospects of dying; but Gareth's objection to Prevention seems much more compelling, since following that course would lead to his near certain demise. But Frick also thinks that this answer starts to become untenable as the number of miners who stand to benefit under Prevention increases. If, say, there are one thousand individuals in the group whose individual risk would be reduced from 3 to 1 percent, then Prevention would save a total of twenty statistical lives (albeit at the cost of

Gareth's death), and it seems to be the morally right course of action despite the compelling personal objection to it that Gareth has at the point in time when the action is to be carried out.[68]

The conclusion that Frick draws from such examples is a form of pluralism, according to which contractualism identifies one class of high-order wrong-making properties among others.[69] He characterizes this consideration as a form of equity, and notes that, while it represents a very important moral reason for action, it is not the only class of moral considerations that count in favor of actions. Another such consideration is human well-being; this is something that has independent normative significance, representing a property that can on its own contribute to making an action right or wrong, all things considered. Thus, in *Miners (1 vs. 100)*, equity will plausibly be dispositive, and Rescue will be the right thing to do in virtue of Gareth's powerful personal objections to Prevention. But in *Miners (1 vs. 1,000)*, though Gareth's individual objections to Prevention remain much more powerful than the objections to Rescue of any of the one thousand other miners, the aggregate benefits to them mean that considerations of well-being outweigh considerations of equity. The balance of reasons has tipped, and it is now the case that Prevention is the right course of action, all things considered.

This line of reasoning dovetails with arguments that have been advanced by other philosophers against the relational version of contractualism for which I have been advocating. Thus, as noted in the preceding section, Parfit argues that theories of this kind yield the wrong answer in a range of hypothetical scenarios in which aggregate welfare (sometimes supplemented by considerations of non-identity) appears to make a difference to moral thought. Here are just two of the several examples of this kind that he has to offer.

In *Case Four*, our only alternatives are as follows:[70]

	Future days of pain	
	For Blue	For each of some number of other people
We do nothing	100	100
We do A	0	100
We do B	90	90

Here, it seems that Blue has powerful personal reasons for rejecting both Nothing or B, since these would each leave her much worse off than she would be if we were to do A; these objections, moreover, seem significantly weightier than the objections of any of the other individuals to our doing A, since they would only be modestly better off if we did B instead. But Parfit notes that this reasoning is insensitive to questions about the number of individuals who stand to benefit from our doing B, in a way that is clearly mistaken. If, for instance, there are a million people in the B-beneficiary group, it would surely be wrong to do A rather than B, even though Blue continues to have a powerful personal objection to the latter. The number of individuals whose well-being is affected by our actions appears in this way to make a difference to moral thought.

Consider, next, Parfit's *Case Seven*, where the alternatives are as follows:[71]

| If we do A | A thousand X-people would be conceived and live for 41 happy years | and a thousand Y-people would be conceived and live for 40 happy years |
| If we do B | The same X-people would be conceived and live for 40 happy years | and a thousand different Z-people would be conceived and live for 80 happy years |

Parfit thinks it is obvious that we should do B in this situation, and argues that this conclusion cannot be defended in the individualist terms of Scanlon-style contractualism. After all, each of the X-people has a nontrivial personal objection to B, insofar as it would deprive him or her of a year of happy life. But Parfit maintains that there is no individual who has a personal objection to A, in the form either of a complaint that it leaves him or her worse off than he or she otherwise would have been (since the Y-people would not so much as have existed in the alternative scenario), or of a complaint that it subjects him or her to a noncomparative harm or burden (since A gives the Y-people forty happy years of life).[72] If we restrict ourselves to personal objections within contractualist reasoning, Parfit therefore contends, we will be forced to choose A, which is clearly the wrong answer.

The intuitions evoked by these hypothetical cases seem consistent with a point made in section 6.3 above, concerning the status of human life as a source of reasons that are ancillary to relational morality. In the simple two-rock rescue case, the fact that more would be saved by going to Rock 2 seems to be an independent consideration that counts in favor of doing so. Thus, even if my ex ante argument fails and saving more rather than fewer isn't something that any of the individuals affected by our actions have a claim against us to do, there still may be some reason to try to save the larger group on Rock 2. Human life and human well-being seem to matter to us for their own sake, as factors that make a difference to practical thought even when they are not laundered into the currency of moral claims.

But what kind of difference should these considerations make? Parfit, seeking a unified account of the moral, urges that we should accommodate them by giving up the individualist restriction within a contractualist framework that seeks principles everyone can rationally will. We should think, not about the personal objections that individuals have, on their own behalf, to candidate principles for the general regulation of behavior, but should also take into account the impartial and impersonal reasons that individuals might have for choosing such principles. As we saw in section 5.4, however, to give up or otherwise relax the individualist restriction would be to sacrifice the relational aspect of contractualist reasoning that precisely gives it much of its appeal. In particular, we would lose the insight that contractualism otherwise can provide into the different kinds of normative significance characteristic of morality, both for individual deliberation and for relations of interpersonal accountability. Contractualism, in the relational form that retains the restriction to objections based on personal interests, identifies, at the very least, one significant class of considerations that can make it the case that actions are generically right and wrong, in the sense of being things that are to-be-done or not-to-be-done. Even if we depart from Parfit on this point, however, we might still agree that his hypothetical cases bring out the difference that aggregate well-being sometimes makes to practical thought. Seen in this light, the cases apparently lend further support to a pluralistic approach to the moral such as Frick's.

I should like to make two main points in response to this suggestion. First, however, a preliminary comment. Parfit himself concedes that his hypothetical cases are highly artificial in their "unrealistic" hyperprecision.[73] This is something of an understatement. The fact is that we never, in human life, encounter choices between options that are known in advance to involve such definite and finely calibrated distributions of benefits and burdens to affected parties. In this respect, his cases are much less realistic even than the sometimes fantastic variants involving runaway trolleys that figure in discussion about the permissibility of harming some to save others. Another respect in which the examples are unrealistic concerns the alternatives for action that are taken as given in their presentation. In *Miners (1 vs. 1,000)*, for instance, it is just stipulated that the only resources available for the program that would save twenty statistical lives are those that could have been expended to rescue Gareth. But this is in fact a strange and implausible assumption, along several different dimensions. Ordinarily, public agencies make decisions about future investments in public safety, striking a balance between programs for emergency response and different programs for emergency prevention. It is hard to think of a context in which resources would be diverted from an ongoing rescue operation to invest in a program of future mining safety. Doing so, moreover, seems to assume that there are no alternatives available for funding the mine safety program, such as imposing licensing fees on mine operators or taxing the sales of the minerals that they extract (never mind the idea that savings could be achieved in other areas of the state or federal budget, through cuts in the allocations that support weapons procurement or subsidies for industrial agriculture). It is worth considering how much weight should really be attached to intuitions elicited by cases that are, in these and other respects, so remote from anything in our ordinary experience of moral choice.

Having said that, I shall, for purposes of argument in what follows, take these intuitions at face value, conceding that aggregate well-being sometimes appears to possess independent significance for practical thought. The first main point I would make about these intuitions is that the cases that elicit them typically involve contexts of essentially bureaucratic or administrative rationality, in which public authorities are tasked with choosing between different possible distributions of a scarce drug or therapy or other resource, or making decisions about matters of social policy. It is not at all obvious to me that relational morality on its own needs to explain intuitions about appropriate distributions under these special conditions, in which decision-makers are subject to democratic pressures to deploy scarce resources in ways that distribute benefits widely over the affected populations.

What we as individuals owe to the members of future generations, for instance, is that they should not be subject to noncomparative harms or deprivations as a foreseeable result of the choices we have made; as I put it in the preceding section, we should see to it that they are able to live under conditions conducive to their flourishing. These requirements carry over to contexts of collective or political agency, which is why the contemporary behavior of the US and other governments on climate issues involves a collective moral failing in precisely the sense captured by the relational account.

Even when individual claims of this kind are not at issue, however, we sometimes appear to have intuitions about the comparative betterness of different distributions of well-being among the members of present and future populations. But what is the bearing of such convictions on questions about interpersonal morality? Are we really subject to standing moral obligations, as individuals, to see to it that the best outcome should result from individual exertions of our capacities for agency? This is very far from being self-evident. Perhaps the most natural human reaction to at least some of the unrealistically hyperprecise hypotheticals would be to refuse to enter into the thought experiment in the first place, insisting that one is not authorized, just as an individual agent, to make decisions about the distribution of scarce funds for vaccination programs or mine safety policies and the like. By contrast, those bodies that are authorized to make such allocative decisions might naturally be understood to have special responsibilities, which they perhaps owe to the democratic populations on whose behalf they are acting, to see to it that public investments are made in ways that benefit as wide a population as possible.[74] There would then be a role for aggregative reasoning about human well-being to play within these special decision contexts that wouldn't carry over to our deliberations about what we are to do, as individuals.

This approach would grant some place for aggregative considerations within the reflections of authorities about the allocation of public funds. But how exactly should such considerations be taken into account within these contexts? Comparatively unproblematic would be the use of them to guide decision-making about options that are each consistent with the moral claims of individuals who would be affected by them, but that go beyond what is required to meet those individual claims. Thus, public authorities may have some responsibility to bring about optimific outcomes, so long as they do not wrong any of the individuals whose personal interests are at stake, even if we are not as individuals under a requirement to do so.[75] They might, for instance, reasonably decide to invest significant public resources in mine safety programs, shifting some funds for this purpose from the standing search and rescue teams that will be available to respond to future emergencies. Distributing resources in this way may have the predictable effect of placing limits on the means that can be mobilized to save identified individuals at the point in time when future accidents happen in the mining sector. But at the earlier moment when the distributional decision is taken, a shift in resources of this kind might well be justified as a way of reducing significantly the loss of statistical lives.

But the hypothetical cases presented earlier in this section suggest a more challenging possibility. Examples such as Frick's *Miners (1 vs. 1,000)* and Parfit's *Case Four* look like situations in which it is right, once the numbers get sufficiently large, to embark on a course of action that cannot be justified individually to each of the people it might affect (such as Gareth and Blue), and that seems to violate their moral claims. But this is a possibility that might be accommodated by the kind of division of labor I am proposing between individual morality and democratic decision-making. Perhaps it would not be right for me, as an individual, to choose the course of action that would violate someone's relational claims against me. I am under an obligation to respect those claims, and the fact that significant aggregate benefits could be achieved by flouting them in a given case does not make that the right thing for me to do. But things could be different in this respect when it comes to the decisions of duly constituted public authorities. Individual moral claims should certainly constrain their deliberations in some way, setting at least basic limits on what it is acceptable for them to decide to do. But at the same time, the special demands of public accountability might entail that such considerations function differently within this context, so that it is sometimes right for the deliberative bodies to choose social policies that slight some individual claims, in order to make possible a significant benefit to a sufficiently large population (as in the miner's case).[76] The upshot would be that moral claims figure, within this special deliberative context, as inputs into deliberation rather than its conclusions. Their role would then differ, in this respect, from the role I have attributed to relational claims in connection with individual deliberation about what to do. But this is a perfectly coherent possibility, which might well be appropriate to the very different decision contexts that are at issue.

To be maximally concessive, however, I should now like to consider the possibility that intuitions about the significance of aggregate well-being cannot be entirely confined to the public side of this division of deliberative labor. I have already conceded that considerations of human life and human welfare have some independent normative significance for individual thought, and that we might partially explain in terms of them the intelligibility of the feeling that we should save more rather than fewer in cases like the two-rock rescue situation. But once considerations of this kind are conceded to be relevant, it is natural to think that they might continue to exert a pull on us in the very different kind of cases I have been considering in this section, in which actions that violate individual claims produce very large aggregate benefits. My second and final point is that it would be dubious to conclude, even then, that reasons of well-being might be dispositive for reasoning about what it is right for us, as individuals, to do.

Presenting the kind of pluralism that he favors, Frick talks about considerations of equity and human well-being as independent reasons for action, which might be weighed against each other, with the balance tipping in the direction of well-being once the interests of a sufficiently large number of identified or statistical persons are at stake. As I argued in chapter 2, however, it is a mistake to suppose that all reasons for action exhibit the kind of normative significance characteristic of considerations that are to be weighed in the balance. Some normative considerations represent practical requirements, which play a distinctive role within individual deliberation, functioning in the way of presumptive constraints on agency. Aspirational reasons for action that go against a practical requirement may continue to have a grip on us, as a matter of deliberative phenomenology. But it is ordinarily an error to think that they might outweigh considerations that are independently intelligible as practical requirements, as I have shown relational moral obligations to be. Practical requirements are not to be weighed against reasons on the other side, but function, so long as they are in place, to exclude such reasons from deliberative relevance.

It does not follow from this that considerations of human well-being could never conflict with relational morality within contexts of individual deliberation. In order for there to be a competition of the right kind between them, however, it would need to be shown that they do not merely represent reasons for action of some kind or other, but that they ground independent practical requirements. But it is not really clear that this challenge can be met. We have some sense for the capacity of well-being to ground practical requirements within relational moral reasoning, insofar as it represents a personal interest capable of underwriting an individual moral claim. Outside of this context, we also understand well-being as a consideration that counts in favor of actions and responses, perhaps rendering intelligible a preference for one option over another when both are morally permissible (for example, in the two-rock rescue case, on at least some interpretations of it). But aggregate well-being does not seem, beyond these roles, to have obvious normative significance for individual reflection, and it is especially unclear that it represents an independent source of practical requirements. It has a scalar character, for instance, that does not correspond very well to any of our familiar models of a practical requirement (as we saw in section 2.2 above).

But perhaps I am wrong about this. Maybe, despite its scalar character, there is a threshold above which considerations of aggregate well-being become weighty or significant enough that they transmogrify into independent practical requirements, of the kind that might intelligibly ground presumptive constraints on individual agency. They would then represent normative factors that could potentially come into straightforward conflict with the independent requirements of relational morality. Even if all of this is conceded, however, it would still not follow that these requirements of well-being simply outweigh the directed moral duties and claims with which they here compete.

There are cases, as we saw in section 2.4, where practical requirements of one type automatically give way when they threaten to compete with requirements of a different type. This can happen, for instance, when they are connected with roles that are hierarchically subordinated to the status associated with the more important type of requirement. But the imagined competition between requirements of relational morality and of well-being is not of this character. Relational morality derives from our conception of ourselves as members of a world of individuals who are equally real, and whose interests are in some sense of equal significance. Its directed requirements define an ideal way of relating to the other individuals in this extensive class, involving regard for their claims, of a kind that provides normative protection from reactive and other forms of blame. These connected elements in the relational conception of moral obligation suggest that it is normatively fundamental, and not such as to give way in a case of imagined conflict with independent requirements of well-being.

This way of thinking about things is consistent with the argument of chapter 2 of this book, where I noted that there are distinct models of a practical requirement, and that it cannot be ruled out that requirements with distinct sources might sometimes come into conflict with each other. We might put this by saying that there are different kinds of consideration that can make it the case that something is to-be-done or not-to-be-done, insofar as they are independently intelligible as presumptive constraints on individual agency. The pluralism currently under consideration, I am now proposing, is best understood as claiming that considerations of human well-being, once they exceed some unspecified threshold of importance, represent an independent class of practical requirements in this sense. But considerations of this kind, however significant, would not alone be dispositive when it comes to the question of what one should do, all things considered. At most, they would define independent constraints on individual agency, which conflict with, but do not undermine or outweigh, the separate requirements of what we owe to each other.

The not implausible result of this way of conceptualizing things is that individuals faced with some of the challenging hypothetical cases we have been considering would be right to experience them as practical dilemmas. They would owe it to Gareth or to Blue to act in a way that is justifiable specifically to them, taking fully into account the strong personal objections they each have to the actions that would maximize aggregate well-being. But they are also under an independent requirement to perform those same actions, given the cumulative significance of the interests that are at stake in the situation. This may also be the right way of thinking about the more familiar cases that traditionally make even deontologists reluctant to embrace absolute prohibitions on certain forms of problematic conduct. If there are enough lives at stake, we might reluctantly conclude that we are required to do something heinous if it is necessary to avert a humanitarian catastrophe (killing one innocent hostage, say, to prevent the hostage-taker from killing all twenty). But this would coexist with the thought that we would also be acting wrongly, and wronging the one in particular, if we were to choose to avert the catastrophe. Under these circumstances, there would be no single answer to the question of what it is right to do, all things considered. Rather, conscientious agents would feel themselves to be pulled in two different directions at once, unable to respond adequately to all of the practical pressures that are bearing down on them.

I myself would describe these as cases of a conflict between moral and extramoral requirements. Human well-being is a consideration with clear moral significance, but in the present context it is no longer functioning in that guise. As I argued in chapter 3, it is part of our concept of interpersonal morality that it collects considerations that bear normatively on our relations to one another, providing a basis for interpersonal accountability and for reactive and other forms of blame. When human well-being is detached from the framework of relational morality, and considered on its own as a self-standing source of what I have called impersonal requirements, it no longer plays this role. It does not make sense for individuals to hold themselves to standing requirements to promote aggregate well-being, nor would a failure to live up to those requirements on a particular occasion provide other individuals with a reasonable basis for resentment.

There is a tragic cast to the exceptional circumstances in which nonmoral considerations of impersonal well-being tempt us to violate weighty injunctions of relational morality. This is captured by the idea that the impersonal considerations at issue do not undermine the interpersonal obligation that is owed to the victim. This same feature makes it intelligible that conscientious individuals might find themselves unable to violate the victim's moral claims against them, however compelling the impersonal values might be that are at stake. We can perhaps make sense of someone who chooses the outcome that is impersonally best in the aggregate for the affected individuals in the exceptional kind of cases that we have been considering. But it would also be humanly intelligible if agents found that they were unable to do so under these circumstances, given their appreciation for what they independently owe to their fellow moral persons.

Acknowledgments

1. Note the vocabulary that seems so natural when characterizing a situation of this kind: there is a *debt* that is *owed to* another party, etc. This is the structure of relational normativity that will be central in the argument of this book.

Chapter One. Introduction

1. I borrow here, of course, from Scanlon, *What We Owe to Each Other*. As I will discuss in chapter 5, Scanlon's approach embodies a deeply relational conception of morality as a unified normative domain.

2. See Hohfeld, *Fundamental Legal Conceptions*. The Hohfeld-like structure that is important to the relational conception, as I shall develop it, is the basic connection between obligations and claims. Further elements in his scheme, such as permissions and powers, seem to me to be derivative from this basic connection, and to be determined by the specific shape or content of the claims and duties that relational morality defines. I have a moral permission to do X, for instance, just in case there is nobody who has a claim against me that I should do X, and also nobody who has a claim against me that I should not do X. Cf. Scanlon, "Reply to Wenar," at pp. 401–2.

3. For an interpretation of tort law along these lines, see Ripstein, *Private Wrongs*.

4. See Thomson, *The Realm of Rights*, p. 117. In the same vein, see also Raz, *The Morality of Freedom*, pp. 170, 210–16; and O'Neill, "The Great Maxims of Justice and Charity," pp. 224–33.

5. Cf. Foot, *Natural Goodness*, chap. 5.

6. See Scanlon, *What We Owe to Each Other*, pp. 6–7. In the same passage, Scanlon refers to this intermediate domain as the morality of what we owe to each other, which is in obvious alignment with my interpretation of the relevant requirements. Note, however, that there are relational requirements that arise in virtue of the special relationships we stand in to particular individuals, which I would not consider to be moral obligations in the sense here at issue. Interpersonal morality, on my account, is the domain of what we owe to each other just insofar as we are each persons, not insofar as we are friends, relatives, lovers, fellow-citizens, and so on.

7. See sec. 5.1 below for further discussion.

8. A pluralistic picture of this kind is suggested by Kamm in "Owing, Justifying,

and Rejecting," sec. 2; see also Frick, "Contractualism and Social Risk," sec. 9. Kamm and Frick distinguish between moral requirements whose violation is wrong, and those whose violation wrongs someone. See also the works cited in note 4 above, which distinguish, somewhat differently, between the part of morality organized around rights and other moral requirements. (Raz's pluralism, which goes together with skepticism about the interest or depth of any distinction between morality and other normative domains, is developed further in his *Engaging Reason*, chap. 11. Raz's skepticism about what I call interpersonal morality might be compared to Foot's in *Natural Goodness*, though it lacks the commitment to Aristotelian foundations that informs her position.) My own view agrees with those of Raz, Thomson, and O'Neill in taking rights to characterize only a subclass of requirements within the intermediate domain of interpersonal morality. Unlike these philosophers, however, I hold that there is a relational structure that is common to all requirements in this domain, and that lends those requirements coherence and unity.

9. The idea that there are extramoral forms of concern for moral persons is discussed in sec. 6.4 below. The dispute about whether to label these forms of concern "moral" or "extramoral" might appear merely verbal. But by the time they get to the final section of this book, readers will be able to see, I hope, that the considerations I label "extramoral" lack some of the defining normative features that unify the core requirements of interpersonal morality.

10. In keeping with this conception of the project, I have tried to keep the main text of this book as unencumbered as my scholarly conscience would tolerate, relegating many qualifications and details to the endnotes. The endnotes also contain extensive references to contemporary philosophical books and articles in which issues touched on in the text are discussed in greater detail.

11. Several examples are offered in sec. 3.2 below.

12. A stimulating general discussion of directed obligations, from which I have profited, is Thompson, "What Is It to Wrong Someone?"; see also May, "Directed Duties."

13. There is a contrasting view, on which the directed duties generated by promises are unconditional, in the sense that having promised to do X, one owes it to the promisee to do X no matter what; but that these directed duties can sometimes be overridden by other kinds of consideration. See Thomson, *The Realm of Rights*, pp. 85–87, chap. 6; also Hart, "Are There Any Natural Rights?," pp. 185–86; and Kamm, "Owing, Justifying, and Rejecting," pp. 465–66. On this approach, the directed obligations defined by promises, though unconditional, are merely pro tanto or contributory; there is always, in principle, a further question to be answered about whether the promisor is morally obligated to do the thing that is owed to the promisee. The alternative that I favor treats these directed obligations as dispositive, albeit defeasible. I shall return briefly to the contrast between the two approaches in sec. 5.3.

14. For a summary discussion of this phenomenon, see Sreenivasan, "Duties and Their Direction." Sreenivasan's discussion is shaped by two assumptions that I shall eventually reject in what follows: that there are moral duties that are not directed; and that a directed duty might be overridden by other considerations in determining what it is that the agent ought to do, all things considered.

15. A theorist who apparently challenges the idea that directed moral obligations correspond to claims is Løgstrup; see his *The Ethical Demand*. On Løgstrup's view, directed ethical obligations are grounded paradigmatically in natural relations of power and vulnerability between two parties. In the vocabulary I would prefer, these natural relations give the vulnerable parties personal interests that are apt to be affected adversely by what their powerful counterparts might do. But I differ from Løgstrup in thinking that the presence of such interests is not sufficient for a directed obligation; interests provide bases for directed obligations only when they also provide a basis for normative claims or entitlements on the part of the individual whose interests are at stake. (I am indebted to Robert Stern for stimulating exchanges about Løgstrup's approach to directed moral obligation.)

16. See, for example, Sreenivasan, "Duties and Their Direction," pp. 485–86. In the standard example of this phenomenon, A promises B that A will provide a benefit specifically to C; see, e.g., Hart, "Are There Any Natural Rights?," p. 180. Theorists sometimes disagree with Hart about whether C has a claim against A that A provide the benefit in such cases. But few would hold that C has a claim if A's fulfillment of the promise to B would benefit C merely accidentally.

17. Foot, *Natural Goodness*, pp. 47–51.

18. See Owens, *Shaping the Normative Landscape*, chap. 6. Strictly speaking, Owens talks of "bare wrongings," not "bare claims"; but the possibility of bare wrongings presupposes that there are bare claims in the sense discussed in the text (i.e., claims that are not based in nonnormative interests held by the bearer of the claims, such as interests in avoiding harm or in securing the benefits of cooperation). Owens's own view explains bare wrongings by appeal to our specifically normative interests in being able to create new obligations.

19. There is a gesture in the direction of these two aspects to the problem of the normativity of the moral in Scanlon's distinction between the questions of the priority of moral reasons for the agent, and of the importance for other parties of the agent's responsiveness to them; see Scanlon, *What We Owe to Each Other*, chap. 4. I find this distinction suggestive, but underdeveloped in Scanlon's treatment of it in *What We Owe to Each Other*. Talk of the priority of moral reasons for the agent doesn't precisely capture the distinctive features of them, as practical requirements; and the issue of importance is not connected clearly to interpersonal practices of accountability. Later work by Scanlon, however, including his *Moral Dimensions*, offers a more extensive treatment of the interpersonal significance of moral requirements.

20. Exemplary for both tendencies is Parfit's brilliant and magisterial *On What Matters*, vols. 1 and 2. Parfit does not completely ignore either the obligatory character of moral rightness or its connection to responsibility and blame. But these topics are given perfunctory treatment (often in connection with discussions of Kant and other figures from the German tradition), and they are not taken to be central to an account of the normative structure of morality. Some examples: in vol. 1, Parfit notes that there is a "blameworthiness" sense in which actions can be wrong, but it does not figure prominently in his account of right and wrong in the core, "indefinable" sense (see vol. 1, secs. 22 and 54). Parfit also spends some time in vol. 1 arguing against

the Kantian idea that people can deserve to suffer (see, e.g., vol. 1, pp. 257–72); he seems to associate robust practices of interpersonal accountability with this discredited idea, which perhaps helps to explain his tendency to downplay this interpersonal aspect of morality. In vol. 2, there is a discussion of normativity in the "imperatival" sense, in connection with some reflections on Nietzsche's moral philosophy (see vol. 2, sec. 124). But Parfit dismisses imperatival conceptions of morality, arguing that they fail to distinguish normative claims from commands (a failure Parfit takes to have been prevalent culturally in Kant's era). On the view I shall develop, by contrast, imperatival or voluntarist accounts may be understood as attempts to elucidate the character of moral norms as practical requirements (an issue that was clearly very important to Kant himself).

21. Issues of both of these kinds—about the role of morality as a source of obligations, and about its connection to practices of interpersonal accountability— are prominent in the recent work of Stephen Darwall; see, for instance, his *The Second-Person Standpoint*. Although I agree with Darwall about the importance of these issues for moral theory, the account I offer is ultimately very different from his. For relevant discussion, see my "Reasons, Relations, and Commands," which argues that Darwall's "second-personal" conception of morality slides between a relational account and a very different "voluntarist" model. In more recent work, Darwall makes clear that he understands obligation to be, at bottom, voluntarist rather than relational in character; see his "Bipolar Obligation." I discuss the voluntarist approach in more detail in chapters 2 and 3 below.

22. One of the most impressive contributions of this kind is Nagel, *The Possibility of Altruism*. Some other (very disparate) examples of the general strategy include Gewirth, *Reason and Morality*; Hare, *Moral Thinking*; Gauthier, *Morals by Agreement*; and Korsgaard, *The Sources of Normativity*. For critical discussion of the general philosophical ambition to vindicate the authority of the moral, see Williams, *Ethics and the Limits of Philosophy*.

23. This conception of the challenge to moral theory is shared by at least some contemporary theorists. In addition to the works by Darwall referred to in note 21 above, see also Skorupski, *The Domain of Reasons*, part 3, which develops an intricate account of moral obligation and its connections to reasons for blame. The relational account I present differs from the accounts favored by both Darwall and Skorupski, as will emerge in later chapters of this book; but I share with them to some degree a conception of the normative features that we need a moral theory to illuminate.

24. These problems of resolution are illustrated, again, by Parfit's *On What Matters*. Parfit discusses issues in metaethics extensively, devoting hundreds of pages to a defense of nonnaturalistic realism about reasons. (Parfit's more recent *On What Matters*, vol. 3, is largely given over to additional extensive discussions of these same metaethical questions.) But the question of the specific normative significance of morality, as a source of obligations and a basis for accountability relations, is hardly mentioned, let alone addressed, in these pages. When Parfit turns to moral rightness and wrongness in particular, issues about their special normative significance are also invisible, and his argument zooms in closely to focus on first-order intuitions about specific cases (including intuitions elicited by an array of ingenious but highly arti-

ficial hypothetical examples). I don't deny that first-order adequacy is a constraint on an account of moral rightness; but there are also theoretical constraints, deriving from the need to make sense of the special normative significance of moral rightness and wrongness themselves. I am trying to address this need directly, framing my investigation in terms that will keep these distinctive forms of normative significance clearly in focus throughout.

25. A conversation with Selim Berker helped me to see that pluralism about the normative is a commitment of the kind of view I favor.

26. In sec. 5.4, however, I do entertain the possibility of devising an illuminating (but nonreductive) philosophical account of the normative nexus at the heart of morality, considering moral contractualism as an account of this kind.

27. I have been deeply impressed by Scanlon's contractualism since encountering his initial statement of it in his paper "Contractualism and Utilitarianism." For an earlier attempt to come to grips with the theory, see, for instance, my "Scanlon's Contractualism." It has dawned on me only gradually that much of the power of contractualism derives from its articulation of a relational conception of the moral domain, and that this conception could in principle be extracted from the context of contractualism, and defended as a more general way of thinking about the basic normative features of the moral (with contractualism representing a specific theoretical elaboration of the more general relational conception). Scanlon himself, I should add, is sometimes diffident about the relational aspect of his view, and he certainly does not attach to it the significance that I see it as having. My argument, insofar as it defends contractualism, is therefore offered in a spirit of appropriation rather than faithful interpretation—one that takes much more seriously than Scanlon does his characterization of interpersonal morality as the domain of what we owe to each other.

28. The background assumption here might be that it is a constraint on any theory we might construct about morality and moral rightness that it accommodate our independent intuitions about first-order questions in this domain. The alternative that I favor is in the spirit of the kind of (wide) reflective equilibrium approach sketched by Rawls, which attempts to do justice both to our views about particular cases and to considerations of a more philosophical nature, such as the need to make sense of the characteristic deliberative and interpersonal roles that moral considerations are suited to play. See Rawls, A Theory of Justice, pp. 42–45.

29. For an influential example of a discussion in normative ethics that is couched in terms of intuitions about moral reasons and the comparative value of different outcomes, see the treatment of issues in population ethics in Parfit, Reasons and Persons, part 4.

30. Fred Neuhauser suggested to me that my argument might be framed in these terms; the suggestion seems to me apt.

31. A helpful recent discussion of this commitment to the "basic equality" of persons is Waldron, One Another's Equals.

32. My reference to "most of us today" might be taken as an invitation to readers to reflect for themselves about whether they find the postulate of equal standing plausible, and whether they understand there to be requirements that are connected

to the abstract insight it expresses. It may be that the community of those who share these assumptions, and view them as plausible starting points for ethical theorizing, is smaller than I perhaps optimistically take it to be. For a contrasting perspective on the characteristically modern, cosmopolitan conception of interpersonal morality operative in this book, see, e.g., Flanagan, *The Geography of Morals*. Flanagan usefully emphasizes the historical and cultural variety we encounter in understandings of selfhood and ethical attainment, and argues that we can profit, both individually and philosophically, from close attention to differences in ethical outlook across cultures and epochs. I do not disagree; but I also think there is value in working out systematically the modern idea that there is a common framework of relational requirements that are suited to structure our interactions with anyone, and that derive from our acknowledgment that their interests are no less important than ours.

33. See, for example, Singer, *The Expanding Circle*; and Greene, *Moral Tribes*.

34. Scanlon, "Contractualism and Utilitarianism," p. 102. (Scanlon's observation is, strictly speaking, about utilitarianism; but he would surely accept a similar claim about other forms of consequentialism.)

35. On the first issue, see, e.g., Sidgwick, *The Methods of Ethics*, pp. 497–98, and Rawls, *A Theory of Justice*, secs. 5–6; on the second issue, a classic treatment is Williams, "A Critique of Utilitarianism."

36. See, for example, Parfit, *Reasons and Persons*, pp. 453–54; also the epigraph from Nietzsche's *The Gay Science*, sec. 343, that appears at the start of that volume ("at last our ships may venture out again . . . ; the sea, *our sea*, lies open again; perhaps there has never yet been such an 'open sea'"); a similar outlook is implicit in Greene, *Moral Tribes*.

37. Influential expressions of the view that the project of modern moral philosophy has failed are Anscombe, "Modern Moral Philosophy"; and MacIntyre, *After Virtue*. I discuss some of Anscombe's concerns about moral obligation in chapter 2 below.

Chapter Two. The Problem of Moral Obligation

1. Anscombe, "Modern Moral Philosophy."

2. See my paper "The Deontic Structure of Morality."

3. Here and in what follows, I shall mostly use the expressions "practical requirement" and "obligation" interchangeably, to refer generically to normative considerations that function deliberatively as presumptive constraints on agency (as I shall go on to put it). The eventual argument of the chapter will be that moral obligations, in the more specific sense of directed duties, are among the normative considerations that are intelligible to us as obligations or practical requirements in this more generic sense.

4. See Scanlon, *What We Owe to Each Other*, chap. 1, for the idea of reasons as considerations that count in favor of attitudes. For the idea that normativity is to be understood fundamentally in terms of reasons, see Raz, *Engaging Reason*, chap. 4, at p. 67; also Skorupski, *The Domain of Reasons*.

5. See Scheffler, "Relationships and Responsibilities," p. 100.

6. See Raz, *Practical Reason and Norms*.

7. See my "The Deontic Structure of Morality"; also Dancy, "Enticing Reasons"; and Greenspan, "Making Sense of Options," sec. 3.

8. The classic statement of this view is Bratman, *Intention, Plans, and Practical Reason*.

9. Cf. Owens, *Shaping the Normative Landscape*, secs. 15–16; Owens assimilates conscientious responsiveness to obligations to motivation through habit, and attempts to make sense in these terms of some of the distinctive deliberative roles that I am calling attention to.

10. See, again, Bratman, *Intention, Plans, and Practical Reason*.

11. The general idea that there might be a plurality of different kinds of normative consideration is familiar from the work of Jonathan Dancy. See, for example, his *Ethics without Principles*, chap. 3, where Dancy contrasts the favoring relation with other forms of normative relevance, such as intensifying and enabling.

12. Cf. Thomson, *Normativity*, pp. 229–30. Thomson's account is expressed not in terms of reasons and their comparative strength, but in terms of the different considerations that on her view ground "directive" claims about action. Those considerations have to do with being defective as a human being; the difference between directives expressed with "ought" and with "must," on her account, can be traced to the severity of the defects that one would manifest in failing to act on the directives. But this is a matter of differences in degree, not differences in kind or quality.

13. Different versions of this approach are developed in Korsgaard, *The Sources of Normativity*, chap. 3; in Williams, *Ethics and the Limits of Philosophy*, chap. 4, and "Moral Incapacity"; and in Frankfurt, *Necessity, Volition, and Love*. For Korsgaard, the practical "must" expresses a class of genuinely normative considerations that are grounded in our "practical identities," and that are aptly described as obligations. For Williams and Frankfurt, by contrast, it gives expression to psychological incapacities that in turn reflect central aspects of who we are; these authors tend not to speak of obligation in this context, but of practical or volitional necessity. For an illuminating discussion of volitional necessity, see Watson, "Volitional Necessities."

14. See, e.g., Korsgaard, "The Normativity of Instrumental Reason." This general approach could also be interpreted in terms of the voluntarist model, insofar as the constitutive condition of thought and action is taken to be a commitment to comply with the core requirements of rationality (where the commitment in question is understood as a kind of law that one legislates for oneself); cf. the brief discussion of Kantian versions of voluntarism about morality in sec. 2.2 below.

15. See, for instance, Kolodny, "Why Be Rational?"

16. It might be argued that one could be akratic with respect to these requirements, acknowledging their significance for one's conception of who one is, but failing to live up to them on account of temptation or weakness. But it is hard to see much space for genuinely acknowledging something as existentially central to one's conception of what one's life is about while still being weak-willed in this way. The subjective conception of significance that is at work in the account seems to preclude

this kind of backsliding. For Korsgaard, e.g., a practical identity is supposed to be a "description under which you find your life to be worth living and your actions to be worth undertaking"; see *The Sources of Normativity*, p. 101. (Korsgaard's own attempt to accommodate the phenomenon of flouted duty is found on pp. 102–5 of this work. Her strategy appeals to the agent's sense that occasional violations of the alleged duty are consistent with maintenance of the practical identity at issue; but this consideration seems to me to undermine the standing of the normative consideration as a genuine duty on the occasions when it is flouted.)

17. There is a different kind of identity-based strategy, which appeals not to agents' conception of who they are, but rather to objective facts about identity of which the agents might be deeply mistaken. This kind of approach would not encounter the problem of flouted duty, though it is vulnerable to problems of other kinds. (The Aristotelian approach sketched in the following section might be understood as an identity-based strategy of this objective kind.)

18. Scanlon, "Wrongness and Reasons"; "Replies," pp. 435–39; and Parfit, *On What Matters*, vol. 1, pp. 368–70; also sec. 22.

19. See especially Scanlon, "Wrongness and Reasons."

20. See again Scanlon, "Wrongness and Reasons," for a forceful presentation of this concern.

21. Compare the notion of morality in the narrow sense developed in Scanlon, *What We Owe to Each Other*, chap. 4, sec. 7. For an interesting expression of skepticism about the idea that there is a significant context-independent distinction to be drawn between moral and other kinds of reasons, see Raz, *Engaging Reason*, chaps. 11–12. A similarly skeptical attitude seems to me implicit in Williams's critical reflections on what he calls "the morality system"; see his *Ethics and the Limits of Philosophy*, esp. chap. 10.

22. On the concept/conception distinction, see Rawls, *A Theory of Justice*, p. 5. On my understanding, a conception of moral rightness is an attempt to identify a high-level property that rightness might be taken to consist in, and that makes sense of the more abstract features that define the modern concept of the moral right.

23. In what follows, I shall (unless otherwise noted) use variants of the expressions "moral" and "morality" to refer to specifically interpersonal morality, in the sense I have roughly sketched here.

24. Nagel, *The Possibility of Altruism*, p. 14.

25. See Parfit, *Reasons and Persons*, p. 27, for this way of using the vocabulary of "agent-neutral" and "agent-relative" in relation to ethical theories. Compare the notion of an "agent-centered" restriction introduced and discussed in Scheffler, *The Rejection of Consequentialism*, e.g., p. 80; as Scheffler makes clear there, an agent-centered restriction in his sense need not involve an absolute prohibition on an agent's performing actions of a certain specified type.

26. The discussion here might be considered an homage to Anscombe's brisk critical survey of modern accounts of moral obligation in "Modern Moral Philosophy," pp. 170–73. Where Anscombe devotes a couple of sentences to each approach she

discusses, I offer a couple of paragraphs, in deference to contemporary scholarly expectations.

27. Reflecting on this aspect of their position, utilitarians might accept that theirs is a revisionist conception of the moral (perhaps by denying that agent-relativity is as important to the modern concept of the moral as I have contended). Alternatively, they might attempt to accommodate this element in the modern concept by showing that individuals will generally do better, by the lights of the utilitarian standard of right conduct, if they treat it in practice as giving them agent-relative goals (so that they strive to keep their own promises, e.g., rather than to promote the neutral value of promissory fidelity).

28. I have suggested that any reasonable conception of practical requirements should construe them as merely defeasible constraints on agency, insofar as circumstances can change unexpectedly in ways that alter what we are required to do. But defeasibility is a matter of degree. The difficulty with the utilitarian conception is not that it defines requirements that are defeasible, but that it renders moral rightness hostage in an exceptional degree to circumstantial fortune of this kind.

29. It is sometimes suggested that maximizing is constitutively rational, and that rationality intelligibly functions as a constraint on the formation of our intentions. But maximizing is crucially unlike the core elements of structural rationality that, as I suggested in sec. 2.1, intuitively strike us as constraints on deliberation. It is, for instance, difficult to assimilate it to the dominance and identity models that have proven helpful in thinking about demands of noncontradiction and means-end consistency. Moreover, it is controversial (to say the least) to assume that maximizing is a constitutively rational ideal.

30. A conclusion that at least some consequentialists have been happy to embrace; see, for instance, Norcross, "Reasons without Demands."

31. Mill, *Utilitarianism*, pp. 47–48.

32. These arguments do not apply to the most prominent contemporary versions of rule consequentialism, such as those defended by Parfit in *On What Matters*, vol. 1, or by Hooker in *Ideal Code, Real World*. To the extent these approaches offer accounts of the obligatory character of morality, their accounts do not appeal to the idea of maximization.

33. Anscombe, "Modern Moral Philosophy." The Aristotelian alternative that she recommends for contemporary ethics is one that does without the special notion of a "moral" obligation; I discuss this approach at the end of the present section.

34. For a sketch of such a view, see Wolf, "Moral Obligations and Social Commands."

35. Wolf addresses these concerns in "Moral Obligations and Social Commands," pp. 360–64. She notes that social commands might be said to give rise to obligations only when the behavior they command is morally valuable in some way. But this stipulation still leaves us with the problem of what she calls "false negatives," which are apparent obligations that a given society neglects to enforce through the exertion of social pressures. The question of whether we are under a moral obligation to offer reparations to the descendants of slaves is not settled, as it seems to me, by observing

that we do not as a society command each other to act in this way. Consideration of such cases moves Wolf to suggest that moral obligations might be determined not by what a society actually commands its members to do, but by the commands that it would be appropriate for a society to lay down, which moves the position in the direction of the hypothetical version of voluntarism that I go on to consider in the text.

36. Darwall, *The Second-Person Standpoint*; see also his "Bipolar Obligation." Darwall understands the issuing of demands by representative members of the moral community to involve their being addressed to an agent through the reactions characteristic of blame. Two other approaches that interestingly tie moral obligation to critical reactions in the register of blame are Greenspan's in "Making Room for Options," sec. 4; and Skorupski's in *The Domain of Reasons*, chap. 12.

37. See Darwall, "Bipolar Obligation," pp. 36–37. For a more general discussion of some of these issues, see my "Reasons, Relations, and Commands." I return to the question of the relation between obligation and responsibility relations in the next chapter; I argue, in sec. 3.4, that the voluntarist cannot do justice to the reasons we have to hold people to moral demands, which have to do with the fact that they define moral obligations in some sense that is independent of their being addressed by members of the moral community to each other.

38. Cf. Watson, "Morality as Equal Accountability," p. 40.

39. For an overview of this historical development in the moral philosophy of the modern period, see Schneewind, *The Invention of Autonomy*. Freud, of course, also interpreted moral development as a process involving the internalization of social relations of authority.

40. A contemporary defense of this general approach is Korsgaard, *The Sources of Normativity*. The commentaries included in this volume raise versions of the questions I have briefly posed in the text for the general Kantian strategy. See, in addition, Street, "What Is Constructivism in Ethics and Metaethics?"; also my "Constructivism about Normativity."

41. See Foot, *Natural Goodness*; also Thompson, *Life and Action*.

42. The conception of identity relevant to this development of the identity-based approach to obligation is different from that emphasized in sec. 2.1 above. It is the conception of one's objective species nature, not a subjective conception of who one fundamentally is or what one's life is about.

43. See Foot, *Natural Goodness*, p. 79.

44. Proponents of Aristotelian approaches are typically skeptical about the modern concept of moral obligation that I have been discussing in this section, preferring a framework that attaches little systematic significance to the distinction between moral and nonmoral reasons and requirements. Theorists of this stripe will be fairly untroubled by their inability to do justice to a concept whose coherence or importance they are anyway inclined to question. But the attractions of Aristotelianism as a theoretical framework for ethics may be diminished somewhat if there is an alternative approach that makes sense of the modern notion of moral obligation that Anscombe and others have rejected.

45. Foot, *Natural Goodness*, p. 48.

46. Her explanation for this dissatisfaction is that other human virtues, such as resourcefulness and persistence in pursuit of the truth, would lead a scholar such as Maklay to want to photograph the Malay servant for scientific purposes, in a way that is at odds with the force of the promissory reason; see *Natural Goodness*, p. 50. But there is a natural response to this worry within the framework of Foot's approach, which is that the resourceful and persistent commitment to the truth is not a virtue if it leads an agent to act in ways that are incompatible with other virtues, such as trustworthiness. (This response would reflect a commitment to the thesis of the unity of the virtues, on at least one natural interpretation of it.)

47. Foot, *Natural Goodness*, p. 51 (emphasis mine). Foot draws here on Anscombe, "Rules, Rights and Promises."

48. I return to the idea that directed duties are the joint property of the parties that they bind in sec. 4.2 below.

49. See, for instance, Feinberg, "The Nature and Value of Rights," pp. 243–44; also Darwall, "Bipolar Obligation," pp. 25–27.

50. See Scheffler, *The Rejection of Consequentialism*, chap. 4, for an especially forceful presentation of this puzzle.

51. Inducing the mysterious stranger to bring about the state of affairs in which promissory fidelity is maximized would count as my doing what I could to advance this agent-neutral goal, and so be a way of fulfilling my promise to you.

52. I offer some further comments about agent-relativity in sec. 4.4 below.

53. Proponents of different theories might understand them to be accounts of the modern concept of moral rightness, because they are attempts to do justice to the basic elements of that concept. But if the relational account is the most plausible such theory, then those who reason correctly about moral rightness will understand it in terms of the property of what we owe to each other, just insofar as we are persons.

54. Cf. Raz, *Practical Reason and Norms*.

55. I assume here provisionally, as it seems to me most natural to do, that these are claims about what it is morally right or wrong to do, in the relational sense I have been trying to explicate. As I explain in sec. 4.1 below, however, promissory obligations are sometimes understood to involve a distinctive, pre- or nonmoral form of normativity that is implicitly relational in structure. On this kind of view, there is a promissory form of rightness, involving self-standing obligations that are owed to another party, that might be registered in deliberation as a presumptive constraint on agency.

56. See, for example, Smith, *The Moral Problem*, chap. 3. Cf. Parfit's discussion of "deontic reasons" in his *On What Matters*, vol. 1, pp. 448–51; also Owens, *Shaping the Normative Landscape*, p. 69: "[obligations] are not factors in the practical deliberations of the conscientious agent." As noted earlier, Owens's alternative assimilates responsiveness to obligations to motivation by habit; but this seems to me to give obligation too little work to do in the perspective of deliberation. (The conscientious agent should be aware of a feature of obligations that makes them suited to figure as defeasible constraints in reflection about what to do.)

57. The original buck-passing theory is Scanlon's account of goodness, developed in chap. 2 of his *What We Owe to Each Other*. For an application of this terminology

to debates about the normative significance of moral rightness, see Darwall, " 'But It Would Be Wrong.' "

58. This fetishism objection is pressed by Smith in *The Moral Problem*, sec. 3.5.

59. This point is helpfully emphasized by Darwall in " 'But It Would Be Wrong.' "

60. I believe this gives rise to a further potential problem for voluntarist approaches, concerning the content of the attitudes through which responsibility is attributed by one party to another (e.g., by the claimholders who address moral demands to agents). I return to this issue in sec. 3.4 below.

61. Private law systems of right figure prominently in Michael Thompson's illuminating discussion of relational or (as he calls it) "bipolar" normativity, in "What Is It to Wrong Someone?" The idea that there are distinct "orders of right" (or systems of relational obligations and claims) plays a central role in the argument of Thompson's paper; I discuss one strand in that argument in sec. 4.2 below.

62. To be clear, I am not appealing here to idea that the relational requirements of morality are obligations for us, because we are constitutively committed to complying with them in virtue of our fundamental identity as persons. There is an identity-based argument for moral requirements that takes this general form, but it is not the argument I am here sketching. My idea, instead, is along the following lines: if there are requirements that we owe to others, just insofar as they are persons who might be affected by our actions, then these requirements will be inescapable for us, because we necessarily occupy the situation that triggers them. Relational moral requirements differ, in this respect, from the relational requirements of certain games.

63. This claim is defended in my "Duties of Love."

64. See my "Scanlon's Contractualism," sec. 3, for a discussion of the relational values enabled by both morality and friendship. The phrase "interpersonal recognition" is inspired in part by Scanlon's talk of "mutual recognition" in *What We Owe to Each Other*, chap. 5. Scanlon understands mutual recognition to constitute the valuable form of relationship that is enabled by morality, and that helps to explain the reason-giving force of moral requirements. It strikes me as potentially misleading, however, to characterize the relational value at issue in these contexts as mutual recognition, since the value at issue can be realized even in cases in which the agent's acknowledgment of the claims of another party is not reciprocated. I return to this issue in sec. 4.4 below.

65. A different possibility might be one in which a single individual has two distinct claims against the agent that cannot in the nature of the case both be satisfied. But this seems less plausible, as a model for intramoral conflict of obligation. The fact that the allegedly conflicting claims are assigned to a single person threatens to undermine their force, as self-standing entitlements. Thus prospective claimholders would not seem entitled to complain about my behavior if I have done what was necessary to live up to other claims that they themselves have against me.

66. I noted in sec. 2.1 above that obligations are typically registered in deliberation through the formation of intentions, which operationalize their function as presumptive constraints on agency. But it is a familiar fact that many of our intentions have a hierarchical structure, establishing clear relations of priority between our more fun-

damental goals and those subordinate to them. On this general point, see Raz, *The Morality of Freedom*, pp. 292–93; also Scanlon, *What We Owe to Each Other*, pp. 121–23.

67. This idea is interestingly defended by Scheffler, "Membership and Political Obligation."

68. See (again) my "Duties of Love." For a recent discussion of friendship that emphasizes its source in values distinct from the moral, see Nehamas, *On Friendship*. Also highly relevant here is Niko Kolodny, "Love as Valuing a Relationship."

69. For this suggestion, see Scanlon, *What We Owe to Each Other*, pp. 164–66. This line of thought would assimilate friendship to the treatment of political membership sketched above, according to which the special values at issue in the two cases are conditioned by or subordinated to the requirements of morality. A different way to assimilate the cases would be to treat political membership, like friendship, as involving an inherent susceptibility to generate independent requirements that might conflict with those of morality.

70. See Bernard Williams, "Moral Luck," for the discussion of Gauguin; and "Persons, Character, and Morality," for his treatment of the compatibility of impartial moral obligation with the attitudes characteristic of intimate relationships.

71. We might put this by saying that the relational obligations of morality are pervasive, even if they do not necessarily override the other kinds of obligations with which they might conceivably conflict. For a thoughtful discussion of the pervasiveness and alleged overridingness of morality, see Scheffler, *Human Morality*, chap. 2.

Chapter Three. Morality as a Social Phenomenon

1. They are not denying that it is a platitude that moral rightness is a source of obligations; to do that would be to offer an alternative interpretation of the abstract concept of moral rightness, rather than the kind of skeptical position I am sketching in the text.

2. I develop some of these themes at greater length in my paper "Rightness and Responsibility."

3. Strawson, "Freedom and Resentment," pp. 79–80.

4. Strawson, "Freedom and Resentment," pp. 79–80.

5. I discuss this and other aspects of Strawson's position in my paper "Emotions and Relationships."

6. See my *Responsibility and the Moral Sentiments*, chap. 2.

7. The idea that accountability relations involve a form of "moral address," whereby demands or expectations are addressed by one agent to another, is an important and interesting theme in the work of Gary Watson on responsibility. See, for instance, Watson's "Responsibility and the Limits of Evil," and also his "Two Faces of Responsibility." I discuss this theme in my paper "Moral Address."

8. A recent collection of papers on this topic, which reflect the complexity of the phenomenon and the range of approaches that may be taken to it, is Coates and Tognazzini, *Blame*.

9. See my "Dispassionate Opprobrium." For a similar view, see Wolf, "Blame, Ital-

ian Style." The reactive approach is, I believe, implicit in Strawson's "Freedom and Resentment"; it is also a theme in my *Responsibility and the Moral Sentiments*.

10. On the importance of adjustments in one's ways of relating to people who have acted wrongly, see Scanlon, *Moral Dimensions*, chap. 4.

11. A still different aspect of the distinctively modern concept of interpersonal morality, to which I shall return, is its commitment to the postulate of the equal standing of all.

12. For a defense of the idea that intentions or attitudes are generally irrelevant to questions about the permissibility or wrongness of what we do, see Scanlon, *Moral Dimensions*, chaps. 1–3. For purposes of discussion in this chapter, we do not need to insist that permissibility is in all cases independent from questions of intent or attitude, only that it is in many cases independent. For a penetrating discussion of this general issue, see Kolodny, "Scanlon's Investigation."

13. For all I have said here, these actions might sometimes include purely mental performances, such as a failure to manage one's malicious or antagonistic attitudes toward others in accordance with reasonable expectations. For discussion of this possibility, see (again) Kolodny, "Scanlon's Investigation."

14. I would emphasize that the attitudes relevant to blame reactions must be construed widely, to include such things as thoughtlessness, lack of due care or consideration, negligence, lack of attention, and so on. These sorts of characteristics might be understood as global features of a person's attitudes, and they sometimes render blame reactions warranted or fitting.

15. This point is an important theme in recent work on accountability by Pamela Hieronymi; see, for example, "The Force and Fairness of Blame."

16. I have elsewhere suggested that traditional forms of global skepticism about responsibility may best be understood as appeals to a concern about the fairness of holding people responsible, given the implication of our actions in a larger world of natural causal processes; see my *Responsibility and the Moral Sentiments*, chap. 4. Standards of fairness govern actions rather than attitudes; they bear on our accountability practices, then, at the moment of reflection described in the text, where we acknowledge our implication in the economy of disesteem, and face a practical question about whether to affirm or to renounce it, as a basis for our continuing interactions with the persons who are its target. I return to this theme in sec. 3.3 below, in connection with the question of the nature of forgiveness.

17. A very different basis for distancing ourselves from participation in the economy of disesteem might be that doing so is counterproductive, serving as an obstacle to the establishment of a more just social order, going forward. This might conceivably be the case, even if it is granted that wrongdoing makes it fitting to respond with reactive or other forms of blame. For a forceful (if, to my mind, unconvincing) statement of this critical position, see Nussbaum, *Anger and Forgiveness*; also relevant here is Flanagan, *The Geography of Morals*, chaps. 8–9. A more positive assessment of the familiar practice of angry blame is offered by Miranda Fricker in her "What's the Point of Blame?"

18. Foot, *Natural Goodness*.

19. See, e.g., Singer, *Practical Ethics*, pp. 213–15.

20. Cf. Sidgwick's sympathetic discussion of the possibility of an esoteric morality, in his *The Methods of Ethics*, book 4, chap. 5.

21. By the same token, a conscientious effort to comply with the utilitarian principle will notoriously not suffice to provide protection from the opprobrium of others. We can easily imagine circumstances in which it might be optimific, and therefore required by utilitarian lights, to react to such a conscientious agent with the reactions characteristic of blame.

22. I offer some additional remarks about utilitarian or consequentialist conceptions of rightness, and their significance for interpersonal accountability, at the start of sec. 3.3 below.

23. It is not in general true that the traits constitutive of virtues are responses solely to the reasons provided by the fact that those traits are virtuous. People who are just, for instance, correctly take their promissory commitments to be serious reasons for action, and respond to those reasons appropriately. In the present case, however, it seems there is no independent account on offer of what the first-order reasons for blame might be, which leaves us only with the reasons that are provided by the fact that such reactions are virtuous; these reasons, I maintain, are reasons of the wrong kind. To anticipate the argument that follows: if one could take for granted a relational account of interpersonal morality, then one could argue that virtuous agents respond correctly to the reasons for blame that are provided by deliberate offenses against relational requirements. But the account of ethical virtue, on this approach, would not be an individualistic alternative to the relational story, but a supplement to it.

24. Note, again, that for all I have said here, these blameworthy performances might include some purely mental actions, involving failure, e.g., to manage malicious or derogatory emotions and feelings toward another person.

25. There are versions of both perfectionism and consequentialism that might come closer to accommodating the point I have emphasized about the social significance of rightness. Consider rule consequentialism, in the version that holds that actions are wrong just in case they would be prohibited by general rules that it would be optimific for the members of community to internalize and to follow (where internalization precisely involves a tendency to blame people when they exhibit attitudes of indifference toward those general rules). This theory seems to do a better job than the perfectionism considered in the text at acknowledging the idea that moral rightness needs to be understood in relation to interpersonal practices of accountability. But it still gives a distorted account of this relation. Reactive and other forms of blame are directly responsive to reasons, construed as considerations that make them individually fitting or warranted, whereas the rule consequentialist appeals to evaluative considerations of a very different kind, about whether it would generally be optimific to hold agents responsible for complying with a given set of requirements. For a recent statement and defense of the kind of rule consequentialism under discussion here, see Hooker, *Ideal Code, Real World*.

26. An impressive recent statement of this general approach is Adams, *Finite and Infinite Goods*.

27. See Adams, *Finite and Infinite Goods*, pp. 252–53 and 257, on this point. On this way of developing the divine command theory, the obligations created by determinations of the divine will ultimately trace back to relational duties of gratitude toward God, which are prior to and independent of the issuance of commandments by God. So interpreted, the divine command theory is not an alternative to the relational account of interpersonal obligation, but presupposes it. I return in sec. 3.4 below to the ways in which voluntarist approaches distort our reasons for complying with moral obligations and addressing them to other parties through our accountability practices.

28. Cf. Watson, "The Trouble with Psychopaths," pp. 315–16.

29. Fricker, "What's the Point of Blame?," p. 173.

30. Watson, "The Trouble with Psychopaths," p. 316.

31. Hieronymi, "Reflection and Responsibility," p. 31.

32. For a historical example of the same basic point, compare the following characterization by Adam Smith of the object of such reactive attitudes as resentment: "To bring him [sc. the wrongdoer] back to a more just sense of what is due to other people, to make him sensible of what he owes us, and of the wrong that he has done to us, is frequently the principal end proposed in our revenge, which is always imperfect when it cannot accomplish this"; see Smith, *The Theory of the Moral Sentiments*, p. 115 (part II, sec. III, chap. I).

33. Strawson, "Freedom and Resentment," p. 77.

34. Strawson, "Freedom and Resentment," p. 80.

35. Strawson, "Freedom and Resentment," p. 84.

36. For a more detailed development of these points, see my "Emotions and Expectations."

37. I return to this theme in sec. 4.4 below.

38. Many culpable failures of causal reasoning can be traced to our natural tendency to overweight our own interests within moral reflection. Flawed reasoning of this kind is often strategically rooted in partiality; the faulty empirical reasoning of most climate change skeptics, for instance, seems clearly to be motivated by their concern to protect their own narrowly economic and political interests. (It is in this way a form of ideology, in the pejorative sense.) Cases of this kind could therefore be described as ones in which agents disregard the consequentialist requirement to attach equal weight to the interests of those potentially affected by their actions.

39. This aspect of apology is emphasized in Helmreich, "The Apologetic Stance."

40. Recent works that take up these issues include Allais, "Wiping the Slate Clean"; Garrard and McNaughton, "In Defense of Unconditional Forgiveness"; Griswold, *Forgiveness*; Hieronymi, "Articulating an Uncompromising Forgiveness"; and Pettigrove, *Forgiveness and Love*.

41. This claim is a minor exaggeration, insofar as there are contexts in which we seem to attribute the standing to forgive to certain third parties. Thus, close friends of the victim might intelligibly say to the perpetrator of a serious wrong that they will never forgive the perpetrator for what was done to the victim. This kind of standing, however, is arguably still positional, insofar as it presupposes that the person who possesses it stands in a special relation of some kind to the party who was wronged.

Third-party forgiveness is not exactly bestowed on behalf of the victim; but it proceeds out of recognition of the victim's privileged entitlement to complain, which may be taken to extend to the third party in virtue of their special relationship to the victim. For an interesting discussion of this elusive and complex phenomenon, see Chaplin, "Taking It Personally."

42. See Scanlon, *Being Realistic about Reasons*, chap. 2, on "pure normative claims," which often articulate relations of dependency between normative and nonnormative facts or circumstances.

43. It has been argued that there are cases in which a person is wronged by an action, without having a right or claim against the agent that is directly flouted through the action. See Cornell, "Wrongs, Rights, and Third Parties." On Cornell's view, the cases at issue involve wrongful actions that cause adverse effects for parties who do not have rights or claims against the agent. But the notion of wrongful action in play here is relational rather than individualistic, insofar as Cornell assumes that someone's rights have been violated by the action that is wrongful; the suggestion is that such actions wrong not only the agent whose rights are violated, but also other parties who are adversely affected by those actions. I explain in sec. 6.1 why I do not find this proposal plausible; for the present, the important point is that, though it attaches significance to the fact that third parties are harmed by wrongful actions, it does this within a relational rather than an individualistic framework.

44. See Ripstein, *Private Wrongs*, chap. 8.

45. This may ultimately be what Ripstein means with the somewhat misleading talk about rights surviving their own violation. See, e.g., *Private Wrongs*, pp. 240–41, where he writes, "The thought that something can be repaired does not mean that damage and repair is just as good [as no wrongdoing at all]; it means that whatever can be done to repair a wrong must be done because it is a wrong that requires repair." See also pp. 249–51, where Ripstein argues, against a proposal due to John Gardner, that the duty of repair has a directional element that cannot be explained merely in terms of the survival of reasons for action that originally counted in favor of the primary duty that was breached by the tortfeasor. These ideas are very close to what I have in mind in characterizing the secondary duty of repair as a residue of a claim that was flouted by the original wrong.

46. Scanlon talks in this connection about the "impairment" of the agent's relationships through acts that disregard moral claims, in his *Moral Dimensions*, chap. 4. I find this somewhat misleading, since it implies that there is an antecedent relationship between the agent and the claimholder that is eligible to be impaired. I come back to this issue in secs. 3.4 and 4.4 below.

47. Cf. Fricker, "What's the Point of Blame?," where blame is characterized as serving to bring about a convergence in moral understanding. If we are looking for a constructive function of blame, however, it seems to me important to emphasize convergence of understanding within the nexus defined by relational requirements. It is through blame and remorseful acknowledgment of wrongdoing that the relational rupture constituted by wrongdoing can be repaired, as the parties converge in a shared affirmation of what they owe to each other.

48. See Wolf, "Moral Obligations and Social Commands."

49. An analogous point applies to divine command theories that emphasize the sanctions attached by God to failures to comply with divine law. Helpful in this connection is the discussion of the "sanction theory" of obligation in Owens, *Shaping the Normative Landscape*, sec. 13.

50. See Wolf, "Moral Obligations and Social Commands"; and Adams, *Finite and Infinite Goods*, chap. 11.

51. See Adams, *Finite and Infinite Goods*, pp. 252–53 and 257, on the primacy of the relationship to God in a divine command theory of obligation. For Adams, the primary reasons that are associated with obligations are reasons of gratitude to God, rather than reasons associated with the avoidance of divine sanctions. One potential problem for this approach, discussed in note 27 above, is that it threatens to ground voluntarist obligations in a primordial obligation of the relational kind, namely a duty of gratitude that is owed by the individual to the divine lawgiver. This would obviously undermine the voluntarist's ambition to offer an alternative theoretical account of obligation. (It is interesting, however, that in ordinary cases of gratitude, directed obligations of gratitude have a discretionary character, something that is hard to reconcile with the role Adams ascribes to gratitude in relation to compliance with divine commands; compare the discussion of imperfect duties of gratitude in sec. 6.2 below.) But however these reasons of gratitude are understood, they still seem to be reasons of the wrong kind for compliance with moral obligations, insofar as they involve the subject's relation to the lawgiver rather than to the persons potentially harmed or injured when the obligations are flouted.

52. See Darwall, "Bipolar Obligation," pp. 36–37; also Wolf, "Moral Obligations and Social Commands," p. 250.

53. A version of this objection also applies to the interesting account of obligation offered by John Skorupski in *The Domain of Reasons*, chap. 12. Skorpuski argues, very roughly, that an action is right or obligatory if it would be blameworthy for agents to perform it in their current epistemic condition. But—as Skorupski is well aware—on this approach, thoughts of right or obligation are transparent to the person who might blame the agents for what they have done. To me, by contrast, it seems that our paradigmatic forms of reactive blame, such as resentment, precisely reflect an understanding of the targeted agents as having acted wrongly, indeed as having wronged another party through their action.

54. For a statement of what is essentially this picture, see Darwall, "Bipolar Obligation." On the general contrast between private and criminal law as involving a contrast between relational and monadic conceptions of "deonticity," see Thompson, "What Is It To Wrong Someone?," sec. 4.

55. Strawson, "Freedom and Resentment," pp. 83–84.

56. For a contrasting view, see Lacey and Pickard, "To Blame or to Forgive?" Despite their best efforts (see especially sec. 3), Lacey and Pickard do not succeed in establishing that something recognizable as forgiveness is really intelligible in the criminal justice context. Whatever public authorities might be doing in forswearing negative emotions and attitudes toward an offender, their doing so would lack the quality of forgiveness, precisely insofar as it is not the action of someone who is understood to have been wronged by the offense.

57. Cf. the discussion of "authoritative motivation" in Scheffler, *Human Morality*, chap. 5.

58. See Adams, *Finite and Infinite Goods*, p. 257.

59. In sec. 5.1 below, I discuss in more detail the extension of moral status to individuals who, for a variety of reasons, may not be able to assert claims against others on their own behalf.

60. See Scanlon, *What We Owe to Each Other*, chap. 4, sec. 8, on the idea of "trusteeship" and the scope of morality.

61. See Scanlon, *Moral Dimensions*, chap. 4.

62. On this point, see my "Dispassionate Opprobrium," secs. 3–4.

63. Indeed, it is something of a challenge for the nonreactive understanding of blame to make sense of the extended forms of blame, such as those intuitively available to third parties and to the agents of wrongdoing. If A wrongs B, then A may have acted in ways that give B reason to modify B's behavior toward A, going forward. But A's behavior toward B need not reflect any disregard for third parties, and so it will not necessarily give those parties reasons to modify their behavior toward A. The extended or vicarious forms of blame, it seems to me, are much more naturally interpreted in reactive terms.

64. Feinberg, "The Nature and Value of Rights."

65. Feinberg, "The Nature and Value of Rights," p. 250. Feinberg does not explicitly relate the performative sense of claiming to the practice of interpersonal accountability and blame, thinking of it rather in juridical terms (see, e.g., p. 251). But for reasons that have emerged in this section, it seems to me that reactive and other forms of blame are the most basic ways in which claims are asserted performatively in our moral practices.

Chapter Four. Relational Requirements without Relational Foundations

1. Williams, *Ethics and the Limits of Philosophy*, pp. 174 and 180.

2. Williams, *Ethics and the Limits of Philosophy*, p. 187.

3. This aspect of promissory obligation is emphasized in the classic account found in Scanlon, *What We Owe to Each Other*, chap. 7.

4. A solution to this problem is sketched in Kolodny and Wallace, "Promises and Practices Revisited."

5. See, for example, Raz, *The Morality of Freedom*, chap. 7; and Owens, *Shaping the Normative Landscape*.

6. A different nonmoralized account of promissory obligation, due to Margaret Gilbert, traces it to the nature of joint commitment rather than to some existing practice or convention. I consider Gilbert's approach in sec. 4.2 below.

7. See Thompson, "What Is It to Wrong Someone?"

8. Thompson himself emphasizes this potential difficulty with the Humean conception of the distinctively moral order of right; see "What Is It to Wrong Someone?," sec. 14. I return to his position in sec. 4.2 below.

9. Not only are there relationship-based moral obligations that the parties stand under in cases of this kind; there may also be independent "duties of love" that are

constitutively connected to the valuable forms of interpersonal relationship that are at issue. For a discussion of this possibility, see my paper "Duties of Love."

10. Raz, "Numbers," p. 210. Raz identifies three kinds of relationship that can give rise to directed duties: commitments or undertakings, thick social bonds, and the kinds of interaction between people that generate debts of gratitude. Compare Hart's comment, in his "Are There Any Natural Rights?," at p. 179, note 7, that (directed) obligations arise "out of the relationship of the parties."

11. Tomasello, *A Natural History of Human Morality*.

12. Tomasello, *A Natural History of Human Morality*, p. 86.

13. Greene, *Moral Tribes*.

14. On the distinction between System 1 and System 2 processes, see Kahnemann, *Thinking, Fast and Slow*.

15. See, for instance, Greene, *Moral Tribes*, chaps. 9–10. Cf. Parfit, *Reasons and Persons*, pp. 85–86.

16. Tomasello, *A Natural History of Human Morality*, pp. 158–63.

17. This would be to follow Williams and Tomasello, and to reject the more skeptical attitude of Greene.

18. See Greene, *Moral Tribes*, pp. 202–4; also Singer, *The Expanding Circle*.

19. Scheffler, "The Practice of Equality." See also his "What Is Egalitarianism?," and "Choice, Circumstance, and the Value of Equality."

20. Scheffler, "The Practice of Equality," pp. 25–31.

21. Scheffler, "The Practice of Equality," pp. 35–37. For a different take on the application of the ideal of equality to relationships between intimates, see Shiffrin, "Promising, Intimate Relationships, and Conventionalism."

22. Cf. Scheffler, "Membership and Political Obligation." Though not specifically about demands of political equality, this article defends the idea that political obligations arise from the value of a specific kind of social relation, one that involves membership in a common political community.

23. Cf. Scheffler, "What Is Egalitarianism?," p. 191: "human relations must be conducted on the basis of an assumption that everyone's life is equally important, and that all members of society have equal standing." Scheffler's primary concern is with contexts, such as political membership and friendship, in which there are thick "human relations" to be "conducted" on an egalitarian rather than an inegalitarian basis. My point is that a recognizably similar idea can be situated within the more abstract context of morality, where it is a question of comporting oneself on the basis of "the assumption that everyone's life is equally important." The deliberative constraint that operationalizes this assumption is one that acknowledges limits on one's conduct that flow from the fact that others have claims against one, just insofar as they are persons.

24. Thompson thinks of the relational part of morality as a conception of justice; there are other ethical requirements that are not bipolar in the same sense, determined, e.g., by the other virtues that humans need in order to do well. See "What Is It to Wrong Someone?," p. 337. In this Aristotelian vocabulary, the relational account of interpersonal morality I am developing in this book could be described as an account of justice. Unlike some Aristotelians, however, such as Philippa Foot and per-

haps Thompson himself, I resist the suggestion that we should think of justice in this sense as fundamentally continuous with the other ethical virtues; see the discussion of the perfectionist strategy in sec. 2.2 above. The relational features that distinguish demands of morality or justice from other ethical reasons, on my approach, are essential to their standing as first-personal obligations and as a basis for relations of accountability; these features constitute the unity of the normative domain that I have been referring to as interpersonal morality.

25. Thompson, "What Is It to Wrong Someone?," pp. 361–62, 373.

26. Thompson, "What Is It to Wrong Someone?," p. 373.

27. Thompson, "What Is It to Wrong Someone?," sec. 11 (this condition appears to be the "chief lemma" to which Thompson refers in the heading to this section).

28. Cf. Thompson, "What Is It to Wrong Someone?," p. 351 (for talk about "foot-hold"), p. 364 (for the reference to a "common source").

29. Thompson refers to this as the "received" conception of justice; see "What Is It to Wrong Someone?," sec. 10.

30. Thompson, "What Is It to Wrong Someone?," secs. 14–15.

31. Thompson, "What Is It to Wrong Someone?," sec. 16.

32. The following criticisms are fairly hastily sketched, and do not do full justice to Thompson's remarkably rich and suggestive paper, which I strongly recommend that readers engage with for themselves.

33. Thompson, "What Is It to Wrong Someone?," p. 372.

34. See, for instance, Thompson, "What Is It to Wrong Someone?," p. 379.

35. Thompson considers a similar story in "What Is It to Wrong Someone?," pp. 380–82. He complains that this strategy for isolating a common order of right threatens to be circular, insofar as it attempts to specify a form of bipolarity "by reference to the manifold it induces" (p. 381). But I fail to see anything circular in the movement of thought described in the text. (Indeed, since I reject Thompson's first condition, it seems to me open to us to specify a still more extensive form of moral bipolarity, by reference, e.g., to a manifold that includes all individuals capable of concept-governed agency, regardless of whether they are competent with distinctively bipolar concepts.)

36. I draw primarily on the following texts by Gilbert: "Obligation and Joint Commitment," "Three Dogmas about Promising," and "Scanlon on Promissory Obligation."

37. See, for example, Gilbert, "Obligation and Joint Commitment," sec. 6, where she contrasts obligations of joint commitment with the obligations that appear to arise in other contexts, and suggests that the latter, insofar as they do not involve joint commitments, may be obligations only in a different (perhaps nondirected) sense.

38. See, for instance, Gilbert, "Three Dogmas about Promising," pp. 306–8, 312–13.

39. Gilbert, "Three Dogmas about Promising," p. 313.

40. Cf. Gilbert, "Three Dogmas about Promising," p. 306: "Olive owes Roger her going to Chicago tomorrow, if and only if, in an as yet unspecified intuitive sense, Roger can appropriately regard Olive's act of going to Chicago tomorrow *as his*." So being able to regard an action as one's own, in the intuitive sense, is necessary and sufficient for having a right against the agent to its performance.

41. Gilbert, for her part, apparently sees joint commitments in a much more

extensive array of situations than seems to me intuitively plausible. See, for example, her "Mutual Recognition and Some Related Phenomena," sec. 3.

42. It is not entirely clear that this is the sense in which Gilbert takes it to be intuitive that the actions of agents involved in joint commitments belong to both parties. Some of her formulations, at least, leave open an interpretation according to which, e.g., Roger can regard Olive's going to Chicago as his, just insofar as he has a claim against her that she so act; see, for instance, "Three Dogmas about Promising," p. 313. But if this is what she means, I see no explanatory work being done by the appeal to joint commitment.

43. For a different and to my mind more plausible account of the relation between joint commitment and directed obligation, see Alonso, "Shared Intention, Reliance, and Interpersonal Obligations."

44. See, for instance, Scanlon, *Moral Dimensions*, p. 140, who speaks of the relationship we stand in to others as "fellow rational beings."

45. Thompson, "What Is It to Wrong Someone?," pp. 351 and 364. Cf. my "Dispassionate Opprobrium," secs. 3–4.

46. See, for example, Williams, "Internal and External Reasons"; also Schroeder, *Slaves of the Passions.*

47. Examples include Korsgaard, *The Sources of Normativity*; and Street, "Constructivism about Reasons."

48. We might put this by saying that there are reasons that both agent and claimholder have in virtue of the obtaining of the directed duty, even if they can "have" those reasons only if there is epistemic warrant for people in their position to believe that they obtain.

49. On this kind of position, we should be reluctant to say that "there are" reasons that the moral nexus grounds, given the lack of the attitudes in the two parties that constitute reasons in the first place.

50. See, again, Street, "Constructivism about Reasons."

51. We could also think of this position as a kind of reductionism, insofar as it reduces relational normativity to individual normativity.

52. An impressive example of an argument to this effect is Korsgaard, *The Sources of Normativity*. For critical discussion, see my "Constructing Normativity."

53. On this point, see my paper "The Argument from Resentment."

54. It is an interesting further question what the best alternative is to the individualist accounts that render directed obligations and claims problematic. The most promising approach, in my view, would be a nonnaturalist realism about the normative that leaves open the possibility that reasons are not conditioned by the subjective attitudes of the agent, and that tolerates a plurality of distinct normative relations (including those at issue in practical requirements, in aspirational reasons for action, and in fittingness-based reasons for attitudes).

55. Scanlon, *What We Owe to Each Other*, chap. 4.

56. See Williams, "Utilitarianism and Moral Self-Indulgence."

57. See my "Dispassionate Opprobrium," secs. 3–4.

58. These remarks apply only to the individuals who are in the core of the manifold

of moral persons, insofar as they are both bearers of moral claims, and capable of acting in compliance with directed moral obligations themselves. As I noted earlier, however, it is possible that this manifold extends to include individuals who have claims against us, even though they are not subject to reciprocal obligations toward us. In these cases, too, our concern to honor their claims cannot be derivative from anything like mutual recognition, since the claimholders are not capable of reciprocating our acknowledgment of their claims. For further discussion, see sec. 5.1 below.

59. A prominent example of this tendency is John Stuart Mill's appeal to the "desire to be in unity with our fellow creatures" in chap. 3 of *Utilitarianism*, p. 30; see also p. 33, where Mill glosses the object of this desire in terms of a "harmony" between one's aims and feelings and those of the others with whom one shares social life.

60. We might think of this as the "method" of running it up the flagpole to see if they salute.

61. This idea figures saliently throughout Scanlon's *What We Owe to Each Other*; see, e.g., p. 5. See also Nagel, "War and Massacre," pp. 67–68; Nagel here contrasts justifications that might be launched to the world at large with justifications that are targeted specifically at the potential victims of one's conduct, and suggests that moral permissibility is plausibly associated with justifications of the latter kind. A similar conception of justifiability to other individuals figures in the essays collected in Forst's *Das Recht auf Rechtfertigung*.

62. On eudaimonistic reflection and morality more generally, see my "The Rightness of Acts and the Goodness of Lives."

63. Cf. the discussion of friendship and morality in my "Scanlon's Contractualism," sec. 3.

64. See, especially, Scanlon, *What We Owe to Each Other*, chap. 4, sec. 5; for further discussion, see (again) my "Scanlon's Contractualism," sec. 3.

Chapter Five. From Interests to Claims

1. See Thompson, "What Is It to Wrong Someone?," p. 354.

2. In the same section, however, I also reject the idea that the possibility of convergence in thought of this kind is a condition for the possibility of a bipolar order of right.

3. The absurdity of this idea reflects a commitment to the idea that "ought" implies "can," in the most basic and plausible version of that idea. The normative significance of moral obligations—both for agents, as presumptive constraints on deliberation, and for others affected by their conduct, as bases of interpersonal accountability relations—presupposes that those subject to them should have the capacity to grasp that the requirements obtain and to regulate their conduct accordingly. These capacities are missing in agents who, at a given point in time, do not possess basic facility with relational normative concepts.

4. An illuminating treatment of cases in which claims might be assigned to individuals who are not able to assert them on their own behalf is Scanlon, *What We Owe to Each Other*, chap. 4, sec. 8. Scanlon's discussion is couched in terms of the idea of

justification to the individual (via the mechanism of a trustee); I focus instead on the idea of vicarious assertion of claims on behalf of the claimholder. These ideas converge, insofar as there is no basis for vicarious blame in cases in which the agent's behavior can be justified appropriately (by reference to the interests of the individual affected, considered as bases for specific moral claims against the agent).

5. Cf. Thompson, "What Is It to Wrong Someone?," pp. 359–60, 376–77. Thompson thinks it is a general condition for membership in a manifold of persons that thoughts about the corresponding order of right should be a typical or normal attainment for the individuals who belong to it. I reject the general condition, but feel that reference to what is normal for members of our species is helpful in thinking about individual humans who suffer the kind of severe disabilities or diseases that are here at issue.

6. See, for example, Scanlon, *What We Owe to Each Other*, chap. 6, sec. 5, and his *Moral Dimensions*, chap. 4. See also Smith, "Attributability, Answerability, and Accountability."

7. Some questions about it are raised in my "Scanlon's Contractualism," sec. 2; see also Watson, "The Trouble with Psychopaths."

8. We might plausibly understand reason to involve capacities to respond to normative considerations as such, in particular the capacity to adjust one's attitudes to the recognition that there are reasons for making such adjustments. See, for example, Raz, "Reason, Rationality, and Normativity." The protests to which I refer in the text are not rational responses in this sense, insofar as they do not involve the capacity to grasp normative contents. But they are responses to facts about actions and attitudes that we can recognize as constituting wrongs; this is what I meant in saying that we can understand the protesting creatures to be incipiently in touch with such normative considerations.

9. Prudence is often contrasted with morality, insofar as it involves one's treatment of oneself rather than one's treatment of other individuals. But within a relational conception of it, the moral should be understood as matter of what we owe to individuals as persons; and at least some duties to oneself, if intelligible, would seem to count as moral in this sense.

10. For a stark expression of this kind of puzzlement, see Hart, "Are There Any Natural Rights?," pp. 181–82. Hart considers duties to oneself "absurd," in part because he thinks the rights to which they correspond give one normative authority over the actions of the party who is bound by the duty. But in the cases at issue, it appears that one "authorizes" the actions that allegedly violate duties to oneself through one's voluntary choice to perform them.

11. It has been questioned whether one can be wronged only if one has an antecedent claim; I return to this issue in sec. 6.1.

12. For this general conception of the issue, as well as some comments on the theoretical alternatives, see Sreenivasan, "Duties and Their Direction"; "A Hybrid Theory of Claim Rights," pp. 262–64; May, "Moral Status and the Direction of Duties"; and Wenar, "The Nature of Claim-Rights."

13. See Hart, *Essays on Bentham*, p. 183.

14. For a "definition" of rights that influentially emphasizes the interests of right-holders, see Raz, *The Morality of Freedom*, chap. 7.

15. Examples are Sreenivasan, "A Hybrid Theory of Claim Rights"; and Wenar, "The Nature of Claim-Rights."

16. See Thompson, "What Is It to Wrong Someone?," sec. 5, for an interesting discussion of the prospects for a reductionist account of bipolar notions (with particular attention to Raz's analysis in terms of individual interests). In saying that I take relational norms as a theoretical primitive, I do not mean that there is no prospect of an illuminating analysis or account of their structure in a given domain, such as that of morality. The point, rather, is that any such analysis or account will implicitly deploy relational notions, and hence not be well understood as a reduction of the relational to the nonrelational. I come back to this issue in sec. 5.4 below.

17. I do not mean to suggest that we can never act in ways that affect the deceased in morally relevant respects. Failure to honor the wishes of one's deceased parents in some matter of importance to them (as expressed, e.g., in their will) could plausibly be described as wronging them. As our temporal distance from the deceased greatly increases, however, it becomes correspondingly more difficult to affect their personal interests in significant ways. (An exception might be cases in which a distant predecessor established a significant institutional legacy, on terms that much later generations might fail to respect or to honor.)

18. I address the topic of moral argument in more detail in the following sections.

19. Classic treatments include Scanlon, "Preference and Urgency"; and Nagel, *The View from Here*, chap. 8.

20. Owens, *Shaping the Normative Landscape*, chaps. 5–6.

21. Cf. Scanlon, *What We Owe to Each Other*, pp. 211–13.

22. The Raz quotation is from his *The Morality of Freedom*, p. 191. Since Hohfeldian rights are claims against some other parties, it seems that Raz's point applies to the justification of at least some claims; it does not matter, for present purposes, whether Raz would agree with me that there are some claims that do not involve assignable moral rights. For a contemporary account of promissory obligation that appeals to normative interests of this specific kind, see (again) Owens, *Shaping the Normative Landscape*.

23. For instance, Owens's account of promissory obligation, which appeals to claim interests, has at least two features that distinguish it from the kind of moral justification I am interested in elucidating. First, Owens makes clear that he is not offering a specifically moral account of the obligations generated by promises; and second, he attributes explanatory significance to claim interests only in conjunction with facts about the social practices through which claims are recognized. See *Shaping the Normative Landscape*, especially chap. 6. I am not sure I understand the explanatory project that is meant to be shaped by these assumptions. But it is surely very different from the explanatory task I am here sketching, which is to make sense of the assignment of a moral claim to a specific individual.

24. Cf. F. M. Kamm, *Morality, Mortality, Volume II*, especially chap. 10.

25. It seems to me important to distinguish what we might call pure claim inter-

ests—whose object is just one's possession of a normative claim—from a distinct interest we might have in possessing normative claims that are socially recognized. Once this distinction is drawn, it begins to seem doubtful to me that we really have pure claim interests. (I am not convinced that it matters that much to us to have specific claims that are not honored if they are not at least acknowledged by the members of our social world, as considerations that give us warrant for resentment and complaint.) But interests of neither kind will, by themselves, be capable of rendering intelligible our concern that our claims should actually be honored by the agents against whom they are held.

26. See, for example, Thomson, *The Realm of Rights*, chaps. 3–5. Thomson frames her discussion in terms of the question of whether rights or claims are absolute, denying that this is the case. She puts this by saying that it is not always the case that agents ought all things considered to respect or "accord" the claim right. But she also says that it is sometimes "permissible" for the agent to infringe claim rights that are held against them; see *The Realm of Rights*, p. 123. The latter formulation suggests that the issue is at least in part whether there is a specifically moral objection to infringing claim rights. See also Sreenivasan, "Duties and Their Direction," sec. 1; Hart, "Are There Any Natural Rights?," pp. 185–86; Kamm, "Owing, Justifying, and Rejecting," pp. 465–66; and Skorupski, *The Domain of Reasons*, p. 312.

27. See Ross, *The Right and the Good*. For a helpful recent discussion of Ross's conception of a prima facie duty, see Hurka, *British Ethical Theorists from Sidgwick to Ewing*, chap. 3.

28. Cf. Ross, *The Right and the Good*, p. 20, where Ross notes that a prima facie duty "is in fact not a duty, but something related in a special way to a duty." What is "morally significant" to Ross, it appears, is not being a prima facie duty per se, but being an act "of a certain kind (e.g. the keeping of a promise)"; cf. *The Right and the Good*, p. 19. But I confess that Ross is not as clear on these points as one might have wished. For discussion, see (again) Hurka, *British Ethical Theorists from Sidgwick to Ewing*, chap. 3. As Hurka notes, Ross developed a different conception of prima facie duties in his later *Foundations of Ethics*, one that appeals to relations of fittingness. But on neither approach do deontic concepts, as such, appear to play a contributory role in relation to obligation *sans phrase*.

29. A helpful discussion of this general point, in application to the positions of both Ross and Prichard, is Dancy, "More Right Than Wrong."

30. For a different take on the relation between claims and Hohfeldian rights, see Feinberg, "The Nature and Value of Rights," pp. 253–54. Feinberg takes claims to be considerations that provide prima facie grounds for asserting a claim in interpersonal practice, which however might not be conclusive. Rights are specified by valid claims, i.e., claims that there is conclusive (epistemic and practical?) reason to assert.

31. Ross allowed that there are some prima facie duties that are conditional in this way (including some of those generated by promises), and duties of this kind are not "outweighed" when the conditions of their validity are not satisfied. See Ross, *Foundations of Ethics*, pp. 94–99.

32. These points bear on the characterization of the deliberative role of directed

obligations that was offered in chap. 2, where I suggested that they properly function as presumptive constraints on further deliberation and action. One might have
thought that the constraints are merely presumptive, because in any given case there
is the further question of whether it might be permissible to infringe the claim that
was acknowledged. But in fact the idea is a different one: that even if a moral claim
and the connected directed obligation obtain in the present circumstances, things
might change, going forward, in such a way as to undermine the claim that previously
obtained (e.g., through the occurrence of an emergency).

33. Residues are also sometimes said to include the appropriateness of compunction or regret about the action that one has performed in cases of this kind; but on no
plausible view is there a duty to feel these things.

34. It would also be natural in such circumstances to apologize to the person
whose property rights one had violated. This is somewhat puzzling, however, since—
as we saw in sec. 3.3 above—apology literally involves an acknowledgment of wrongdoing, and there is by hypothesis no wrong that has been committed in the kinds
of cases we are discussing. I think the kind of apology that seems to make sense in
such cases reflects the "nameless virtue," identified by Susan Wolf, whereby we take
responsibility in an expansive sense for our actions and the harms they may cause.
Trespassers who refuse to apologize, insisting legalistically that their action involved
no strict wrongdoing, seem to lack the generosity characteristic of this virtue. See
Wolf, "The Moral of Moral Luck."

35. Cf. the discussion of "traces" of outweighed prima facie duties in Hurka, *British
Ethical Theorists from Sidgwick to Ewing*, sec. 8.3. See also Kamm, *Morality, Mortality,
Volume II*, chap. 12, p. 317.

36. This is a point emphasized by Hurka, *British Ethical Theorists from Sidgwick to
Ewing*, pp. 70–72, 78.

37. The same consideration might explain the appropriateness of compunction
or regret in these cases. Conscientious agents will be concerned about the effects of
their actions on the personal interests of those affected by them, as bases of moral
claims against them. But once one has regard for those interests, that concern might
intelligibly be a source of regret that one was forced to act in a way that would damage
them (a regret or compunction that may persist, even after one has honored all of the
fallback claims that those same interests may generate). This kind of compunction
or regret, however, will have a very different basis from the positional responses to
wrongdoing discussed in sec. 3.3 above, such as remorse and the associated duties to
apologize and make amends. These duties are genuine residues of claims, insofar as
they presuppose that moral claims were in place that the agent flouted (so that the
agent could be said to have wronged the bearer of the claims). In the cases here at
issue, by contrast, compunction or regret reflects an independent concern for the
interests that ground a person's moral claims, one that might persist even under conditions in which there is no claim that has been flouted.

38. Though the relational conception can make sense of non-absolute deontological constraints of various kinds, I should acknowledge that it may have difficulty with
one particular case in which familiar deontological constraints are sometimes under-

stood to be defeated or undermined. This is the case in which a violation of moral constraints on our treatment of individuals could avert a disaster that would otherwise befall a large number of other persons. To make sense of such cases—which are staples in discussions of so-called threshold deontology—it would be most natural to assume that the interests of the people who are threatened by the disaster could somehow be aggregated together in the moral reasoning that goes to determining what we are permitted or required to do. But reasoning of this kind does not seem consistent with the relational conception, as I have been developing it in this book. I discuss in the next section the significance of the distinction between personal interests and impersonal reasons to the relational account of moral reasoning; secs. 6.3–6.4 take up in more detail some cases in which essentially aggregative considerations might appear relevant to reflection about what it is permissible for an agent to do.

39. For discussion of cases with this structure, see Kamm, *Morality, Mortality, Volume II*, chap. 12.

40. See Scheffler, *Human Morality*, pp. 31–33, for a very helpful survey of different ways in which an effective responsiveness to moral considerations could be realized through an agent's deliberative processes and dispositions.

41. Relevant here are the discussions of utilitarianism in secs. 2.2 and 3.2 above.

42. A further respect in which the position differs from some forms of intuitionism is that the propositions grasped through rational intuition do not describe abstract principles, but claims about the rightness of particular acts. An intuitionism of this kind might aptly be compared to the "particularism" developed by Dancy; see, e.g., his *Moral Reasons*.

43. In support of this conclusion, it might be said (in the spirit of particularism) that there are too many distinct ways in which personal interests might bear on questions about the assignment of claims to an individual, and that the normative significance of such interests in the context of relational moral reflection interacts too multifariously with other relevant factors to permit illuminating general procedures or principles to be specified.

44. The primary statement of this view is Scanlon, *What We Owe to Each Other*.

45. On "personal" reasons that people have for objecting to candidate principles, see Scanlon, *What We Owe to Each Other*, chap. 5.

46. There is, strictly speaking, a gap between the interests that figure in contractualist reasoning and the concrete interests of individuals who have actual moral claims. Contractualist reasoning, about principles for the general regulation of behavior, is somewhat idealized, and it considers the personal interests associated with representative positions or roles that individuals might occupy under the normative regimes that are up for assessment (such as the position of recipient of a promissory commitment, or addressee of a lie). Cf. Scanlon, *What We Owe to Each Other*, chap. 5, sec. 4, on "generic" reasons for objecting to principles. The actual moral claimholder, in real life, will be an individual who occupies such a position or role in fact. Such individuals will, in virtue of occupying these roles, have personal interests that ground reasonable objections to principles that permit agents, e.g., to break promises made to the claimholders, or to address to them claims known to be false. (For further

discussion of this issue, to which I am indebted, see Jonker, "In Defense of Directed Duties," chap. 1.)

47. Scanlon's own account of promissory obligation, which appeals to the value of assurance in support of a principle of fidelity, is presented in his *What We Owe to Each Other*, chap. 6. For discussion, see Kolodny and Wallace, "Promises and Practices Revisited."

48. Thus, though promisees and third-party beneficiaries have interests of similar kinds that might adversely be affected by the promisor's failure to perform, it makes a crucial difference that the adverse effects on the third party are not foreseeable by the promisor at the point in time when the promise is undertaken. This tells against the assignment of primary claims to third parties not to be disadvantaged by the actions of promisors, which is the idea that is under consideration in the present context. But the issue of foreseeability does not necessarily tell against the different idea that there is a generic secondary claim not to be harmed by actions that violate primary claims, once these have been assigned to individuals; I return to this idea in sec. 6.1 below.

49. Gilbert, "Scanlon on Promissory Obligation." A similar criticism is developed by Darwall in his "Demystifying Promises."

50. Gilbert, "Scanlon on Promissory Obligation," p. 282.

51. See Gilbert, "Scanlon on Promissory Obligation," sec. 3, for this argument.

52. Gilbert, "Scanlon on Promissory Obligation," pp. 284–85. Gilbert might have added, as well, that having the power to release the agent from a directed duty is also not necessary for having a right or a claim. Some claims might be inalienable, and this possibility poses a challenge to the so-called will theory of rights or claims.

53. Cf. Scanlon, "Reply to Wenar," p. 404: "in a contractualist account of promises promisees are singled out in two ways: by the central role that their interest in assurance has in justifying principles of fidelity and by the way in which those principles must make promissory obligations sensitive to their wills." Scanlon mentions both of these aspects of the contractualist account of promising because he wishes to emphasize its ability to accommodate ideas that are prominent in the "interest" and "will" theories of rights. But I believe the first aspect is the one that is ultimately fundamental to the implicitly relational structure of contractualist morality.

54. Scanlon, *What We Owe to Each Other*, pp. 11–12.

55. Scanlon, "Wrongness and Reasons"; see also Scanlon, "Replies," pp. 435–39.

56. These different conceptions are in competition with each other, in part, because they are attempts to identify different high-level properties that make actions right or wrong in the to-be-done or not-to-be-done sense. But they are also in competition because they differently fill in the abstract and somewhat indeterminate concept of moral rightness and wrongness. Thus competing substantive conceptions will emphasize different aspects of the abstract concept of moral rightness that they are trying to specify. (Consequentialists, for instance, typically attach less importance to the interpersonal aspect of the moral than do some other theoretical approaches—to a degree, I believe, that gives their accounts a somewhat revisionist character.) Note that Scanlon himself originally spoke of his theory as an account of morality in the narrower sense "having to do with our duties to other people"; see *What We Owe to*

Each Other, p. 6. This suggests that his account might be one that answers to a specifically relational concept of morality, a suggestion that would make it hard to see it as a competitor to other moral theories (insofar as they do not similarly construe the domain they are describing in relational terms). It therefore seems to me more fruitful to think of the account as a substantive conception that fills in a more abstract concept of the moral right (construed, perhaps, as a set of duties that concern other people, considered as individuals whose interests are equally important, and that also have the deliberative and interpersonal features discussed in chaps. 2 and 3 above).

57. Construed as a theory of moral rightness, contractualism might appear to have reductionist ambitions, insofar as the main elements of the theory (including personal interests, reasons for rejecting candidate principles, and so on) seem intelligible within a nonrelational context. But the way these elements are combined in the theory seems to incorporate an essentially relational structure, in the ways I have tried to explain in the text. The result is not, I think, helpfully understood as a reduction of the relational to the nonrelational, but rather as an elucidation of relational morality (via an account of the nature of moral principles and the form of reasoning through which they are justified). An even more clearly nonreductionist approach to understanding directed obligations and their correlative claims might be to see them as specifications of some essentially relational ideal. For examples of this general strategy, see, for instance, Ripstein's account of the private law of torts, in his *Private Wrongs*, which derives specific claims and directed duties from the fundamentally relational idea that no person is in charge of another person and his or her means. See also the account of rights sketched in Zylberman, "The Very Thought of (Wronging) You," which appeals to a basic ideal of independence and nondomination. These ambitious approaches are attractive in many respects; but I worry that the relational ideals to which they appeal do not provide a perspicuous basis for the full range of directed obligations that make up interpersonal morality. (The ideals are in some ways too abstract, so that it is difficult to derive from them specific moral obligations, and in other ways too determinate, describing values that do not seem to apply to some ways of wronging others.)

58. He sometimes characterizes specific moral duties, such as the duty of promissory fidelity, in relational terms, as duties owed to another party; see, e.g., *What We Owe to Each Other*, p. 316. But it is striking that the terms "claim" and "right" do not even appear in the index of this book.

59. See Scanlon, "Reply to Wenar," pp. 402–3. Note that I have not suggested that we might explain why certain actions are obligatory by appeal to the claims of other parties. This is connected to a point emphasized in sec. 5.3, namely that claims represent conclusions of moral deliberation, rather than inputs into reflection about what people are obligated to do. (The specific moral reasoning that explains why a duty is owed to another party will also, itself, explain the assignment of a claim to that party.) It does not follow that the relational structure of the moral is not significant, only that its significance lies elsewhere, in the light it sheds on larger normative features of morality.

60. Parfit, *On What Matters*, vol. 2, secs. 21–23.

61. For a critical discussion of this debate, see Kumar, "Contractualism on the Shoal of Aggregation."

62. See Scanlon, "How I Am Not a Kantian."

63. See Scanlon, "Contractualism and Justification."

64. One might stipulate that each of the persons on Rock 2 has a claim to be rescued, in virtue of the fact that they are members of the larger group of individuals with symmetrical personal interests in being saved. But on this interpretation of it, the contractualist account of reasonable rejectability would not shed much light on this assignment of claims, precisely insofar as it becomes detached from the idea that claimholders have a distinctive personal objection or complaint about actions that violate their claims. (The persons on Rock 2 have personal objections, on Scanlon's latest proposal, to the actions that violate their stipulated claims. But their personal objections are not distinctive, but precisely comparable to the objection that the individual on Rock 1 has to the rescuer's saving the Rock 2 people, an objection that by hypothesis does not correspond to a moral claim.) In sec. 6.3 below, I develop a different relational explanation of the idea that there is a moral requirement to save the individuals on Rock 2.

65. Parfit, *On What Matters*, vol. 1, secs. 22, 54. Parfit at one point concedes that Scanlon's theory will lose the idea that moral obligations are owed to specific individuals, and that those individuals would be wronged if we flouted them, if the individualist restriction is given up; see *On What Matters*, vol. 2, pp. 241–42. My point is that in losing these things, the theory is deprived of precisely the elements that contribute in large measure to its interest and appeal.

Chapter Six. Some Practical Consequences

1. Raz, "Numbers," p. 210.

2. This would be a specifically moral obligation that is owed by children to their parents, one that applies in virtue of more general principles that specify what we owe to each other. I think there are, in addition, sui generis directed duties that are owed to each other by the parties to relationships of this kind. For discussion, see my "Duties of Love."

3. For further discussion of such issues, see Scheffler, "Relationships and Responsibilities"; and Kolodny, "Love as Valuing a Relationship"; also my "Duties of Love."

4. Shiffrin has argued that promises serve to redress imbalances of power and vulnerability that naturally develop in the context of relationships between intimates; see her "Promising, Intimate Relationships, and Conventionalism." She appeals to this consideration, however, to explain why participants in such relationships require the power to undertake promissory commitments, not to elucidate the force of such commitments once they are made.

5. Cornell, "Wrongs, Rights, and Third Parties."

6. Hart, "Are There Any Natural Rights?," p. 180.

7. Cf. Shiffrin, *Speech Matters*, pp. 19–26. Note that the situation would be different if the third party overheard the lie as a result of covert surveillance that could not have been anticipated by the agent.

8. Compare the treatment of the *Palsgraf* case, and others with this structure, in Ripstein, *Private Wrongs*, chap. 4. Ripstein defends and develops Cardozo's thought, in *Palsgraf*, that the defendants cannot have wronged the plaintiff, because there is a contradiction in "the idea of owing [a] duty to someone who is unforeseeable" (p. 90).

9. See Cornell, "Wrongs, Rights, and Third Parties," note 26, pp. 121–22. Cornell quotes Anscombe, who writes, in her "Modern Moral Philosophy," at p. 184, that "a man is responsible for the bad consequences of his bad actions." (I note that Anscombe's main interest, in the larger passage in question, is in the somewhat different claim that people are not responsible for the bad consequences of good actions; also, that her core conception of good and bad actions is very different from the relational one that Cornell himself presupposes.)

10. See Cornell, "Wrongs, Rights, and Third Parties," p. 140. Insofar as this is the case, it seems, after all, that "every wrong can be traced to a rights violation," which is a claim Cornell disavows on p. 142. One theoretical peculiarity of Cornell's favored approach is that it operates with a disunified conception of wrongs. Some wrongs essentially violate rights; others are not understood to consist in rights violations, though they presuppose that the harmful consequences in which they consist can be traced to rights violations. It is an advantage of the alternative I propose that it sees every wrong as itself the violation of a claim.

11. It might be asked why, if we are willing to go this far, we do not also assign to people claims not to be harmed in consequence of actions that fall short of what the agent ought to do, even if those actions do not flout primary moral claims. Thus, I might akratically sleep in rather than going to the library first thing in the morning, as is my customary practice; and this might, unbeknownst to me, cause my neighbor to get fired from her job. (Perhaps she developed the habit of leaving for work only when she saw that I was on my way to the library, and so was late on the fateful day, missing an important meeting with her boss.) But I feel no intuitive pull toward thinking that there might be secondary moral claims in cases of this kind. Bad consequences of bad actions seem imputable to the agent, at most, only in cases where the badness of the actions involves neglect of the social responsibilities of agency. Moral claims not to be harmed thus seem secondary in the way described in the text, insofar as they are parasitic on primary moral claims that are flouted through the actions that violate them. Their assignment perhaps reflects a general concern we have, as moral persons, that agents should be attentive to their interpersonal responsibilities.

12. On enforceability as a condition of rights, see Wenar, "The Nature of Claim-Rights," sec. 10. On identification of an agent to whom the corresponding duty can be assigned, see O'Neill, *Towards Justice and Virtue*, p. 129. On general conditions of enforceability, see James, "Rights as Enforceable Claims," pp. 133–47.

13. For the suggestion that enforceability might apply to juridical but not necessarily to moral rights, see Zylberman, "The Very Thought of (Wronging) You," p. 162.

14. Compare defensive liberty rights, such as our right to freedom from bodily trespass, which is held against any agent we might come into contact with. The class of people who are bound by the correlative directed duty in such cases, though extensive, seems much more clearly defined than the class of individuals against whom secondary claims not to be harmed might be held.

15. On inalienable moral rights, see Sreenivasan, "A Hybrid Theory of Claim Rights," pp. 259–61.

16. Specificity is of course a matter of degree. Even in cases of rights to positive performance, there is some discretion that agents have to determine specifically how they are going to fulfill their directed duties. Having promised to meet you at the airport, I have leeway to decide for myself which bridge to take to get there, how long in advance I will arrive, etc. The general idea is that moral claim rights will seem firmly in place in proportion to the degree to which the directed duties connected with them are more determinate. The duties at issue in cases of gratitude, it seems, are at the less determinate end of the spectrum.

17. Note that this conception obviously does not transfer over to the context of an individual's relationship to God, where—as I observed in secs. 3.2 and 3.4—some voluntarists appeal to gratitude to explain our reasons for complying with divine commands. But whatever conception of gratitude is thought to be in place there, it will lack the element of discretion characteristic of the gratitude we owe to other human agents. (The normative considerations that support our compliance with divine commands should not be such as to leave it up to us whether or when to so comply!) The reasons of gratitude that appear to figure in some divine command theories therefore represent a different normative phenomenon from the imperfect duty of gratitude that often obtains in interpersonal relations, one that would require a very different kind of account.

18. I am indebted here to the illuminating discussion in Herman, "Being Helped and Being Grateful."

19. See Herman, "Being Helped and Being Grateful," p. 398.

20. See, for example, Singer, *The Most Good You Can Do.*

21. A starkly contrasting position, in the spirit of the Effective Altruism movement, is defended by Pummer in "Whether and Where to Give." Whereas I maintain that we have discretion to act suboptimally in discharging our moral obligations of mutual aid, Pummer contends that if we are making charitable contributions, we (often) have to give to the most effective aid organizations, even when it would not be wrong to give nothing.

22. This is an important theme in the work of Bernard Williams; see, for instance, his "A Critique of Utilitarianism."

23. The resulting account would have affinities with the approach sketched by Murphy in *Moral Demands in Nonideal Theory.* For critical discussion of this approach, see Cullity, *The Moral Demands of Affluence,* chap. 5.

24. A powerful statement of the maximally demanding view is offered by Unger in *Living High and Letting Die.* Note that the question of the level of contribution expected of individuals is distinct from the question of whether individuals have

discretion to direct their efforts in suboptimal (but still effective) directions. A perfectly coherent position might be that we are each required to contribute most of our income (beyond the minimal level necessary to support our basic needs) to charitable causes that address acute human welfare deficits; but that it is open to us to devote all of those contributions (say) to local programs that support the homeless in our community, rather than to efforts to prevent malarial infections farther afield.

25. For any given agent, we might ask two questions: (a) what is the range of eligible actions open to the agent to provide assistance to others in acute need (i.e., actions that are over some reasonable threshold of expected effectiveness)?; (b) which specific individuals would benefit from the assistance that is made possible by each of those available actions? It is a commonplace that the resulting class of potential beneficiaries, for those of us in the modern world, is extremely extensive, since there are so many easy actions open to us that would make available benefits to people who are extremely remote from us. (Consider online donations to aid organizations with global reach.)

26. See, again, Murphy, *Moral Demands in Nonideal Theory*, for a broadly similar view. Murphy emphasizes the fact that our duties of mutual aid give us a common, agent-neutral aim; my discussion differs in stressing the relational character of those duties, and the nature and extent of the claims with which they correspond.

27. Cf. Cohen, "Who Is Starving Whom?"

28. Compare the comment of Theano Laoumis of Lesbos, Greece, describing the response of fellow islanders to the thousands of migrants who washed up on their shores in 2015: "You didn't know who to save first, there were so many people. But we did save them. It was only natural." Quoted by Alderman, "Greek Villagers Rescued Migrants."

29. Cf. Cullity, *The Moral Demands of Affluence*, pp. 75–77. Though he admits that a fair share view applies more naturally to collective projects than to direct emergencies, he ultimately rejects it even there. But it may be relevant that he draws the distinction somewhat differently than I have done. For me, the idea is that we need different principles to explain our duties in regard to ongoing collective efforts to address structural problems of acute human need, and in direct emergency situations in which only a few individuals are even in a position to respond. Cullity, by contrast, distinguishes collective endeavors from individual direct action, and notes that some situations that require a collective response have the character of direct emergencies. For me, the latter are not situations that call for a fair share solution, so the fact that that approach would deliver some counterintuitive verdicts in the emergency context is not an objection. But the issues are complicated, and there is of course much more to be said about them.

30. See Cullity, *The Moral Demands of Affluence*, e.g., secs. 5.3–5.5, also chap. 10.

31. The locus classicus for discussion of this problem is Parfit, *Reasons and Persons*, part 4. Parfit's discussion is shaped by the assumption that any theory must recognize that beneficence is at least a part of morality, and that beneficence in turn involves "our general moral reason to benefit other people, and to protect them from harm" (*Reasons and Persons*, p. 371). The challenge is to develop a principle of beneficence

that can accommodate our intuitions about a range of hypothetical cases involving populations of different sizes and welfare levels (what he calls "Theory X"). His final attempts at meeting this challenge are his "Can We Avoid the Repugnant Conclusion?," and "Future People, the Non-Identity Problem, and Person-Affecting Principles." I myself am doubtful that moral philosophy really needs a Theory X in Parfit's sense, in part because the essentially consequentialist conception of beneficence latent in his discussion—as a matter of our general "moral" reason to benefit people and protect them from harm—seems to me questionable. On the latter point, see Scheffler, *Why Worry About Future Generations?*, chap. 1.

32. An important challenge in thinking about this issue is posed by the fact that our personal behavior, considered on its own, would apparently make little difference to the overall trajectory of environmental degradation or climate change. As we saw in the discussion of mutual aid above, contractualism invites us to consider, in the first instance, the effects of general compliance with candidate principles by the people whose behavior they purport to regulate. It is clear that continued complacency on the part of all of us who live in affluent and resource-intensive parts of the world would have significant cumulative effects on the life circumstances of future generations.

33. Where quality might take into account not only the aggregate well-being or happiness of the people who inhabit each of the future scenarios we might help to bring about, but also the distribution of happiness and suffering among those people.

34. See, for example, the approach implicit in Shiffrin, "Wrongful Life, Procreative Responsibility, and the Significance of Harm." Broadly similar positions are defended, e.g., by Harman, "Can We Harm and Benefit in Creating?"; Woodward, "The Non-Identity Problem"; and Kumar, "Who Can Be Wronged?"

35. Parfit, *On What Matters*, vol. 2, chap. 22.

36. Parfit, *On What Matters*, vol. 1, p. 419; cf. *On What Matters*, vol. 2, pp. 234–35.

37. On the plausibility of a noncomparative conception of harm, see Parfit, *On What Matters*, vol. 2, pp. 233–34. What Parfit fails to appreciate is that this noncomparative conception of harm can be combined with an essentially comparative account of moral reasoning to yield a relational framework for thinking about the moral dimension of cases involving the non-identity problem. See, e.g., his "Future People, the Non-Identity Problem, and Person-Affecting Principles," pp. 125–26, where he argues that in many cases of this kind, we cannot restrict ourselves to thinking about the effects of our actions on people who will actually exist, but must also think about how other, merely possible people would have fared if we had acted otherwise. But comparisons of this sort are entirely consistent with the relational approach I have been defending. Indeed, as I argued in sec. 5.4, they are built into the contractualist account of relational moral reasoning, which is essentially comparative, and hence requires us, in cases that involve the non-identity problem, to compare the objections of the actual individuals whom our actions cause to exist with the objections that different people would have had if we had acted otherwise. For a sympathetic recent discussion of contractualist reasoning about obligations to future generations, see Kumar, "Wronging Future People." Kumar rightly emphasizes the generality of

the moral principles determined by contractualist reasoning, as well as the fact that they define duties that are owed to future people; but he somewhat downplays the essentially comparative character of moral justification, which seems to me important for understanding cases involving the non-identity problem in relational terms.

38. For discussion of this case, see Frick, "Conditional Reasons and the Procreation Asymmetry"; also his "Zukünftige Personen und Schuld ohne Opfer."

39. See Parfit's discussion of the "no difference view," in *Reasons and Persons*, pp. 366–69.

40. For discussion of some other cases that involve similarly eccentric retrospective attitudes, see my book *The View from Here*. Consideration of such cases lends support to the idea that one can have a moral claim against someone, even if it is not the case that one rationally prefers, all things considered, that the claim should not have been violated; contrast Frick, "Zukünftige Personen und Schuld ohne Opfer," sec. 11.

41. See, e.g., Greaves, "Population Axiology." For further discussion of issues in this area, see, e.g., Broome, "Should We Value Population?"; Broome, *Weighing Lives*; McMahan, "Causing People to Exist and Saving People's Lives"; and McMahan, "Problems of Population Theory."

42. Parfit, *Reasons and Persons*, p. 369.

43. While this inference is tempting, I note that it elides two very different kinds of judgments, those about the value of outcomes and those about the rightness of actions, in ways characteristic of consequentialist approaches. See also Parfit, *On What Matters*, vol. 2, chap. 22, which similarly bases conclusions about what it is right for individuals to do on somewhat elusive intuitions about, e.g., "the goodness of outcomes and peoples' complaints" (p. 227).

44. See, for example, Parfit, *Reasons and Persons*, pp. 393–94. Also relevant here is Jan Narevson's telling observation that "we are in favor of making people happy, but neutral about making happy people," in his "Moral Problems of Population," p. 80. (Even the first part of Narveson's slogan is potentially misleading, however: we may be in favor of making people happy, but it isn't clear that we have a moral obligation to do so. To think that we do is arguably to fall back on the questionable assumption that beneficence, construed in broadly consequentialist terms, is at least part of any sane moral outlook.)

45. For this way of thinking about the content of our duties regarding future generations, see Scheffler, *Why Worry About Future Generations?* Scheffler argues, among other things, that our concern to meet this standard has important sources outside of morality, e.g., in our relation to the values around which our own lives are organized. While I agree with him about this, I also think there are obligations of interpersonal morality that derive from the relation we will stand in to future individuals, and that these moral obligations are similar in content to the nonmoral norms that Scheffler describes.

46. Scanlon originally suggested that there is a personal objection that could be brought by an individual in tiebreakers; when it is a question of saving one person on Rock 1 vs. saving two people on Rock 2, the two people on Rock 2 could each object,

on his or her own behalf, to a principle that permits you to go to either rock; the personal objection would be, roughly, that his or her presence makes no difference to the moral verdict about what it is permissible to do. See *What We Owe to Each Other*, chap. 5, sec. 9. But there are many situations in which the presence or absence of a given individual makes no difference to the question of what it is permissible for an agent to do. If aggregation is permitted, the presence of the single individual on Rock 1 makes no difference of this kind; similarly, in the rescue situation described in the text, where there are several on Rock 2, each of them could individually say that his or her presence makes no difference, even if it is morally required to save the greater number. Cf. Raz, "Numbers," pp. 204–6. Scanlon now favors a different approach to cases of this kind, arguing that the number of individuals on Rock 2 with equivalent personal interests in being saved might make it unreasonable for the person on Rock 1 to reject principles requiring that you go to Rock 2; see his "Contractualism and Justification." I offer a brief critical discussion of this proposal in sec. 5.4 above, noting that it appears to sacrifice the relational structure that makes contractualism attractive in the first place.

47. See, e.g., the classic discussions in G. E. M. Anscombe, "Who Is Wronged?"; and Taurek, "Should the Numbers Count?"

48. For an interesting suggestion of this kind, see Munoz-Dardé, "The Distribution of Numbers and the Comprehensiveness of Reasons." In particular, she proposes that the impersonal value of human life might represent a good reason for action, one that renders it intelligible that the rescuer might choose to save more rather than fewer, without making it obligatory so to act. See also Anscombe, "Who Is Wronged?"; and Scanlon, "Contractualism and Justification." (Note: though I shall continue to refer to impersonal reasons of human life and human well-being in what follows, the relevant considerations should be understood to include, potentially, the well-being of all members of the manifold of moral persons, including nonhuman claimholders, if there are such.)

49. In a different kind of case, of course, there might be compelling personal reasons that tip the balance in the other direction, in favor of saving the person on Rock 1. Maybe that person is a close friend of yours, someone who has a claim against you as a friend to be given special consideration. This is a consideration that figures in Taurek's discussion in "Should the Numbers Count?"

50. Cf. Kumar, "Contractualism on Saving the Many." Kumar argues that once the symmetrical objections of the individuals who find themselves on the different rocks have been determined to neutralize each other, one for one, we are to consider the objections of the remaining individuals on Rock 2 in a second stage of contractualist reasoning. I am suggesting, by contrast, that the earlier objections of everyone to principles permitting the rescuer to save fewer are dispositive, once we recognize that the later objections of individuals to principles requiring the rescuer to save those on the other rock are inconclusive.

51. For a brief critical discussion of similar proposals, see Kamm, *Morality, Mortality, Volume I*, p. 120; and Otsuka, "Saving Lives, Moral Theory and the Claims of Individuals," pp. 123–24. It is perhaps an advantage of this approach that it does justice to

a desideratum articulated by Scanlon in "Contractualism and Justification," namely that the explanation for why we should save more in a "disjoint" case such as Rock 1 vs. Rock 2 should also explain why we should save more rather than fewer in a "subset" case, where there is a single group of potential rescuees, and saving more rather than fewer members of this group would not impose significant additional costs on us. The ex ante argument sketched in the text applies equally to cases of both kinds. Note, however, that there is a different objection to saving fewer in the subset case that does not carry over to disjoint cases. In the subset case, some individuals in the larger set of prospective rescuees have a personal objection, at the time of the rescue operation, to principles that permit us to save fewer members of their group; and there is no similar objection at that time that individuals in the subset have to principles that require us to save more.

52. This is a common objection to the general approach I have sketched; see the texts by Kamm and Otsuka referred to in the preceding note.

53. Note that something like this assumption may be necessary to explain, in relational terms, why the rescuer is not permitted to save none in cases in which, e.g., there is the same number of individuals on each rock. Those individuals have symmetrical personal objections, which cancel each other out, to principles that require the rescuer to save those on the other rock. But what is the personal objection to principles that permit the rescuer to save nobody? One basis for it would be the idea that all of the individuals could reject such a principle, since their ex ante likelihood of being saved in such a situation will be enhanced if the rescuer is required to save those on one rock or the other. But this seems to assume, again, that the occurrence of the emergency functions in the way described in the text, as a kind of natural lottery.

54. This is of course an echo of Anscombe's question in "Who Is Wronged?"

55. This would be another case, like that of mutual aid, in which individuals have claims against agents to do things that will not necessarily benefit them in particular in the end. Cf. Munoz-Dardé, "The Distribution of Numbers and the Comprehensiveness of Reasons," p. 196: "Justifying *to* you a duty to save does not mean there is a duty to save *you.*"

56. See, again, my *The View from Here.*

57. Two classic early contributions are Foot, "The Problem of Abortion and the Doctrine of the Double Effect"; and Thomson, "Killing, Letting Die, and the Trolley Problem." A helpful recent discussion, which includes commentary from leading contributors that provides something of an overview of the current debate, is F. M. Kamm, *The Trolley Problem Mysteries.*

58. Sometimes the intuition about the trolley driver is put in terms of a conflict of negative duties, with a duty not to kill one rationally outweighed by a duty not to kill the five; see, e.g., Foot, "The Problem of Abortion and the Doctrine of the Double Effect," pp. 27–28. But these would not be directed obligations, as the relational account understands them, since (like Hohfeld-style rights) they figure as inputs into moral reflection rather than outputs of such reasoning; cf. sec. 5.3 above.

59. Kamm, *The Trolley Problem Mysteries,* pp. 16–18.

60. For expression of skepticism that these different ways of causing harm to one

in the course of saving others make a moral difference, especially in the context of contractualist reasoning, see Parfit, *On What Matters*, vol. 1, sec. 53.

61. Indeed, this has become one of the fixed points in discussions about trolley cases. But Thomson, who introduced this case in the first place, has since had second thoughts about whether it really would be permissible for the bystander to switch the trolley onto the siding; see her "Turning the Trolley."

62. Similar considerations apply to Scanlon's Case One, in which Grey would lose a few years of life by giving up an organ to White, and White would gain many more years if the donation were made; see Scanlon, "How I Am Not a Kantian," p. 136; also Parfit, *On What Matters*, vol. 2, p. 192. In considering a principle requiring people to sacrifice organs in situations of this kind, it is important to take into account not merely the years of life that Grey and White would each lose under this principle and the alternatives to it, but the objections that both of them would have to a set of social arrangements in which their bodies were constantly available for beneficent public appropriation.

63. Cf. Scanlon, "How I Am Not a Kantian," p. 138, on the possibility of a "moral standoff" within contractualist reasoning. Scanlon is considering here what he calls Case One, described in the preceding note. The idea is that Grey and White might each have comparably powerful personal objections to principles that either require Grey to donate the organ, or permit Grey not to make the donation. For further discussion of this case, see Scanlon's more recent "Contractualism and Justification."

64. For a vigorous statement of this worry, see Fried, "Can Contractualism Save Us from Aggregation?"

65. See Frick, "Contractualism and Social Risk"; see also James, "Contractualism's (Not So) Slippery Slope"; and Kumar, "Risking and Wronging." The vaccine example, and the terms in which it is discussed, are borrowed loosely from Frick's persuasive discussion of this general approach. Note that the contrast between "ex ante" and "ex post" objections here refers to objections that individuals have before and after the actions up for assessment are carried out. The ex ante objections at issue in my discussion of the two-rock rescue situation in the preceding section, by contrast, are objections that individuals have at a still earlier point in time, before they know what rescue situations they will find themselves in at all.

66. See, yet again, Wallace, *The View from Here*.

67. Frick, "Contractualism and Social Risk," p. 212.

68. Frick, "Contractualism and Social Risk," sec. 8.

69. Frick, "Contractualism and Social Risk," sec. 9.

70. Parfit, *On What Matters*, vol. 2, p. 197.

71. Parfit, *On What Matters*, vol. 2, p. 232.

72. See Parfit, *On What Matters*, vol. 2, p. 234. The reasoning is questionable, however. Note that humans have noncomparative interests in being able to live as long as it is typical for members of their communities to survive, something that is a condition for their being able to sustain projects and relationships through their different natural stages. Even people who will enjoy forty happy years have a powerful objection on their own behalf to being brought into a scenario in which it is known

in advance that their lives would be cut short in medias res. (To say nothing of the comparative and noncomparative objections that their friends, parents, children, and life partners would have, on their own behalf, to losing the person to whom they are related in these ways in the person's prime of life.) This objection seems more powerful than the comparative objection that the X-people would have to scenario B (involving the loss of a single year of happy life); and of course, there is no similar noncomparative objection that any of the Z-people could bring against our choosing B. For these reasons, it seems to me that Case Seven is not genuinely problematic for a relational interpretation of contractualism, and that Case Four and Frick's *Miners (1 vs. 1,000)* better illustrate the limits of the kind of reasoning implicit in this approach to interpersonal morality. I shall therefore mainly focus on the latter cases in the discussion that follows; but the remarks I make about those cases could also apply to Case Seven if readers disagree with the relational treatment of it I have just sketched.

73. Parfit, *On What Matters*, vol. 2, p. 234.

74. Cf. Scanlon, "How I Am Not a Kantian," p. 139. Speaking of decisions by public officials, Scanlon here writes, "Producing the best consequences might be the correct standard in these cases not because it is the basis of morality but because it is what is owed to people in situations of that kind, by agents who stand in a certain relation to them." This suggestion would admittedly need careful development. If there is a directed special obligation here, for instance, it will presumably be owed to all of the individuals in the jurisdiction of the public officials, considered collectively. Thus, each member of the group might have a basis for complaint if, for instance, the officials were to underinvest in mine safety programs, in order to support overly robust search and rescue teams. But these claims would be based in interests that individuals share, insofar as they are members of the polity to whom consideration is owed, by officials whom they have entrusted to make decisions about the allocation of public funds. So all members of the polity might be wronged by the decision to overinvest in rescue rather than prevention, including people who end up benefiting personally from such a decision.

75. Cf. James, "Contractualism's (Not So) Slippery Slope," sec. 5.

76. Cf. Munoz-Dardé, "The Distribution of Numbers and the Comprehensiveness of Reasons," secs. 7–8. Munoz-Dardé proposes that there are limits on the claims that individuals can reasonably make on scarce public resources in contexts of social choice, limits that are sensitive to the numbers of individuals who stand to benefit in other ways if resources are made available to address their needs. Considering Frick's *Miners (1 vs. 1,000)*, Scanlon tentatively explores a similar proposal in "Contractualism and Justification"; but he does not limit the reasoning to contexts of social choice by authorized public officials, which undermines the cogency of the proposed form of argument. (Considered as a question of interpersonal morality, I don't see how the impartial value represented by even twenty statistical lives can make it unreasonable for the trapped miner to reject principles that would almost certainly entail his or her death.)

Adams, Robert Merrihew, *Finite and Infinite Goods: A Framework for Ethics* (Oxford: Oxford University Press, 1999).

Alderman, Liz, "Greek Villagers Rescued Migrants. Now They Are the Ones Suffering," *New York Times*, August 17, 2016, https://www.nytimes.com/2016/08/18/world /europe/greece-lesbos-refugees.html.

Allais, Lucy, "Wiping the Slate Clean: The Heart of Forgiveness," *Philosophy & Public Affairs* 36 (2008), pp. 33–68.

Alonso, Facundo M., "Shared Intention, Reliance, and Interpersonal Obligations," *Ethics* 119 (2009), pp. 444–75.

Anscombe, G. E. M., "Modern Moral Philosophy," as reprinted in Mary Geach and Luke Gormally, eds., *Human Life, Action and Ethics: Essays by G. E. M. Anscombe* (Charlottesville: Imprint Academic, 2005), pp. 169–94.

Anscombe, G. E. M., "Rules, Rights and Promises," as reprinted in her *Ethics, Religion and Politics: The Collected Philosophical Papers of G. E. M. Anscombe*, vol. 3 (Minneapolis: University of Minnesota Press, 1981), pp. 97–103.

Anscombe, G. E. M., "Who Is Wronged? Philippa Foot on Double Effect: One Point," as reprinted in Geach and Gormally, eds., *Human Life, Action and Ethics*, pp. 248–51.

Bratman, Michael, *Intention, Plans, and Practical Reason* (Cambridge, Mass.: Harvard University Press, 1987).

Broome, John, "Should We Value Population?," *Journal of Political Philosophy* 13 (2005), pp. 399–413.

Broome, John, *Weighing Lives* (Oxford: Oxford University Press, 2004).

Chaplin, Rosalind, "Taking It Personally: Third-Party Forgiveness, Close Relationships, and the Standing to Forgive," in Mark Timmons, ed., *Oxford Studies in Normative Ethics*, vol. 8 (Oxford: Oxford University Press, forthcoming).

Coates, D. Justin, and Neal A. Tognazzini, eds., *Blame: Its Nature and Norms* (New York: Oxford University Press, 2013).

Cohen, Jonathan, "Who Is Starving Whom?," *Theoria* 47 (1981), pp. 65–81.

Cornell, Nicolas, "Wrongs, Rights, and Third Parties," *Philosophy & Public Affairs* 43 (2015), pp. 109–43.

Cullity, Garrett, *The Moral Demands of Affluence* (Oxford: Oxford University Press, 2006).

Dancy, Jonathan, "Enticing Reasons," in R. Jay Wallace, Philip Pettit, Samuel Scheffler, and Michael Smith, eds., *Reason and Value: Themes from the Moral Philosophy of Joseph Raz* (Oxford: Clarendon Press, 2004), pp. 91–118.

Dancy, Jonathan, *Ethics without Principles* (Oxford: Oxford University Press, 2004).

Dancy, Jonathan, *Moral Reasons* (Oxford: Blackwell, 1993).

Dancy, Jonathan, "More Right Than Wrong," in Mark Timmons and Robert N. Johnson, eds., *Reason, Value, and Respect: Kantian Themes from the Philosophy of Thomas E. Hill, Jr.* (Oxford: Oxford University Press, 2015), pp. 101–18.

Darwall, Stephen, "Bipolar Obligation," as reprinted in his *Morality, Authority, and Law: Essays in Second-Personal Ethics I* (New York: Oxford University Press, 2013), pp. 20–39.

Darwall, Stephen, " 'But It Would Be Wrong,' " as reprinted in his *Morality, Authority, and Law*, pp. 52–72.

Darwall, Stephen, "Demystifying Promises," as reprinted in his *Honor, History, and Relationships: Essays in Second-Personal Ethics II* (Oxford: Oxford University Press, 2013), pp. 131–54.

Darwall, Stephen, *The Second-Person Standpoint: Morality, Respect, and Accountability* (Cambridge, Mass.: Harvard University Press, 2009).

Feinberg, Joel, "The Nature and Value of Rights," *Journal of Value Inquiry* 4 (1970), pp. 243–57.

Flanagan, Owen, *The Geography of Morals: Varieties of Moral Personality* (New York: Oxford University Press, 2016).

Foot, Philippa, *Natural Goodness* (Oxford: Clarendon Press, 2001).

Foot, Philippa, "The Problem of Abortion and the Doctrine of the Double Effect," as reprinted in her *Virtues and Vices and Other Essays in Moral Philosophy* (Oxford: Blackwell, 1978), pp. 19–32.

Forst, Rainer, *Das Recht auf Rechtfertigung: Elemente einer konstruktivistischen Theorie der Gerechtigkeit* (Frankfurt am Main: Suhrkamp Verlag, 2007).

Frankfurt, Harry, *Necessity, Volition, and Love* (Cambridge: Cambridge University Press, 1992).

Frick, Johann, "Conditional Reasons and the Procreation Asymmetry," unpublished manuscript (version 11, PDF file, updated May 2018).

Frick, Johann, "Contractualism and Social Risk," *Philosophy & Public Affairs* 43 (2015), pp. 175–223.

Frick, Johann, "Zukünftige Personen und Schuld ohne Opfer," in Markus Rüther and Sebastian Muders, eds., *Worauf es ankommt: Derek Parfits praktische Philosophie in der Diskussion* (Hamburg: Felix Meiner Verlag, 2017), pp. 113–45.

Fricker, Miranda, "What's the Point of Blame? A Paradigm Based Explanation," *Noûs* 50 (2016), pp. 165–83.

Fried, Barbara, "Can Contractualism Save Us from Aggregation?," *Journal of Ethics* 16 (2012), pp. 39–66.

Garrard, Eve, and David McNaughton, "In Defense of Unconditional Forgiveness," *Proceedings of the Aristotelian Society* 103 (2004), pp. 39–60.

Gauthier, David, *Morals by Agreement* (Oxford: Oxford University Press, 1986).

Gewirth, Alan, *Reason and Morality* (Chicago: University of Chicago Press, 1978).

Gilbert, Margaret, "Mutual Recognition and Some Related Phenomena," as reprinted in her *Joint Commitment: How We Make the Social World* (Oxford: Oxford University Press, 2013), pp. 324–37.

Gilbert, Margaret, "Obligation and Joint Commitment," *Utilitas* 11 (1999), pp. 143–63.

Gilbert, Margaret, "Scanlon on Promissory Obligation," as reprinted in her *Joint Commitment*, pp. 271–95.

Gilbert, Margaret, "Three Dogmas about Promising," as reprinted in her *Joint Commitment*, pp. 296–324.

Greaves, Hilary, "Population Axiology," *Philosophy Compass* 12 (2017), doi: 10.1111/phc3.12442.

Greene, Joshua, *Moral Tribes: Emotion, Reason, and the Gap between Us and Them* (New York: Penguin Books, 2014).

Greenspan, Patricia, "Making Room for Options: Moral Reasons, Imperfect Duties, and Choice," *Social Philosophy and Policy* 27 (2010), pp. 181–205.

Griswold, Charles L., *Forgiveness: A Philosophical Exploration* (New York: Cambridge University Press, 2007).

Hare, R. M., *Moral Thinking: Its Levels, Method and Point* (Oxford: Oxford University Press, 1981).

Harman, Elizabeth, "Can We Harm and Benefit in Creating?," *Philosophical Perspectives* 18 (2004), pp. 89–113.

Hart, H. L. A., "Are There Any Natural Rights?," *Philosophical Review* 64 (1955), pp. 175–91.

Hart, H. L. A., *Essays on Bentham: Jurisprudence and Political Theory* (Oxford: Oxford University Press, 1982).

Helmreich, Jeffrey S., "The Apologetic Stance," *Philosophy & Public Affairs* 43 (2015), pp. 75–108.

Herman, Barbara, "Being Helped and Being Grateful: Imperfect Duties, the Ethics of Possession, and the Unity of Morality," *Journal of Philosophy* 109 (2012), pp. 391–411.

Hieronymi, Pamela, "Articulating an Uncompromising Forgiveness," *Philosophy and Phenomenological Research* 62 (2001), pp. 529–55.

Hieronymi, Pamela, "The Force and Fairness of Blame," *Philosophical Perspectives* 18 (2004), pp. 115–48.

Hieronymi, Pamela, "Reflection and Responsibility," *Philosophy & Public Affairs* 42 (2014), pp. 3–41.

Hohfeld, Wesley Newcomb, *Fundamental Legal Conceptions* (New Haven: Yale University Press, 1964).

Hooker, Brad, *Ideal Code, Real World: A Rule-Consequentialist Theory of Morality* (Oxford: Oxford University Press, 2003).

Hurka, Thomas, *British Ethical Theorists from Sidgwick to Ewing* (Oxford: Oxford University Press, 2014).

James, Aaron, "Contractualism's (Not So) Slippery Slope," *Legal Theory* 18 (2012), pp. 263–92.

James, Susan, "Rights as Enforceable Claims," *Proceedings of the Aristotelian Society* 103 (2003), pp. 133–47.

Jonker, Julian David, "In Defense of Directed Duties" (Dissertation: University of California, Berkeley, 2017).

Kahnemann, Daniel, *Thinking, Fast and Slow* (New York: Farrar, Strauss, and Giroux, 2011).

Kamm, F. M., *Morality, Mortality, Volume I: Death and Whom to Save from It* (Oxford: Oxford University Press, 1993).

Kamm, F. M., *Morality, Mortality, Volume II: Rights, Duties, and Status* (New York: Oxford University Press, 1996).

Kamm, F. M., "Owing, Justifying, and Rejecting," as reprinted in her *Intricate Ethics: Rights, Responsibilities, and Permissible Harm* (New York: Oxford University Press, 2007), pp. 455–90.

Kamm, F. M., *The Trolley Problem Mysteries*, Eric Rakowski, ed. (New York: Oxford University Press, 2015).

Kolodny, Niko, "Love as Valuing a Relationship," *Philosophical Review* 112 (2003), pp. 135–89.

Kolodny, Niko, "Scanlon's Investigation: The Relevance of Intent to Permissibility," *Analytic Philosophy* 52 (2011), pp. 100–123.

Kolodny, Niko, "Why Be Rational?," *Mind* 114 (2005), pp. 509–63.

Kolodny, Niko, and R. Jay Wallace, "Promises and Practices Revisited," *Philosophy & Public Affairs* 31 (2003), pp. 119–54.

Korsgaard, Christine M., "The Normativity of Instrumental Reason," in Garrett Cullity and Berys Gaut, eds., *Ethics and Practical Reason* (Oxford: Clarendon Press, 1997), pp. 215–54.

Korsgaard, Christine M., *The Sources of Normativity* (Cambridge: Cambridge University Press, 1996).

Kumar, Rahul, "Contractualism on Saving the Many," *Analysis* 61 (2001), pp. 165–70.

Kumar, Rahul, "Contractualism on the Shoal of Aggregation," in R. Jay Wallace, Rahul Kumar, and Samuel Freeman, eds., *Reasons and Recognition: Essays on the Philosophy of T. M. Scanlon* (New York: Oxford University Press, 2011), pp. 129–54.

Kumar, Rahul, "Risking and Wronging," *Philosophy & Public Affairs* 43 (2015), pp. 27–49.

Kumar, Rahul, "Who Can Be Wronged?," *Philosophy & Public Affairs* 31 (2003), pp. 99–4117.

Kumar, Rahul, "Wronging Future People: A Contractualist Proposal," in Axel Gosseries and Lukas H. Meyer, eds., *Intergenerational Justice* (Oxford: Oxford University Press, 2009), pp. 251–72.

Lacey, Nicola, and Hannah Pickard, "To Blame or to Forgive? Reconciling Punishment and Forgiveness in Criminal Justice," *Oxford Journal of Legal Studies* 35 (2015), pp. 665–96.

Løgstrup, Knud Eljer, *The Ethical Demand* (Notre Dame: University of Notre Dame Press, 1997).

MacIntyre, Alasdair, *After Virtue: A Study in Moral Theory*, 2nd ed. (Notre Dame: University of Notre Dame Press, 1984).

McMahan, Jeff, "Causing People to Exist and Saving People's Lives," *Journal of Ethics* 17 (2013), pp. 5–35.

McMahan, Jeff, "Problems of Population Theory," *Ethics* 92 (1981), pp. 96–127.

May, Simon Căbulea, "Directed Duties," *Philosophy Compass* 10 (2015), pp. 523–32.

May, Simon Căbulea, "Moral Status and the Direction of Duties," *Ethics* 123 (2012), pp. 113–28.

Mill, John Stuart, *Utilitarianism* (Indianapolis: Hackett Publishing Co., 1979).

Munoz-Dardé, Véronique, "The Distribution of Numbers and the Comprehensiveness of Reasons," *Proceedings of the Aristotelian Society* 105 (2005), pp. 207–33.

Murphy, Liam B., *Moral Demands in Nonideal Theory* (Oxford: Oxford University Press, 2000).

Nagel, Thomas, *The Possibility of Altruism* (Princeton: Princeton University Press, 1978).

Nagel, Thomas, *The View from Here* (New York: Oxford University Press, 1986).

Nagel, Thomas, "War and Massacre," as reprinted in his *Mortal Questions* (Cambridge: Cambridge University Press, 1979), pp. 53–74.

Narveson, Jan, "Moral Problems of Population," *The Monist* 57 (1973), pp. 62–86.

Nehamas, Alexander, *On Friendship* (New York: Basic Books, 2016).

Norcross, Alastair, "Reasons without Demands: Rethinking Rightness," in James Dreier, ed., *Contemporary Debates in Moral Theory* (Oxford: Blackwell Publishing, 2005), pp. 38–53.

Nussbaum, Martha, *Anger and Forgiveness: Resentment, Generosity, and Justice* (New York: Oxford University Press, 2016).

O'Neill, Onora, "The Great Maxims of Justice and Charity," in her *Constructions of Reason* (Cambridge: Cambridge University Press, 1989), pp. 224–33.

O'Neill, Onora, *Towards Justice and Virtue: A Constructive Account of Practical Reasoning* (Cambridge: Cambridge University Press, 1996).

Otsuka, Michael, "Saving Lives, Moral Theory, and the Claims of Individuals," *Philosophy & Public Affairs* 34 (2006), pp. 109–35.

Owens, David, *Shaping the Normative Landscape* (Oxford: Oxford University Press, 2012).

Parfit, Derek, "Can We Avoid the Repugnant Conclusion?," *Theoria* 82 (2016), pp. 110–27.

Parfit, Derek, "Future People, the Non-Identity Problem, and Person-Affecting Principles," *Philosophy & Public Affairs* 45 (2017), pp. 118–57.

Parfit, Derek, *On What Matters*, vols. 1 and 2, Samuel Scheffler, ed. (Oxford: Oxford University Press, 2011).

Parfit, Derek, *On What Matters*, vol. 3 (Oxford: Oxford University Press, 2017).

Parfit, Derek, *Reasons and Persons* (Oxford: Oxford University Press, 1984).

Pettigrove, Glen, *Forgiveness and Love* (Oxford: Oxford University Press, 2012).

Pummer, Theron, "Whether and Where to Give," *Philosophy & Public Affairs* 44 (2016), pp. 77–95.

Rawls, John, *A Theory of Justice*, rev. ed. (Cambridge, Mass.: Harvard University Press, 1999).

Raz, Joseph, *Engaging Reason: On the Theory of Value and Action* (Oxford: Oxford University Press, 1999).

Raz, Joseph, *The Morality of Freedom* (Oxford: Clarendon Press, 1986).

Raz, Joseph, "Numbers: With and without Contractualism," as reprinted in his *From Normativity to Responsibility* (Oxford: Oxford University Press, 2011), pp. 193–210.

Raz, Joseph, *Practical Reason and Norms*, 2nd ed. (Princeton: Princeton University Press, 1990).

Raz, Joseph, "Reason, Rationality, and Normativity," as reprinted in his *From Normativity to Responsibility*, pp. 85–101.

Ripstein, Arthur, *Private Wrongs* (Cambridge, Mass.: Harvard University Press, 2016).

Ross, W. D., *Foundations of Ethics* (Oxford: Clarendon Press, 1939).

Ross, W. D., *The Right and the Good* (Oxford: Clarendon Press, 1930).

Scanlon, T. M., *Being Realistic about Reasons* (Oxford: Oxford University Press, 2014).

Scanlon, T. M., "Contractualism and Justification," in M. Frauchiger and M. Stepanians, eds., *Themes from Scanlon* [tentative title] (Berlin: De Gruyter, forthcoming).

Scanlon, T. M., "Contractualism and Utilitarianism," in Amartya Sen and Bernard Williams, eds., *Utilitarianism and Beyond* (Cambridge: Cambridge University Press, 1982), pp. 103–28.

Scanlon, T. M., "How I Am Not a Kantian," in Derek Parfit, *On What Matters*, vols. 1 and 2, Samuel Scheffler, ed. (Oxford: Oxford University Press, 2011), vol. 2, pp. 116–39.

Scanlon, T. M., *Moral Dimensions: Permissibility, Meaning, Blame* (Cambridge, Mass.: Harvard University Press, 2008).

Scanlon, T. M., "Preference and Urgency," *Journal of Philosophy* 72 (1975), pp. 655–69.

Scanlon, T. M., "Replies," *Ratio* 16 (2003), pp. 424–39.

Scanlon, T. M., "Reply to Wenar," *Journal of Moral Philosophy* 10 (2013), pp. 400–405.

Scanlon, T. M., *What We Owe to Each Other* (Cambridge, Mass.: Harvard University Press, 1998).

Scanlon, T. M., "Wrongness and Reasons: A Re-examination," in Russ Shafer-Landau, ed., *Oxford Studies in Metaethics*, vol. 2 (Oxford: Oxford University Press, 2007), pp. 5–20.

Scheffler, Samuel, "Choice, Circumstance, and the Value of Equality," as reprinted in his *Equality and Tradition: Questions of Value in Moral and Political Philosophy* (New York: Oxford University Press, 2010), pp. 208–35.

Scheffler, Samuel, *Human Morality* (New York: Oxford University Press, 1992).

Scheffler, Samuel, "Membership and Political Obligation," *Journal of Political Philosophy* 26 (2018), pp. 3–23.

Scheffler, Samuel, "The Practice of Equality," in Carina Fourie, Fabian Schuppert, and Ivo Wallimann-Helmer, eds., *Social Equality: On What It Means to Be Equals* (Oxford: Oxford University Press, 2015), pp. 21–44.

Scheffler, Samuel, *The Rejection of Consequentialism: A Philosophical Investigation of the*

Considerations Underlying Rival Moral Conceptions (Oxford: Oxford University Press, 1982).

Scheffler, Samuel, "Relationships and Responsibilities," as reprinted in his *Boundaries and Allegiances: Problems of Justice and Responsibility in Liberal Thought* (New York: Oxford University Press, 2002), pp. 97–110.

Scheffler, Samuel, "What Is Egalitarianism?," as reprinted in his *Equality and Tradition*, pp. 175–207.

Scheffler, Samuel, *Why Worry About Future Generations?* (Oxford: Oxford University Press, 2018).

Schneewind, Jerome, *The Invention of Autonomy* (Cambridge: Cambridge University Press, 1997).

Schroeder, Mark, *Slaves of the Passions* (Oxford: Oxford University Press, 2010).

Shiffrin, Seana Valentine, "Promising, Intimate Relationships, and Conventionalism," *Philosophical Review* 117 (2008), pp. 481–514.

Shiffrin, Seana Valentine, *Speech Matters: On Lying, Morality, and the Law* (Princeton: Princeton University Press, 2014).

Shiffrin, Seana Valentine, "Wrongful Life, Procreative Responsibility, and the Significance of Harm," *Legal Theory* 5 (1999), pp. 117–48.

Sidgwick, Henry, *The Methods of Ethics*, 7th ed. (Indianapolis: Hackett Publishing Company, 1981).

Singer, Peter, *The Expanding Circle: Ethics, Evolution, and Human Progress* (Princeton: Princeton University Press, 2011).

Singer, Peter, *The Most Good You Can Do: How Effective Altruism Is Changing Ideas about Living Ethically* (New Haven: Yale University Press, 2015).

Singer, Peter, *Practical Ethics*, 3rd ed. (New York: Cambridge University Press, 2011).

Skorupski, John, *The Domain of Reasons* (Oxford: Oxford University Press, 2010).

Smith, Adam, *The Theory of the Moral Sentiments* (London: Penguin Books, 2009).

Smith, Angela, "Attributability, Answerability, and Accountability: In Defense of a Unified Account," *Ethics* 122 (2012), pp. 575–89.

Smith, Michael, *The Moral Problem* (Oxford: Blackwell, 1994).

Sreenivasan, Gopal, "Duties and Their Direction," *Ethics* 120 (2010), pp. 465–94.

Sreenivasan, Gopal, "A Hybrid Theory of Claim Rights," *Oxford Journal of Legal Studies* 25 (2005), pp. 257–74.

Strawson, P. F., "Freedom and Resentment," as reprinted in Gary Watson, ed., *Free Will*, 2nd ed. (Oxford: Oxford University Press, 2003), pp. 72–93.

Street, Sharon, "Constructivism about Reasons," in Russ Shafer-Landau, ed., *Oxford Studies in Metaethics*, vol. 3 (Oxford: Oxford University Press, 2008), pp. 207–46.

Street, Sharon, "What Is Constructivism in Ethics and Metaethics?," *Philosophy Compass* 5 (2010), pp. 363–84.

Taurek, John, "Should the Numbers Count?," *Philosophy & Public Affairs* 6 (1977), pp. 293–316.

Thompson, Michael, *Life and Action: Elementary Structures of Practice and Practical Thought* (Cambridge, Mass.: Harvard University Press, 2008).

Thompson, Michael, "What Is It to Wrong Someone? A Puzzle about Justice," in R. Jay Wallace, Philip Pettit, Samuel Scheffler, and Michael Smith, eds., *Reasons and Values: Themes from the Moral Philosophy of Joseph Raz* (Oxford: Clarendon Press, 2004), pp. 333–84.

Thomson, Judith Jarvis, "Killing, Letting Die, and the Trolley Problem," *The Monist* 59 (1976), pp. 204–17.

Thomson, Judith Jarvis, *Normativity* (Chicago: Open Court, 2008).

Thomson, Judith Jarvis, *The Realm of Rights* (Cambridge, Mass.: Harvard University Press, 1990).

Thomson, Judith Jarvis, "Turning the Trolley," *Philosophy & Public Affairs* 36 (2008), pp. 359–74.

Tomasello, Michael, *A Natural History of Human Morality* (Cambridge, Mass.: Harvard University Press, 2016).

Unger, Peter, *Living High and Letting Die* (New York: Oxford University Press, 1996).

Waldron, Jeremy, *One Another's Equals: The Basis of Human Equality* (Cambridge, Mass.: Harvard University Press, 2017).

Wallace, R. Jay, "The Argument from Resentment," *Proceedings of the Aristotelian Society* 107 (2007), pp. 295–318.

Wallace, R. Jay, "Constructing Normativity," *Philosophical Topics* 32 (2004), pp. 451–76.

Wallace, R. Jay, "Constructivism about Normativity: Some Pitfalls," in James Lenman and Yonatan Shemmer, eds., *Constructivism in Practical Philosophy* (Oxford: Oxford University Press, 2012), pp. 18–39.

Wallace, R. Jay, "The Deontic Structure of Morality," in David Bakhurst, Brad Hooker, and Margaret Olivia Little, eds., *Thinking about Reasons: Essays in Honour of Jonathan Dancy* (Oxford: Oxford University Press, 2013), pp. 137–67.

Wallace, R. Jay, "Dispassionate Opprobrium: On Blame and the Reactive Sentiments," in R. Jay Wallace, Rahul Kumar, and Samuel Freeman, eds., *Reasons and Recognition: Essays on the Philosophy of T. M. Scanlon* (New York: Oxford University Press, 2011), pp. 348–72.

Wallace, R. Jay, "Duties of Love," *The Aristotelian Society Supplementary Volume* 86 (2012), pp. 175–98.

Wallace, R. Jay, "Emotions and Relationships: On a Theme from Strawson," in David Shoemaker and Neal Tognazzini, eds., *Oxford Studies in Agency and Responsibility*, vol. 2 (Oxford: Oxford University Press, 2014), pp. 119–42.

Wallace, R. Jay, "Moral Address: What It Is, Why It Matters," in David Shoemaker and Neal Tognazzini, eds., *Oxford Studies in Agency and Responsibility*, vol. 5 (Oxford: Oxford University Press, forthcoming).

Wallace, R. Jay, "Reasons, Relations, and Commands: Reflections on Darwall," *Ethics* 118 (2007), pp. 24–36.

Wallace, R. Jay, *Responsibility and the Moral Sentiments* (Cambridge, Mass.: Harvard University Press, 1994).

Wallace, R. Jay, "Rightness and Responsibility," in D. Justin Coates and Neal A. Tognazzini, eds., *Blame: Its Nature and Norms* (New York: Oxford University Press, 2013), pp. 224–43.

Wallace, R. Jay, "The Rightness of Acts and the Goodness of Lives," in R. Jay Wallace, Philip Pettit, Samuel Scheffler, and Michael Smith, eds., *Reasons and Values: Themes from the Moral Philosophy of Joseph Raz* (Oxford: Clarendon Press, 2004), pp. 385–411.

Wallace, R. Jay, "Scanlon's Contractualism," *Ethics* 112 (2002), pp. 429–70.

Wallace, R. Jay, *The View from Here: On Affirmation, Attachment, and the Limits of Regret* (New York: Oxford University Press, 2013).

Watson, Gary, "Morality as Equal Accountability: Comments on Stephen Darwall's *The Second-Personal Standpoint*," *Ethics* 118 (2007), pp. 37–51.

Watson, Gary, "Responsibility and the Limits of Evil," as reprinted in his *Agency and Answerability: Selected Essays* (Oxford: Clarendon Press, 2004), pp. 219–59.

Watson, Gary, "The Trouble with Psychopaths," in R. Jay Wallace, Rahul Kumar, and Samuel Freeman, eds., *Reasons and Recognition: Essays on the Philosophy of T. M. Scanlon* (New York: Oxford University Press, 2011), pp. 307–31.

Watson, Gary, "Two Faces of Responsibility," as reprinted in his *Agency and Answerability*, pp. 260–88.

Watson, Gary, "Volitional Necessities," as reprinted in his *Agency and Answerability*, pp. 88–122.

Wenar, Leif, "The Nature of Claim-Rights," *Ethics* 123 (2013), pp. 202–29.

Williams, Bernard, "A Critique of Utilitarianism," in J. J. C. Smart and Bernard Williams, *Utilitarianism: For and Against* (Cambridge: Cambridge University Press, 1973), pp. 77–150.

Williams, Bernard, *Ethics and the Limits of Philosophy* (Cambridge, Mass.: Harvard University Press, 1985).

Williams, Bernard, "Internal and External Reasons," as reprinted in his *Moral Luck: Philosophical Papers 1973–1980* (Cambridge: Cambridge University Press, 1981), pp. 20–39.

Williams, Bernard, "Moral Incapacity," as reprinted in his *Making Sense of Humanity and Other Philosophical Papers 1982–1993* (Cambridge: Cambridge University Press, 1995), pp. 46–55.

Williams, Bernard, "Moral Luck," as reprinted in his *Moral Luck*, pp. 20–39.

Williams, Bernard, "Persons, Character, and Morality," as reprinted in his *Moral Luck*, pp. 1–19.

Williams, Bernard, "Utilitarianism and Moral Self-Indulgence," as reprinted in his *Moral Luck*, pp. 40–53.

Wolf, Susan, "Blame, Italian Style," in R. Jay Wallace, Rahul Kumar, and Samuel Freeman, eds., *Reasons and Recognition: Essays on the Philosophy of T. M. Scanlon* (New York: Oxford University Press, 2011), pp. 332–47.

Wolf, Susan, "Moral Obligations and Social Commands," as reprinted in her *The Variety of Values: Essays on Morality, Meaning, and Love* (New York: Oxford University Press, 2014), pp. 233–54.

Wolf, Susan, "The Moral of Moral Luck," as reprinted in Cheshire Calhoun, ed., *Setting the Moral Compass: Essays by Women Philosophers* (New York: Oxford University Press, 2004), pp. 113–27.

Woodward, James, "The Non-Identity Problem," *Ethics* 96 (1986), pp. 804–31.

Zylberman, Ariel, "The Very Thought of (Wronging) You," *Philosophical Topics* 42 (2014), pp. 153–75.

abuse example, 150–51

accountability: and bipolar thought, 149–50, 257n3; and claims, 104; and consequentialism, 22, 87–88; and (directed) obligations, 13, 238n21; and divine command theories, 80–81; and equal standing, 22, 106; and fairness, 248n16; and individualism, 134; and individualist restriction, 226; and modern morality, 67, 69, 75–86; and moral right and wrong, 71–72, 75–86; and normativity, 14; and objective *versus* participant attitudes, 69–70; and obligation, 238n21; and public policy, 229; and relational morality, 12–14, 16, 22–23, 66–67, 86–95, 98–99, 103–4, 115, 149–50; and rescue from rocks example, 215; and rights, 197; and social life, 71, 75–76, 80, 81–82; and standards of right and wrong, 66; and subjective facts, 128–29, 132–33; and suffering, 238n20; and utilitarianism, 86–87. *See also* claims; expectations or demands; foreseeability; reactive attitudes and emotions

Adams, Robert Merrihew, 149n26, 250n27, 252n51

affection, 65. *See also* families; friends

After Virtue (MacIntyre), 240n37

agent-neutrality, 38, 39, 51, 52, 135, 242n25, 243n27, 245n51, 268n26

agent-relativity: agent-centeredness *versus*, 242n25; and antecedent interactions, 106–7, 135–36; and deliberation, 38, 51–52, 136; and (directed) obligations, 17–18, 135–45; and first-order moral issues, 38; and morality as ideal, 135–45; overview, 51; and relational morality, 53, 137–38; and universality, 135; and utilitarianism, 39, 243n27; and virtue theory, 45–46; and voluntarism, 42

aggregation (numbers): and beneficence, 268n31; and circumstances, 232–33; and contractualism, 273n60; and deontological constraints, 262n38; and ex ante considerations, 272n51; and extramoral concerns, 221–33; and first-order moral issues, 215–19; and happiness/suffering, 269n33; and harm, 272n60; and individualist restriction, 186–88; and mutual aid, 268nn28,29; and noncomparative interests, 213–14, 273n72; and presumptive constraints, 230–33; and public officials' decisions, 274nn74,76; and relational morality, 19, 20, 191–92, 210, 221, 262n38. *See also* rescue from rocks example; trolley examples

allocation of resources, 192, 227, 228, 274

Alonso, Facundo M., 256n42

amends, 92–94. *See also* apologies; forgiveness; moral repair

ancestors, 160, 259n17

anger, 70–71, 74, 112–13, 248n17. *See also* reactive attitudes and emotions

Anger and Forgiveness (Nussbaum), 248n17

animals, nonrational, 101–2, 120–21, 258n8. *See also* nonhumans

Anscombe, G.E.M., 24–25, 31, 38, 41, 47, 240n37, 242n26, 243n33, 244n44, 266n9. *See also* divine command theories antecedent interactions: and agent-relativity, 106–7, 135–36; and (directed) obligations, 16, 136, 194, 195–96; and foreseeability, 194; and gratitude, 118, 135–36, 193; and interests and claims, 162–63; and moral wrongs, 258n11; and mutual aid, 209; and personal relationships, 16, 17, 18, 110–11, 125, 253n9; and promissory obligation, 107, 109–10, 114–15; and universality, 111. See also joint commitment; personal relationships

anti-individualism, 125–34

apologies, 13, 89–90, 90–91, 92, 94, 250n39, 261nn34,37

"Are There Any Natural Rights?" (Hart), 236n13, 237n16, 254n11, 258n10, 260n26, 265n6

Aristotelian approaches, 46, 120, 122, 236n8, 242n17, 243n33, 244n44, 254n24

artificial persons, 152–53

artists examples, 64, 65

aspirations, 164

assurance interests, 108, 161–62, 165, 169, 175, 181–82, 263n57. See also fidelity

attitudes of agents, 10–11, 78. See also disregard or indifference; intentions; subjective (psychological) facts

"authoritative motivation," 253n57

authority, 14–15, 31, 33–34, 238n22, 244n39. See also divine command theories; law and legislative authorities; public officials' decisions; social command theories

autonomy, 8, 161–62, 165, 168–69

aviation disaster example, 171, 173

avoidance and withdrawal, 71, 74, 102–3, 113, 129, 195

backsliding, 242n16

basics needs, 164

Being Realistic about Reasons (Scanlon), 251n42

beneficence, 25, 206, 207, 268n31, 270n44, 273n62. See also charity; gratitude; mutual aid

Berker, Selim, 239n25

biological humans, 3, 150–51. See also species nature

bipolar thought: and accountability, 149–50, 257n3; and animals, 258n8; and convergence of understanding, 257n2; and manifold of moral persons, 119, 120–22, 147, 148–56, 159, 246n61, 255n35, 258n5; and nonhumans, 152; and relational morality, 18, 146–47, 259n16; and universality, 120, 150; and virtues, 254n24. See also deliberation (moral reasoning)

blame: and aggregation, 231; characterized, 70; communicative, 83; and convergence of understanding, 251n47; and criminal law, 99; and (directed) obligations, 71, 84, 253n65; and disregard, 66, 79, 82–83, 84, 94, 249n25; as enforcement, 199; and epistemic conditions, 252n53; and equal standing, 87–88; and expectations or demands, 66, 70–71, 73, 74–75, 248nn9,10; and forgiveness, 90–91; and group norms, 12; impersonal, 100; and individualism, 75–76, 77–79, 132–33; and intentions, 102–3; and interpersonal recognition, 94–95; juridical account of, 253n65; and moral injury, 84, 88–89; and moral right and wrong, 72, 73–74; nonreactive, 102–3, 129; Parfit on, 237n20; reasonable, 73–74; and reasons, 238n23, 249n25; and relational morality, 13, 15, 83, 95–104, 252n53; and rule consequentialism, 249n25; self-, 101; and social command theories, 96, 244n36; and social life, 129; and subjective facts, 128–29; and third parties, 253n57; and utilitarianism, 77–78, 249n21; vicarious, 151, 258n4; and virtues, 79, 249nn2,25. See also accountability; reactive attitudes and emotions; resentment and other forms of blame

Blame (Coates and Tognazzini), 247n8

bodily integrity/trespass, 168–69, 267n14

British Ethical Theorists from Sidgwick to Ewing (Hurka), 260nn27,28, 261nn35, 36 buck-passing theory, 56, 245n57

"'But It Would Be Wrong'" (Darwall), 246n57

"Can We Avoid the Repugnant Conclusion?" (Parfit), 269n31

Case Four (Parfit), 224–25, 228–29, 232, 274nn72,74

Case One (Scanlon), 273nn62,63

Case Seven (Parfit), 225, 274n72. *See also* public officials' decisions

catching a flight example, 219

Chaplin, Rosalind, 251n41

charity, 80. *See also* beneficence; gratitude; mutual aid

child killed by drunk driver example, 196

children and infants, 77, 101–2, 120–21, 150–51, 152, 158, 193–94, 265n2. *See also* families

circumstances (conditionality) (emergencies): and aggregation, 232–33; and blame, 73–74; and claim duties, 173–74; and dominance model, 30; and miners example, 227; and mutual aid, 208–9; and presumptive constraints, 28, 261n32; and promissory obligation, 6–7, 170–71, 175–76, 236n13, 260n31; and relational morality, 175; and secondary obligations, 28–29. *See also* aggregation (numbers); directed obligations/duties: conflicts of; epistemic constraints; historical conditionality; presumptive constraints

claim interests: deliberation, 164–70; and justification, 165–70, 259nn22,23; and moral wrongs, 251n43; and resentment, 260n25; and social practices, 259nn23,25; and special standing, 167, 169

claim rights (Hohfeldian): characterized, 2; and claims, 260n30; and deliberation, 172; and (directed) obligations, 157, 172; and gratitude, 2, 9, 20, 192, 201–6; and justification of claims, 259n22; and ownership, 124; and permissibility, 170–71, 201, 260n26; and problem cases, 190, 191;

and relational morality, 2–3, 235n2; and secondary claims, 199–200

claims: and accountability, 82, 104; and apologies, 90, 94; and attitudes of agents, 11; and attitudes of claimholders, 98–101; bare, 237n18; and bipolar thought, 149–50, 153–55; and blame, 84; and claimholder's reflections, 59; conflicts of, 246n65; and consequentialism, 88; constitutive conditions of, 1, 10, 16, 18, 49–50, 51, 53, 58, 60–61, 80, 83, 85, 124; and cosmopolitan morality, 18, 53; and deliberation, 18–19, 147, 165–76, 178, 179, 180–81, 186, 264n59; and (directed) obligations, 6, 8, 19–20, 237n15, 257n58, 264n59; without directed obligations, 257n58; and disregard, 10, 85; fallback, 173–75; and forgiveness, 92; and friendship, 16; and Hohfeldian rights, 260n30; inalienable, 263n52; and interests, 7–8, 10, 18–19, 82, 147, 156–65, 176–89; and interpersonal morality, 66; and interpersonal recognition, 62, 141; and joint commitment, 124; and Malay servant example, 164–65; and manifold of persons, 146, 159–60; and moral nexus, 15–16, 23; and moral wrongs, 251n43, 266n9; and natural goodness, 76–77; and normative interests, 147, 165, 176–89, 237n18; overview, 6–9; and persons, 60–61, 61–62, 107; and presumptive constraints, 51; and property rights, 124; "pure normative," 251n42; and rational agency, 16; and reactive attitudes, 80; and relational morality, 1, 2, 6–9, 18, 19–22, 49–50, 58–59, 60, 131, 158, 172–73, 178, 198–99; and resentment, 83, 99–100; residual, 173–74, 251n45, 261nn33,37; and retrospective attitudes, 270n40; and rights, 2–3, 8–9, 20, 103, 259n22, 260n30; without rights, 200–210; and Scanlon, 264n58; secondary, 191, 198–200, 251n45, 266n11, 267n14; and social interaction, 103; and sports example, 60–61; third-party, 251n43; and trustees, 102, 257n4;

claims (*cont.*)
and voluntarism, 58, 96. *See also* accountability; circumstances (conditionality) (emergencies); claim interests; disregard or indifference; expectations or demands; foreseeability; moral repair; nonidentity problem; persons; rights; selfstanding obligations; special (privileged) standing

climate change, 86–87, 160, 211–12, 213, 227, 250n38, 269n32. *See also* global responsibility

Coates, D. Justin, 247n8

coercion, physical (force), 140, 199

collaboration. *See* joint commitment (collaborative agency)

commands, normative, 238n20. *See also* divine command theories; social command theories

commune example, 165

communicative blame, 83

compassion, 100–101

compensation, duties of, 175

competition, 113

compunction, 261nn33,37

concept/conception distinction, 36, 242n22

conditionality. *See* circumstances (conditionality) (emergencies); historical conditionality; presumptive (defeasible) constraints

conflicts: of (directed) obligations, 20, 28–29, 32–33, 62–65, 173, 192, 231–32, 246n65; intergroup, 113, 114; and moral life, 141; and prima facie duties, 173, 174; and wellbeing, 192, 230–32. *See also* circumstances (conditionality) (emergencies)

congenital ailment example, 213–14

consequences, 266n9

consequentialism: and accountability, 22, 87–88; and beneficence, 268n31, 270n44; and blame, 249n25; and (directed) obligations, 41, 243n30; and equal standing, 22–23, 116–17; indirect, 158–59; and moral rightness, 270n43;

and mutual aid, 206; and relational morality, 263n56; rule, 243n32, 249n25. *See also* individualist restriction; maximizing; utilitarianism

constitutive conditions: of claims, 82; of concept of the moral, 69; of (directed) obligations, 124; of friendship, 144–45; of groups, 112; of identity as persons, 246n62; of joint commitments, 122–23; of mutual recognition, 139–40; of personal relationships, 139, 144, 145, 254n9; of rationality, 243n29; of reasons, 128, 130, 256n49; of self-concept, 133; and of thought action, 31, 104, 241n14; of virtuous traits, 249n23

constructivism, 126

consumption example, 77

contempt, 11, 79, 83, 132

contracts, 2, 50, 193–94, 194–95, 223–33

contractualism: and aggregation, 273n60; *and Case Seven*, 225; and claims and interests, 19, 178–89; and gratitude, 204–5; and individualist restriction, 186–89, 212–13, 225–26, 265n65; and interests, 262n46; and moral right and wrong, 35, 184–85, 188–89; and mutual recognition, 136; and non-identity problem, 212–13; and principles, 19, 179–89, 198, 204, 223, 226, 262n46, 264n57, 269n32, 270n37; and relational morality, 19, 147, 179, 184, 185–86, 187, 188–89, 208, 224–27, 239n25, 264n57, 269n37, 270n46; and secondary claims, 198–99. *See also* Frick, Johann; Kumar, Rahul; Parfit, Derek; Scanlon, T. M.

"Contractualism and Justification" (Scanlon), 265n63, 271n48, 272n51, 273n63, 274n76

"Contractualism and Social Risk" (Frick), 236n8, 273nn65–69

"Contractualism and Utilitarianism" (Scanlon), 239n27, 240n34

"Contractualism on Saving the Many" (Kumar), 271n50

conventional wisdom, 22

convergence of understanding, 251n47, 257n1

cooperation, 16, 106, 112–13, 237n18

Cornell, Nicolas, 195–99, 251n43, 266nn9,10

corporations example, 152–53

cosmopolitan morality: and bipolar thought, 120; and class of persons, 18–19, 37; and consequentialism, 88; and deliberation, 37–38, 52–54; described, 17; and (directed) obligations, 53–54; and divine command theories, 42–43; and equal standing, 37–38; and individualism, 130; and interpersonal morality, 23, 37, 118; and joint agency, 113; and Kantian ethics, 44; and perfectionism, 46; and relational morality, 17, 52–54, 88–89, 120, 240n32; and utilitarianism, 39; and voluntarism, 42. See also manifold (class) of moral persons; modern morality; universality

cost-benefit analyses, 178

"A Critique of Utilitarianism" (Williams), 240n35, 267n22

Cullity, Garrett, 268n29

culture, 112, 240n32. See also social life, relations, practices, and conventions

Dancy, Jonathan, 241n11, 260n29, 262n42

Darwall, Stephen, 238nn21,23, 244nn36,37, 245n49, 246nn57,59, 252nn52,54, 263n49

debt model, 19–20, 116, 194, 235n1. See also gratitude; promissory obligation

the deceased, 259n17

deceit, 135. See also duplicity; misleading statements example

deep structure of realm of impartial morality, 16

defective human beings, 241n12

deliberation (moral reasoning): and agent-relativity, 38, 51–52, 136; and aggregated well-being, 192, 229; and claims and interests, 18–19, 147, 164–76, 165–76, 178, 180–81, 186; and contractualism, 178–89; and cosmopolitan morality, 37–38, 52–54; and (directed) obligations, 1, 50–51, 54–

65, 171–75, 176, 179, 245n56; and disregard, 82; and egalitarianism, 117; and equal standing, 37–38, 142, 250n38; and esteem/disesteem, 129, 248nn16,17; and foreseeability, 200; and gouty-toed stranger, 195; and habit, 176–77, 241n9, 245n56; and high-level property, 36–37; and individualist restriction, 226; individual versus public, 228–29; and intentions, 29; and interpersonal morality, 16, 35–37, 172; and joint commitment, 123; and justification, 175–76; and maximizing, 243n29; and moral right and wrong, 56–57; and moral theories, 13, 24–25, 30–37, 39–47, 67, 178–89; and natural history of morality, 113–14; and normativity, 14, 16; overviews, 1, 12, 13, 16, 18–19, 24–25; and permissibility, 19, 176–77; and personal relationships, 136; and persons, 254n23; and plurality of considerations, 241n11; practical reasoning distinguished from, 147; and prima facie duties, 170–72, 174; and relational morality, 16, 25, 47–50, 52–58, 149, 170, 175, 180–81, 186, 201; and responsiveness, 262n40; and rights, 170–71; and self-consciousness, 176–77; and social meanings, 56; and trolley examples, 272n58; unintelligibility of, 24–25, 38; and voluntarism, 34. See also bipolar thought; epistemic constraints; eudaimonistic reflection; intentions; interests; intuition; justification; moral right and wrong; moral theories; presumptive (defeasible) constraints; principles; reasons; rights

demands. See expectations or demands

democratic legitimacy, 34

"Demystifying Promises" (Darwall), 263n49

deonticity: and aggregation, 232; and deliberation, 55, 67, 68, 69, 172–73; and (directed) obligations, 49; and interests, 147; and moral theories, 30–34, 37, 39–47; and practical requirements, 26–27, 29;

deonticity (*cont.*)

and prima facie duties, 171–75; and promissory obligations, 29, 51; and reasons, 57, 245n56

dependency and equality, 203–5

descendants (future generations), 19, 160, 210–15, 227, 270n45

determinism, 75

"Directed Duties" (May), 236n12

directed obligations/duties: and agent-relativity, 17–18, 135–45; and anti-individualism, 125–34; and beneficence, 207; and conditionality, 236n13; conflicts of, 20, 28–29, 32–33, 62–65, 173, 192, 231–32, 246n65; constitutive conditions of, 124; and cosmopolitan morality, 18; and deliberation, 13; domain of, 105; and equal standing, 23; extension of, 118; imperfect duties, 19, 20, 155, 201–10; and individualism, 126–27, 134; and interests, 163, 237n15; interpersonal, 21; and joint commitment, 122–23, 256n43; and law conception of ethics, 25; and manifold of persons, 18–19, 110; and moral injury, 11; and moral nexus, 15–16, 23; and moral right and wrong, 67–86; and mutual recognition, 136, 139–40; and nonnormative relations, 106, 107–25; and normativity, 14; to oneself, 155–56, 258nn9,10; overview, 5–6, 34–47; pervasiveness/overridingness of, 247n71; and presumptive constraints, 12, 29–34, 51, 115, 158, 175, 236n13, 245n56; and problem cases, 190, 191; reflexive, 155–56, 204–5; and relational morality, 5–6, 16, 47–54, 58–59, 105–7, 115, 131, 158; and rights, 2, 8–9, 157, 235n2; secondary, 28–29, 89–95, 93, 251n45; and social command theories, 95–96; and social life, 13, 71, 123; Thompson on, 236n12; and universality, 122; and virtue theory (perfectionism), 44–47; and voluntarism, 41–44. *See also* accountability; agent-relativity; claims; deliberation; nondirected duties; non-identity problem; obligations; personal relationships; practical requirements; prima facie duties; promissory obligation *and other duties;* rescue from rocks *and other examples;* self-standing obligations

disabilities, 258n5

disapprobation, 72, 74, 75, 100, 102. *See also* reactive attitudes and emotions

disapproval, moral, 71, 74

discretion: and claimholder, 50, 51, 57; and divine command theories, 267n17; and emergency mutual aid, 209; and forgiveness, 90, 91; and gratitude, 193, 202–3, 203–4, 252n51, 267nn16,17; and imperfect duties, 20; and mutual aid, 201, 205–10, 267n21, 268nn24,25; and practical requirements, 27, 49; and relational morality, 49–50, 123; and rights, 201, 202–3, 267n16; and specificity, 267n16; and will theory of rights, 157

diseases, 258n5

disregard or indifference: and antecedent relationships, 251n45; and bipolar thought, 153–54; and blame, 66, 79, 82–83, 84, 94, 249n25; and claim interests, 169; and climate change skepticism, 250n38; and consequentialism, 87, 88; and of expectations demands, 66; and gallery opening example, 182; and gratitude, 204; and impairment of relations, 102–3; and moral injury, 10–11, 13, 170, 195–96; and moral repair, 92–93; and moral right and wrong, 74; and reactive attitudes, 85–86, 185; and relational morality, 82, 85; and rescue from rocks example, 218–19; and rule consequentialism, 249n25; and secondary claims, 199–200; and third parties, 197–99, 253n57

"The Distribution of Numbers and the Comprehensiveness of Reasons" (Munoz-Dardé), 271n48, 272n55, 274n76

diversity, 32

divine command theories: and accountability, 80–81; and beneficence, 25; and (directed) obligations, 25; and discretion, 267n17; and gratitude, 250n27, 252n51, 267n17; and moral right and wrong, 41–43; and relational morality, 250n27, 252n51; and sanctions, 252nn49,51; and social relations, 31, 80; and universality, 41–42. *See also* Anscombe, G.E.M.; commands, normative

The Domain of Reasons (Skorupski), 238n23, 240n4, 244n36, 252n53

dominance model, 3, 31–32, 32–33, 39, 40, 243n29

drunk driver example, 196

duplicity, 135. *See also* deceit; misleading statements example

duties. *See* directed obligations/duties; nondirected duties; obligations; prima facie duties

"Duties and Their Direction" (Sreenivasan), 236n14, 237n16, 258n12, 260n26

Effective Altruism, 205–6, 267n21

egalitarianism, 117–18, 142. *See also* equal standing

elderly persons, 150, 151

emergencies. *See* circumstances (conditionality) (emergencies)

emotions, 249n24. *See also* anger *and other emotions*; reactive attitudes and emotions

empathy, 112–13, 116

enforceability, 199, 266n12

Engaging Reason (Raz), 236n8, 240n4, 242n21

enjoyment, 160

entitlement, 6

epistemic constraints, 29, 74, 126–28, 130, 252n53, 256n48, 260n30. *See also* misleading statements example; subjective (psychological) facts

equality and dependency, 203–5

"equally real," 37, 46, 53, 60, 63, 64, 88, 110, 116, 131, 143, 148, 231

equal standing: assumption of, 239n32; and

blame, 87–88; and consequentialism, 87–88, 116–17; and contractualism, 180–81; and cosmopolitan morality, 37–38; and deliberation, 37–38, 142, 250n38; and (directed) obligations, 23; and divine command theories, 42; and gratitude, 203–5; and interpersonal domain, 125; and interpersonal morality, 21–23, 106, 248n11; and interpersonal recognition, 86; and justification, 176, 179; and manifold of persons, 125; and modern morality, 116; and personal relationships, 117, 254n17, 254n23; in political life, 117; and relational morality, 115, 254nn21,23; and universality, 117; and utilitarianism, 39. *See also* cosmopolitan morality; dependency and equality; mutual recognition

equity, 229–30

esteem/disesteem, 43, 75, 129, 248nn16,17

The Ethical Demand (Løgstrup), 237n15

Ethics and the Limits of Philosophy (Williams), 238n22, 241n13, 242n21, 253nn1,2

Ethics without Principles (Dancy), 241n11

eudaimonistic reflection, 144–45

evolution, 116. *See also* biological humans; natural history of morality

ex ante considerations, 20, 200, 204, 216–23, 225, 272nn51,53, 273n65

exceptions. *See* circumstances (conditionality) (emergencies)

expectations or demands: and accountability, 70–71, 247n7; and blame, 70–71, 73, 74–75; and (directed) obligations, 118; disregard of, 66; and moral injury, 170; and moral right and wrong, 72–73; and promissory obligation, 73, 107, 108; and reactive attitudes, 13, 80; reasonable, 74; and resentment, 84–85; and social command theories, 96–97. *See also* ex ante considerations

extra-moral concern for persons, 4, 192, 221–33, 236n9

extraterrestrials examples, 118–19, 159, 160, 161. *See also* nonhumans facts, nonnormative, 91–92, 251n42. *See also* climate change; reasoning, empirical

fairness, 108, 165, 248n16, 268n29

families: and agent-relativity, 135–36; and antecedent interactions, 110–11; and natural history of morality, 112–13; and relational morality, 16; self-standing domain *versus,* 125; and third-party harm, 197; and voluntarism, 33–34. *See also* children

Feinberg, Joel, 103, 104, 253n65, 260n30

"fellow creatures" (Mill), 257n59

fellow humanity, 125

"fellow rational beings," 256n44

fetishism, 56, 57

fidelity, 118, 163n53, 190, 263n47, 264n58. *See also* assurance interests

Finite and Infinite Goods (Adams), 252n51

first-order moral issues: and agent relativity, 38; and aggregation, 215–19; and claims, 169; and (directed) obligations, 176, 191, 192–210; and foreseeability, 192–200; and hypothetical cases, 15, 20–21; and imperfect duties, 201–10; and individualist restriction, 186–87; and non-identity problem, 210–15; and reasons *versus* responsiveness, 237n19; and relational morality, 14–15, 19, 22–23, 54, 190–92; and rights, 191, 201–10; and self-standing requirements, 115; and third-party harm, 195–99, 221–33; and virtues, 138. *See also* aggregation (numbers); hypothetical cases; intuition; political obligations; promissory obligation *and other duties;* rescue from rocks *and other examples*

fittingness, 260n28

Flanagan, Owen, 240n32, 248n17

flat-tire example, 123, 201, 203

flying to Chicago example, 123–24, 255n40, 256n42

Foot, Philippa, 7, 44–45, 46, 47–49, 76–77, 236n8, 245n46, 254n24, 272n58. *See also* virtue theory (perfectionism)

force (coercion, physical), 140, 199

foreseeability, 7, 19–20, 160, 182, 191, 192–200, 214, 227, 263n48, 266nn7,8

forgiveness, 13, 67, 89, 90–92, 94, 100–101, 250nn40–41, 252n56

Forst, Rainer, 257n58

Foundations of Ethics (Ross), 260n28

Frankfurt, Harry, 241n13

"Freedom and Resentment" (Strawson), 248n9

Freud, Sigmund, 244n39

Frick, Johann, 223–27, 229–30, 236n8, 273n65

Fricker, Miranda, 83–84, 248n17, 251n47

friendship: and agent-relativity, 135–36; and antecedent interactions, 110–11; and claims and directed obligations, 16, 61, 64, 110–11, 136, 193–94; constitutive conditions of, 144–45; and equal standing, 87, 117, 142; and library book return example, 176; and mutual recognition, 140; and natural history of morality, 112; and nonmoral values, 247nn68,69; political membership compared, 247n69; and promissory obligation, 176, 182; and relational morality, 125, 141; and rescue from rocks example, 271n49; and third-party forgiveness, 250n41; and third-party harm, 197. *See also* personal relationships

future generations (descendents), 19, 160, 210–15, 227, 269n32, 270n45. *See also* non-identity problem

"Future People, the Non-Identity Problem, and Person-Affecting Principles" (Parfit), 269nn31,37

gallery reception example, 9–10, 11, 182

games examples, 246n62. *See also* sports examples

Gardner, John, 251n45

The Gay Science (Nietzsche), 240n36

generosity, 261n34

The Geography of Morals (Flanagan), 240n32, 248n17

Gewirth, Alan, 238n22

Gilbert, Margaret, 122–24, 182–83, 184, 253n6, 255nn37,40,41, 256n42, 263n52

global responsibility, 248n16. *See also* climate change

goodness of agent's own life, 18

gouty-toed stranger example, 107, 123, 138, 195

gratitude: and antecedent interactions, 118, 135–36, 193; and artificial persons, 153; and claim rights, 2, 9, 20, 192, 201–6; and consequentialism, 270n44; and (directed) obligations, 16, 111, 135, 191, 192–200, 193, 201; and discretion, 193, 202–3, 203–4, 252n51, 267nn16,17; and divine command theories, 250n27, 252n51, 267n17; and natural history of morality, 112–13; and prima facie duty, 172, 174; and reasons, 252n51, 267n17; and relational morality, 123, 190, 191, 192–200, 204, 205; and rights, 9, 202–5. *See also* beneficence; charity; mutual aid

Greene, Joshua, 112–13, 114, 116, 240n36, 254n17

Greenspan, Patricia, 244n36

groups, 12, 112, 113–14. *See also* accountability; social life, relations, practices, and conventions

guilt, 74, 101. *See also* reactive attitudes and emotions

habit, 176–77, 241n9, 245n56

handicapped person example, 213–14

happiness, 39, 213, 214, 225, 269n33, 270n44, 273n72

harassment, 153

Hare, R. M., 238n22

harm: and aggregation, 272n60; avoiding, 237n18; moral injury distinguished from, 9–10; noncomparative, 269n37; risks of, 221–22; third-party, 182, 195–99, 221–33, 250n41, 251n43, 253n57. *See also* moral injury or wrong

Hart, H.L.A., 157, 183, 196, 237n16, 254n11, 258n10

health, physical and mental, 160

Hieronymi, Pamela, 83

high-level, right-making properties, 35, 36–37, 55, 69, 125, 184, 224, 242n22, 263n56. *See also* "to-be-done"/"not-to-be-done" (right and wrong in generic sense)

highway example, 120

historical conditionality, 36, 240n32

historical interactions. *See* antecedent interactions; natural history of morality

Hohfeld, Wesley Newcombe, 2. *See also* claim rights

Hooker, Brad, 243n32, 249n25

hostage-taking example, 232

"How I Am Not a Kantian" (Scanlon), 265nn62,63, 273n63, 274n74

Human Morality (Scheffler), 253n57, 262n40

human nature, 120, 248nn16,17. *See also* species nature

Humean theories, 109–10, 114, 120, 122, 126, 128–29, 133, 253n8. *See also* individualism; subjective (psychological) facts

Hurka, Thomas, 260nn27,28, 261nn35,36

"A Hybrid Theory of Claim Rights" (Sreenivasan), 259n15, 267n15

hypothetical cases, 15, 20–21, 212–14, 226–27, 238n24, 239n28. *See also* intuition; miners *and other specific examples*

Ideal Code, Real World (Hooker), 243n32, 249n25

ideals, 264n57

identity-based accounts: and conflicts of obligation, 65; and maximizing, 243n29; and mistaken objective identity, 242n17; and "must," 241n13; and perfectionism, 45; and presumptive constraints, 64; and reasons, 30–31, 32–33, 35; and relational morality, 246n62; species nature *versus*, 244n42; and subjective facts, 133–34, 241nn13,16; tribal, 16, 112, 113; and weakness of will, 241n16. *See also* roles, social; tribes

ideology, 250n38

imbalances, 193–95, 203, 265n4. *See also* power and vulnerability

impairment of relationships, 102–3, 251n45

imperfect duties, 19, 20, 155, 201–10. *See also* gratitude; mutual aid *and other imperfect duties*

impersonal morality, 64–65, 100, 114

"In Defense of Directed Duties" (Jonker), 263n46

independence, 264n57. *See also* dependency and equality

indifference. *See* disregard or indifference

indignation, 15, 70, 74, 77, 78, 99–101, 151. *See also* reactive attitudes and emotions

individualism: anti-, 125–34; and blame, 75–76, 77–79, 132–33; and forgiveness, 91–92; and manifold of persons, 131–32; and moral repair, 92–94; and presumptive constraints, 133–34; and relational morality, 4, 17, 76–86, 106–7, 125–34, 251n43; and subjective attitudes of agent, 256n53; and universality, 131–32, 134. *See also* Foot, Philippa; Humean theories; identity-based accounts; subjective facts; virtue theory *and other individualistic theories*

individualist restriction, 186–89, 212–13, 225–26, 265n65

infants and children, 77, 101–2, 120–21, 150–51, 152, 158, 193–94, 265n2. *See also* families

information, limited, 29. *See also* epistemic constraints

injury. *See* moral injury or wrong

installment payments example, 194–95

intentions, 27–28, 29, 50–51, 102, 246n66, 248n12

interests: assurance, 108, 161–62, 165, 169, 175, 181–82, 263n47 (*see also* fidelity); characterized, 160; and claims, 7–8, 10, 18–19, 82, 147, 156–65, 176–89; and claims and wrongs, 147, 156–65; and the deceased, 259n17; and deliberation, 18–19, 147, 165–76, 178, 180–81, 186; and deon-

ticity, 47; and (directed) obligations, 163, 237n15; and interpersonal recognition, 163–64; and justification, 163, 165–66, 170, 176–77; and Malay servant example, 164–65; noncomparative, 213–14, 273n72; and non-identity problem, 211–12; nonnormative, 237n18; normative, 147, 165, 176–89, 237n18; of others, 18–19; and phases of life, 156; political, 250n38; and private law, 156–65; and promissory obligation, 175; reasons *versus*, 186; and reductive accounts, 259n16; and relational morality, 18–19, 21, 23, 158–59, 162–64, 178, 262n43; and runaway trolleys examples, 220; second-order, 168–69, 199; and universality, 23; and vaccine example, 222–23. *See also* claim interests; equal standing; harm; second-order normative consequences; third-party beneficiaries; virtue theory *and other theories*; well-being, individual *and other interests*

"Internal and External Reasons" (Williams), 256n46

interpersonal morality: and accountability, 76; and aggregation, 188; characterized, 3–4; and claimholders, 66; and contractualism, 187, 188; and cosmopolitan morality, 23, 37, 118; and deliberation, 16, 35–37, 172; and (directed) obligations, 12; domain of, 3–4, 36, 125, 235n6, 239n27, 255n24; and equal standing, 106; extension of, 116; and extra-moral requirements, 232, 236n9; and games example, 60; and gratitude, 267n17; and ideals, 264n57; and manifold of persons, 148; and miners example, 274n76; and morality, 242n23; and moral right and wrong, 35–36, 67–76, 72, 185; and moral theories, 35–38; and perfectionism, 78; and personal relationships, 17; and relational morality, 21, 25, 158, 166; and rights, 236n8; Scanlon on, 237n19; and secondary claims, 266n11; and transactional obligation, 54. *See also* accountability; equal standing; foreseeability; future generations; interpersonal recognition; modern morality; social life, relations, practices, and conventions

interpersonal recognition: and blame, 94–95; and claims, 62, 141; friendship distinguished from, 145; and interpersonal morality, 246n64; and justifiability, 187; mutual recognition *versus*, 141, 142–43, 257n60; and promissory obligations, 195; and reactive attitudes, 85–86; and relational morality, 18, 163, 195

intuition: and beneficence, 269n31; and consequentialism, 270n43; and joint commitment, 255n40; and moral theories, 239nn28–29; questionable, 196–97; and relational morality, 3, 4, 5, 19, 147, 176–89; and rights, 8. *See also* hypothetical cases

intuitionism, 19, 262n42

The Invention of Autonomy (Schneewind), 244n39

inviolability, 166

jettisoning excess cargo example, 107, 108, 111

joint commitment (collaborative agency), 112, 116, 122–24, 126, 130, 141, 255nn37,40,41, 256nn42,43

Jonker, Julian, 263n46

juridical rights, 199

justice, 80, 248n17, 249n23, 254n24, 255n29. *See also* law and legislative authorities

justification: and claim interests, 165–70, 259nn22,23; comparative, 270n37; and contractualism, 187; directed, 257n61; and interests, 163, 165–66, 170, 176–77; and mutual aid, 208; and normative interests, 165; overview, 176–77; and permissibility, 257n61; and relational morality, 176–89. *See also* circumstances (conditionality) (emergencies); deliberation; reasons

Kamm, F. M., 220, 235n8, 271n51, 272n57

Kantians, 35, 44, 120, 132, 237n20, 241n14, 244n39, 244n40

kidney donation example, 175

kindness, 16

Kolodny, Niko, 247n68

Korsgaard, Christine M., 238n22, 241n13, 242n16, 244n40

Kumar, Rahul, 269n37, 271n50

Lacey, Nicola, 252n56

Laoumis, Theano, 267n26

law and legislative authorities: and allocation of resources, 192; and authority, 34; and conflicts of obligations, 63; criminal law model, 98–99, 100–101, 252nn54,56; and (directed) obligations, 25, 59; and Hohfeldian rights, 2; and interests, 156–65; private law model, 93, 98–99, 100–101, 103, 119, 148, 246n62, 252n54, 264n57; and relational morality, 158; and utilitarianism, 41. *See also* contracts; *Palsgraf v. Long Island Railroad Co.*; public officials' decisions; rights

Legos example, 89–90

liberty rights, 200

library book return example, 176

life, goodness of agent's own, 18

Life and Action (Thompson), 244n41

Living High and Letting Die (Unger), 268n24

Løgstrup, Knud Eljer, 237n15

love, 64, 65, 110–11, 133, 194, 197, 253n9

"Love as Valuing a Relationship" (Kolodny), 247n68

loyalty, 111

MacIntyre, Alasdair, 240n37

"Making Room for Options" (Greenspan), 244n36

malaria-reducing example, 160, 164, 205, 268n24

Malay servant example, 7–8, 47–54, 161–62, 164–65, 166, 245n46 manifold (class) of moral persons: and agent-relativity, 135–36; and bipolar thought, 120–22, 147, 150, 255n35, 258n5; and claim interests, 166; and claims, 146, 159–60; and (directed) obligations, 18, 110, 122–23; and individualism, 131–32; and interests, 166; and mutual recognition, 140–41, 256n58; and reflexive obligations, 155–56; and relational morality, 3, 16, 17, 18–19, 37, 106, 111–25, 148, 149, 155, 190–91; and Scanlon, 264n57; and social bonds, 113–14, 116; and universality, 148; well-being of, 271n48. *See also* bipolar thought; interpersonal recognition; mutual recognition; orders of right; persons; strangers; universality

maximizing, 243nn29,30. *See also* consequentialism

May, Simon Căbulea, 236n12

"Membership and Political Obligation" (Scheffler), 254n22

mentally impaired people, 101–2, 120–21, 150–52

mercy, 100–101

The Method of Ethics (Sidgwick), 249n20

Mill, John Stuart, 41, 257n59

miners example, 223–24, 226–27, 228–29, 232, 274nn72,76

misleading statements example, 196–97, 266n7. *See also* deceit; duplicity

mobbing, 153

modern morality: and accountability, 67, 69, 75–76; and antecedent relationships, 17; and moral right and wrong, 68–69, 72–73; overviews, 107; and relational morality, 134

"Modern Moral Philosophy" (Anscombe), 24–25, 266n9. *See also* cosmopolitan morality; equal standing; interpersonal morality; manifold (class) of moral persons; moral right and wrong; persons; self-standing obligations

moral deficiencies *versus* failings, 3

Moral Demands in Nonideal Theory (Murphy), 267n23, 268nn23,26

The Moral Demands of Affluence (Cullity), 268n29

Moral Dimensions (Scanlon), 237n19, 248nn10,12, 251n46, 253n61, 256n44, 258n6

moral domain, 16, 255n24. *See also* manifold (class) of moral persons

"Moral Incapacity" (Williams), 241n13

moral injury or wrong: and aggregation, 228; and antecedent claims, 258n11; and apologies, 90–91; and attitudes of agents, 10–11; bare, 237n18; and blame, 88–89; and claims, 251n43, 266n9; and claims and interests, 156–69; and disregard, 10–11, 13, 170; and foreseeability, 192–200; and forgiveness, 92; harm distinguished from, 9–10; and interests, 147; moral wrong *versus*, 236n8; and mutual aid, 208; and Pilates class example, 170; and reactive attitudes, 84; and relational morality, 9–11, 85, 251n43; and resentment, 83; and rights, 195–96, 197, 266n9; and secondary claims, 191; and trolley examples, 220–21; and vaccine example, 223. *See also* disregard or indifference; harm; moral repair

morality, 1–5, 16, 69, 242n23. *See also* interpersonal morality; modern morality; moral right and wrong; natural history of morality; normativity; social life, relations, practices, and conventions

Morality, Mortality (Kamm), 271n51

The Morality of Freedom (Raz), 235n4, 247n66, 253n5, 259nn14,22

"morality of right and wrong" (Scanlon), 3–4

"the morality system" (Williams), 242n21

"Moral Luck" (Williams), 247n70

moral nexus, 15–16, 23. *See also* relational morality

moral norms, 14. *See also* authority; moral right and wrong; normativity; reactive attitudes and emotions; social life, relations, practices, and conventions

"Moral Obligations and Social Commands" (Wolf), 243n35

moral reasoning. See deliberation; moral theories; practical reasoning

moral repair, 67, 89, 92–95, 251nn45,47

moral right and wrong: and accountability, 71–72, 75–76, 76–86, 81, 83; and blame, 72, 73–74; and claims, 105; and consequentialism, 270n43; and contractual moral reasoning, 184–85, 188–89; defined, 105; and deliberation, 56–57; and expectations or demands, 72–73; and hypothetical cases, 20–21; and individualism, 76–81; and individualist restriction, 226; and interpersonal morality, 35–36, 67–76, 72, 185; and modern morality, 68–69, 72–73; and "morality of right and wrong" (Scanlon), 3–4; and moral theories, 34–38; and natural history of morality, 113; and normativity, 14, 68–69, 239n24; and obligation, 247n1; Parfit on, 238n24; and reactive emotions, 75; as reason, 56; and relational morality, 56–57, 81–86, 105, 185–86; and rescue from rocks example, 218–19; wrongs versus, 236n8. See also deliberation (moral reasoning); first-order moral issues; high-level, right-making properties; interpersonal morality; intuition; moral injury or wrong; moral theories; permissibility/impermissibility; reasons; rights; "to-be-done"/"not-to-be-done" (right and wrong in generic sense)

Morals by Agreement (Korsgaard), 238n22

moral standing. See bipolar thought; equal standing; interpersonal recognition; manifold (class) of moral persons; mutual recognition; persons; rights; special (privileged) standing

moral theories: Anscombe on, 242n25; and authority of moral norms, 14–15; and deliberation, 13, 24–25, 30–37, 39–47, 67,

178–89; and deonticity, 30–34, 37, 39–47; historical development of, 244n39; and moral right and wrong, 34–38; and presumptive constraints, 30–35; and relational morality, 12, 126. See also contractualism and other theories; high-level, right-making properties; normativity: metaethics of; Scanlon, T. M. and other theorists

Moral Thinking (Hare), 238n22

Moral Tribes (Greene), 240n36

moral wrong. See moral injury or wrong; moral right and wrong

"More Right Than Wrong" (Dancy), 260n29

mother as third-party beneficiary example, 196

Munoz-Dardé, Véronique, 271n48, 272n55, 274n76

Murphy, Liam B., 267n23, 268nn23,26

"must," 27, 30, 34, 241nn12,13. See also practical requirements; "to-be-done"/"not-to-be-done" (right and wrong in generic sense)

mutual aid: and aggregation, 268nn28,29; and claim rights, 9; and claims, 19, 20; and discretion, 201, 205–10, 267n21, 268nn24,25; emergency, 208–9; and relational morality, 191, 205, 206, 207–8, 268n26; and rights, 201–2, 205–10. See also beneficence; gratitude; organ donation example

mutual recognition: and agent-relativity, 137; and bipolar thought, 152, 153; and directed obligations, 136, 139–40; and interpersonal morality, 246n64; interpersonal recognition versus, 141, 142–43, 257n60; and manifold of persons, 140–41; and relational morality, 107, 136. See also equal standing; interpersonal recognition

Nagel, Thomas, 37, 148, 238n22, 257n61. See also "equally real"

"nameless virtue," 261n34

Narevson, Jan, 270n44

natural goodness, 76–77. *See also* Foot, Philippa

Natural Goodness (Foot), 236n8

natural history of morality, 16, 106, 112–14, 116

naturalistic conceptions of ethics, 120

"The Nature and Value of Rights" (Feinberg), 103, 253n65, 260n30

Necessity, Volition, and Love (Frankfurt), 241n13

Nehamas, Alexander, 247n68

Neuhauser, Fred, 239n30

Nietzsche, Friedrich, 238n20, 240n36

nondirected duties, 158, 236n14, 255n37

nondomination, 264n57. *See also* power and vulnerability

nonhumans, 152, 271n48. *See also* animals, nonrational; extraterrestrials examples

non-identity problem, 191, 210–15, 269n37. *See also* future generations

nonmoral norms, 270n45

nonnaturalistic realism, 238n24, 256n53

nonnormative relations, 106, 107–25

nonreductive realism, 14

normative ethics. *See* first-order moral issues

normativity: and backsliding, 242n16; bipolar, 246n61; and (directed) obligations and accountability, 14; metaethics of, 14–15; and moral norms, 16; and moral right and wrong, 14, 68–69, 239n24; and Parfit, 237n20, 238n24; pre- or nonmoral, 245n55; and reasons, 15, 240n4; and relational morality, 126, 238n23, 257n3, 264n59; unity of domain of, 255n24. *See also* accountability; deliberation (moral reasoning); directed obligations/duties; morality; moral theories; self-standing obligations

Normativity (Thomson), 241n12

norms. *See* normativity

norms, nonmoral, 270n45

"Nowheresville," 103

"Numbers" (Raz), 254n10, 265n1, 271n46

Nussbaum, Martha, 248n17

objective attitude, 69–70

obligations, 25, 34–47, 247n1. *See also* directed obligations/duties; nondirected duties; practical requirements; volitional necessity

"Obligations and Joint Commitment" (Gilbert), 255n37

One Another's Equals (Waldron), 239n31

O'Neill, Onora, 236n8

On Friendship (Nehamas), 247n68

online donations example, 268n25

On What Matters (Parfit), 237n20, 238n24, 242n18, 243n32, 245n56, 265nn60,65, 269n37, 273nn60,62,70–72, 274n73

opprobrium, 12, 78, 86, 249n21

orders of right, 109, 119–21, 148–49, 159, 246n61, 253n8, 255n35, 257n2, 258n5

organ donation example, 273n62

Otsuka, Michael, 271n51

"ought implies can," 257n3

"ought to do," 27, 56, 157, 172, 210, 215, 236n14, 241n12, 257n3, 260n26, 266n11

Owens, David, 237n18, 241n9, 245n56, 252n49, 259nn22,23

"Owing Justifying, and Rejecting" (Kamm), 235n8

pain, freedom from, 160

Palsgraf v. Long Island Railroad Co., 196, 197, 266n8

Parfit, Derek: and aggregation, 273n72, 273nn60,62,70–72; and artificial cases, 215; and beneficence, 268n31; and individualist restriction, 186–87, 212–14, 224–26, 265n65, 270n39, 274n73; and intuition and reasons, 239n29; and moral right and wrong, 34, 35, 188–89, 237n20, 242n18, 270n43; on noncomparative harm, 269n37; on reasons, 238n24, 245n56; and rule consequentialism, 243n32. *See also* "Can We Avoid the Repugnant Conclusion?"; *Case Four*; *Case Seven*; "Future People, the Non-Identity Problem, and Person-Affecting Principles"; *On What Matters*; *Reasons and Persons*

participant attitude, 70, 84–85

particularism, 262n42

peremptory normative constraints, 68

perfectionism. *See* virtue theory

permissibility/impermissibility: and apology, 89–90; and claim rights, 170–71, 201, 260n26; defined, 235n2; and directed justification, 257n61; and equal standing, 22; and ex ante objections, 219–20; and gallery reception example, 162; and intentions or attitudes, 248n12; and justifications, 257n61; and killing, 218; and moral wrongs, 4; and mutual recognition, 140; and physical coercion, 199; and presumptive constraints, 12; and property rights, 2; and sacrifice of basic needs, 164; Scanlon on, 248n12. *See also* deliberation (moral reasoning); moral right and wrong

personal relationships: and agent-relativity, 137; and antecedent interactions, 16, 18, 110–11, 125; constitutive conditions of, 139, 144, 145, 254n9; and demands and expectations, 70–71; and (directed) obligations, 16, 17, 65, 135–36, 192–95, 202, 254n10; and equal standing, 117, 254n17, 254n23; and eudaimonistic reflection, 144–45; and imbalances, 265n4; impairment of, 102–3, 251n45; and objective attitude, 69–70; and relational morality, 113–14, 141; and thick ties, 192. *See also* antecedent interactions; friendship *and other personal relationships*; gratitude; mutual recognition

persons: artificial, 152–53; and biological species, 3, 150–51; and claims, 60–61, 61–62, 107; class of, 18–19; and conflicts of obligations, 63; and deliberation, 254n23; and (directed) obligations, 60–61, 111; extra-moral concern for, 4, 192, 221–33;

and interest of claimholders, 163–64; and interpersonal morality, 266n11; and natural history of morality, 116; and normative interests, 165; oneself as, 258n9; and relational morality, 13, 245n53, 246n62. *See also* equal standing; interpersonal morality; interpersonal recognition; manifold (class) of moral persons; moral domain; mutual recognition

phases of lives, 150–51, 156

Pickard, Hannah, 252n56

Pilates class example, 72–73, 169

pluralism, 3–44, 32, 224, 226, 229–30, 231, 235n8, 239n25. *See also* Raz, Joseph

political life, 117, 247n69, 250n38, 254n22

political obligations and rights, 63–64, 199

political rights, 199

The Possibility of Altruism (Nagel), 238n22

power and vulnerability, 237n15, 265n4. *See also* nondomination

practical reasoning, 147. *See also* deliberation (moral reasoning); practical requirements

Practical Reasons and Norms (Raz), 245n54

practical requirements, 1, 15, 26–34, 49, 173, 240n3. *See also* disregard or indifference; individualist restriction; "must"; obligations; presumptive (defeasible) constraints; relational requirements; "to-be-done"/"not-to-be-done" (right and wrong in generic sense)

"Preference and Urgency" (Scanlon), 259n16

presumptive (defeasible) constraints: and accountability, 12; and aggregation, 230–33; and bipolar thought, 149, 153; conflicting, 231; and cost-benefit analyses, 178; and deliberation, 26–47, 60–61, 68, 170, 172–73; and deonticity, 27, 29, 172–73; and (directed) obligations, 12, 29–34, 51, 115, 158, 172–75, 236n13, 245n56; and duties and claims, 172–75; and equal standing, 117–18; and high-level property, 36–37; and identity, 64; and moral right, presumptive (defeasible) constraints: (*cont.*) 35–36; and moral theories, 30–35; overview, 28–29; and practical requirements, 27, 28–29, 240n3; and promissory obligation, 6, 7, 51, 175, 236n13; and reasons, 26–34, 50, 55–56, 172–73; and relational morality, 12, 55, 175; and Scanlon's contractualism, 184; and sports example, 59–61; and subjective facts, 126–28, 133–34; transactional duties as, 51; unconditional constraints *versus*, 28–29; and utilitarianism, 39–41, 243n28. *See also* circumstances (conditionality) (emergencies); obligations; prima facie duties

prima facie duties, 171–72, 174, 260nn27,28,31

principles: and claims and interests, 19; and contractualism, 19, 179–89, 198, 204, 223, 226, 262n46, 264n57, 269n32, 270n37; and ex ante considerations, 20; and miners example, 274n76; and mutual aid, 206–7, 209, 210; and non-identity problem, 211; and organ donation example, 273nn62–63; and particularism, 262nn42–43; and personal relationships, 114; and promissory obligation, 108–10; and relational morality, 109–10, 140–41, 143, 208, 215–21, 262n43, 264n57, 268n29; and rescue from rocks example, 215–21, 271nn46,50, 272n53. *See also* agent-relativity *and other principles;* utilitarianism *and other moral theories*

private law of torts, 93–94

Private Wrongs (Ripstein), 251n45, 264n57, 266n8

privileged standing. *See* special (privileged) standing

procreative decisions example, 213–14

promise to meet at airport example, 267n16

promise to meet student example, 55–56, 262n46

"Promising, Intimate Relationships, and Conventionalism" (Shiffrin), 254n22, 265n4

promissory obligation: and accountability, 81–82; and agent-relativity, 39, 51–52, 135, 243n27; and antecedent interactions, 107, 110–11; and blame, 73–74; and circumstances, 6–7, 170–71, 175–76, 183, 236n13, 260n31; and claim interests, 167, 169; and claims, 59; and coercion, 199; conditionality of, 6–7, 183; and contractualist moral reasoning, 181–82; and cosmopolitan morality, 52–54; and debt model, 194; and deliberation, 28; and deonticity, 29, 51; and directionality, 6, 182–83; and discretion, 267n16; and exceptions, 62, 170–71; and expectations, 73, 107, 108; generalization of, 114–15; and Hohfeldian rights, 259n22; and interests, 175; and intuitive understanding, 15–16; and justification, 180; and moral reasoning, 171–72, 180; nonmoralized account of, 253n6; overview, 5–9; and perfectionism, 45–46; and personal relationships, 136; and prima facie duty, 174, 260nn28,31; reasons *versus*, 29; and relational morality, 6, 47–54, 109–12, 114–15, 176; and rights, 183; and self-standing obligations, 109–10, 245n55; and social command theories, 96; and social practices, 108–11, 253n6; and special (privileged) standing, 183; and subjective facts, 108, 134; and third-party beneficiaries, 156, 157–58, 181–82, 183, 237n16; and third-party injury, 196; and transactions, 16, 110; and utilitarianism, 39, 40, 243n27. *See also* assurance interests; contracts; Malay servant *and other examples*

property rights examples, 2, 124, 171, 173, 174, 202, 203, 261n34

prudence, 155, 258n9

psychological facts. *See* subjective (psychological) facts

public officials' decisions, 20, 215, 221–33, 227, 252n56, 274nn74,76. *See also* law and legislative authorities

Pummer, Theron, 267n21

rain example, 55

rational force, 27

rationality, 16, 31, 241n14, 243n29. *See also* practical reasoning; will

Rawls, John, 239n28

Raz, Joseph: on aggregation, 271n46; on attitude adjustment, 258n8; and claim interests, 166; and on claims rights, 259n22; and exclusionary reasons, 241n6; on exclusionary reasons, 26, 50; on individual interests, 259n16; on intentions, 247n66; on interest in rights, 165, 166; and interpersonal morality, 236n8, 336n8; and normativity and reasons, 240n4; on personal relationships, 111, 114–15, 192–95, 202, 254n10; on reasons, 55, 240n4, 241n6, 242n21, 245n54; and rights, 235n4, 259nn14,22; on right wrong, 265n1

reactive attitudes and emotions: and accountability, 70–71; adjustment of, 258n8; and claims, 80; and disregard, 85–86, 185; and legal analogies, 98–99, 100–101; and moral injury, 84; and mutual aid, 210; overveiw, 70; and presumptive constraints, 12; and reasons, 15, 74–75, 79, 83, 127, 130, 237n19; and relational morality, 13–14, 248n9; and special standing of claimholders, 99–100; vicarious, 151–52. *See also* avoidance and withdrawal; expectations or demands; resentment *and other attitudes*

"realm of rights" (Thomson), 2

The Realm of Rights (Thomson), 260n26

"Reason, Rationality, and Normativity" (Raz), 258n8

Reason and Morality (Gewirth), 238n22

reasoning, empirical, 250n38. *See also* climate change; facts, nonnormative

reasoning, moral. *See* deliberation (moral reasoning); moral theories; practical reasoning

reasons: and attitude adjustments, 258n8; and blame, 238n23, 249n25; for blame, 238n23; constitutive conditions of, 128,

130, 256n49; and (directed) obligations, 13, 15, 32, 34, 172, 173, 256n48; and discretion, 27; exclusionary, 26, 50; and gratitude, 252n51, 267n17; and hypothetical cases, 21; impartial, 186; and intuition, 239n29; and morality, 35–36; nonmoral, 215, 242n21, 244n44; and nonnaturalist realism, 256n53; and normativity, 15, 240n4; and presumptive constraints, 26–34, 50, 55–56, 172–73; and prima facie duty, 172; and reactive attitudes, 15, 74–75, 79, 83, 237n19; and relational morality, 16, 256n49; rightness or wrongness as, 56; subjective facts *versus*, 106, 126–29, 130, 131–32, 133, 256n54; and virtues, 249n23; and voluntarism, 244n37, 250n27. *See also* dominance model; identity-based accounts; interests; justification

Reasons and Persons (Parfit), 239n29, 240n36, 254n15, 268n31, 270nn39,42,44

reception example, 9–10

Das Recht auf Rechtfertigung (Forst), 257n61

reciprocity, 111

redress, 93–94

reductive accounts, 16, 158–59, 162, 256n51, 259n16

refugees example, 209, 268n27

regret, 27, 219, 223, 261nn33,37

The Rejection of Consequentialism (Scheffler), 242n25

relational morality: overviews of, 1–12, 105; overviews of argument for, 12–23, 66, 104, 115, 126, 146, 190–91. *See also* accountability; claims; contractualism *and other theories*; deliberation (moral reasoning); directed obligations/duties; manifold (class) of moral persons; moral right and wrong; universality

relational requirements, 126, 235n6. *See also* claim rights; claims; directed obligations/duties; self-standing obligations

relations, nonnormative, 106, 107–25

relationships. *See* personal relationships; social life

remedy, 93–94

remorse, 251n47

"Replies" (Scanlon), 263n56

"Reply to Wenar" (Scanlon), 235n2, 258n12, 263n53, 264n59

rescue from rocks example, 187–88, 215–19, 225–26, 265n64, 270n46, 271nn49,50, 272nn53,54,55, 273n65

resentment: and aggregation, 232; and artificial persons, 152–53; and claim interests, 260n25; described, 99–100; and esteem/disesteem, 129; and forgiveness, 90; and guilt, 101; and individualism, 132–33; and moral wrongs, 252n53; and mutual aid, 208; and phases of life, 150–51, 156; and Pilates class example, 169–70; and relational morality, 13, 83–84, 187, 250n32; and secondary claims, 199; and utilitarianism, 77–78. See also reactive attitudes and emotions

resource depletion, 211–12

respect, 8, 48

responsibility. See accountability

responsiveness, 262n40

The Right and the Good (Ross), 260n27–29,31

right and wrong. See moral right and wrong; "to-be-done"/"not-to-be-done" (right and wrong in generic sense)

rights: alienability of, 202; and claims, 2–3, 8–9, 20, 259n22, 260n30; claims without, 200–210; and deliberation, 170–71; and (directed) obligations, 2, 157; and discretion, 201, 202–3, 267n16; and duties to oneself, 258n10; and ex ante determinacy, 200; and first-order moral issues, 191, 201–10; and foreseeability, 192–200; and gratitude, 9, 202–5; inalienable, 202; interest theory of, 157–58, 263n53; and interpersonal morality, 236n8; liberty, 267n14; and moral injury, 195–96, 197, 266n9; political, 199; and promissory obligations, 183; and relational morality, 2–3, 158, 200, 201; and Scanlon, 264n58;

and social interaction, 103; and third-party harm, 195–99; will theory of, 157–58, 263nn52,53. See also claim rights; enforceability; equal standing; moral repair

Ripstein, Arthur, 93, 251n45, 264n57, 266n8

roles, social, 61, 262n46. See also artists examples; friends and other roles; identity

Roman private law, 148

romantic partners. See love

Ross, W. D., 171–72, 174, 260n27, 260nn28,29,31

Rousseau, Jean-Jacques, 75

sacrifice, 111

sanctions, 41, 43, 75, 96

sanction theory, 252n49

satisfaction, 160

satisficing, 27, 50, 57

"Saving Lives, Moral Theory, and the Claims of Individuals" (Otsuka), 271n51

Scanlon, T. M.: on aggregation, 270n46, 272n51; and on assurance fidelity, 263n53; and buck-passing theory, 56, 245n57; and consequentialism, 22, 240n34; and deliberation, 186; on disregard, 102, 251n46; and "duties to other people," 263n56; and equal standing, 179; on "fellow rational beings," 256n44; on friendship/political membership, 247n69; on impairment, 102–3, 251n46; and individualist restriction, 187–88, 225, 265n65; and interests, 180, 262n46; on justification, 257n4; on morality, 242n21; and moral right and wrong, 3, 34, 35, 185; on mutual recognition, 136, 246n64; and organ donation example, 273nn62,63; on permissibility/wrongness, 248n12; on promissory obligation, 253n3, 263nn47,53; on public officials' decisions, 274nn74,76; on "pure normative claims," 251n42; and reasons and attitudes, 240n4; and reasons and reaction, 237n19; and on reasons principles, 262n44; and relational morality, 147, 179, 184–86, 235nn1,6, 239n27, 259n16, 262n44,

263n56, 264nn57,58; and rescue from rocks example, 265n64, 270n46, 271n48, 272n51; and right and wrong, 242nn18–20; and special standing, 183; and trustees, 258n4; on utilitarianism, 240n34. See also *Being Realistic about Reasons*; contractualism; "Contractualism and Justification"; "Contractualism and Utilitarianism"; "How I Am Not a Kantian"; *Moral Dimensions*; "Preference and Urgency"; "Replies"; "Reply to Wenar"; *What We Owe Each Other*; "Wrongness and Reasons"

"Scanlon on Promissory Obligation" (Gilbert), 263n52

"Scanlon's Investigations" (Kolodny), 248nn12,13

Scheffler, Samuel, 26, 117–18, 142, 242n25, 253n57, 254nn22,23, 262n40, 269n31, 270n45

Schneewind, Jerome, 244n39

Schroeder, Mark, 256n46

secondary claims, 191, 198–99, 199–200, 266n11

secondary interests, 168–69, 199

secondary obligations, 28–29, 89–95, 93, 251n45

second-order normative consequences, 56–57, 168–69, 251n45

second-person "morality" (Tomasello), 112–13

The Second-Person Standpoint (Darwall), 238n21, 244n36

self-blame, 101

self-concepts, 133

selfhood, 240n32

self-indulgence, moral, 138–39, 143

self-standing obligations: and agent-relativity, 137; and antecedent interactions, 162; and anti-individualism, 115–25; and conflicts of claims, 246n65; and first-order moral issues, 115; and individualism, 130–31; and political membership, 247n69; and promissory obligations,

109–10, 245n55; and relational morality, 17, 106, 162–63; and social practices, 109–10. *See also* mutual recognition

Shaping the Normative Landscape (Owens), 237n18, 241n9, 245n56, 252n49, 253n5, 259nn20,22,23

"Shared Intention, Reliance, and Interpersonal Obligations" (Alonso), 256n43

Shiffrin, Seana Valentine, 254n22, 265n4

shipwreck example, 175

"Should the Numbers Count" (Taurek), 271nn47,49

Sidgwick, Henry, 39, 249n20

Singer, Peter, 116

Skorupski, John, 238n23, 240n4, 244n36, 252n53

slavery, 157, 243n35

sleeping-in example, 266n11

Smith, Adam, 250n32

social command theories, 42–43, 95–97, 100, 243n35, 244n36. *See also* authority; commands, normative; law; sanctions

social life, relations, practices, and conventions: and basic resources, 211–12; and bipolar thought, 120, 122; and blame, 129, 253n65; and claim interests, 259nn23,25; and claims, 259n23, 260n25; and cosmopolitan morality, 37; and deliberation, 56; and (directed) obligations, 13, 71, 123; and divine command theories, 31, 80; and inclusive domain of persons, 113–14, 116, 137; and interpersonal morality, 21, 35, 37, 60, 67, 72; and Mill, 257n59; and modern morality, 244n39; and morality, 14; and moral theories, 149n25; and obligations, 9, 71; personal relationships *versus*, 111; and promissory obligation, 108–10, 114–15, 253n6, 259n23; and relational morality, 14, 81–82, 104, 107, 111, 125, 146, 197–98, 208; and rescue from rocks, 216; and responsibility, 69, 266n11; and rights and claims, 103; and universality, 110; and voluntarism, 31, 33–34, 100. *See also* accountability; culture; groups; interpersonal

social life (*cont.*)
   morality; interpersonal recognition; law
   and legislative authorities; natural history of morality; promising *and other*
   practices; roles, social; social command
   theories; social ties, thick
social ties, thick, 122, 192, 193–94, 254nn10,22.
   See also friendship; political life
The Sources of Normativity (Korsgaard),
   238n22, 241n13, 242n16, 244n40,
   256nn47,52
special (privileged) standing: and accountability, 98–101; and claim interests, 167,
   169; and contractualism, 184, 187; and
   (directed) obligations, 122; and disregard,
   82; and joint commitment, 124; and
   moral wrongs, 166; and promissory obligation, 183; and relational morality, 166–
   67, 250n41. *See also* third party, harm of;
   third-party beneficiaries
species nature, 112, 116, 152, 258n5. *See also*
   biological humans; evolution; human
   nature
sports examples, 59–61, 63, 158
Sreenivasan, Gopal, 236n14, 237n16, 258n12,
   259n15, 260n26, 267n15
Stern, Robert, 237n15
strangers, 107, 113–14, 118–19, 139, 193. *See*
   also gouty-toed stranger example;
   nonhumans
Strawson, P. F., 69, 70, 84–85, 99–100, 248n9
subjective (psychological) facts: and accountability, 128–29, 132–33; and bipolar
   thought, 153; incapacities, 241n13; and individualist accounts, 256n53; and information, 29; and joint projects, 112; and
   nonnaturalist realism, 256n54; obligations *versus*, 133; and practical identity,
   241nn13,16, 244n42; and presumptive
   constraints, 126–28, 133–34; and promissory obligation, 108, 134; reasons *versus*,
   106, 126–29, 130, 131–32, 133, 256n54; and
   relational morality, 106, 128, 129–30; and
   universality, 131–32. *See also* attitudes of

agents; deliberation (moral reasoning);
   epistemic constraints; foreseeability;
   Humean theories; intentions; interests
suffering, 238n20, 269n33
surgical procedure example, 202
sympathy, 112
System 1 and System 2 processes, 254n14

"Taking It Personally" (Chaplin), 251n41
talents, 155
Taurek, John, 271n49
temporal distance, 160
temptation, 241n16
theological framework, 25, 31
Theory X, 269n31
third party, harm of, 182, 195–99, 221–33,
   250n41, 251n43, 253n57
third-party beneficiaries, 7, 156, 157–58, 162,
   181–82, 183, 196, 198, 237n16, 251n43
third-party claims, 251n43
third-party forgiveness, 250n41
Thompson, Michael: and antecedent relationships, 125; and bipolar thought, 119–
   22, 148, 246n61, 254n24, 255n35, 258n5,
   259n16; and (directed) obligations,
   236n12; on directed-obligations, 236n12;
   on Humean conception of moral right,
   253n8; on justice, 254nn24,29, 255n29;
   and natural goodness, 244n41; and on
   private criminal law, 252n54; and relational morality, 246n61, 254n24; and self-
   standing order of right, 109–10. See also
   Life and Action; virtue theory (perfectionism); "What Is It to Wrong
   Someone?"
Thomson, Judith Jarvis, 2, 236n8, 241n12,
   260n26, 273n61
thought and action, 31, 104, 241n14. *See also*
   deliberation (moral reasoning)
"Three Dogmas about Promising" (Gilbert), 255nn36–40, 256n42
Timmy's consent example, 183
"to-be-done"/"not-to-be-done" (right and
   wrong in generic sense), 34–36, 49–50,

55–57, 184–85, 188–89, 226, 231, 237n20, 263n56. *See also* high-level, right-making properties; moral right and wrong; "must"; practical requirements

"To Blame or to Forgive?" (Lacey and Pickard), 252n56

Tognazzini, Neal A., 247n8

Tomasello, Michael, 112–13, 113–14, 254n17

torts, 2, 93, 164n57, 197, 251n45

transactional obligation, 16, 50–54, 110

transcendental arguments, 16

tribes, 16, 112, 113, 119, 121

trolley examples, 219–21, 226, 272n58, 273n61

The Trolley Problem Mysteries (Kamm), 272nn57,59

trust, 48, 74, 102, 111, 129, 168–69, 245n46

trustees, 102, 253n60, 258n4

Unger, Peter, 268n24

unity of interpersonal domain, 4, 36

unity of moral realm, 21, 226, 255n24

"unity with fellow creatures" (Mill), 257n59

universality (of morality): and agent-relativity, 135; and antecedent interactions, 111; and bipolar thought, 120, 150; and directed-obligations, 122; and divine command theory, 41–42; and equal standing, 117; and individualism, 131–32, 134; and interests, 23; and manifold of moral persons, 148; and natural history of morality, 113–14; and relational morality, 23, 111, 113–14, 119, 121, 124, 131–32, 134; and social conventions, 110; and subjective facts, 131–32; and utilitarianism, 113–14. *See also* manifold (class) of moral persons

universalizability, 35

universities example, 152

utilitarianism: and accountability, 86–87; and agent-relativity, 39, 243n27; and blame, 77–78, 249n21; and cosmopolitan morality, 39; and defeasible constraints, 243n28; and empathy domain, 116; group morality *versus*, 114; as individualistic, 77;

and moral right and wrong, 35, 39–41; and obligations, 39–41; and opprobrium, 249n21; and relational morality, 41; Scanlon on, 240n34; and self-indulgence, 138; and universality, 113–14; Williams on, 267n22. *See also* consequentialism; Greene, Joshua *and other utilitarians*

vacation decision example, 28, 29

vaccine for children example, 222–23, 273n65

values, 18–19, 35–36, 270n45

"The Very Thought of (Wronging) You" (Zylberman), 264n57, 266n13

vices, 27

virtue theory (perfectionism): and accountability, 78, 79, 81; and agent relativity, 45–46; and bipolar thought, 254n24; and blame, 79, 249nn23,25; and claim-rights, 2; and cosmopolitan morality, 46; and (directed) obligations, 44–47; and interests, 46, 138–39; and Malay servant example, 245n46. *See also* Foot, Philippa; justice *and other virtues*; Thompson, Michael

volitional necessity, 241n13

voluntarism: and accountability, 81; and attitudes, 246n60; and cosmopolitan morality, 42; and deliberation, 34; and (directed) obligations, 41–44, 58, 96–97, 144n36, 238nn20,21; and gratitude, 252n51, 267n17; hypothetical, 244n35; and practical requirements, 31, 33–34, 238n20; private law model *versus*, 100; and rationality, 241n14; and reasons, 244n37, 250n27; and relational morality, 25, 58–59, 238n21, 252n51, 258n10. *See also* Darwall, Stephen; divine command theories; social command theories

voluntary acts, 5, 155–56, 193, 194, 217

vulnerability and power, 237n15, 265n4

Waldron, Jeremy, 239n31

"War and Massacre" (Nagel), 257n61

warning, duties of, 175
Watson, Gary, 82, 83, 247n7
weakness of will, 27, 241n16
well-being, individual, 20, 160, 161–62, 182,
192, 230–32. *See also* aggregation (numbers); future generations; mutual aid;
non-identity problem
"What is Egalitarianism" (Scheffler),
254n23
"What Is It to Wrong Someone?" (Thompson), 236n12, 246n61, 252n54, 253nn7,8,
255nn27–29, 256n45, 258n5, 259n16
"What's the Point of Blame?" (Fricker),
248n17, 251n47
What We Owe to Each Other (Scanlon),
235nn1,6, 237n19, 240n4, 242n21, 245n57,
246n64, 247nn66,69, 253nn60,3, 256n55,
257nn61,64,4, 258n6, 259n21, 262n44,
263nn47,56, 264n58, 271n46
"Whether and Where to Give" (Pummer),
267n21
"Who Is Wronged?" (Anscombe),
272nn53,54
Why Worry about Future Generations?
(Scheffler), 269n31, 270n45

the will, 3, 4, 26, 65, 67–86, 69, 84–85
Williams, Bernard: on authority of the
moral, 238n22; and conflicts of duty, 64–
65; and (directed) obligations, 105–6, 111,
241n13, 247n70; on intimate relationships, 247n70; and "morality system,"
242n21; on moral self-indulgence, 138–
39; and mutual aid, 267n22; and relational morality, 254n17. *See also* "A Critique of Utilitarianism"; *Ethics and the
Limits of Philosophy*; "Internal and External Reasons"; "Moral Incapacity";
"Moral Luck"
withdrawal and avoidance, 71, 74, 102–3, 113,
129, 195
Wolf, Susan, 243n35, 261n34
wronging. *See* moral injury or wrong
"Wronging Future People" (Kumar),
269n37
"Wrongness and Reasons" (Scanlon),
242nn18–20
"Wrongs, Rights, and Third Parties" (Cornell), 251n43, 266nn9,10

Zylberman, Ariel, 264n57, 266n13

A NOTE ON THE TYPE

This book has been composed in Arno, an Old-style serif typeface in the classic Venetian tradition, designed by Robert Slimbach at Adobe.